SUICIDE *of the* WEST

ALSO BY JONAH GOLDBERG

Liberal Fascism
Tyranny of Clichés

SUICIDE *of the* WEST

How the Rebirth of Tribalism, Populism,

Nationalism, and Identity Politics Is Destroying

American Democracy

———————

JONAH GOLDBERG

CROWN
FORUM
NEW YORK

Copyright © 2018 by Jonah Goldberg

Published in the United States by Crown Forum, an imprint of the Crown
Publishing Group, a division of Penguin Random House LLC, New York.
crownforum.com

CROWN FORUM with colophon is a registered trademark of Penguin
Random House LLC.

Library of Congress Cataloging-in-Publication data is available upon request.

ISBN 978-1-101-90493-0
Ebook ISBN 978-1-101-90494-7

Printed in the United States of America

Jacket illustration: Zak Tebbal

10 9 8 7 6 5 4 3

First Edition

To Lucianne Goldberg, happy warrior.

Contents

PART I

INTRODUCTION

Stumbling upon a Miracle

THERE IS NO GOD IN THIS BOOK.

The humans in this story are animals who evolved from other animals who in turn evolved from ever more embarrassing animals and before that from a humiliating sea of ooze, slime, meats, and vegetables in the primordial stew. We pulled ourselves out of the muck, not some Garden of Eden. Indeed, if the Garden of Eden ever existed, it was a slum. We created the Miracle of modernity all on our own, and if we lose it, that will be our fault too.

This book assumes that the Almighty does not guide human affairs and does not intercede on our behalf. God is not in the picture. Well, He is in the picture in the sense that the *idea* of God—and gods—play a very large role in human affairs. But my assumption is that God is in our heads and hearts, not in the heavens above.

The only concession to my own beliefs lies in the word "assumes" just above. I am making this assumption for the purposes of an argument. I am not an atheist, but I think it is useful to play one for the argument I want to make, as a means of guiding the reader through a way of thinking about the world.

In Enlightenment-based democracies, claims that something is true because God says so are inherently suspect because part of the point of the Enlightenment was to create a space where people can disagree about what God wants from us—if He wants anything at all. That's why the highest form of argument in a democracy is one based on facts grounded in reason and decency. I won't deny I'm passionate in parts of this book, but I try not to let the passion get ahead of the facts or the argument. That is because I think persuasion matters, though you wouldn't know it from the last few years in American life. On the right and the left, persuading your opponents is out of fashion, replaced by the mandate to rile up your supporters. I am weary of that, particularly on my own "side." So I'm taking a gamble and doing this the old-fashioned way.

For the purposes of this book, I assume that nearly all the important truths about good and evil or freedom and tyranny are not self-evident. But they can be discovered. The truths we know we have figured out for ourselves—over a really, really, really long time. After thousands of generations of trial and error, we discovered "best practices" out there in the world, like prizes in some eternal scavenger hunt. If the concepts of right and wrong were as universally obvious to everyone as, say, hot and cold, the library shelves groaning under the weight of tomes chronicling war and barbarity would instead lie empty.

And for those who can't suspend their faith in God and believe He revealed to us all we need to know, that's fine. All I ask is you bear in mind that He took His time revealing it all. The Jews, never mind Jesus, show up very late in the story of humanity. And long after the Ten Commandments and the Bible appeared, most of humanity still spent thousands of years ignoring divine instruction.

BUT JUST AS GOD can't get credit, neither can any of His more popular substitutes. There is no dialectic, inevitability, teleology, or hidden algorithm that made human success a foregone conclusion. What happened *happened*, but it didn't *have* to happen that way. There is no "right side of history." Nothing is foreordained.

If you cannot let go of the idea that there is a great plan to the universe—that we as individuals, a nation, or a species have some inevitable destiny—that's fine too. All I ask of you is to consider a secondary proposition: *We have no choice but to live by the assumption that this is the case.*

For instance, many philosophers, physicists, and neuroscientists have depressingly compelling arguments that there is no such thing as free will. Brain scans reveal that many of our conscious decisions were already made subconsciously before they popped into our heads. It looks an awful lot like free will is a story our brains tell us.

But here's the problem: Even if you believe there is no such thing as free will, it is impossible to live any kind of decent life based on that belief. Even if our personal choices are some deep fiction, we still have to convince ourselves to get out of bed in the morning. We are still obligated as a society to judge people as if they make their own choices.

The same goes for every nation and civilization. You can believe that cold, impersonal forces drive humanity to a certain destiny like wind drives a leaf, but we still have to argue about whom to elect president, what Congress should do, and what schools should teach. Prattle on about how free will is a delusion to your friends at the bar all you like; you're still going to have to choose to go to work in the morning.

We all understand in our bones that choices matter—paradoxically because we have no choice but to think that way.

JUST TO BE CLEAR, I am not arguing for some kind of nihilism or moral relativism. The philosopher Richard Rorty famously wrote in *Consequences of Pragmatism*:

Suppose that Socrates was wrong, that we have *not* once seen the Truth, and so will not, intuitively, recognise it when we see it again. This means that when the secret police come, when the torturers violate the innocent, there is nothing to be said to them of the form "There is something within you which you are betraying. Though you embody the practices of a totalitarian society which will endure forever, there is something beyond those practices which condemns you."

This thought is hard to live with, as is Sartre's remark:

"Tomorrow, after my death, certain people may decide to establish fascism, and the others may be cowardly or miserable enough to let them get away with it. At that moment, fascism will be the truth of man, and so much the worse for us. In reality, things will be as much as man has decided they are."[1]

I think there is much truth to this. What societies decide is right or wrong becomes what *is* right and wrong for most of the people who live in them. But I think the lessons of history show that societies can choose poorly—and that this can be proved empirically through facts and reason. Some cultures are better than others, not because of some gauzy metaphysical claim, but because they allow more people to live happy, prosperous, meaningful lives without harming other people in the process. Because this is true, it is incumbent upon all of us to fight for a better society, to defend the hard-learned lessons of human history, and to be grateful for what we have accomplished. This book begins and ends with that simple idea.

With all this in mind, let me review, not necessarily in perfect order, what lies in the middle of this book.

My argument begins with some assertions: Capitalism is unnatural. Democracy is unnatural. Human rights are unnatural. The world we live in today is unnatural, and we stumbled into it more or less by accident. The natural state of mankind is grinding poverty punctuated by horrific violence terminating with an early death. It was like this for a very, very long time.

Imagine you're an alien assigned with keeping tabs on *Homo sapiens* over the last 250,000 years.[2*] Every 10,000 years you check in.

In your notebook, you'd record something like this:

Visit 1: Semi-hairless, upright, nomadic apes foraging and fighting for food.
Visit 2: Semi-hairless, upright, bands of nomadic apes foraging and fighting for food. No change.
Visit 3: Semi-hairless, upright, bands of nomadic apes foraging and fighting for food. No change.

Except for a few interesting details about their migrations and subsequent changes in diet, forms of rudimentary tools, and competition with Neanderthals, you'd write the same thing roughly *twenty-three times* over 230,000 years. On the twenty-fourth visit, you'd note some

* Traditionally the date for the emergence of *Homo sapiens* is around 200,000 years ago. More recent research suggests that the first *Homo sapiens* may have existed in the area that is today Morocco some 300,000 years ago. I split the difference.

amazing changes. Basic agriculture and animal domestication have been discovered by many of the scattered human populations. Some are using metal for weapons and tools. Clay pottery has advanced considerably. Rudimentary mud and grass shelters dot some landscapes (introducing a new concept in human history: the *home*). But there are no roads, no stone buildings worthy of the label. Still, a pretty impressive advance in such a short period of time, a mere 10,000 years.

Eagerly returning 10,000 years later, our alien visitor's ship would doubtless get spotted by NORAD. He might even get here in time to see Janet Jackson play the halftime show at the Super Bowl.

In other words, nearly all of humanity's progress has taken place in the last 10,000 years. But this is misleading. It's like saying between Jeff Bezos, Mark Zuckerberg, and me, our combined net worth is more than $150 billion. Because for most of that 10,000 years, the bulk of humanity lived in squalor. Indeed, there are many who argue—plausibly—that the agricultural revolution made things *worse* for most of humanity. Our diet got less diverse, and, for the vast majority of us, our days were now defined by tedious, backbreaking labor.

The startling truth is that nearly all of human progress has taken place in the last three hundred years (and for many of the billions of non-Westerners lifted out of crushing poverty thanks to capitalism, it's happened in the last thirty years). Around the year 1700, in a corner of the Eurasian landmass, humanity stumbled into a new way of organizing society and thinking about the world. It didn't seem obvious, but it was as if the great parade of humanity had started walking through a portal to a different world.

Following sociologist Robin Fox and historian Ernest Gellner, I call this different world "the Miracle." And we made it, even if we didn't really know what we were doing. "Unique among species," Fox writes, "we created the novel environment, and the supernovel environment that followed on the Miracle, by ourselves and for ourselves."[3]

The Miracle is about more than economics, but economics is the best way to tell the story of humanity's quantum leap out of its natural environment of poverty. Until the 1700s, humans everywhere—Europe, North and South America, Asia, Africa, Australia, and Oceania—lived on the equivalent of one to three dollars a day. Since then, human prosperity has been exploding across the world, starting in England and Holland with the rest of Western Europe and North America close behind. Debate climate change all you like. This is the most important "hockey stick" chart in all of human history:[4]

GDP, 1990 international dollars, millions

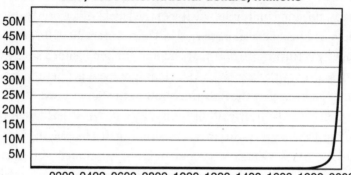

I have included an appendix of charts chronicling the transformation of the Miracle in detail, arguably way too much detail. If you need further persuading on this point, I encourage you to read it. If you don't, feel free to skip right on by.

But it is crucial that the reader goes into the rest of this book appreciating just how different humanity's environment has become in a blink of an eye, in evolutionary terms. As economist Todd G. Buchholz puts it, "For most of man's life on earth, he has lived no better on two legs than he had on four."[5] For the first time in human history, the great challenge is not survival but coping with abundance.

As I discuss at length, the Miracle was the product of a profound and unprecedented transformation in the way humans thought about the world and their place in it. The prosperity of the Miracle didn't happen because of the scientific revolution or from accumulating private property or conducting trade. All of those things played important roles, but science, technology, trade, and property existed in countless civilizations prior to the Miracle, and yet we could not achieve escape velocity from the status quo of one to three dollars per day. Ideas changed everything. This new thinking, which I call the Lockean Revolution, was a wide and deep change in popular attitudes. It held that the individual is sovereign; that our rights come from God, not government; that the fruits of our labors belong to us; and that no man should be less equal before the law because of his faith or class. Of course, such a revolutionary way of viewing the world wasn't universally accepted or implemented overnight, but the mental switch had been flipped.

For the first time in human history, the state itself was more than a glorified criminal enterprise. The emergence of the state thousands of years ago was a beneficial precondition for the emergence of the Miracle, but that doesn't change the fact that the state begins as a means of exploitation. All states prior to the Miracle were designed for the betterment of the tiny slice of humans at the top. Everywhere around the world, rulers saw the masses as little more than instruments of their will. To be sure, humans invented all sorts of theologies and ideologies, such as the divine right of kings, that rationalized these systems as something more noble (and some were better than others), but when put to the test, the interests of rulers always came first.

And yet, these systems endured for thousands of years. In fact, most humans live in societies where the old rules still largely apply. Why? Because there is something about tyranny, monarchy, and authoritarianism that "works," by which I mean there is something in our wiring that finds such systems *natural*.

Which brings us to human nature, the subject of Chapter 1. The first primates with the Latin prefix *Homo* appear in the fossil record just under six million years ago. *Homo sapiens* has been around for between 200,000 and 300,000 years. The Miracle began three hundred years ago. That's a half dozen human lifetimes.*

Evolutionary change does not work on this short a time line. The needle barely moves over 10,000-year increments. In other words, everyone reading this book carries the same basic programming of the humans who toiled in the wheat fields of Mesopotamia or carried spears through the forests of Africa, Germany, or Vietnam. And even

---

* Think of it this way. My father was born when Oliver Wendell Holmes was on the Supreme Court. Holmes fought in the Civil War, under Lincoln. Lincoln was a young man working on a farm in Indiana when John Quincy Adams was president. In 1775, John Quincy Adams, as a boy, heard the gunfire at the Siege of Boston, where George Washington commanded the colonial forces. Washington was born in 1732, at the dawn of the Miracle. That's five lifetimes. If you want to make it six, Washington's father was born in 1694—and died at the ripe age of forty-eight, about fourteen years past the average life expectancy for an Englishman or colonial at the time.

if you account for the view that certain populations have distinct traits that have evolved in shorter periods of time than the last ten or twenty millennia, such differences would be trivial against the backdrop of the innate programming we acquired over the last 200,000 to 300,000 years, never mind the last five to six million.

For all intents and purposes, human nature holds constant as the world changes around us. This is a truth better comprehended from literature than from science. When we read about characters in the distant past or the distant future, what makes them recognizable to us is that they are still *us*: human beings with all of the normal joys, desires, and fears we all experience.

Stated plainly, from the perspective of our genes, we weren't meant to live like we do today, with wealth, rights, and freedom, and all their fruits. As I describe in the chapter on human nature, our natural condition isn't merely poor, it's *tribal*.[6]

For all of human—and most of primate[7]—history until the dawn of the agricultural revolution, humans lived in small, often wandering, groups. This means that all of human politics, religion, and economics—to the extent we can use such words—was *personal*. Tribes and bands do have internal politics. We are imbued with a very strong "coalition instinct" that helps us forge alliances based on loyalty and reciprocity. But, again, these are personal, face-to-face interactions. Our understanding of our place in the universe, our sense of self in relation to others, was defined by a small handful of people who had to work cooperatively to survive.

In short, all meaning was tribal. And as the great economist and philosopher Friedrich Hayek observed, humans are still programmed to understand the world in personal and tribal terms.

The secret of the Miracle—and of modernity itself—stems from our ability to hold this tendency in check. It is natural to give preferences to family and friends—members of the tribe—and to see strangers as the Enemy, the dangerous Other. Nearly all higher forms of social organization expand the definition of "us" to permit larger forms of cooperation. Religion teaches that coreligionists are allies, even when they are strangers. The nation-state tells us that fellow citizens are part of the glorious *us*. Even modern racism plays this role, as does communism, fascism, and nearly every other modern-ism.

We will get into all of these -isms soon enough. But the two most important ones for now are liberalism—by which I mean not partisan Democrats or progressives but the original Enlightenment-based understanding of natural rights and limited government—and capitalism. Rightly understood, capitalism isn't a separate ideology or system from liberalism. But separating them out here might be helpful.

In later chapters, I spell out how liberalism and capitalism created the Miracle and how the United States of America is the fruit of the Miracle. But the key point to understand for the arc of this book is that both are unnatural. The idea that we should presume strangers are not only inherently trustworthy but also have innate dignity and rights does not come naturally to us. We have to be taught that—carefully taught. The free market is even more unnatural, because it doesn't just encourage us to see strangers to be tolerated; it encourages us to see strangers as *customers.*

The invention of money was one of the greatest advances in human liberation in all of recorded history because it lowers the barriers to beneficial human interaction. It reduces the natural tendency to acquire things from strangers through violence by offering the opportunity for commerce. A grocer may be bigoted toward Catholics, Jews, blacks, whites, gays, or some other group. But his self-interest encourages him to overlook such things. Likewise, the customer may not like the grocer, but the customer's self-interest encourages her to put such feelings aside if she wants to buy dinner. In a free market, money corrodes caste and class and lubricates social interaction.

Violence, the natural way to get what you want from strangers, is zero-sum. I hit you with a rock and take your apple. There is one apple-eating winner and there is one apple-less loser with a lump on his head. Trade is mutually beneficial, because the apple buyer needs an apple and the apple seller needs the buyer's money for something else. Trade builds trust and encourages strangers to see each other as equals in a transaction. Labor and commerce in a market order create objective metrics to judge people by. "I don't care if so-and-so is [black, Jewish, gay, Catholic], he does a good job and shows up on time." Liberalism, by enforcing the rule of law and recognizing the rights of everybody, especially property rights, makes trade easier, and trade makes liberalism more desirable.

The Miracle comes out of this worldview. It is the product of a bourgeois revolution, an eighteenth-century middle-class ideology of merit, industriousness, innovation, contracts, and rights. Capitalism is the most cooperative system ever created for the peaceful improvement of peoples' lives. It has only a single fatal flaw: *It doesn't feel like it.*

The market system is so good at getting people—from all over the world—to work together that we barely notice how much we're cooperating. Liberalism, meanwhile, by refusing to give people direction and meaning from above—as every ancient system did, and every modern totalitarianism does—depends on a healthy civil society to provide the sense of meaning and belonging we all crave. Civil society, as I explain later, is that vast social ecosystem—family, schools, churches, associations, sports, business, local communities, etc.—that mediates life between the state and the individual. It is a healthy civil society, not the state, that civilizes people. We come into this world no different than any caveman, Viking, Aztec, or Roman came into this world: humans in the raw, literally and figuratively. Starting with the family, civil society introduces us to the conversation about the world and our place in it.

When civil society fails, people fall through the cracks. The causes of failure can take many forms, as can the consequences. But one thing holds fairly constant: When we fail to properly civilize people, human nature rushes in. Absent a higher alternative, human nature drives us to make sense of the world on its own instinctual terms: That's tribalism.

The easiest illustration of this is the way young men from dysfunctional homes and atomized communities have fallen in with street gangs for thousands of years in every corner of the globe. The gangs offer meaning and a sense of belonging and operate according to the us-versus-them logic of tribalism. Heroic community leaders understand this far better than the rest of us. That is why virtually every intervention with at-risk youth involves getting young men and women to find healthier attachments in civil society, often through sports, but also through voluntarism, vocational training, music, art, and other productive pursuits.

The same dynamic repeats itself with terrorists, the Klan, the

Mafia. and cults of every stripe. Getting these modern tribalists to find meaning elsewhere—in family, work, faith—is the only way to civilize them.

This is not a new problem. It is a problem that begins with modernity itself.

In his book *Tribe: On Homecoming and Belonging*, Sebastian Junger recounts how the English colonies in North America were vexed by a bizarre problem: Thousands of white European colonists desperately wanted to be Indians, but virtually no Indians wanted to be Europeans. "When an Indian child has been brought up among us, taught our language and habituated to our customs," Benjamin Franklin explained in a letter to a friend in 1753, "if he goes to see his relations and make one Indian ramble with them, there is no persuading him ever to return." However, Franklin added, when whites were taken prisoner by the Indians, they'd go native and want to stay Indians, even after being returned to their families. "Tho' ransomed by their friends, and treated with all imaginable tenderness to prevail with them to stay among the English, yet in a short time they become disgusted with our manner of life . . . and take the first good opportunity of escaping again into the woods."[8]

As Junger observes, this phenomenon seemed to run against all of the assumptions of civilizational advance. And yet it kept happening, thousands of times over.[9] Why? Because there is something deeply seductive about the tribal life. The Western way takes a lot of work.

But this is not just a phenomenon of the poor and poorly educated or of strangers in the New World. The pull of the tribe is inscribed on every human heart, and it can take highly intellectual and sophisticated forms. In later chapters, I argue that the sense of alienation we feel toward liberal democratic capitalism should rightly be understood as *romanticism*. Nailing down the meaning, history, and forms of romanticism, as we will see, is a tricky business. But I agree with the scholars who argue that romanticism begins with the French philosopher Jean-Jacques Rousseau. The core of romanticism, for Rousseau and those who followed, is the primacy of feelings. Specifically, the feeling that the world we live in is not right, that it is unsatisfying and devoid of authenticity and meaning (or simply requires too much of us and there must be an easier way). Secondarily, because our feelings tell us that the world is out of balance, rigged, artificial, unfair, or—most often—oppressive and exploitative, our natural wiring drives us to the belief that *someone must be responsible.* The evil string pullers take different forms depending on the flavor of tribalism. But the most common include: the Jews, the capitalists, and—these days on the right—the globalists and cultural Marxists.

Thus, I argue, romanticism has never gone away, even if the period we call the romantic era has been consigned to stodgy library books. Liberal democratic capitalism does not give us much by way of meaning; it merely gives us the freedom to find it in civil society and the marketplace. And for some—many!—that is not enough. And so we seek out new theories, causes, and ideologies that have all the answers and promise to take us out of this place to some imagined better world of harmony, equality—for the right people, at least—authenticity, and meaning.

Marx, for all his talk of scientific socialism, was an incurable romantic, convinced that malevolent forces—Jews, the ruling class, industrialists, "capital"—were exploiting the masses.[10] He in turn argued—"prophesied" is the better word—that, if the masses, the workers of the world, bound together in tribal solidarity, they could overthrow their masters and deliver humanity to some glorious new realm where we would live essentially the way man lived in Eden. Nazism shared many of the same theories about who resided behind the curtain, manipulating the German people. Hitler's vision of the end of history was different from Marx's, but he shared the dream that his tribe would reach the Promised Land.

It is my contention that all rebellions against the liberal order of the Miracle are not only fundamentally romantic in nature but *reactionary.* They seek not some futuristic modern conception of social organization. Rather, they seek to return to some form of tribal solidarity where we're all in it together. Romanticism is the voice through which our inner primitive cries out "There must be a better way!"

But—spoiler alert!—*there isn't one.* This is it. Look around, everybody: You're standing at the end of history. In terms of economics, no other system creates wealth. We can get richer, and we can solve many of the problems that still plague modern society. The remedies for those problems might require more intervention by government or less. But, in the final analysis, we cannot improve upon the core assumptions of the Miracle. Every other kind of economics—if there even is any other kind of economics*—concerns itself not with creating wealth but with how to redistribute it. That is not economics; that is *politics*.

This brings us to the second main theme of this book: corruption.

This desire to return to our authentic selves cannot be eradicated (nor should we try). But it can be channeled. Just as we have an innate need and desire to eat, that desire has to be cultivated in the right way if we are to live healthy lives. I argue that political ideas and movements based upon the romantic idea of following our feelings and instincts can best be understood as *corruption*. To the modern ear, "corruption" suggests petty criminality, particularly among politicians. But this is a pinched and narrow understanding of what corruption really is. "Corruption" literally means decay, rot, and putrefaction.

In other words, corruption is the natural process of entropy by which nature takes back what is hers. Rust will eat away at iron until it rejoins the soil. Termites will eat any wood home given the only two ingredients they need: opportunity and time. The only way to fight off nature's greedy claws is through human care. Any boat owner knows that there is no substitute for upkeep and vigilance. And so it is with the Miracle.

Because every generation enters this world with its natural wiring intact, every generation must be convinced anew that the world they have been blessed to be born into is the best one. Corruption isn't about giving in to the seduction of bribery; it is about giving in to the seduction of human nature, the angry drumbeats of our primitive brains and the inner whispers of our feelings.

When I started this book, no one thought Donald Trump would run for president, never mind *become* president, including Trump himself. But his emergence proved beneficial for my larger thesis, even if it wasn't necessarily beneficial for our society. I argue that the right's

---

* Irving Kristol observed that there are no non-capitalist economic theories. I think that is right. The moment a supposedly alternative economic system stops recognizing the role that markets and prices play, it ceases to be economics and becomes some romantic ideology that borrows from the language of economics to sound more attractive or authoritative.

embrace of Donald Trump's brand of politics represents a potentially catastrophic surrender of conservative principles, and a sign of how deeply the corruption has set in.

But Trump's rise is a symptom of our larger problems, not the cause of them. It must be understood, at least in part, as a backlash against the left's turn to identity politics, which is just another form of tribalism. Tragically, that backlash has yielded or at least solidified a new identity politics all its own. The Miracle ushered in a philosophy that says each person is to be judged and respected on account of their own merits, not the class or caste of their ancestors. Identity politics says each group is an immutable category, a permanent tribe. Worse, it works from the assumption that what benefits one group must come at the expense of another.

The rise of the populisms and nationalisms of the left and the right that have come to define so much of our politics today are manifestations of corruption. The Miracle works on the assumption that the individual is the moral center of our system, and the individual armed with reason, facts, the law, or simply morality (and hopefully all four) on his side should win any contest with an angry throng shouting with tribal passion. As I argue in Part Two, the genius of the Constitution lay in enshrining that principle into law.

And finally, there is the last theme of this book. I do not offer many public policy proposals to remedy our problems, in large part because I do not think our problems are fundamentally policy problems. The crisis that besets our civilization is fundamentally psychological. Specifically, we are shot through with *ingratitude* for the Miracle. Our schools and universities, to the extent they teach the Western tradition at all, do so from a perspective of resentful hostility toward our accomplishments. It is not that the story they tell is pure fiction—though that happens—but that it is, at best, half-true.

Consider Howard Zinn's *People's History of the United States*. Published in 1980, it has sold millions of copies and remains one of the mostly widely used texts in America.[11]

At the beginning of *A People's History*, Zinn confesses that he only wants to tell the story of America from the perspective of the oppressed:

Thus, in that inevitable taking of sides which comes from selection and emphasis in history, I prefer to try to tell the story of the discovery of America from the viewpoint of the Arawaks, of the Constitution from the standpoint of the slaves, of Andrew Jackson as seen by the Cherokees, of the Civil War as seen by the New York Irish, of the Mexican war as seen by the deserting soldiers of Scott's army, of the rise of industrialism as seen by the young women in the Lowell textile mills, of the Spanish-American war as seen by the Cubans, the conquest of the Philippines as seen by black soldiers on Luzon, the Gilded Age as seen by southern farmers, the First World War as seen by socialists, the Second World War as seen by pacifists, the New Deal as seen by blacks in Harlem, the postwar American empire as seen by peons in Latin America.[12]

All of these things should be taught. But the idea now is that knowing this story is the *only story worth knowing*. That *this and only this* is the story of America. By turning the Founders into nothing more than greedy white racists, by decrying Columbus as nothing more than a genocidal murderer, by arguing that slavery is a uniquely Western and American sin, by claiming that "Western civilization" and "American exceptionalism" are nothing more than euphemisms for "racism" and "imperialism," the *ressentiment*-drenched intellectuals at the commanding heights of our culture seek to make the story of the Miracle into a Curse, leaving them as the only legitimate storytellers of our civilization.

By no means do the majority of Americans subscribe to the Zinn view of America. But a majority of Americans, I believe, are ungrateful for what the Miracle has brought us. Sometimes this ingratitude manifests itself as simply taking one's good fortune for granted. And that is enough to destroy a civilization. Because maintaining a civilization, fighting off corruption, takes *work*. If we don't teach people to hold what they have precious, they simply won't bother defending it against those who think what we have is evil.

Just as the spoiled children of the wealthy are often ungrateful for the opportunities provided by their parents, we as a society are ungrateful for our collective inheritance. The system we live under is like the proverbial goose that lays the golden egg.

You are probably familiar with the story, but I think it would be instructive to look at it more closely. There are many versions of the fable going back to Aesop and antiquity, but two of the oldest versions in the West come from France and England.

In the classic French version, the story goes something like this: A cottager and his wife discovered a hen that laid a golden egg every day. After thinking about it, they deduced that the hen must contain a great lump of gold in its gut. In order to get the gold, they killed it. Having done so, they found to their surprise that the hen differed in no respect from their other hens. The unwise duo had neither a hoard of gold nor any more golden eggs.[13]

William Caxton's earlier version (1484) is slightly different, and more faithful to Aesop's. This time, it is a single farmer. Not happy with one egg a day, he orders the goose to double its quota to two. The goose replied that it couldn't ("And she sayd to hym / Certaynly/ my mayster I maye not . . ."). The farmer is furious at the remarkably generous—and polite!—creature and kills it.[14]

The moral of both versions is usually the same: Greed is bad. Wanting more than you have leads to having nothing at all. But the truth is the lessons are actually quite different.

In the first version, the cottager and his wife use their reason; in the second, the farmer succumbs to his rage. The practical consequences are the same—no more golden eggs—but the mistakes stem from different kinds of folly. The cottagers are not insane to think that a bird that produces golden eggs might have gold inside it. The farmer, however, is crazy not to take the word of a magic goose when it insists it can't do better than one golden egg per day (an enormous amount of wealth in the fifteenth century). And to get so angry at the bird that you kill it is true lunacy.

Yes, both stories are about greed. But what really unites them is *ingratitude*.

What would *you* do if you found a goose that laid a golden egg every day? It seems reasonable to think that a wise person would take care of the goose, making it as comfortable as possible. You would feed it better than you otherwise would a conventional goose. You might put a fence around its shelter. If the goose politely told you that it needed certain things to keep up its production, you would take these requests seriously. To borrow from another ancient proverb, don't look a gift horse in the mouth.

These two versions of the goose that lays the golden egg speak to the two kinds of assaults befalling the Miracle. In one, sheer rage driven by the feeling that "I deserve more!" leads to the creature's death. In the other, intellectual hubris drives the couple to think they can out-smart this Miracle that literally waddled into their lives as a gift. The first is an analogue to the populist rage that churns on the left and the right. The second is a mirror of the mind-set of supposed intellectuals who are convinced they are smarter than the market and the system they inherited. And both stories highlight the ingratitude that defines our times.

Let me close with another parable of sorts, probably more familiar to the reader.

In the opening scene of *The Godfather* (both the book and the film), Don Corleone is receiving visitors on his daughter's wedding day. Sicilian tradition holds that he must grant any favor asked of him on this day. His first supplicant is Amerigo Bonasera, the undertaker.[15]

"I raised my daughter in the American fashion," Bonasera says in the book that inspired the movie. "I believe in America. America has made my fortune. I gave my daughter her freedom and yet taught her never to dishonor her family."

Alas, the daughter found an American boyfriend who tried to rape her. "She resisted. She kept her honor." The boyfriend and another boy beat her viciously in retaliation. "I went to the police like a good American," he says. But, despite being arrested and convicted, the boys receive a slap on the wrist from a lenient, probably corrupt judge. "They went free that very day. I stood in the courtroom like a fool and those bastards smiled at me. And then I said to my wife: 'We must go to Don Corleone for justice.'"

Don Corleone breaks the silence to ask, "Why did you go to the police? Why didn't you come to me at the beginning of this affair?"

Bonasera dodges the question and asks, "What do you want of me? Tell me what you wish. But do what I beg you to do." He then whispers in the Don's ear that he wants the boys killed.

The Don tells the undertaker he's getting carried away, that this punishment is unreasonable. The undertaker replies, flatly, "I will pay you anything you ask."

This infuriates Don Corleone. In a voice Mario Puzo describes as "cold death," the Don answers: "We have known each other many years, you and I . . . but until this day you never came to me for counsel or help. I can't remember the last time you invited me to your house for coffee though my wife is godmother to your only child. Let us be frank. You spurned my friendship. You feared to be in my debt."

The undertaker mutters, "I didn't want to get into trouble."

Don Corleone interrupts him with a wave of his hand. "No. Don't speak. You found America a paradise. You had a good trade, you made a good living, you thought the world a harmless place where you could take your pleasures as you willed. You never armed yourself with true friends. After all, the police guarded you, there were courts of law, you and yours could come to no harm. You did not need Don Corleone. Very well. My feelings were wounded but I am not that sort of person who thrusts his friendship on those who do not value it—on those who think me of little account."

The Don smiles derisively. "Now you come to me and say, 'Don Corleone give me justice.' And you do not ask with respect. You do not offer me friendship. You come into my home on the bridal day of my daughter and you ask me to do murder and you say 'I will pay you anything.' . . . [W]hat have I ever done to make you treat me so disrespectfully?"

The undertaker responds, "America has been good to me. I wanted to be a good citizen. I wanted my child to be American."

The Don applauds sardonically and says: "Well spoken. Very fine. Then you have nothing to complain about. The judge has ruled. America has ruled. Bring your daughter flowers and a box of candy when you go visit her in the hospital. That will comfort her. Be content. After all, this is not a serious affair, the boys were young, high-spirited, and one of them is the son of a powerful politician. . . . So give me your word that you will put aside this madness. It is not American. Forgive. Forget. Life is full of misfortunes."

The two argue about the nature of justice versus vengeance. And once again the undertaker asks, "How much shall I pay you?" The

Don, furious, turns his back on Bonasera and asks, "Why do you fear to give your first allegiance to me?" He lectures the undertaker about the delays and corruption of the American system. "You go to the law courts and wait for months. You spend money on lawyers who know full well you are to be made a fool of. You accept judgment from a judge who sells himself like the worst whore in the streets . . . [But if] you had come to me for justice those scum who ruined your daughter would be weeping bitter tears this day. If by some misfortune an honest man like yourself made enemies, they would become my enemies . . . and then, believe me, they would fear you."

The undertaker finally understands and pleads: "Be my friend. I accept."

When Bonasera relents and asks Don Corleone to be his friend, he is turning his back on America. He is rejecting—not without cause, of course—the Lockean worldview, the Miracle, in favor of the more natural and eternal political order. It works on the assumption that there is no extended order of abstract rules and contracts, there is only power, loyalty, reciprocity, alliances, honor, and friendship. Right and wrong are defined by what is good for our tribe. It is no coincidence that the name Amerigo Bonasera, translated from the Italian, means "Good night, America."

The moral universe of *The Godfather* is the moral universe of all politics before the Miracle. It is natural. It lurks beneath the surface in every society and in every soul. It is there waiting to reclaim the Miracle and restore humanity to nature. And all it takes for nature to succeed is for us to let it. Nothing is guaranteed. Nothing is written. All that is good in the world requires work. I hope this book helps in the task that falls on every one of us.

1

Human Nature
Our Inner Tribesman

Human nature is real. Few statements are less controversial among the people who study the subject and more controversial among people who don't.

It is fair to say that no reputable psychologist, neuroscientist, linguist (including Noam Chomsky), or economist disputes the fact that human beings come preloaded with a great deal of software. Indeed, the fashionable metaphor today is not software but "apps"—as in the applications we have on our smartphones. Different situations trigger different apps, and sometimes these apps can be in conflict.

All of the serious debates about nature versus nurture start with the premise that there is already a lot built into our nature. The only question is what we can add on top of nature or what apps we can override. Think of a car. We all generally agree that a car comes with an engine, four wheels, and a steering wheel. These things come standard. That's nature. Nurture provides the options, and there are a great many options. But no matter how many add-ons you buy, a car is not going to be a helicopter.

In his enlightening book *Just Babies: The Origins of Good and Evil*, psychologist Paul Bloom chronicles a remarkable number of experiments conducted on infants and toddlers. (Rest assured: No babies were harmed in the process.) He demonstrates that babies as young as six months already come preloaded with a number of psychological traits that suggest an innate moral sense. For instance, infants between six and ten months old were shown puppet plays. One puppet would be trying to get up a hill. Another puppet would either come to the hill-climbing puppet's aid or it would get in the way, stymieing the climber's efforts. Afterward, the babies were given a choice between the mean puppet and the nice puppet. The babies almost uniformly preferred the nice puppet over the jackass puppet. When a similar study was performed with twenty-month-old toddlers, the kids would reward the nice puppet with candy and punish the bad puppet by taking its candy away.[1] Other studies confirm that we are all born with some very basic programming about empathy, altruism, cooperation, and other moral intuitions.

Bloom takes great care in pointing out that, just because we are born with a kind of moral sense, that doesn't mean we are therefore moral. Rather, we are born with moral taste buds. How we use them depends on the environment we grow up in and, crucially, how we define "morality."

One of the most important findings of not just Bloom but thousands of researchers across numerous disciplines is that we are all born with a natural distrust of strangers. Very young babies can identify language; their cries even have regional accents. "Young babies can recognize the language that they have been exposed to, and they prefer it to other languages even if it is spoken by a stranger," Bloom reports. "Experiments that use methodologies in which babies suck on a pacifier to indicate their preferences find that Russian babies prefer to hear Russian, French babies prefer French, American babies prefer English, and so on. This effect shows *up mere minutes after birth, suggesting that babies were becoming familiar with those muffled sounds that they heard in the womb*" [emphasis mine].[2]

Interestingly, our brains dedicate an enormous amount of resources to facial recognition. We are born with an intense interest in human faces. No doubt there are many reasons for this. For instance, much early human communication was done nonverbally and that's still true for humans today, particularly before we learn to speak. One can debate whether reading faces was important in the past or today, but our ability to *recognize* faces was clearly more vital in the past. Being able to instantly recognize kin or friends from strangers could mean the difference between life and death. (It's telling that our ability to identify faces is actually much more sophisticated than our ability to verbally articulate the differences between faces. Most of us can instantly distinguish between, say, Matt Damon's face and Matthew

McConaughey's. But can you instantly explain what makes their faces so different?)

The desire for unity and distrust of strangers are universal human tendencies—but just tendencies. While I don't think they can be wholly taught out of us, they certainly can be tempered and channeled in productive ways. It is a common cliché among certain tribes of humanists to say something like "There is no race but the human race," which of course is just a more secular version of "We are all children of God" and similar endearing platitudes. All things being equal, I think this is a benign cliché and worth incorporating into our civilizational dogma. But I should point out that, of all the systems ever created that actually put this belief into practice, none has been more successful on the ground than the market. The market lowers the risk—or "price"—of distrust by letting very different peoples and cultures find common interest.

The distrust of strangers and the craving for unity are important themes in this book, because they illuminate a much broader fact: Ideology is downstream of human nature. Children and adults are constantly told that one needs to be taught to hate. This is laudable nonsense. We are, in a very real sense, born to hate every bit as much as we are born to love. The task of parents, schools, society, and civilization isn't to teach us not to hate any more than it is to teach us not to love. The role of all of these institutions is to teach what we should or should not hate.

Bloom writes that "just about all the readers of this book believe that it's wrong to hate someone solely because of the color of his or her skin. But this is a modern insight; for most of human history, nobody saw anything wrong with racism."[3] All good people are supposed to hate evil, but the definition of what constitutes evil is rather expansive across time, and refining the definition of evil is the very essence of what civilizations *do*.

Every culture ever known has things it hates and things it loves. And every political ideology ever known has some group it considers the Other. The pro-Nazi philosopher Carl Schmitt famously said, "Tell me who your enemy is, and I will tell you who you are."[4] Fascism is supposedly defined by its demonization of "the other." Obviously, in Nazi Germany, the Other was best represented by the Jew.

But communism had its Others too. They went by such names as the bourgeois, or the ruling class, or the kulaks. Contemporary liberalism has a host of Others it hates. We've all probably met avowed lovers of tolerance who talk about how much they hate intolerant people—but only *certain kinds* of intolerant people. I've lost count of the number of times I've heard people insist that the slightest prejudice against Muslims is evil and then proceed to explain how awful evangelical Christians are.

The anthropologist Richard Shweder compiled a useful list of things that different societies have thought was praiseworthy, neutral, or appalling:

> masturbation, homosexuality, sexual abstinence, polygamy, abortion, circumcision, corporal punishment, capital punishment, Islam, Christianity, Judaism, capitalism, democracy, flag burning, miniskirts, long hair, no hair, alcohol consumption, meat eating, medical inoculations, atheism, idol worship, divorce, widow marriage, arranged marriage, romantic love marriage, parents and children sleeping in the same bed, parents and children not sleeping in the same bed, women being allowed to work, women not being allowed to work.[5]

In other words, the capacity for humans to think certain things are "naturally" good or bad is remarkably elastic. But there's a difference between elastic and infinite. For example, incest has been a taboo everywhere. Obviously the strength of that taboo has varied, but no society has celebrated it. (Alas, that taboo has been steadily weakening in American popular culture.) Similarly, there's no society in the world—now or known to have existed—where people didn't give preference to relatives and friends over strangers, a point I'll be coming back to quite a bit in later chapters.

Anthropologist Donald E. Brown compiled a list of attributes that describe "the Universal People"—i.e., everybody, everywhere. "Human universals—of which hundreds have been identified—consist of those features of culture, society, language, behavior, and mind that, so far as the record has been examined, are found among all peoples known to ethnography and history."[6] The list is too long to reprint here.

But some of the most important, for our purposes at least, include coalitions; conflict; cooperation and cooperative behavior; corporate statuses; collective decision making; divination; ethnocentrism; entification (treating patterns and relations as things); envy; etiquette; fear; feasting; folklore; food sharing; gift giving; gossip; government; group living; (collective) identity; in-groups (as distinguished from out-groups); in-group biases in favor of close kin (as distinguished from distant kin groups); kin terms translatable by basic relations of procreation; kinship statuses; judging others; law (rights and obligations); law (rules of membership); leaders; magic; magic to increase life; magic to sustain life; male and female and adult and child seen as having different natures; males dominating the public/political realm; males more aggressive; males more prone to lethal violence; males more prone to theft; moral sentiments; myths; narrative; overestimating objectivity of thought; planning; planning for the future; preference for own children and close kin (nepotism); prestige inequalities; private inner life; promise; property; psychological defense mechanisms; rape; rape proscribed; reciprocal exchanges (of labor, goods, or services); reciprocity, negative (revenge, retaliation); reciprocity, positive (recognition of individuals by face); redress of wrongs; rites of passage; rituals; role and personality seen in dynamic interrelationship (i.e., departures from role can be explained in terms of individual personality); sanctions; sanctions for crimes against the collectivity; sanctions including removal from the social unit; self distinguished from other; self as neither wholly passive nor wholly autonomous; self as subject and object; self as responsible; self-image, awareness of (concern for) what others think; self-image, manipulation of; self-image, wanted to be positive; social structure; socialization; socialization expected from senior kin; socialization includes toilet training; spear; special speech for special occasions; statuses and roles; statuses ascribed and achieved; statuses distinguished from individuals; statuses based on something other than sex, age, or kinship; succession; sweets preferred; symbolism; symbolic speech; taboos: tabooed foods; tabooed utterances; taxonomy; territoriality; trade; and turn taking.

Again, this is only a partial list.

One of the most interesting taboos in American life is the taboo against discussing human nature. This is an entirely modern prohibition. The ancient Greeks and Romans, not to mention every major world religion, considered human nature not only real but an essential subject for study and contemplation. I think there are multiple overlapping reasons—many of them laudable—for our aversion to the subject. Our civilization has struggled to live up to the ideals of universal equality enshrined in the Declaration of Independence, the U.S. Constitution, and similar canons. Discussion of human nature inevitably bleeds into debates about genetic differences between groups or claims that certain behaviors or choices are "unnatural." Discussion of human nature also grinds against the idea that the individual is unconstrained by external—or internal!—restraints, a nearly unique dogma of the West. Another reason why "human nature" sounds like fighting words is that it is at loggerheads with the French Enlightenment tradition that believes in the "perfectibility of man."

But while some of these concerns are valid, the fact is the human universals identified by Brown apply to blacks and whites, Asians and aborigines. I am agnostic about the issue of racial differences, in part because I'm not clear on why they should matter even if they exist. Most of the good work on the subject—there's a great deal of awful work as well—focuses on large aggregate and statistical differences between populations. Whatever may or may not explain these differences has no bearing whatsoever on how we should treat individuals as a matter of law, manners, or morality.

But one of the sources of the taboo against discussions of human nature does need addressing: the idea of the noble savage.

Jean-Jacques Rousseau is often credited with coining the phrase "noble savage," though that honor belongs to John Dryden, who wrote in *The Conquest of Granada* (1670):

I am as free as nature first made man,
Ere the base laws of servitude began,
When wild in woods the noble savage ran.[7]

"The concept of the noble savage was inspired by European colonists' discovery of indigenous peoples in the Americas, Africa, and (later) Oceania," Steven Pinker writes. "It captures the belief that humans in their natural state are selfless, peaceable, and untroubled, and that blights such as greed, anxiety, and violence are the products of civilization."[8]

Again, Rousseau didn't coin the term, but he was the great popularizer of this myth. He wrote in 1755:

> So many writers have hastily concluded that man is naturally cruel, and requires civil institutions to make him more mild; whereas nothing is more gentle than man in his primitive state, as he is placed by nature at an equal distance from the stupidity of brutes, and the fatal ingenuity of civilised man.[9]

"Rousseau reversed the poles of civilization and barbarism," writes Arthur Herman. "His paeans of praise for primitive man, the 'noble savage' . . . who lives in effortless harmony with nature and his fellow human beings, were meant as a reproach against his refined Parisian contemporaries. But they were also a reproach against the idea of history as progress."[10] For Rousseau, the advent of private property, the development of the arts, and the general advancement of human health and prosperity were actually giant steps backward.

Rousseau is considered by many to be the father of romanticism. And for a seminar on intellectual history, that is a fine way to describe him. But it is my argument that romanticism shouldn't be understood as a school of art, literature, or philosophy but as a school of rebellion against the unnatural nature of the Enlightenment and all of the Enlightenment's offspring: capitalism, democracy, natural rights, and science. The romantic spirit rebels against the iron cage of modernity, demanding a return to an imagined authenticity in harmony with nature. Romantic rebellion is less an argument and more of a primal yawp. It is a feeling that the world around us is dehumanizing, fake, artificial, and oppressive. "Romanticism is precisely situated neither in choice of subject nor in exact truth, but in a mode of feeling," explained the French poet Charles Baudelaire (the man who coined the term "modernity," as it happens).[11]

I will be returning to this point throughout the chapters that follow, but for now the important point is that this idea, this *feeling*, that modern man is corrupt and unnatural—or, more specifically, has been corrupted by modern society—suffuses vast swaths of our culture. It fuels a host of ideological and religious assumptions about past "golden ages" and nostalgic nostrums about how things used to be better in previous generations.

Romanticism is neither right nor left, because it is a pre-rational passion written into the human heart. It manifests itself in different ways and at different times across the ideological spectrum. It has been the fuel behind nationalism, populism, radicalism, and various forms of "reactionary" politics. It is also the wellspring of most of the great art of the last three hundred years, speaking to, and for, the parts of the soul that cannot speak through reason and science alone.

In short, it is a rebellion against the unnatural constraints of modern civilization. It shouts "I am not a number!" or "I am not a machine!" or "The man can't keep me down!"

A common thread between various forms of left-wing romanticism, including assorted flavors of Marxism, and right-wing libertarianism and anarchism is that they make much of the fact that the state—or even civilization itself—is a form of institutionalized violence. As we will see, this is largely true. Where this insight goes off the rails is when it is assumed the past was less violent, that humans lived in peace and harmony in some golden age before the enslaving force of the state imposed itself.

"The idea that violence is rooted in human nature is difficult for many people to accept," writes Francis Fukuyama in *The Origins of Political Order: From Prehuman Times to the French Revolution*. "Many anthropologists, in particular, are committed, like Rousseau, to the view that violence is an invention of later civilizations, just as many people would like to believe that early societies understood how to live in balance with their local environments. Unfortunately, there is little evidence to support either view."[12] Deirdre McCloskey rightly observes that "conquest, enslavement, robbery, murder—briefly, force—has characterized the sad annals of humankind since Cain and Abel."[13]

According to Steven Pinker, author of *The Better Angels of Our Nature: Why Violence Has Declined*, if similar proportions of people died from violence in the twentieth century as did in most prehistoric societies, the death count of the twentieth century—allegedly the "bloodiest century"—would not be 100 million but two billion, or twenty times greater.[14] This is because roughly one-third of primitive humans in small-scale societies died from raids and fights alone (though this is somewhat misleading, since the death rate for males is twice that of females).[15]

"To minimize risk, primitive societies chose tactics like the ambush and the dawn raid," writes Nicholas Wade in *Before the Dawn: Recovering the Lost History of Our Ancestors*. "Even so, their casualty rates were enormous, not least because they did not take prisoners. That policy was compatible with their usual strategic goal: to exterminate the opponent's society. Captured warriors were killed on the spot, except in the case of the Iroquois, who took captives home to torture them before death, and certain tribes in Colombia, who liked to fatten prisoners before eating them."[16] For generation after generation, day in and day out, warfare was *normal.*

This is no longer a debated point among most serious scholars. People who think we once lived in glorious harmony with each other—and the environment—aren't scientists, they're poets and propagandists. The evidence for mankind's blood-soaked past can be found in the archaeological record, DNA analysis, the writings of ancient commentators and historians, and the firsthand reports of those remaining societies that have so far resisted modernity.

Napoleon Chagnon, the famous—and famously controversial—anthropologist, lived among the Yanomamö people in the Amazon for long stints starting in the 1960s and ending in the 1990s. He found that killing was a central institution of life.[17] Roughly 44 percent of men over the age of twenty-five had participated in killing someone. One-third of adult male deaths were from violence and more than two-thirds of men over the age of forty had lost at least one close relative to violence.[18]

Chagnon found that the Yanomamö culture lived in a state of "chronic warfare." The most common motives for raids and battles revolved around efforts to steal women, recover stolen women, or seek revenge for past abductions of women. Of course, men went to war for other reasons: blood feuds were particularly popular. But Chagnon did not find much evidence to confirm the prevailing orthodoxy of the day that warfare was "modern" and that to the extent primitive societies resorted to war it was because of scarce resources, specifically "protein scarcity." This is a version of a very common assumption: that scarcity of resources is the chief cause of war. Obviously, this is not outlandish. But it is exaggerated. Wars are very often the by-product of pride, honor, and a desire for status.[19]

The barbarity of the past is hardly defined solely by the prevalence of war. Consider just two of the most obvious examples of what we today consider barbaric behavior: torture and slavery.

Torture, the deliberate infliction of pain or agony for punishment, fun, or profit, is the international pastime of premodern man (and it hardly died out suddenly in the 1700s either). In ancient societies many forms of torture were the preliminary rituals of human sacrifice. The Aztecs routinely burned victims alive, removed them from the flames, and then cut out their still-beating hearts.[20] The Mayans skipped the burning for the most part and simply pinned their live victims to an altar and cut out their hearts.[21]

The Assyrians deserve their status in the torture hall of fame. Flaying—by which the skin is removed while the victim is still alive—was particularly popular. Staking was even more revered. The best torturers were able to do it in a way that left the staked alive and suffering for days.[22] The Persians were inventive as well. One method involved simply forcing a person to stand in a room full of very fine ash for as long as he could. When he collapsed from fatigue, he would inhale the ashes and slowly suffocate.

That seems preferable, however, to "sitting in the tub." In this practice, the victim was placed in a wooden tub with only their head sticking out. The executioner would then paint the victim's face with milk and honey. Flies would begin to swarm around the victim's nose and eyelids. The victim was also fed regularly and fairly soon they would virtually be swimming in their own excrement. At which stage maggots and worms would devour their body. One victim apparently survived for seventeen days. He decayed alive.[23] (Scaphism, a variant of this technique, involved more or less the same thing, but with the victim tied to boats or logs.)

If you're the sort of person who enjoys this sort of thing, the Internet is a smorgasbord of lists of torture methods, from sewing animals into living victims so they would have to eat their way out, to using fire to force rats to eat their way in. The ancient Greeks would not even *consider* confessions unless elicited by torture. The Romans had the same practice.[24] They also perfected crucifixion, from which we get the word "excruciating." The Chinese had *lingchi*, or death by a thousand cuts.

The centrality of torture as a tool of statecraft around the world cannot be exaggerated. But few societies put more time, energy, and ingenuity into the practice than medieval Europeans.[25]

Diehard members of the cult of the Noble Savage may want to say all of the cultures and civilizations were subsequent to man's fall from grace. But there is simply nothing in the archaeological record to support that. "We need to recognize and accept the idea of nonpeaceful past for the entire time of human existence," writes Stephen A. LeBlanc, co-author with Katherine E. Register of *Constant Battles: Why We Fight*. "Though there were certainly times and places during which peace prevailed, overall, such interludes seem to have been short-lived and infrequent. . . . To understand much of today's war, we must see it as a common and almost universal human behavior that has been with us as we went from ape to human."[26]

Then there's slavery.

IT IS SURELY TRUE that slavery was less common among primitive man than among the societies that arose after the agricultural revolution. That is not because primitive man was more moral; it is because primitive man was so much *poorer*. Slaves are a very large expense for nomadic bands. Guarding an enemy who doesn't want to be part of the group is costly and dangerous. Children can be taken in as assets—a common practice in many primitive societies, notably among American Indians—and women can be forced into marriage, very often a kind of slavery. But captured warriors from another tribe are a liability. Better to kill them, often theatrically, for the amusement of the victors.

After the agricultural revolution roughly 11,000 years ago, slavery emerges almost everywhere. The most ancient texts make reference to it. The Bible takes it as a given in human affairs. The Code of Hammurabi says that freeing a slave is a crime punishable by death.[27] There are records of slavery in China going back to 1800 B.C.[28]

For understandable reasons, America's shameful experience with slavery informs the way we talk about the institution. That's right and proper. But it also distorts our understanding of it. As Thomas Sowell has chronicled, Americans tend to believe—because it is what they are taught—that slavery is an inherently racist institution.[29] Some even seem to believe that slavery is a uniquely American sin. America certainly must take ownership of its use of slaves and the central role racism played in it. But the conventional understanding gets the causality backward. American racism stems from slavery, not the other way around.

Historically speaking, there are two remarkable aspects of American slavery. The first is the hypocrisy. Other societies relied on slavery more than we did, and some were arguably crueler to their slaves (though American slavery was plenty cruel). But none of those societies were founded on principles of universal human rights and dignity. The Romans, Greeks, Chinese, and Egyptians were not hypocrites for keeping humans in bondage; they sincerely believed that it was natural (even Aristotle said so).[30] But America was born with the Declaration of Independence and the words "All men are created equal." That is irreconcilable with slavery, no matter the rationalization.[31]

Which brings us to the second remarkable thing about American slavery. Against the backdrop of the last 10,000 years, the amazing thing about American slavery is not that it existed but that we put an end to it. In the context of the last thousand years, there were many efforts to abolish slavery. Many failed and many more were only half measures, establishing various forms of de facto slavery, such as serfdom. Over the nineteenth century, slavery was outlawed across much of Europe and in most northern colonies and states in America. England abolished the slave trade in 1807. The Dutch followed in 1814.[32] The Congress of Vienna, which determined the fate of post-Napoleonic Europe, condemned slavery.[33] Britain would abolish slavery in all of its colonies in 1834, though the Dutch would not follow suit until 1863.[34]

America, meanwhile, though it banned the slave trade in 1808,[35] was otherwise tardy, and the effort was bloody and painful. But we officially ended the practice in 1865, with the passage of the Thirteenth Amendment.

The timing was not coincidental. "The fact is that slavery disappeared only as industrial capitalism emerged," writes economist

Don Boudreaux. "And it disappeared first where industrial capital-ism appeared first: Great Britain. This was no coincidence. Slavery was destroyed by capitalism."[36] Adam Smith not only opposed slav-ery on moral grounds* but also considered it incompatible with the free market. "It appears, accordingly, from the experience of all ages and nations, I believe, that the work done by free men comes cheaper in the end than the work performed by slaves."[37] He also wrote that "whatever work he does beyond what is sufficient to purchase his own maintenance, can be squeezed out of him by violence only, and not by any interest of his own."[38]

The fact that we needed a war to end the institution demonstrates that not everybody saw the light all at once. Nor is it altogether accu-rate to say that the war was launched to end slavery, though the war would never have started absent slavery. But what is true is that a lib-eral democratic order—and by extension a modern economy—cannot last while tolerating slavery. An array of internal contradictions led to the Civil War. As Abraham Lincoln put it, "I believe this government cannot endure, permanently half slave and half free." And, famously invoking Jesus's admonition, "A house divided against itself cannot stand."[39]

Take the Declaration of Independence out of it, and American slavery was *normal*. MIT economists Daron Acemoglu and Alexan-der Wolitzky write:

> Standard economic models of the labor market, regardless of whether they incorporate imperfections, assume that transactions in the labor market are "free." For most of human history, how-ever, the bulk of labor transactions have been "coercive," mean-

---

* Smith writes in *The Theory of Moral Sentiments*, "There is not a negro from the coast of Africa who does not . . . possess a degree of magnanimity which the soul of his sordid master is too often scarce capable of conceiving. Fortune never exerted more cruelly her empire over mankind, than when she subjected those nations of heroes to the refuse of the jails of Europe, to wretches who possess the virtues neither of the countries which they come from, nor of those which they go to, and whose levity, bru-tality, and baseness, so justly expose them to the contempt of the vanquished." Adam Smith. "V.1.19.: Of the Influence of Custom and Fashion upon our Notions of Beauty and Deformity." *The Theory of Moral Sentiments*. Library of Economics and Liberty. http://www.econlib.org/library/Smith/smMS5.html

ing that the threat of force was essential in convincing workers to take part in the employment relationship, and thus in determining compensation. Slavery and forced labor were the most common forms of labor transactions in most ancient civilizations, including Greece, Egypt, Rome, several Islamic and Asian Empires, and most known pre-Colombian civilizations . . ."[40]

In other words, the very notion that humans can sell their services or labor in a free market is a remarkably recent idea. Conversely, while almost all socialist and communist doctrine claims to oppose slavery—including so-called wage slavery in the case of the Marxists—the reality of socialism taken to its logical conclusion has often led to slavery in the form of forced labor. Command economies are just that: *command* economies. The Soviet Union, Nazi Germany, communist China, and North Korea have all widely used forced labor. China's laogai system was set up in the 1950s and modeled on the Soviet Union's gulag. "Laogai" means reform through labor, and the ostensible idea was to create committed Communists by forcing them to be indoctrinated to communism with the aid of backbreaking labor. The system became a profit center for party leaders and exists to this day, though the government has ditched the name "laogai" in favor of *jianyu,* or "prison." But the practice endures. In the 2000s, it was revealed that administrators continued to profit from prisoners even after they worked them to death, by selling the organs of slaves.[41]

That China continued to rely on slave labor even after it embraced "capitalism" isn't an indictment of capitalism, properly understood, but of authoritarianism. Authoritarian regimes can make profits, but that doesn't make them free-market systems. The slaveholding rulers of the South got very rich, but everyone else stayed poor—or enslaved—because others were denied the full scope of liberty and rights necessary for capitalism to work. It's a good thing China has embraced some market principles, because history shows that the development of a strong middle class creates a demand for responsive and accountable government. But China will not be a free country until the Communist Party is laid on the ash heap of history, where it belongs. As for now, it should be understood as a de facto authoritarian aristocracy, as we will see.

Disciples of the noble savage and radical egalitarians aren't the only constituencies vexed by the reality of human nature. Partisans for the free market often run up against the inconvenient fact that *Homo sapiens* and *Homo economicus* are not synonyms.

The phrase *Homo economicus*, economic man, emerges as a criticism of John Stuart Mill and other thinkers who were seen—usually unfairly, particularly in the case of Adam Smith—as reducing humans to purely rational, profit-maximizing, economic beings. It's not at all clear to me that Mill actually believed that man was purely a profit maximizer and it is clear to me that Smith did not. In other words, *Homo economicus* is one of those terms, like "social Darwinism," that has few if any adherents but is especially useful as an intellectual epithet. Mill was quite clear that his definition of man as a profit maximizer was bound to the study of economics:

Geometry presupposes an arbitrary definition of a line, "that which has length but not breadth." Just in the same manner does Political Economy presuppose *an arbitrary definition of man, as a being who invariably does that by which he may obtain the greatest amount of necessaries, conveniences, and luxuries, with the smallest quantity of labour and physical self-denial with which they can be obtained in the existing state of knowledge* [emphasis mine].[42]

An expert on football would have a definition of *Homo footballis* that would ignore what the players did off the field. Is it any scandal that an economist would have a definition of people that was contingent on economic activity?

Still, it is true that, historically, many economists and free-market ideologues have all too often looked at human behavior through a narrow economic lens. And, to be fair, Marxism has a tendency to reduce all questions to economic concerns as well. The old adage "If all you have is a hammer, every problem looks like a nail" seems apposite. Some free-market ideologues often sound like they believe in *Homo economicus.*

Regardless, the fact is that humans are not defined by the pursuit of profit, even if they often pursue profit. Many critics of capitalism find the idea of "economic man" a useful straw man in their indictment of capitalism, because bound up in the idea of economic man is the idea that "greed is good," in the words of Oliver Stone's straw man Gordon Gekko in 1987's *Wall Street*.

Wherever you come down on these issues, it's fair to say that we tend to think that humans are motivated by financial greed far more than they are. To be sure, greed is a staple of human nature, but greed for money has only been around for as long as money has been around—and, in evolutionary terms, that hasn't been a very long time. Surely reasonable people can agree that greed predated money. One can easily see why greed for food and other basic resources would evolve. We can imagine countless circumstances in human history where the altruistic man starved to death, while the greedy one lived another day and hence passed on his genes.

But just as greed—or covetousness—is natural, so is altruism. Without altruism, it is unlikely the human race would have made it this long. Altruism can be driven by compassion, another universal human tendency. But it also is closely linked to gift exchange, reciprocity, and cooperation. Long before there were coins, the economy of primitive man was governed by gift exchange and reciprocity: I do this thing for you; you do something for me. I give you a hunk of meat; you help me fend off a bully eager to rob me. (The social economy of prisons—arguably the closest approximations to a state of nature in modern society—works according to these principles.) Richard Leakey and Kurt Lewin have ascribed the essence of the survival of the human species to the concept of reciprocity. Small bands of early humans could only survive if they learned to share resources "in an honored network of obligation."[43] It is a well-established finding in anthropology, psychology, and sociology that people who violate the norms of reciprocity are shunned by the larger group. Even among criminal organizations—prison gangs, the Mafia, etc.—the rules of reciprocity must be honored within the group. People who over-adhere to these norms—the generous, the philanthropic, etc.—are admired and often endowed with authority, political or moral, over others. The "big men" who lead many primitive societies often earned their status by the perceived justness with which they distributed resources to the group.[44]

Which brings us to admiration. Of course, all other things being equal, people want to be rich rather than poor. But what they want even more is to be admired, respected, and valued. Adam Smith understood this—and so much else about human nature—in his *Theory of Moral Sentiments*:

> Man naturally desires, not only to be loved, but to be lovely; or to be that thing which is the natural and proper object of love. He naturally dreads, not only to be hated, but to be hateful; or to be that thing which is the natural and proper object of hatred. He desires not only praise, but praiseworthiness; or to be that thing which, though it should be praised by nobody, is, however, the natural and proper object of praise. He dreads, not only blame, but blame-worthiness; or to be that thing which, though it should be blamed by nobody, is, however, the natural and proper object of blame.[45]

A desire to be admired is hardwired into us, just as it is in chimpanzees. There's no debate about this, as far as I can tell, among the diverse range of disciplines that look at such things. The researchers, however, focus less on the concept of admiration and more on the idea of "status." Status is the essence of chimpanzee politics, as Frans de Waal persuasively argued at book-length in his *Chimpanzee Politics: Power and Sex Among Apes*.[46] It would be a strange believer in evolution who thought that something that was central to the life of our nearest genetic cousins is irrelevant to us.

Sociologists distinguish between two kinds of status in all human societies: ascribed status and achieved status. "Ascribed status" refers to what you are born with. Royalty is the quintessential example of ascribed status: the belief that some people are just born better or worse thanks to their lineage or parents. In numerous societies, India arguably the most famous, the whole of the population was divided up into different categories of ascribed status called castes. These castes set the acceptable parameters of virtually every meaningful pursuit in life, including the places one could live, whom one could marry, and even what kind of occupations one could hold. Europe's caste system was perhaps less austere but no less binding, with categories of serfs, peasants, nobility, and other rankings of humans' innate worth.

One of the greatest yet among the least appreciated achievements of the American Revolution was the decision to abolish such things. One very good reason it's so unappreciated is that we maintained another version of applied status: slavery. In the Roman tradition of slavery, slaves were not born, they were made. The child of a slave did not inherit that status. In the American South, defenders of slavery realized that this common tradition of slavery was incompatible with their system, so they adopted the Aristotelian notion that some people are simply slaves by nature, making slavery an ascribed status.[47]

Though we have abandoned formal, legal, and applied status in America, the desire for status it is still a fact of our lives. If you had a typical grade school or high school experience, you know that status seeking is the very heart of adolescent social life. Adolescents talk not of status but of popularity, though this is not that meaningful a distinction. Cliques are all about status. So are the petty and often cruel contests that define the politics of the locker room and the playground. The same goes for prisons.

More broadly, one need only look at the enduring success of political dynasties to see that inherited status still plays a big role in our culture. Kennedys, Bushes, Clintons, Roosevelts, Romneys—we ascribe status to the progeny of famous people whose worth and honor is unearned by their own actions. In marketing terms, certain last names and bloodlines have in effect become a kind of inherited title, though today we would call it a "brand."

This is even more the case outside of politics. We cavalierly talk about "Hollywood royalty" without really understanding what we mean by that. Out of a concern for my eternal soul, I've vowed never to write about the Kardashians, but I think I am not putting it in too much peril to simply note that we treat that ridiculous band of airheads and slatterns as some sort of celebrity gentry.[48]

This is natural. Every family has within it a spark of dynastic ambition. I'm reminded of Tywin Lannister's sermon to Jaime Lannister on the importance of family in *Game of Thrones*: "Your mother's dead. Before long I'll be dead, and you and your brother and your sister and all of her children, all of us dead, all of us rotting underground. It's the family name that lives on. It's all that lives on. Not your personal glory, not your honor, but family. You understand?"[49]

Status is closely linked to our natural instinct for authority and hierarchy—an instinct that is found in just about every species of animal that lives in groups. Dogs, chickens, and apes have hierarchies and pecking orders. Jonathan Haidt notes that these impulses are so baked into us they manifest themselves in language. "The urge to respect hierarchical relationships is so deep that many languages encode it directly," he writes. "In French, as in other romance languages, speakers are forced to choose whether they'll address someone using the respectful form (*vous*) or the familiar form (*tu*). Even English, which doesn't embed status into verb conjugations, embeds it elsewhere. Until recently, Americans addressed strangers and superiors using title plus last name (Mrs. Smith, Dr. Jones), whereas intimates and subordinates were called by first name. If you've ever felt a flash of distaste when a salesperson called you by first name without being invited to do so, or if you felt a pang of awkwardness when an older person you have long revered asked you to call him by first name, then you have experienced the activation of some of the modules that comprise the Authority/subversion foundation."[50]

Haidt's use of the word "foundation" refers to part of the Moral Foundations Theory he and other researchers formulated. He lays it all out in his path-breaking book *The Righteous Mind: Why Good People Are Divided by Politics and Religion*. If you can read that book and not come away confident that there is something called "human nature," you might as well put down this book too.

Moral Foundations Theory holds that there are six components to moral sentiments that form the basis of all forms of moral reasoning. They are: care, fairness, liberty, loyalty, authority, and sanctity. How these foundations are applied and interact explain all of the variations in human cultures and societies when it comes to how we define right and wrong.

Indeed, the need for norms of behavior is another universal facet of human nature. As we've seen, there is a lot of variability in the kinds of norms we establish, but the need for norms is uniform across all societies. And certain basic rules of conduct or moral behavior seem to be universal—and pre-rational—as well. When someone cuts in line in front of us at the grocery store, there is a chemical reaction in our brains that fills us with anger. Our reaction is often quite disproportionate to the harm actually done to us. That's because we evolved to see the stakes in norm violations to be much greater than they are at the local Walmart or Kroger. A norm violation on the African savannas could be a matter of life and death.

Paul Bloom recounts how the innate and universal tendency of children to tattle on their siblings and classmates seems to be an early form of norm enforcement. One key indicator of this is that kids rarely make up stuff when they rat out each other. Psychologists Gordon Ingram and Jesse Bering studied tattling by children in an inner-city school in Belfast and found that "the great majority of children's talk about their peers' behavior took the form of descriptions of norm violations."[51]

Norms matter evolutionarily because they are the sinew of all cooperation. If primitive man lived a solitary life, as Thomas Hobbes believed, norms wouldn't matter. But we evolved in groups, specifically tribes. Without cooperation, we would still be a mid-tier species, not the planet's apex predator. And cooperation is impossible without norms, or rules. Think about it for just a moment and this becomes obvious. A hunting party cannot work as a group unless it has agreed upon rules, including lines of authority. What separates an army from a rabble is that the soldiers know their place and their duties, even when they're not being supervised.

Charles Darwin himself speculated about how cooperativeness—altruism, reciprocity, consensus around norms, and, most of all, unity—was the key to human survival. The tribe that works together survives to pass its genes on. "If . . . the one tribe included . . . courageous, sympathetic and faithful members, who were always ready to warn each other of danger, to aid and defend each other," Darwin observed, "this tribe would without doubt succeed best and conquer the other."[52] Cooperation explains the evolution of language, religion, warfare, and almost every uniquely human endeavor. But the drive and desire to cooperate isn't just a society-wide phenomenon. Politics, long before we had the word "politics," has been about forming coalitions: within the band, the tribe, or any other social unit. Chimpanzees and humans alike form coalitions around all manner of interests. These coalitions are like subtribes, and they are every bit as prone to the logic of us-versus-them as the tribe as a whole is to foreign enemies. As we will see, the dire shape of our politics today is a function of this tendency, as Americans break up into "tribal" coalitions against other Americans they only see as "the other."

Adherence to norms is impossible without some collective understanding that norms must be enforced. Paul H. Robinson and Sarah M. Robinson's book *Pirates, Prisoners, and Lepers: Lessons from Life Outside the Law* brilliantly and, to my mind, incontrovertibly demonstrates how notions of punishment and retribution are not merely universal (a relatively uncontroversial point) but absolutely necessary for cooperation. This is much more controversial. A growing number of criminologists and ethicists see punishment itself to be illegitimate and dangerous. David Garland, a professor of sociology and law at New York University, insists: "It is only the mainstream processes of socialization (internalized morality and the sense of duty, the informal inducements and rewards of conformity, the practical and cultural networks of mutual expectation and interdependence, etc.) which are able to promote proper conduct on a consistent and regular basis."[53] Another scholar claims "the institution of criminal punishment is ethically, politically, and legally unjustifiable ... [A] society concerned about protecting all of its members from violations of their claims of right should rely on institutions other than criminal punishment."[54]

But, as the Robinsons show, with exhaustive citations from both psychological research as well as the historical record, cooperation is unsustainable without some kind of sanction against those who do not cooperate. If you and nine of your friends are tasked with digging a ditch in the hot sun on the promise that you will all be rewarded at the end of the day with a great meal, how long will you tolerate an able-bodied free rider who sits in the shade under a tree as you toil in discomfort? How likely is it that the group will include the slacker in the meal at the end of the day? Countless laboratory and real-life experiments show that the free rider will be punished, certainly with scorn, and usually with exclusion from the reward.

This instinct to enforce group norms manifests itself everywhere from primitive tribes to sports teams and even, as the Robinsons demonstrate, to utopian hippie communes where everyone is supposed to be free to let their freak flags fly. And whenever the instinct is not enforced by a central authority or the collective itself—or both—the unit disintegrates. Even a young Bernie Sanders was kicked off his commune because he was less interested in doing the work of socialism than he was in talking about the need for socialism.[55]

Instead, let us move on to a final, crucial facet of human nature: meaning. We are creators of meaning. What do I mean by "meaning"? Simply that we have a natural tendency to imbue things, practices, people, events, ideas, and everything else around us with significance beyond the rational and material. Just consider the meaning we invest in eating food. The family dinner, breaking bread with old friends, Thanksgiving—we invest in these things meaning far beyond the need for sustenance. There's a vast anthropological and sociological literature dedicated to the role eating plays in every culture. The primary form of what social scientists call "gift exchange" has always been, at least until very recently, the sharing of food.[56]

For millennia food—preparation, blessing, sharing—has been the sinew of society. Many major religious holy days in Judaism, Christianity, and Islam involve food—either the communal eating of it or the communal abstention from it. Indeed, when some Christian denominations take *Communion*—i.e., joining not just the community of fellow Christians but entering into the body of the church itself—they do so by eating the transubstantiated flesh of Jesus. Depending on the denomination, this is a solemn moment or a celebratory one, but in all cases the significance is greater than merely snacking on "my little cracker," in the words of Donald Trump.[57]

In subsistence societies, a great feast combined every aspect of life. It was a celebration, a cause for thanksgiving as well as entertainment. The feast was also the keystone of politics: the Big Man's authority derived in very large part from how he distributed food at such gatherings to members of the clan or tribe. The feast was also a vital tool of diplomacy. Peace with an enemy tribe was often brokered and usually celebrated at a feast. Marriages, one of the central tools of alliance making, were both sealed and solemnized with a great feast.[58]

The Hebrew Bible is crammed with countless rules about what kind of animals we can eat, how they must be prepared, etc. The modern mind looks at such rules and says, *Ah, that was about hygiene,* or some such. But that misses the forest for the trees. No doubt, hygiene played a role in such norms, but to say Kashrut ("kosherism") is just the ancient version of a sign saying "Employees must wash hands" is absurd. Prior to the scientific revolution, we did not compartmental-ize meaning as we do today.

Think of it this way: For some primitive tribes a tree was many things—a source of fuel, a resource for shelter and tools, a plaything for children, perhaps a source of food, and a manifestation of some divine purpose or entity. Separating the practical ways of seeing a tree from the transcendent ones is a modern invention. To the extent any-one does believe we are simply *Homo economicus* and nothing more, they blind themselves to the vast scope of meaning that cannot be reduced to economic inputs.

Ernest Gellner argues that, in the transition to modernity, we lost something that defined how humans saw the world until three hun-dred years ago.[59] We used to layer meaning atop meaning, horizon-tally, like one sheet of tinted film atop another. Utility and sacredness, habit and ritual, convenience and tradition, metaphor and fact—each lay atop one another, producing a single lens through which we viewed the world. The scientific revolution changed that. We now hold each sheet of film separately and look at the world through it. We have one sheet for religion. Another for business. Yet another for family. We pick up each one like a special and separate magnifying glass for each specimen.

This division of mental labor has helped to produce enormous prosperity, cure diseases, reduce violence, and liberate humanity from millennia of superstitions that held individual humans from realizing their potential.

But it has also produced enormous challenges, because this way of seeing the world is unnatural. Our modern tendency to put different aspects of our lives into distinct silos—religion over here, entertain-ment here, food here, politics over there—is wholly alien to how man evolved to live. In our evolutionary natural habitat, we stack meaning atop meaning. Family is a sacred bond, but it is also a survival mecha-nism. Food is sustenance, but it is also an opportunity for community and sacralization. Politics isn't an artificial mechanism or a separate sphere of life, blocked off from religion, survival, or community; it is how every important question of daily life is answered, and it is how

God, or the gods, or our ancestors, wanted us to live—all at the same time.

By separating out the different meanings of our lives, each one seems more diluted, less all-encompassing and fulfilling. We miss the unity of the pre-Enlightenment mind. And so we yearn to restore meaning where it isn't. We yearn to end the division of labor and find ways of life that are "authentic" and "holistic." We attach ourselves to ideologies that promise unity, where we are all part of the same family or tribe. We flock to leaders on the left and the right who promise to tear down walls and end division—but always on our terms. So much of the rhetoric about the evils of money and the "capitalist system" isn't really about money but about how so much of our lives has been chopped up by this division of psychic and spiritual labor, banishing the ecstasy of the transcendent from our daily lives. This, in short, is the romantic temper. The romantic wants to pull down the walls of compartmentalized lives and restore a sense of sacred or patriotic unity of meaning and purpose.

Still, just because the modern mind compartmentalizes more than the ancient one did doesn't mean the walls are as high and as sturdy as we think. They are being broken down every day, in our own minds and in the larger community. That is because our inner tribesman doesn't like this world, and he is desperate to get back to where he came from. The problem is that seeking such unity in all things is the first step in leaving the Miracle of modernity. The desire to decompartmentalize every facet of life—work, family, politics, economics, art, etc.—is a reactionary one. It is the totalitarian temptation, and a corruption of the civilization we are blessed to live in. And it is utterly natural.

2

CORRUPTING THE MIRACLE
When Human Nature Strikes Back

Naturam expelles furca, tamen usque recurret. ("You may drive nature out with a pitchfork, but she will keep coming back.")

—HORACE[1]

Freedom is a fragile thing and is never more than one generation away from extinction. It is not ours by inheritance; it must be fought for and defended constantly by each generation, for it comes only once to a people. Those who have known freedom and then lost it have never known it again.

—RONALD REAGAN, 1967[2]

IN WILLIAM GOLDING'S CLASSIC NOVEL *LORD OF THE FLIES*, A group of British schoolboys get stranded on a deserted island. These adolescents are in some respects the pinnacle of Western civilization. But without supervision, the children almost instantly forget the rules of society. Brimming with testosterone, adrenaline, and all of the sexual confusions of adolescence, they fall back on primitive instinctual mechanisms. They form coalitions not just to hunt but to vie for status, safety, and power. They become tribal, cruel, and superstitious. In their paranoia, they create a demon that they both fear and worship. They mount a pig's rotting head on a pike and call it "the Lord of the Flies" (the literal translation of "Beelzebub")[3] and worship it as their god. But the beast explains to gentle and stubbornly civilized Simon that the pig head is not in fact the real beast. The beast is not "something you could hunt and kill," because the real beast resides inside all of the children themselves.[4]

That internal beast is human nature. It cannot be killed; it can only be tamed. And even then, constant vigilance is required.

The story of civilization is, quite literally, the story of taming, directing, channeling, or holding at bay human nature. It is human nature to take what you want, particularly from a stranger—if you can get away with it. It is human nature to kill—again, particularly strangers—if you don't like them or feel threatened by them. It is human nature to grant favors to family and friends. Civilizations—all of them—establish rules of one kind or another to direct or channel human nature toward productive ends. What counts as productive ends has evolved over time. For most of the last 10,000 years, productive ends were defined as "what is good for the rulers." Since the Enlightenment, the definition has improved. The modern ideologies of socialism, nationalism, and democracy all claim that the ends of a just society must be the betterment of "the people." But, human nature being what it is, the elites of every society often find ways to benefit nonetheless. And definitions of "the people" often turn out to be quite selective.

When a politician uses his power and authority for personal gain, we call that "corruption." And that's fine. But this understanding of corruption is but one small tentacle of the larger beast. The older, more authentic meaning of "corruption," according to the *Oxford English Dictionary*, was: "The destruction or spoiling of anything, esp. by disintegration or by decomposition with its attendant unwholesomeness; and loathsomeness; putrefaction."[5]

This understanding of corruption was once central to our view of the world and our place in it. The phrase, "ashes to ashes, dust to dust" doesn't appear in the Bible—it's from the Book of Common Prayer—but that was the idea.[6] Genesis 3:19 gets to the heart of it: "By the sweat of your face you shall eat bread, till you return to the ground, for out of it you were taken; for you are dust, and to dust you shall return." Hamlet observes that "a man may fish with the worm that hath eat of a king, and eat of the fish that hath fed of that worm."[7]

Prior to the scientific revolution, corruption was more than a metaphor in our daily lives. Everyday cuts and scrapes could invite death if they got infected. Without refrigeration, uncured food began to turn almost instantly. Wood, a universal building material, was always losing the battle against rot and decay. How to hold at bay the corrupting power of nature was an obsession in everyday life. Think about what we mean when we talk about "decadent" societies, civilizations, or empires. "Decadent" comes to us from the Medieval Latin *decadentia*, meaning decay or decaying. A decaying civilization, like a decaying house, is one that has given itself over to natural forces of entropy.

From the very first societies that could call themselves "civilized," the job of policy makers—whether kings, priests, or legislators and bureaucrats—was to fend off the corrupting power of human nature. When man's law disappears or loses its force, nature's law returns—quickly.

THIS IS MOST OBVIOUS when people resort to violence. When a political partisan or religious zealot picks up a gun and goes on a killing spree, we all intuitively grasp that violence represents an enormous step backward. But that language is inadequate. It is actually a form of rot, a regression to the mean, an expression of the natural savagery of humanity.

A common feminist slogan is that men must be "taught not to rape." Some seem to believe this is a stance against some camp of pro-rape pedagogy out there. But on its plain meaning, the feminists are right: Men must be taught not to rape because rape is natural. Rape was considered by countless societies to be the natural extension of military conquest. When the Yanomamö capture a woman, the whole raiding party gets to rape her. She is then brought to the village, where anyone else who wants to rape her may do so. Afterward, she is forced to be some man's wife.[8]

In his article "Explaining Wartime Rape," Jonathan Gottschall, a scholar of this grim subject, reviews the prevalence and ubiquity of wartime rape and concludes: "In short, historical and anthropological evidence suggests that rape in the context of war is an ancient human practice, and that this practice has stubbornly prevailed across a stunningly diverse concatenation of societies and historical epochs . . ."[9]

It is significant that both rape and prohibitions against rape are universal to all societies. It wasn't a question of morality but of situational ethics. It all depended on whom one raped and for what reason. Even among the !Kung or the Yanomamö, rape *within* the tribe or family or band was usually considered taboo. But rape—or murder—of *the Other* was not merely tolerated; it was celebrated. Women were legitimate spoils of war, from prehistoric times until just about the day before yesterday, in every corner of the globe.[10]

There's a lot of talk about "rape culture" in America, as if America is somehow too tolerant of rape. Since we should have zero tolerance for rape, this claim is in some very narrow sense true. But the reality is that America—and the West generally—is less tolerant of rape than any society in human history.

Now, when I say that rape is natural, I do not mean that all men are equally disposed to be rapists. It surely came easier for some prehistoric men than for others. And rape—like violence generally—is far more prevalent among men. But my point is that the social norms against rape are modern inventions, artificial constructs of our civilization. That doesn't mean these norms are bad; it makes them important and noble and worthy of protection.

The key point here, however, is that when we witness the evil of rape, some part of us recognizes it for what it is. It is not an expression of capitalist culture but a regression to man's basest self. Long before feminism took up the cause of fighting rape, civilization had been working to make it unacceptable. Rape is a tangible manifestation of the corruption of civilized behavior. If you want to return to the time of the mythical noble savage, you want to return to a time when rape was a routine and acceptable practice in human affairs.

A KEY TOOL FOR getting humans to play by rules nobler than those of the jungle is the idea of virtue. Definitions of virtue vary across time and place, but they are united by the idea that virtuous people adhere to a moral code above mere selfishness. Virtue requires denying one's baser instincts—i.e., human nature—and doing what is right. This is why C. S. Lewis argued that "courage is not simply *one* of the virtues, but the form of every virtue at the testing point . . ."[11] Or, as John Locke said, "Fortitude is the guard and support of the other virtues . . ."[12] In short, virtue takes effort.

"Man's one resource in the face of Fortune and blind circumstance was his virtue," writes Arthur Herman. "Originally, *virtus* meant courage in battle, but it came to include manly integrity in all spheres of life. Virtue was the inner strength necessary to overcome the 'slings and arrows of outrageous Fortune,' as Shakespeare put it, and to forge one's own destiny."[13] In other words, virtue is no longer just courage in military battle but courage in the battle against human nature. No principle is truly held lest it comes at a price.

At least until the rise of modern doctrines of progress—Whiggism, Hegelianism, Marxism, and progressivism generally—which all shared a teleological faith in inevitable human improvement, the metaphorical power of corruption and the eternal cycles of life informed nearly all literature, philosophy, theology, and, most importantly, daily life. It explained why nearly every society believed that civilizations mirrored the ages of man. It was the footnote to every explanation of why love fades, faith fails, and man disappoints God.

One of the dumbest tropes of smart people is the notion that modern science deposed man as the "center of the universe."[14] Yale's John Bargh says that Galileo "removed the Earth from its privileged position at the center of the universe." The *Britannica Concise Encyclopedia* tells us that Galileo's "dethronement of Earth from the center of the universe caused profound shock . . ."

It is a modern conceit that the center is a place of privilege and honor. As I wrote in my last book, "Before Copernicus the general consensus among Western scientists and theologians was, in accordance with Aristotle, that the Earth was either at, or was, the anal aperture of the universe, literally."[15]

In 1486, Giovanni Pico, a leading philosopher of the Italian Renaissance, penned his *Oration on the Dignity of Man*, commonly referred to as the manifesto of the Italian Renaissance. In it he observed that the Earth resided in "the excremetary and filthy parts of the lower world." Two centuries earlier, Thomas Aquinas concluded that, "in the universe, the earth—that all the spheres encircle and that, as for place, lies in the center—is the most material and coarsest of all bodies." In Dante's *Inferno*, the lowest pit of Hell is at the exact center of the planet, which historian Dennis Danielson describes as the "dead center of the universe."[16]

This fetid world was, in short, not merely corrupt but corrupting. The ideal, the pure, the true, lay in the next world, and the man of virtue and integrity fought against the baser, natural temptations that pulled his gaze from what was good and noble.

"I know that after my death you will become utterly corrupt and will turn from the way I have commanded you to follow," Moses tells the Israelites. "In the days to come, disaster will come down on you, for you will do what is evil in the LORD's sight, making him very angry with your actions."[17]

In the Book of James, Jesus proclaims: "You adulterous people! Do you not know that friendship with the world is enmity with God? Therefore whoever wishes to be a friend of the world makes himself an enemy of God."[18]

Catholic priests, nuns, and monks turn their back on worldly temptations because they are the path to corruption.

This idea that human nature is corrupting of all that is divine, noble, or good is not merely the stuff of philosophers and theologians. It has been the central problem of politics and administration since the agricultural revolution.

In his *Origins of Political Order,* Francis Fukuyama demonstrates that there are certain universal characteristics of all human societies, fixed features of the human condition that political orders must work with rather than deny or erase if they are to be successful. The first of these:

> Inclusive fitness, kin selection, and reciprocal altruism are default modes of sociability. All human beings gravitate toward the favoring of kin and friends with whom they have exchanged favors unless strongly incentivized to do otherwise.[19]

Without "strong countervailing incentives," Fukuyama argues, "the natural human propensity to favor family and friends—something I refer to as patrimonialism—constantly reasserts itself."

He adds that "organized groups—most often the rich and powerful—entrench themselves over time and begin demanding privileges from the state. Particularly when a prolonged period of peace and stability gives way to financial and/or military crisis, these entrenched patrimonial groups extend their sway, or else prevent the state from responding adequately."[20] The details vary, but the themes remain constant. Elites succumb to the temptations of human nature, and, in their corruption, the civilization loses the integrity that made greatness possible in the first place.

This observation, offered in the language of social science, can be found in the poetry of Shakespeare (particularly the Roman plays), countless cautionary tales from the Bible, and nearly every history of every fallen empire. Mancur Olson writes:

> Many have been puzzled by the mysterious decline or collapse of great empires or civilizations and by the remarkable rise to wealth, power, or cultural achievement of previously peripheral or obscure peoples. The collapse of the Roman Empire in the West and its defeat by scattered tribes that would otherwise have been of no account is only one of many puzzling examples. On repeated occasions the imposing empires of China have decayed to the point where they could fall prey to far less numerous or sophisticated peoples like the Mongols or to uprisings by poor peasants in remote provinces. The Middle East provides several examples of such collapsed empires, and so do the Indian civilizations of Meso-America; even before the Aztec empire was destroyed by a small contingent of Spaniards there had been a succession of empires or cultures, each of which seems to have been supplanted by a previously obscure tribe, its grand pyramids or cities abandoned to the wilderness. The pattern was not greatly different in the Andes, or at Angkor Wat, or in still other places.[21]

This pattern, he notes, was well known when Herodotus put pen to papyrus. "The cities that were formerly great, have most of them become insignificant; and such as are at present powerful, were weak in olden time. I shall therefore discourse equally on both, convinced that human happiness never continues long in one stay."[22]

Historians and political scientists focus on elites for wholly understandable reasons: By definition, that's where the power is. If one robs banks because that is where the money is, one who studies power studies those who wield it. (Also, elites tend to leave written records of their doings, which makes it possible to study them. Even "social histories" of marginal groups depend heavily on the evidence left behind by their masters, employers, and rulers.)

But this emphasis can distort our understanding of things. If one understands the history of decaying civilizations as purely the history of corrupted elites, it's only natural to believe that the problem lies with elites themselves. This leads to a lot of populist fantasies that "people-powered movements" are immune to the sins and temptations that define the rich and powerful. But elites are humans, and so it follows that the problems of elites are problems with humans themselves. Civilizations can also die when the masses are corrupted too.

Today, there's a low-simmering Jacobin fever aimed at the so-called one percent. This bland description of economic elites is logically ludicrous, given that it is a fact of math that there will always be a top one percent. A Bernie Sanders of a Stalinist bent could, in theory, liquidate the ranks of the top one percent and, in that very act, create an entirely new top one percent. Remove the top floor of a building and the next floor down becomes the top floor. The only way to ensure there is no top is to tear down the whole structure to the foundation.

One could replace the top economic echelon with a random sampling from the broader cadres of the bottom hundredth percentile. Is there any compelling testimony, other than that of campus Marxists and folk song lyricists, that would convince a reasonable person that the same problems that bedevil the current one percent would not, in short order, infect the new one percent? Meet the new boss, same as the old boss.

Neighborhood grocers give jobs to sons and nephews with just as much certitude about the rightness of what they are doing as hedge fund managers and New York real estate moguls. In fact, they probably feel more justified, as mom-and-pop shops do not have teams of lawyers and compliance officers charged with the task of fending off the corruptions of nepotism. Employing your children to work for the family concern—a farm, a store, whatever—is seen as wholly natural, because it is.

Indeed, nepotism is a good illustration of the eternal struggle between civilization and human nature. The word itself is instructive. It's derived from the Italian *nepotismo*, drawn from the Latin *nepos* for "grandchild" and the root of "nephew."[23]

The Catholic Church's struggle with nepotism lasted centuries. As best they could, priests were expected to follow the biblical admonition not to become "friends with this world" so that they could better serve it. Jesus led a chaste life and never married. Paul instructed followers to be celibate if at all possible.[24] And Christians, never mind leaders of the Church, were instructed to be as Christlike as possible. Nonetheless, there was no enforced, uniform rule on priestly celibacy in the Western Church for a thousand years[25] (and male priests can marry in the Eastern rite churches, but only before becoming priests). As humans are wont to do, priests often put their own desires, or the needs of their families, ahead of the Church. Various councils advised priests to be celibate and not have children as a measure to combat the image of priestly self-indulgence and corruption, but they didn't take hold for the most part.

Over time, the clergy became a parallel aristocracy. Priests left property to their children and built coalitions and dynasties within the Church. In response, Pope Benedict VIII banned the children of priests from inheriting property in the early eleventh century.[26] It wasn't until the Second Lateran Council in 1139 when the Church fully barred priests from marriage.[27]

While such rules proved relatively effective for the rank and file of the priesthood, the age-old story of the elites at the top exempting themselves from the rules they applied to others reasserted itself. Cardinals gave in to their carnal desires. Bishops built up their wealth and land holdings. And even the popes themselves tended toward creating their own "papal dynasties." This is how the term "nepotism," or "nephew-ism," was born. So-called cardinal-nephews were often, in fact, actual nephews, and sometimes "nephew" was a euphemism for the cardinal's own offspring. One of the most important power centers of the Church was the curial office of the superintendent of the ecclesiastical state. From 1566 until 1692—126 years!—that office was held by a cardinal-nephew.

The Borgia pope Callixtus III installed two of his nephews as cardinals. One of them, Rodrigo, eventually became pope himself, as

Alexander VI. He, in turn, made his mistress's brother a cardinal, who later became Pope Paul III. He went on to make two of his nephews cardinals.[28] This practice continued until 1692, when Pope Innocent XII issued a papal bull, *Romanum decet Pontificem*, limiting the pope's ability to bestow estates or privileges on any relatives.[29]

More than any other major institution of Western civilization, the Catholic Church was dedicated to rejecting the natural temptations of human nature. Or, if you prefer, it was—and is—dedicated to channeling human nature in productive and virtuous directions. When the Church fell short of these principles, it opened itself up to charges of the purest form of hypocrisy. Martin Luther's disgust with nepotism was one of his four central indictments of the Catholic Church. But what exactly was the heart of Luther's complaint? That the Church had become *too worldly*, a euphemism for the broader understanding of corruption.

Hypocrisy is often a terrible failing but it is more often a misunderstood one. Hypocrisy is the act of violating an ideal or principle you admonish others to follow. Too many people believe that hypocrisy is an indictment of the ideal as much as it is the hypocrite. This is folly. A world without hypocrisy is a world without ideals. A glutton may be a hypocrite by counseling others not to be gluttonous, but that doesn't mean the advice is wrong. Hence La Rochefoucauld's famous line that "hypocrisy is a tribute vice pays to virtue." And what is vice? Well, definitions vary. But a generic one might be: inappropriately giving in to our natural instincts and desires—the opposite of virtue.

The corruption that beset the Church can best be understood as nature reasserting itself—in this case, human nature. The Church responded by implementing new rules that made it more difficult for officials of the Church to give in to the whispered temptations emanating from their own genes. That is what civilizing institutions *do*, and the world would be worse off if, in a desire to avoid the charge of hypocrisy, they lifted all restraints on natural behavior.

Every human institution has faced similar trials. Again, the first tool of political power is not money or force or law; it is family. Every primitive society was governed first and foremost through an intricate web of family alliances. Social scientists call this "familism." Every monarchy and empire was similarly held in place by a network of rela-

tions by blood and marriage. Indeed, marriage—particularly polygamous marriage—was a tool of statecraft on every populated continent
for millennia. A king who took many wives was rewarded with many
children he could in turn marry off to cement alliances. The first
Ch'in emperor is said to have had over 3,000 wives and concubines.[30]

This practice had enormous political advantages for the emperor,
but it came with equally massive administrative problems. The Chinese response was to create a legendarily merit-based civil bureaucracy. Entrance exams were seen as an antidote to nepotistic patronage.
And compared to what came before, the Chinese bureaucracy was
an impressive advance. But, again, you can chase nature out with
a pitchfork—or, in this case, a civil service test—but nature invariably returns. The bureaucrats used their positions of power much the
same way priests in the Catholic Church did. They built up personal
dynasties—coalitions of common interest—rewarded their friends
and family, and enriched themselves at the public's expense.[31]

One famous reform to keep the bureaucrats on the straight and
narrow was to take the principle of priestly celibacy one step further:
castration. Many empires used eunuchs as trusted aides and servants
on the assumption that a man with no children would not be tempted
to enrich his own family (and a man without fully functioning male
equipment would not be seduced by other temptations). The practice
certainly had some merit, hence its ubiquity and endurance across
many civilizations and centuries. But, again, you can separate a man
from his genitals, yet you cannot separate him from his nature. Even
eunuchs have relatives. Indeed, some families would deliberately geld
one of their sons solely for the purpose of having one of their own
in a position of power. (In Europe, many second or third sons were
similarly encouraged to become figurative eunuchs in service to the
Church for similar reasons.) A Chinese saying captures the problem
well: "When a man becomes an official, his wife, children, dogs, cats,
and even chickens fly up to heaven."[32]

The Janissaries of the Ottoman Empire offer a similar example of
the difficulty in banishing human nature. Sultan Murad I created the
Janissaries, or "new soldiers," in 1383.[33] They served as a kind of Praetorian Guard, loyal only to the emperor. In theory, this loyalty was
derived from the fact that the Janissaries had no other family to speak

of. The Janissaries were Christian children stolen from their families, usually in the Balkans, at a young age and transported to the capital and other major cities. Scouts would scour the provinces for the most promising Christian youth—Muslims couldn't be slaves—and would tear them from their families. The children were then raised in Turkish families, constantly supervised by eunuchs, and groomed to have no allegiances other than to their master, the sultan. This idea should be familiar to anyone who read Plato's *Republic*, where the guardians are plucked from their natural parents to avoid nepotism in all its forms. (Socrates even suggests that the guardians should not be informed that they have human parents.)[34]

The Janissaries were slaves, but they were richly rewarded ones, thanks to the remarkably merit-based system they were conscripted into. Trained not only for war but for administration, they studied numerous languages, mathematics, and, of course, the Koran. Janissaries literally ran the Ottoman Empire as generals, ministers, provincial governors, and bureaucrats. Some, such as Sokollu Mehmed Pasha, even rose to the rank of grand vizier; Sokollu served three different sultans and was, effectively, the prime minister of the Ottoman Empire. Because the civil service was only open to foreigners, the Ottoman Empire was a true historical oddity: a slave empire ruled by the slaves.[35]

But it didn't last. Once again, this brilliant system for contradicting or at least compensating for human nature was undone by human nature. Over time, as with all groups where a strong collective identity is formed, coalitional self-interest is soon to follow. The key ingredients to this transformation everywhere in human history seem to be power and time. The longer a cohesive group collectively has the former, it is only a matter of the latter before the group takes advantage of it.

The Janissaries eventually became a predatory or parasitic class, in effect holding the state hostage to their interests. In 1826, Mahmud II decided it was time to finally amputate the once healthy but now corrupted and putrefied limb from the body politic. The Janissaries rebelled, and the uprising was crushed. Thousands of Janissaries died in the ensuing massacre, in what has been called "the Auspicious Incident."[36]

THE LESSON OF THE Chinese eunuchs, Ottoman Janissaries, and countless other groups is the same.[37] Given time and incentives, any group of humans will start to see themselves as a cohesive group, a caste or aristocratic class. Just as any random group of dogs—strays and purebreds alike—will, if put together, quickly form a pack with a collective identity, humans will do the same thing given time and the right inducements. The children in *Lord of the Flies*, contestants on *Survivor*, college students in the Stanford prison experiments, members of the Seattle Seahawks, police, firemen, marines, Copts, Sunnis, teachers' unions, street gangs, college professors—the list is as endless as the subdivision of labor and identity in any society. This natural human tendency is neither bad nor good. It's simply a fact. The capacity to trick our coalitional and tribal instincts to self-organize around identities other than race and kin can be the source of both wonderful things and horrible ones. Unity is a neutral value. Unity's moral status is derived entirely from what the group does. Whatever label you ascribe to the group—class, faction, sect, etc.—the only time self-interested groups or coalitions become a real threat to the larger society is when they claim the power of the state for their own agenda.

As I will discuss at length shortly, America's Founders and other Enlightenment intellectuals understood this implicitly. The remedies for this problem are myriad, but two are worth mentioning here: virtue and pluralism. We have already discussed virtue. Inculcating a profound commitment to certain higher principles is a bulwark against corruption.

The second notion, pluralism, is less obvious but no less important.

In political science and institutional economics, pluralism implies the idea that power should be distributed widely in a society. Nobel Prize–winning economist Douglass C. North and his coauthors argue in *Violence and Social Orders: A Conceptual Framework for Interpreting Recorded Human History* that nearly all of the things we associate with healthy, modern societies are directly attributable to the multiplication of institutions. When you only have a handful of "stakeholders" in a society—usually the priests, the landholding aristocrats, the military, maybe some guilds and bureaucrats, and, of course, the monarch—power is defined by the personal relationships between a tiny handful of elites. They in effect form a ruling coalition against the masses and they design the system for their own benefit. But, at some point, if you have enough different institutions, relationships between elites become "impersonal" for the simple reason that there are too many elites, and too many power centers, to conduct politics through personal relationships. In ideal cases, society hits a tipping point, and elites agree to general rules that bind everyone, including the elites themselves. (They also recognize that the most successful institutions will be open institutions that attract talent from as broad a base as feasible.) Ultimately, this gives birth to the rule of law, which holds that winners are bound by the same rules as losers, and that no one can wield arbitrary power.

The role played by institutions is older and larger than mere party politics, but looking at how party politics operate in developed democratic societies helps illustrate the point. As we've seen count-less times over the last century, any country can hold an election. In many parts of the world, the running joke about elections was "One man, one vote, one time." In other words, once a "democratic" can-didate got into power, he no longer had any use for democracy. The real test is when there's a transfer of power from one party to another. In healthy democratic countries, the party—or parties—out of power still have rights and prerogatives and the ability to make life difficult for the party in power. The parties have bought into a system—i.e., the Constitution—that takes all sorts of options off the table, from using violence against your opponents, to holding on to power after your defined term, to disrespecting the rights of the opposition and the people generally.

This principle emerged from the interplay of institutions. Political parties, after all, evolved as coalitions of elites and elite institutions—i.e., factions—not electoral organizations. And, starting in England, for reasons we will discuss in detail in another chapter, these factions stumbled into a system where respect for dissident or hostile elites and institutions out of power was written into law and, more importantly, into the *culture*. A critical mass of institutions, and a balance of power among them, forced elites—i.e., nobles and the king—to forgo using violence against each other to settle political disputes. This required creating not only political and social space for disagreement but psy-chological acceptance of the idea that people had the right to be wrong.

This was a conceptual breakthrough in the history of humanity. In traditional societies—and modern authoritarian ones as well—the only check on power is power. A king might refrain from crushing a powerful but troublesome nobleman, but not because the *law* prevents him. The only thing truly preventing rulers from destroying rival elites is a *Game of Thrones*-style cost-benefit analysis. Will attacking this lord be too expensive in terms of military resources or gold? Will doing so encourage even more dissent? Will I get in trouble with the Church? And in primitive societies, such calculations were far simpler: Can we take them by surprise? Do we have enough spears? And so on.

Institutional pluralism not only imposed constraints on elites but also constrained what elites could do with the state. In societies where the state picks sides—punishes dissidents, crushes minority faiths, etc.—control of the state becomes everything. In societies where there are a multitude of institutions, a cognitive switch is flipped, and people suddenly understand that everyone has a vested interest in keeping the rules of the game fair for everyone. As we shall see, this was the central insight of the Founders.

And while my use of the term "pluralism" includes all of this, it also includes something even larger. Modernity both requires and creates a *plurality of meaning and identity*, not simply *among* the population, but *within* each and every person. This is in stark contrast to primitive society, where identity and meaning were bound up and inseparable from the tribe. For most of human history, meaning was confined to a very small zone: "us." *Us* could be a tribe, a faith, a city-state, or denizens of a specific class. The rules for *us* were different from the rules for *them*, and there was nothing wrong with using force or the state—the same thing, ultimately—to arbitrarily enforce the rules in your favor.

Tribalism is natural, but it can also be manufactured. Manufactured tribalism is the very essence of identity politics, the heart of aristocracy, and the soul of nationalism. "Identity politics" may be a modern term, but it is an ancient idea. Embracing it is not a step forward but a retreat to the past.

———

WHEN ALL OF YOUR identity is bound up in a single group or cause, your concern for institutions and people outside of your group diminishes or vanishes. The Praetorian who *only* cares for the Guard, as a matter of logic, does not care about his family, his country, his faith, or anything else. The Mafioso who concerns himself solely with *La Cosa Nostra* (literally "our thing") will not concern himself with the law, the country, or conventional notions of morality. An open society is one where we have many allegiances—to family and society, to work and faith, etc. When you have competing or simply multiple allegiances, you open yourself up to the idea that opponents are not enemies. Pluralism creates social and psychological spaces where others are free to pursue their interests too. The religious freedom that emerges from the Treaty of Westphalia allowed for different faiths to operate freely, so long as everyone obeyed certain more or less neutral rules of behavior.

In an open society, a Catholic soldier may have Protestant brothers-in-arms. A Jewish doctor has gentile patients. The African-American policeman counts white officers as fellow brothers of the badge. This may mean we have weaker attachments to any specific identity, but that is the price we pay for peace and freedom. It can also mean that our attachments are stronger, because they came from an informed choice or a leap of faith. Regardless, pluralism requires tolerance and forces us to open ourselves up to the possibility that our identity is not the only true or right one.

This mental division of labor makes modernity possible. The most important division is between what the German sociologists called *gesellschaft* and *gemeinschaft*. The easiest way to remember the difference is the word "sell" in *gesellschaft*. Modern society's most important divide is between the external, impersonal, order of contracts, commerce, and law, and the personal order of family, friends, and community. We all live in both realms simultaneously, even though the rules for these realms could not be more different.

Humans were not designed to live in the market order of contracts, money, or impersonal rules, never mind huge societies governed by a centralized state. We were designed to live in bands, or what most people think of as tribes. The human brain is designed so that we can manage stable social relationships with roughly 150 people. This is called Dunbar's number, after the anthropologist Robin Dunbar.[38] Others have proposed slightly different numbers,[39] but the point remains: We were designed by evolution to be part of a group, but that group was very limited in size. These groups took on a variety of structures, but the basic anatomy was generally the same. There was a Big Man or some other form of chieftain or "alpha." There was little division of labor beyond that which separated men and women, the very young and the very old. In the most basic sense, these bands were socialist or communist in that resources were generally shared. But the genetic programming clearly emphasized *us* over *me*.

We still hold on to that programming and it rubs up against modernity constantly.

My father always used to tell me that the most corrupting thing in business wasn't money but friendship. If a total stranger called my father and offered him a cash payment to hire the stranger's totally unqualified kid, my dad would reply, "Get the hell out of here." But if a lifelong friend called and said that his unqualified son or daughter really needed a break, the answer might still be no, but it would be a much more difficult decision. That's because we are wired to help our friends and family in ways we are not when it comes to strangers.

People who think money is a corrupting force in life fail to appreciate that we simply cannot treat everyone as friends or family. The glory of money—and the rule of law—is that it empowers us to cooperate with strangers. One needn't know, never mind be related to, the butcher one buys a rasher of bacon from. A rich man and a poor man have the right to buy whatever product they wish, so long as they have the required funds to make the purchase. The democratizing power of money is one of the great forgotten advances of humanity.

Family, however, does not operate according to the rules of the market order. Indeed, in my family, we are Communists in the sense that we operate under the maxim "From each according to his ability, to each according to his need." I do not charge my daughter for food, and my wife and I do not present anyone with a bill for the household chores we do. If a friend or relative needs to sleep in my house or borrow my car, that falls under the natural, tribal economy of reciprocity or, more simply, favors. But if a stranger wants to use my car or sleep in my house, the rules are very different.

The problem is that the market order is unnatural. It is a human invention, no less artificial because it was developed over countless generations. And because it doesn't feel natural, it leaves many people cold, particularly those who are impoverished in the currency of gemeinschaft—community, friendship, family. The greatest force in the corruption of modernity is the organized political effort—active in every generation—to impose the rules of gemeinschaft on the gesellschaft. Every anti-capitalist political ideology is a variant of the idea that society should operate like a family, a tribe, a small community where everyone knows each other. Identity politics in all its forms is just a subset of this worldview. It says "My tribe deserves more than your tribe."

It's interesting: What we call corruption in developing or "backward" countries today—tribalism, favoritism, nepotism, self-dealing, patronage, graft, etc.—went by a different word for most of human history: politics. Similarly, Tammany Hall and other political machines of the nineteenth and twentieth centuries are considered pristine examples of corruption, even though most humans who are alive today, or who ever lived, would see that model of politics as so much more authentic and natural than the ideal of "clean government" today.

Spend a few minutes actually studying what activists mean by "social justice" and you will discover that it is often a reactionary effort. It claims the rule of law is a rigged system designed to protect the interests of the patriarchy or white privilege or the "one percent." Social justice holds that abstract rules or timeless principles are inadequate if they do not lead to "redistributive" or "economic" justice. In other words, as Friedrich Hayek famously observed, social justice is about the subjective will to power of a tribal coalition, not universal principles.[40]

Today's identity politics, likewise, holds that objective standards of merit or notions of free speech are invalid, even racist, if they perpetuate the amorphously defined evil of "white privilege." Christian organizations must adopt secular values, because deviation from social justice principles or priorities is a new form of heresy. Recently resurgent white supremacists and various "nationalists" share the same categorical thinking, arguing that the system is rigged toward minorities. All that matters is "winning" for my team or race or coalition. Following the rules or tolerating expression you disagree with has been redefined as surrender. Your enemies' misfortune is your victory, and vice versa.

Again, this is the natural way for humans to think about the world. It is consistent with our basic programming. During Hurricane Harvey, legions of partisans took to Twitter to cheer the fact that Texas was being punished for being a "red state" or for voting for Trump or simply for being Texas. Put the asininity of such expressions to one side. There could be no more human response than to think a terrible storm was sent to punish your enemies. All that was missing was an offering to Baal or Thor of a hundred oxen.

And it is all a corruption of the Miracle.

ENTROPY IS THE NATURAL process of decay, which is just another word for corruption, and as any homeowner who has labored to fend off rust, rot, or mold understands, keeping nature at bay requires effort. Well, the Miracle is our home, and our home requires upkeep.

Humanity did not get an exemption from the second law of thermodynamics. Everything under the sun, and the sun itself, dies, dissipates, and decays. The best we can do is hold entropy at bay, fighting the rust that consumes every alloy and the termites and bacteria that consume every living thing. Without effort, civilization dies, because that is what civilization is: effort. Humanity has been taking off like a rocket since the 1700s, but we have not achieved a stable orbit in the heavens. And even if we did, no orbit is stable over the long run. Eventually gravity claims what is hers.

COMPLACENCY IS A RECIPE for slow-motion suicide. The very first civilizations succeeded by "conquering" nature. Swamps were drained and forests cleared for crops. Animals were tamed and domesticated for food. Shelters were erected to fend off the elements. But the more important effort was keeping human nature under control, at first by regulating the violence that comes so naturally to us. Over the millennia, this effort became more refined, but it was still marked—everywhere—by oppression and exploitation to one extent or another.

That truly began to change once, and only once, in human history. That effort required work, not simply by states—or even especially by states—but also by the people themselves. That task is not over, the work is not done—*and it will never be.* As a species, we are in an endless sea, and we must keep paddling or sink back into the depths. Poverty is natural; wealth takes effort.

Under the best of circumstances, every important endeavor requires work. Every person who has ever been married understands that marriage requires effort. Every athlete understands the importance of practice and training. Every general knows that troops lose their edge unless it is carefully maintained. The Miracle of liberal democratic capitalism is not self-sustaining. Turn your back on its maintenance and it will fall apart. Take it for granted and people will start reverting to their natural impulses of tribalism. The best will lack all conviction and the worst will be full of passionate intensity. Things will fall apart.[41]

In the next chapter I look at how that work began.

PART II

3

The State
A Myth Agreed Upon

How did we get from the world of the hunter-gatherers to the state? A host of thinkers talk of something called "the social contract" as the beginning of modern society. These theories date back to antiquity, but their glory days came around the time of the Enlightenment, when Hugo Grotius, Thomas Hobbes, John Locke, Jean-Jacques Rousseau, Immanuel Kant, and others put forth one version or another of the same basic idea: Men in a state of nature agree to sacrifice some personal freedoms in exchange for security. There are important differences, however, between different notions of the social contract. For example, Hobbes's social contract gave license to an all-powerful state—the Leviathan—to protect humanity from life in a state of nature, which he described as "solitary, poor, nasty, brutish and short."[1] Locke's social contract was much better, insofar as he saw the state as a servant of the people rather than a master of them.

What unites pretty much all of the classical understandings of the social contract is that they are wrong. *There never was any such thing as a real, existing, social contract.* Prior to the Enlightenment, there's no record of any large group of people, primitive or otherwise, voluntarily coming together to write down or agree to the kind of social contract the philosophers describe.[2] It's a useful myth, a vital lie; the social contract is, to borrow a term, a social construct.

TO THE EXTENT there ever was one, the first social contract was—to borrow a phrase from *The Godfather*—an offer the signatories couldn't refuse. And the Godfather in this analogy was a gangster of sorts. He was what Mancur Olson, one of the great economists of the last half century, called "the stationary bandit." Before the stationary bandit, there were only roving bandits.

Roving bandits are exactly what they sound like. They are raiders, warlords, and marauders who sweep into a community and take everything they can: crops, tools, weapons, money, women, children, etc. It should go without saying that the roving bandit was a staple figure of the state of nature. The archaeological record is clear about that.

In the early days of the agricultural revolution, the threat of roving bandits was far greater than in the days of hunter-gatherers. First off, nomadic tribes are moving targets. Agricultural communities are easier prey because they stay in one place. Moreover, when humans settled down to grow crops, they lost their ability to feed themselves sustainably in any other way. Hence, being plundered of their food stores and equipment and having their able-bodied males slaughtered was often a catastrophic event. Because the roving bandits had no intention of returning anytime soon, they also had no interest in leaving anything of value behind.

The consequences of roving bandits were long-lasting for their victims. If you know you are likely to fall prey to whichever band of thieves might come your way, you are unlikely to make many long-term investments. Why toil in the fields or restore your granaries if you know that the Huns or the Cimmerians or whoever will just come back and take it all again? "In a world of roving banditry there is little or no incentive for anyone to produce or accumulate anything that may be stolen and, thus, little for bandits to steal," Olson writes.[3]

Hence, this dynamic becomes a problem for the marauders as well. Just as good hunting grounds or fisheries can be depleted by overuse, you can only raid and plunder the same village so many times before there's not much left to steal, particularly when the victims refuse to make futile long-term investments. It's a vicious cycle that leaves both thief and victim poorer in the long run.

Thus, the stationary bandit is a solution to a very serious problem. Olson first stumbled on this idea while reading Edward C. Banfield's classic work *The Moral Basis of a Backward Society* (1958). Banfield conducted meticulous interviews with residents of a poor village in southern Italy. In one of these interviews he talked to a monarchist who proclaimed that "monarchy is the best kind of government because the King is then owner of the country. Like the owner of a house, when the wiring is wrong, he fixes it."[4]

Later, Olson stumbled on the story of White Wolf, a marauder in 1920s China. The quintessential roving bandit, White Wolf led a small army of raiders around the countryside, terrorizing villages. He was defeated and crushed by an even stronger warlord, Feng Yu-hsiang. The interesting thing is that the villagers welcomed Feng Yu-hsiang as a kind of savior, even though he taxed—i.e., extorted—the local population heavily. Why welcome one warlord over another? Because Feng Yu-hsiang settled down, providing protection from all the other bandits. This protection introduced stability and predictability to the peasants' lives. They may have had to pay too much in taxes, but they also knew they'd be left enough to live on. And so long as they paid, their lives would be spared. The order and predictability of the stationary bandit is, according to Olson, "the first blessing of the invisible hand."[5]

"The invisible hand," a term coined by Adam Smith, has come to describe the social benefits that accrue when individuals are empowered to pursue their own self-interests and specialize economically. By allowing individuals to work to their own ends, the whole of society grows richer, as if guided by an invisible hand. That "as if" is crucial. Smith's detractors often mischaracterize the invisible hand, insinuating that supporters of the free market think there is something guiding coordination, but the whole point is that the coordination simply emerges.

Olson explains how the stationary-bandit model is an improvement over what came before. It's really just math. A stationary bandit has a longer time horizon. He realizes that taking 100 percent of a village's wealth will make him richer right now. But what will he get next year? Nothing. If he takes half this year, he knows there will be something to take next year. He also realizes that if he lets the villagers plant more crops, there will be more for him to tax in the years ahead. This gives the stationary bandit an incentive not just to fend off the roving bandits but to make investments in public goods other than security. He might build roads or lend resources for the digging of new irrigation canals or the clearing of forests to plow new fields.

How much he taxes becomes a simple question of return on investment. "The starting point" for Olson's theory of development "is that no society can work satisfactorily if it does not have a peaceful order and usually other public goods as well."[6] The stationary bandit is the first real provider of a peaceful order, without which the invisible hand can never appear.

Today, the state has an important role in all of this. The state regulates the use of violence and protects the right of the citizens to use their property. Absent the confidence that the police will stop people from plundering the bakeries, the bakers will not bake bread. The stationary bandit was the first entity to serve this function.

Of course, this does not mean that the stationary bandit is a good person. Odds are strong that, more often than not, he was awful from the perspective of the very high moral perch we sit on today and probably from the view of some much lower perches as well (and his hand in the economy was almost surely far from invisible). Thus the classic libertarian indictment of government as a criminal enterprise—most famously stated by Albert Jay Nock, author of *Our Enemy, the State* (1935)—has some merit.[7]

The Mafia works on the same principle of long-term exploitation. They sell protection to businesses, both legal and illegal, in return for "a piece of the action." The don understands that if they rob their "clients" of everything they have all at once, their clients will go out of business.[8]

But what Nock and others failed to appreciate is that there are social benefits to the state's monopoly on violence. For starters, we would not have property rights without the state. Prior to the order and security of the stationary bandit, if a stronger man or army took what was yours, it became his or theirs. Possession is ten-tenths of the law under the laws of nature: The weaker lion cannot sue when the stronger one claims the larger share of the kill.[9]

Because a stationary bandit has an interest in letting his subjects get richer—his slice of the pie gets bigger when the whole pie gets bigger—he must protect the lives and property of his "clients" if they are to keep working for him. He may say everything in his territory belongs to him, and that is true in the sense that, if he wants to take it, he can. But he understands that, in practice, people need a high level of confidence that they will be left a "fair" share of what they make or grow.

To accomplish this in a large society, where the ruler cannot keep a watchful eye on everything under his dominion, requires clearly stated rules. These rules begin as arbitrary edicts from the boss or king, but in short order they become binding—and the introduction of writing gave these rules a kind of universal and fearful authority and, eventually, sacredness. The king always has the right to change his mind, of course. But when petitioners come to court to settle a disagreement, the peasant who most persuasively claims he was following the recognized rules is the one most likely to win. If the king sides with the rule breaker—as he no doubt often did—there's a social and political cost for the king in the sense that he is sowing doubt and instability.

This dynamic probably defined the earliest days of the agricultural revolution, when the first bands and tribes settled down to grow crops. From there, it was almost inevitable that the state as we understand it today would emerge.

How, exactly, did we go from the stationary bandit to the state?

There's a bit of a chicken-or-the-egg problem here. A self-starting state, one that just springs up from a voluntary collaboration of individuals and institutions—what scholars call a "pristine state"—is for anthropologists, sociologists, and political scientists a bit like the lost city of Atlantis. They think it probably existed. They just haven't found it. What they have found are numerous examples of "competitive states."[10] These are states that come into existence when loosely associated or less developed neighboring societies recognize the need to combat already existing states. Since the state-governed societies are usually larger, more organized, and more advanced, they tend to prey successfully on non-state societies, repeating the same cycle of the stationary bandit versus the roving bandit on a larger scale. In response, the prey organize themselves to defend against the predators. (*Game of Thrones* fans might think of Lord Stark calling in his bannermen.) This almost reflexive self-organization into a kind of permanent battle formation happens again and again in human history. As Charles Tilly famously said, "War made the state and the state made war."[11]

This is not to say that there was no first state. Surely someplace deserves that title. But the important point is that states evolved—emerged, really—from what came before them as a problem-solving response to external aggression. (One of the only ways we could get anything like a real world government—at least in our lifetimes—would be if our planet faced an invasion from outer space. It might not happen, but you can see how it might.)

When the conditions are right, we form states. War—i.e., an external threat—is clearly one of those conditions. But an equally important one is population size. When societies are provided with security and order, a number of secondary patterns emerge. Labor becomes more specialized, which produces more wealth. Another outgrowth of large populations and state-provided security is that property rights become ever more secure, at least for the wealthy holders of property. Property holding is itself a kind of division of labor. When you own land, you can extract more productivity or wealth from it. More wealth and security from external foes means more population, and more population means more wealth and security. It's a virtuous cycle. And when societies get bigger, they need even more formal rules to govern them. "Growth will simply not occur unless the existing economic organization is efficient," write economists Douglass C. North and Robert Paul Thomas.[12] And this "entails the establishment of institutional arrangements and property rights."[13]

The agricultural revolution made mass societies possible, and mass societies could only be maintained through force, both physical and psychological. Hunter-gatherer tribes were largely voluntary associations insofar as the group was held together by strong blood ties and mutual dependence. You could leave if you wanted, and some families did when the band got too large.

The philosopher Ernest Gellner argues that, in a state of nature, mankind lived in universal propertylessness. "Hunter/gatherers are defined by the fact that they possess little or no means for producing, accumulating and storing wealth. They are dependent on what they find or kill. Their societies are small, and are characterized by a low degree of division of labour." However, Gellner notes: "Agrarian societies produce food, store it, and acquire other forms of storable wealth."[14] That storable wealth not only creates classes of people; it also serves as a means of social control. Stored food is an insurance plan against crop failures and other calamities.

But storable wealth isn't just food. It also includes the tools for producing more food, and the weapons necessary to protect—or seize—it. Money as a storehouse of value is a relatively recent invention. Before currency, a man was wealthy if he owned livestock, shovels, swords, and slaves, among other means of production. But before the agricultural revolution, there was little use for much of that. Some hunter-gatherers might have carried gold or some other trinkets—seashells are among the first baubles in the archaeological record—but when you have no permanent residence and must stay on the move, wealth was largely restricted to what you could carry and use.

Settled communities are communities of specialized laborers. To understand the power of the division of labor, consider the case of the humble sandwich. In 2015, a man inspired by the canonical libertarian essay by Leonard E. Read, "I, Pencil," set out to make a sandwich from scratch—i.e., with no products he didn't make himself. He grew his own vegetables, distilled salt from seawater, milked a cow, and used the milk to cultivate cheese. He pickled a cucumber in a jar, grew his own wheat, and ground it into flour for bread. He collected his own honey, and killed a chicken himself for the meat. The whole process took him six months and cost him $1,500. At the end of the project, he issued his verdict on his sandwich: "It's not bad. That's about it. It's not bad." Even here, he took shortcuts. He didn't buy the cow or scour the countryside for the seeds, etc.[15]

The specialization inherent to the agricultural revolution creates classes of people in ways never imagined in small bands of hunters. Crops need to be tended to and protected. That means some people will be farmhands, others soldiers. Still others are better suited to work the mills or bake the bread. When you think about what is required to maintain a large agriculture-based society, the number of specialized jobs gets long very quickly: soldiers, farmers, butchers, cobblers, blacksmiths, masons, carpenters, and, of course, slaves and overseers. How do you keep all of these specialists in their assigned roles? Dependence on the state's insurance function is one method. Another is coercion.

Coercion, of course, implies violence, and all societies, including our own, depend on violence to maintain social order to one extent or another. Academics get the shakes when you try to offer a universal definition of the state, but one component is essential and pretty much universally agreed upon: force.

Max Weber famously defined the state as a "monopoly of the legitimate use of physical force within a given territory."[16] Weber would be the first to note that there's a bit more to it than that. States have laws (and the means to enforce them), bureaucracies, and systems of taxation. But for a state to be a state, it must be able to enforce its rules, i.e., its will.

But whether it's the arbitrary whim of a third-century warlord or official guidelines from the Occupational Safety and Health Administration, if there is any lesson to be learned from history it is that, ultimately, laws have to be enforced through violence or the threat of violence.[17] Indeed, the very word "enforce" literally means to use force.[18]

But coercion doesn't only take the form of physical force, and not all compulsion is violence. No society can last long if held together solely by violence, or even the threat of violence. Ideology—by which I mean an internally coherent worldview that tells us how to behave and cooperate—is essential. If violence is the only measure of right and wrong, then the peasant has every incentive to kill his lord if he can get away with it. Large-scale societies need a theology and metaphysics to help everyone "know their place" in the social pecking order. Societies differentiate between legitimate and illegitimate uses of violence by that standard. Even contemporary North Korea, which uses violence and fear more than almost any other state imaginable, still devotes massive resources to the propagation of an ideology for its people. Yes, many people obey the Dear Leader out of fear, but one need only read interviews with defectors or see footage of women openly weeping with joy at the sight of Kim Jong-un to understand that some besotted souls obey their Dear Leader out of love.

"Agrarian societies tend to develop complex social differentiation, an elaborate division of labour," Gellner writes. "Two specialisms in particular become of paramount importance: the emergence of a specialized ruling class, and of a specialized clerisy (specialists in cognition, legitimation, salvation, ritual)."[19] In other words, you need an aristocracy, starting with a monarch, and you need a priesthood of some kind to explain to people why the monarch deserves obedience. As the saying goes in *Game of Thrones*, "The Faith and the Crown. These are the two pillars of the realm. If one should fall, so will the other."[20]

The aristocracy rules primarily through force. The priests use words, specifically, texts. Indeed, the development of writing was arguably the greatest leap forward in the history of human coercion—and cooperation.

The ability to write words probably began with the need to write numbers. Taxing and trade required record keeping. Not only was human memory unequal to the task of reliably storing data about all those bushels of wheat and shipments of rice, but the character of the memorizers also wasn't altogether trustworthy.

"The first to overcome the problem were the ancient Sumerians, who lived in southern Mesopotamia," Yuval Noah Harari writes:

"There, a scorching sun beating upon rich muddy plains produced plentiful harvests and prosperous towns. As the number of inhabitants grew, so did the amount of information required to coordinate their affairs. Between the years 3500 BC and 3000 BC, some unknown Sumerian geniuses invented a system for storing and processing information outside their brains, one that was custom-built to handle large amounts of mathematical data. The Sumerians thereby released their social order from the limitations of the human brain, opening the way for the appearance of cities, kingdoms and empires. The data-processing system invented by the Sumerians is called 'writing.'"[21]

It didn't take long for this system of bookkeeping to evolve into a system for law giving. Even discounting my vanity for my own profession, it is impossible to overstate the revolutionary nature of the written word. Arthur C. Clarke famously said, "Any sufficiently advanced technology is indistinguishable from magic."[22] That was surely the case with the first books and scrolls. From scratchings on a page, wise men and priests could learn things they did not know and tell tales about places far away and events long ago. (Amidst all the talk about how "the cloud" of data storage is some grand new thing under the sun, people seem to forget that The Cloud 1.0 was invented in Mesopotamia thousands of years ago.)

The written word did not merely accelerate the diffusion of information in radical and profound ways; it also made sanctity portable. As Ernest Gellner observed, writing permits solemnity and authority to be decoupled from a verbal context. Prior to writing, sanctity required verbal, face-to-face ritual. Now it could be transported across vast distances as well as stored for future generations.[23]

One of the first lines of Hammurabi's code reads: "Then Anu and Bel called by name me, Hammurabi, the exalted prince, who feared God, to bring about the rule of righteousness in the land . . ." Hammurabi's job was "to destroy the wicked and the evil-doers, so that the strong should not harm the weak; so that I should rule over the black-headed people like Shamash, and enlighten the land, to further the well-being of mankind." The epilogue of the code established Hammurabi's status as the father of the people, as commanded by the gods. "Hammurabi is a ruler, who is as a father to his subjects, who holds the words of Marduk in reverence, who has achieved conquest for Marduk over the north and south, who rejoices the heart of Marduk, his lord, who has bestowed benefits for ever and ever on his subjects, and has established order in the land."[24]

Babylon, the largest city in the world at the time, was the capital of the Babylonian Empire, which stretched through much of modern-day Iraq and Syria. Hammurabi issued his famous code as a way to unify disparate kingdoms, streamline rules across his diverse imperial subjects, and elevate his status as the divine father of his people. It was also a bit of a legacy project. He wanted a permanent record of his supposed wisdom and fairness.

There's debate about how the code's 282 laws were actually incorporated into daily life. But, for our purposes, the most important thing about the Code of Hammurabi was that it, and laws like it, served as the operating software for a vast cooperation network. It did this by establishing clear rules about violence, commerce, and social status.

A citizen living on the coast of the Persian Gulf and a citizen living hundreds of miles up the Euphrates were now bound by the same rules, even though they might never meet each other or lay eyes on their ruler.

Schoolchildren are taught that the Code of Hammurabi is a great moment in human progress, but that does not mean it was what most people today would consider to be a "progressive" document. For instance, law number 15 declares: "If any one take a male or female slave of the court, or a male or female slave of a freed man, outside the city gates, he shall be put to death."[25]

Probably the most famous of Hammurabi's laws were numbers 196 to 199, which established the principle of *lex talionis,* or "an eye for an eye":

196. If a man put out the eye of another man, his eye shall be put out. [An eye for an eye]
197. If he break another man's bone, his bone shall be broken.
198. If he put out the eye of a freed man, or break the bone of a freed man, he shall pay one gold mina.
199. If he put out the eye of a man's slave, or break the bone of a man's slave, he shall pay one-half of its value.[26]

The code also says that if a son strikes his father, the son's hand must be cut off.[27] It's easy to see all of this as barbaric from our vantage point; I certainly do. But it's important to recognize that regulating violence is a huge boon to humans seeking security and order. The whole reason the stationary bandit is welcomed by the peasants is that his predictable use of violence is preferable to the arbitrary violence of the roving bandit. That desire and need for order and security did not vanish with the rise of the state; the nature of the threat did. Military protection from dangers without evolved into police protection from dangers within.

The code was also a huge economic advance. A lot of it deals with commerce. Roughly a third of the 282 edicts pertain to trading practices, credit, and property in one way or another. For instance: "If a merchant give an agent corn, wool, oil, or any other goods to transport, the agent shall give a receipt for the amount, and compensate the merchant therefor. Then he shall obtain a receipt from the merchant for the money that he gives the merchant."[28] Such "best practices" were essential to a sprawling agricultural empire.

Last, the code also put in writing the social hierarchy of the Babylonian Empire. Hammurabi, naturally, was the keystone. Beneath him were the military and the priests, then the citizens, and, finally, the slaves. There was also a more recognizable class system. The Amelu were the elite, comprising the priests, the military, government officials, landowners, and merchants. Below the *amelu* were the *mushkinu*: craftsmen, artisans, farmers, teachers, and other workers. And beneath them were the *ardu,* the slaves. Even the slaves had a hierarchy as spelled out in the code. Slaves could own slaves and run their own businesses in certain circumstances, which sometimes allowed them to buy their freedom.[29]

Part of the genius of the code—and why the people embraced it—was that it took informal rules and unwritten customs and universalized them. Hammurabi was no democrat, but he was deferential to the traditions of his subjects. Indeed, laws are often lagging rather than leading indicators, formalizing what had been an informal rule for a very long time.

This underscores an important point: Written law—which was both civil and religious—reflected existing cultural and psychological norms at least as much as it replaced them. The most obvious example is the principle of "an eye for an eye." The idea of retributive justice is no doubt far older than the code. Indeed, there's overwhelming evidence to support the claim that a desire for retributive justice isn't even an "idea" at all but an instinct we describe as an idea.[30] Regardless, it's important to recognize that rule givers can only work within the confines of human nature. More importantly, we should respect the fact that many of our most important institutions are embedded with deep reservoirs of knowledge. They are evolved problem-solving devices that emerge through a process of discovery and trial and error.

There's a story—possibly apocryphal—about Dwight Eisenhower when he was the president of Columbia University. As the campus was expanding, the school needed to lay down some new sidewalks. One group of planners and architects insisted that the sidewalks be laid out this way. Another group said they must go that way. Both camps believed reason was on their side of the dispute. "Legend has it," writes my *National Review* colleague Kevin D. Williamson, "that Eisenhower solved the problem by ordering that the sidewalks not be laid down at all for a year: The students would trample paths in the grass, and the builders would then pave over where the students were actually walking. Neither of the plans that had been advocated matched what the students actually did when left to their own devices.

"There are two radically different ways of looking at the world embedded in that story," Williamson writes. "Are our institutions here to tell us where to go, or are they here to help smooth the way for us as we pursue our own ends, going our own ways?"[31]

This is an entirely valid, even vital question to ask about our contemporary society. But looking backward at the evolution of the state and other institutions, the best answer one can come up with is "both." The stationary bandit didn't establish himself as a ruler in order to maximize the liberties or opportunities of his victims-subjects-clients. And the state did not emerge for the betterment of the people but for the betterment and security of the rulers. Hammurabi may indeed have had the best interests of his people in mind when he issued his rules for when and how wives should be murdered, slaves mutilated, and children drowned. But I think a reasonable person can also suspect that Hammurabi's motivations were also self-interested.

So when I write that these societies "need" aristocracies, ideologies, etc., I do not mean that anyone set out to build these institutions for any other reason than self-interest. These are naturally occurring phenomena, human universals on mass scale. Just as slime molds spontaneously self-generate out of disparate single-celled organisms under the right conditions, humans self-organize into hierarchical communities under some kind of state.

One fascinating example of this natural human tendency can be found in American prisons. Prison gangs emerged into virtual states within the penal ecosystem. Some even have written constitutions. These de facto governments running American prisons, described by David Skarbek, were a response to the chaos that overtook prison systems in California and Texas. The old code of conduct that dictated how inmates behaved broke down in the 1970s, and the gangs filled the vacuum with a new code enforced by them.[32] These new stationary bandits returned order to the prisons, not the guards. But it's worth keeping in mind that the gang leaders did not intend to impose some new penal social order. The social order emerged from their pursuit of their narrow interests. "This bottom-up process of institutional emergence," Skarbek writes, "was the result of inmate actions, but not the execution of any inmate design."[33]

For most of human history, self-interest came before ideology. The arguments for aristocracy and monarchy—whether in feudal Japan, ancient Rome, or anywhere else before the Enlightenment—were justifications for the authority of the rulers. The Enlightenment changed the formula. Rather than appealing to myth and mystery, the architects of the Enlightenment appealed to reason.

But one thing did not change: The state remains a myth agreed upon. We tell ourselves that the state is a thing, and our belief in it makes it real (just as belief in a nation is the ultimate author of its reality). After all, you can't touch or see the state. You can see buildings and bureaucrats and soldiers, but all of these things are tools or servants of the state, not the state itself. There's no Great and Powerful Oz behind the curtain. There isn't even a rumpled professor. The state exists because people say it does.

When the state disappears, as in the old Soviet Union, what is the only tangible evidence that it's gone? The tanks are still there. The buildings too. The only real proof the state has disappeared is that people stop acting as if it exists. They stop following its orders, which means they refuse to cooperate with each other under the invisible banner of the state.

Yuval Harari argues that virtually all of civilization—religion, corporations, money, ethics, morality, etc.—should really be seen as nothing more than a collection of stories we tell ourselves.

These fictions or social constructions often serve as the software for civilization. Stories allow huge populations to cooperate across vast territories. We tell ourselves the story that paper money has value, and because everyone agrees to respect the story, the money is accepted in lieu of things of intrinsic value. In times of crisis, when we revert back to something closer to the state of nature, the illusion of money's value becomes clear. In the post-apocalyptic, zombie-infested—excuse me, "walker"-infested—state-of-nature world of *The Walking Dead*, money has no value save as kindling or toilet paper.

The funny part is that, in modern-day America, people who come to realize or fear that paper money is not a reliable storehouse of value feel the need to buy gold. But the value of gold is a social construction too. Within the socially constructed world of modern economics, buying gold may be a smart strategy in some circumstances. A Berliner in 1923 would certainly rather have had his money in gold than in German marks. But a Berliner in 1945 might have traded all his gold for food or guns.

Money, of course, is just one of innumerable fictions that define our conception of reality and right and wrong. We tell ourselves that humans have natural or God-given rights. Where is the proof—the physical, tangible, visible proof? Don't tell me a story; show me the evidence. The fact is we have rights because some believe they are in fact God-given, but far more people believe we should act *as if* they are God-given or are in some other way "real."

Economists and other scholars of development don't like to call such things stories. They prefer the term "institution," which is fine by me. At the most basic level, an institution isn't a building or an organization; it's a rule. But before it was a rule, it was a story. And religion—the mother of so many of our stories—is the most important of them all.

Put all issues of theology aside, and just look at religion as a way to get humans who are not related to each other and who do not even know each other to cooperate. Religion provides humans with meaning, for a reason to behave a certain way and to treat others a certain way. A Sunni Muslim who encounters another Sunni Muslim has a story in common, and that shared story leads them to cooperate rather than fight.

It seems silly even to bother to demonstrate that religion has enormous power over how humans conduct themselves, given that it is the one assertion both defenders and critics of religion agree upon. But just to illustrate the point, consider the story of Henry IV in the snows of Canossa.

In 1073, Pope Gregory VII set out to reform investiture in the Holy Roman Empire. Gregory believed the pope, not the Holy Roman emperor, should have the power to appoint bishops and the like. The Holy Roman emperor at the time, Henry IV, liked the power to make such appointments, and he resisted the reforms and denounced Gregory. The pope responded by excommunicating Henry in 1076. This created a crisis for Henry—and the empire. No doubt Henry was worried about his eternal soul, but even if he were a secret atheist, he would have understood that the rest of society believed in the story. One could not remain a king in eleventh-century Europe and be cut off from the Holy Mother Church. Gregory allowed Henry to repent. So arguably the most powerful man in the world walked hundreds of miles over the Alps from Speyer in what is today Germany to the Canossa Castle in the region of Emilia-Romagna in Italy. He then spent three days kneeling, barefoot, in the snow outside the castle, during a blizzard, wearing a hair shirt, fasting, and awaiting forgiveness from the pope.[34]

There is reason to believe that religion itself is an evolutionary adaptation. Group cooperation is the key to human survival, and religion can be an incredibly powerful source of social cohesion, fostering sacrifice for the greater good of the community.

We all pay taxes, obey traffic rules, work at jobs, and do a thousand other things every day in compliance with the intangible rules that emanate from countless fictions agreed upon. It is no great exaggeration to say: "Tell me your stories and I will tell you who you are."

The agricultural revolution created a social landscape as alien to our genetic programming as a colony on Mars. The first city-states had tens or hundreds of thousands of inhabitants living cheek by jowl, competing for resources, mates, and status. Humans adapted to this new environment the only way any animal adapts to any new environment: by applying their nature to it as best they could. The Big Man was replaced by the stationary bandit, who was replaced by a king (or emperor or czar or pharaoh). To be sure, the king used force to keep the people in line. But force was not enough. Humans have an innate need to know their place in society. We have an instinctual hunger for meaning and order.

In short, large populations needed a story. The stories varied in countless details, but the plot and themes were well-nigh universal. That's because the stories that worked were those that tracked with our innate desire for a father figure, a head man, or an alpha ape who cared for us. Scour the anthropological and archaeological record; it's the same story, over and over, for thousands of years. The king is anointed or otherwise chosen by some divine authority to rule over his people, like a father.

If you take the time line of humanity from the first city-states around 4000 B.C. until today, monarchy, broadly defined, has been the default arrangement for human affairs for roughly 99 percent of the period. Monarchy—or, if you prefer, some kind of aristocracy with a solitary paternal figure at the top—defined nearly all human societies until around 1800. There is a reason why Catholic priests are called fathers and the pope is *il Papa*.

And what about after 1800? We will be spending a lot of time on this question in later chapters, but it's worth noting here that the introduction of democracy didn't suddenly erase our natural desire and tendencies to look to father figures. The Soviet Union, allegedly the antidote to all the superstitions that came before it, spared little effort to cast Joseph Stalin as the father of the Motherland.[35] Adolf Hitler, who also rejected the ancient customs of monarchy as well as the modern innovation of democracy, styled himself as the nation's father. Napoleon Bonaparte, Benito Mussolini, Francisco Franco, Mao Tse-tung, Mobutu Sese Seko, Fidel Castro, Hugo Chávez, Vladimir Putin, and virtually every other ostensibly secular authoritarian ruler of the last two centuries has worked assiduously to play the role of father to his children-subjects. George Washington himself was dubbed "the father of his country" for all time before he even left office. His comrades are still remembered as the "Founding Fathers."

In other words, even when we remove the dogmas that elevate monarchy over democracy, the pattern holds more often than not. "Patriotism" comes from the Latin *patria*, meaning fatherland, itself a derivative of *pater*, or "father." This points to why it's not sufficient to say that strongmen imposed this role on their respective populations. The people *asked for it*. They celebrated it. Virtually every cult leader in human memory claimed to be the group's father (or mother) and it was because of this claim—not despite it—that the worshipful formed their flocks. And this yearning has not vanished in the twenty-first century. Recall comedian Chris Rock insisting that we have to do what President Obama wants because "he's the Dad of our country."[36]

Given the thousands of natural experiments across Eurasia, North and South America, and all the other corners of the globe, there's no avoiding the conclusion that this basic idea satisfies some deep innate needs of human beings. If monarchy were unnatural in some profound way, it would not have provided such a stable form of government for thousands of years. If a desire for a fatherly leader to do what's in our best interests weren't hardwired into us, it would not be a staple of political cultures around the globe.

If you emptied a jar of ants onto the surface of some distant habitable planet, they will do exactly what they do here on Earth: start building colonies. Similarly, left to their own devices in an unnatural environment, humans "naturally" organize around a centralized authority. The fact that monarchies of a fashion predate the agricultural revolution only amplifies the point.

And here we need to revisit my argument about corruption. When democracies fall apart, we often say they are "falling" or "slipping backward" into authoritarianism. The breakdown of Venezuela fits this familiar model. This is one form of social entropy. But our language fails us when societies reject democracy and the market in favor of supposedly "future-oriented" models of social organization. When the Bolsheviks took over Russia, Western intellectuals hailed it as a great advance in human affairs. Castro's takeover of Cuba was likewise celebrated as an exciting improvement, a more humane and rational way of organizing politics and economics. What this misses is that all efforts to escape the Miracle of liberal democratic capitalism lead to the same destination.

The categories of left and right tend to mislead us, and so do terms like "forward" and "backward." Thomas More coined the word "Utopia" to mean no place. He contrasted it with the term "eutopia," which means good place. How many millions have died in a quest to find a perfect society that does not and cannot exist? Meanwhile, how many billions have benefited from our discovery of a good place—the oasis that is the Miracle? The point is that there's no direction—left, right, forward, backward—out of the oasis that won't take us back to the desert.

In other words, every effort to do away with liberal democratic capitalism is reactionary, because they all attempt to restore the unity of purpose that defines the premodern or tribal mind. Socialism, nationalism, communism, fascism, and authoritarianisms of every stripe are forms of tribalism. The tribal mind despises division. It despises the division of labor and the inequality it inevitably fosters. It despises the division between the religious and the secular, between the individual and the group, between civil society and the state. Whether it takes the form of religious orthodoxy, communist dogma, the divine right of kings, or some variant of "social justice" theory, the same underlying impulse rules: We must all be in it together. The genius of the Miracle lies in the division of labor, not just in manufacturing or science, but in our own minds. Save in times of war or some other existential crisis, meaning cannot be a mass, collective enterprise without crushing the rich ecosystem of institutions that actually give us meaning and ensure liberty and prosperity.

4

THE BIRTH OF CAPITALISM
A Glorious Accident

W HERE DOES THE MIRACLE COME FROM? ODDLY ENOUGH,
given how much it's been studied and how recent it is, no one
really knows. Or, to be more accurate, no one can really agree. There
is no shortage of theories, but consensus remains remarkably elusive.
And often, when scholars try to synthesize all the scholarship, they
throw their hands up in consternation. Joel Mokyr begins his daunting *A Culture of Growth: The Origins of the Modern Economy* recounting the sudden explosion of prosperity that began in Europe in the
1700s and has been spreading, in fits and starts, around the globe ever
since. "The results were inescapable: nearly everywhere on the planet
men and women lived longer, ate better, enjoyed more leisure, and
had access to resources and delights that previously had been reserved
for the very rich and powerful, or more commonly, had been utterly
unknown."[1]

The names for this event vary. Some call it the Great Enrichment
or the Great Divergence. I prefer the Miracle for a fairly straightforward reason. Miracles defy explanation. Nearly all scholars agree that
the Miracle began in the West, but there's precious little agreement
on why it happened there.[2] In his afterword to the third edition of
the *European Miracle*, Eric Jones surveys the intellectual cacophony
around the question of why modernity happened and, with a mix of
exasperation and jest, writes: "Perhaps there was something supernatural about Europe's rise after all."[3]

Alas, there's no God in this book, and so that explanation is
unavailable to us.[4]

The next best explanation for modernity is: England did it. There's a great deal to recommend this theory of the case. Indeed, if you're using "where" figuratively, then the origins of capitalism and the Miracle remain a mystery. But if you literally mean "where," then we know the answer to that question: England.

"We are still experiencing the aftereffects of an astonishing event," writes Daniel Hannan in his brilliant, unavoidably provocative, and widely misunderstood book, *Inventing Freedom: How the English-Speaking Peoples Made the Modern World*. "The inhabitants of a damp island at the western tip of the Eurasian landmass stumbled upon the idea that the government ought to be subject to the law, not the other way around. The rule of law created security of property and contract, which in turn led to industrialization and modern capitalism. For the first time in the history of the species, a system grew up that, on the whole, rewarded production better than predation."[5]

The original working title of this book was *The Tribe of Liberty*. The reason I liked that title is that Hannan's view is the one I hold nearest to my heart. And for this and other reasons, the idea that liberty was born as a cultural quirk of an obscure people deserves a bit more explication than some of the other theories of where modernity comes from.

A vast sea of literature, dogma, doctrine, and social science has been dedicated to the question of "Why England?"

They can all be summarized with a single statement: England was *weird*. When I say "weird," I do not mean it with a hint of insult. It was gloriously, wonderfully, fantastically weird. Monty Python is weird. My father was weird. Marriage is weird. Most of the joyful and precious things in life are weird, and it is the weirdness that makes them joyful and precious.

Why for the first time ever did this weirdness manifest itself? Daniel Hannan identifies five widely agreed-upon crucial factors:

1. **The development of a nation-state.** One needs a certain amount of cohesiveness and order to let the Miracle emerge. And that only comes from a regime that can "apply laws more or less uniformly to a population bound together by a sense of shared identity."
2. **Closely related to this is a healthy civil society full of competing and complementary institutions that serve to root the**

society and serve as a counterbalance to the arbitrary power of the state or crown. The sovereignty of the individual as a cultural artifact is deeply rooted in, and at least partly derived from, the role of mediating institutions. As Alexis de Tocqueville observed, "The spirit of individuality is the basis of the English character. Association is a means of achieving things unattainable by isolated effort. . . . What better example of association than the union of individuals who form the club, or almost any civil or political association or corporation?"

3. **Island geography.** The importance of being an island is not obvious at first. But it was crucial for two reasons. First, islands have natural protections from foreign invaders. This allowed for England to be less militarized than other nations. War was for the most part reserved for fending off foreign invaders. The Anglo distrust of standing armies is a direct product of this accidental arrangement. Second, and very much related, this made political absolutism less necessary. Kings evolve absolute powers for the same reason "stationary bandits" are welcomed by victimized peasants: to protect the populace from foreign threats. The lack of an absolute ruler not only gave space for civil society and competing power centers to develop, it prevented the king from claiming that he "owned" the country (the people and their stuff), as was common elsewhere.

4. **Religious pluralism.** This strikes me as incontrovertible insofar as religious hegemony in general deters innovation, which, until very recently, was seen as a kind of heresy or apostasy. Prior to the Reformation, religion wasn't a separate sphere of life from work and family. Even laboring differently was seen as a threat to the established order. More on this in a moment.

5. **Last, and Hannan argues most important, common law:** "a unique legal system that made the state subject to the people rather than the reverse."[6]

It's a good list, and Hannan makes a good case for it. But we still have the problem of English weirdness. By that I mean, if modernity arises only once and in one place, it is almost impossible to know for sure *why* it happened there. The scientific method would require a true test, and none is available. If modernity happened someplace else, say Japan, we could compare and contrast and distill the commonalities and come up with a testable hypothesis.

There is one objection to this point: the Netherlands, a great merchant republic, which competes with England as the birthplace of the modern corporation. Perhaps unfairly, I am giving short shrift to the Dutch. The problem is that the two nations were deeply enmeshed in each other's cultures, even when they were at war with each other. Indeed, I think you could make a good case that neither would have become capitalist without the other. It's a bit like the problem of identifying the first state. No one has identified a "pristine state," i.e., one that arises all on its own. Instead, archaeologists and anthropologists can only locate "competitive states": states that emerge in order to compete with or resist some other state. This captures the dynamic between England and Holland.[7] I have no doubt that some partisans of the Dutch would make the case that the Netherlands pulled England into the Miracle, not the other way around. And I am open to that argument. But from the evidence I've seen, the causality works more the other way around, despite numerous Dutch contributions. It's like two great basketball players who become better because of their competition with each other.

Regardless, the spillover from England and the Netherlands to the rest of Europe was rapid in the eighteenth century, again because of virtuous competitive pressure. But also because of the shared cultural assumptions and institutions of Christian Western Europe (Russia is a different matter). "The 'demonstration effect,'" writes Ralph Raico, "that has been a constant element in European progress—and which could exist precisely because Europe was a decentralized system of competing jurisdictions—helped spread the liberal politics that brought prosperity to the towns that first ventured to experiment with them."[8]

As Hannan recounts in loving and patriotic detail, the roots of English democracy stretch deep into antiquity. Sources dating back to at least the 600s show that the English had a social compact between ruler and ruled, one which organically evolved in England long before any of the rules were written down. Kings met with other lords and other leaders out in the open and promised to uphold their duties as a servant of their people. The Roman historian Tacitus noted 2,000 years ago that this was a common practice among Germanic tribes as well. But only England held on to it, perhaps because being an island nation protected it from the wars that wiped out such traditions elsewhere.

J. R. Maddicott, author of the authoritative *Origins of the English Parliament, 924–1327,* draws a line from the early Germanic "Witans" of England to the Magna Carta and to British democracy today: "Substituting 'earls' for 'ealdormen' and 'barons' for 'thegns,' we are not so very far from the general look of an early parliament."[9] He later says that "in other parts of the West, the Germanic and Carolingian legislative tradition died out in the tenth century. Its energetic preservation and promotion in England was quite exceptional. . . . We need not baulk at the notion of English exceptionalism."[10]

Oxford University medieval historian James Campbell agrees. "That representative institutions have their roots in the dark-age and medieval past is not an anachronistic view; rather it is fully demonstrable," he writes. "It does indeed look as if the history of constitutional liberty has important beginnings in Anglo-Saxon England."[11]

The formal mechanisms of democracy are not the only anatomical features of democracy that can be traced to Old Blighty. Feudalism in England was significantly different from feudalism in Western Europe and extremely different from feudalism in Eastern Europe, Russia, China, and the rest of the world.

In most feudal societies, kinship rules basically made the concept of private property, particularly private land, unthinkable. In peasant societies (Alan Macfarlane's term), the serfs worked the land for a host of reasons and, contra Marx, they didn't all have to do with economic exploitation. They had more to do with ancient and tribal attachments to specific plots of dirt. This was their land to work because this was where their ancestors had worked and where their ancestors were buried.

Peasants in most of Europe didn't leave their land to their children, because it wasn't their land to dispose of. They were more like sharecroppers. In Eastern Europe, peasants had views of ownership similar to the Native Americans. They were intergenerational caretakers of the soil, and "ownership" was better understood as an eternal lease. But in England, MacFarlane found that the individual right of landowners to "alienate" their property—i.e., sell it or leave it to people other than their children—was already deeply rooted in English common law by the beginning of the 1500s.[12] Marx and Engels claim in *The Communist Manifesto* that capitalism "has torn away from the family its sentimental veil, and has reduced the family relation to a mere money relation."[13] But as Francis Fukuyama observes, that was demonstrably untrue in England. Centuries before the emergence of Marx's hated bourgeoisie, the English were treating "family" land as just another commodity. Fukuyama cites a study of land transfers in one English district; only 15 percent of transfers went to the owner's family during his lifetime, and 10 percent at death.[14] In other words, farmers could sell their land to strangers. And as early as the twelfth century, "English *villeins* (tenants legally tied to their lands) were buying, selling, and leasing property without the permission of their lords."[15] In other words, private property was an ancient custom in England, predating legal and philosophical justifications for it, sometimes by centuries.

Another, related advantage stemmed from the fact that hereditary castes—a near universal institution around the world—were weirdly weak in England. "On the Continent, seigniorial [baronial] justice was common," Hannan writes. "The great magnates were the law on their own estates. But England, before the Normans came [in 1066], had no feudal aristocracy. It had its great men, as all warrior societies had, and many of them held large estates, though these tended to be fragmented across many counties. But the great men never constituted a hereditary caste with legal privileges—such as, to cite the most notorious example from Europe, exemption from taxation. They were as subject to the law of the land as anyone else."[16] In other words, feudal lords, while extremely powerful on their own lands, were not so powerful that they could serve as absolute monarchs in their little mini-states.

I think Hannan might overstate the point, but the core truth remains. Aristocracy worked differently in England. Hannan attributes this to the fact that, in Europe, Roman law was the norm, while in England it was something of an alien imposition that never took deep root in the soil.[17] Roman law, like Napoleonic law, is "deductive": Lawmakers determine a principle, write it down, and impose it on the society. Common law is an emergent property, bubbling up from the society itself.

Common law evolved case by case, which is why some call it judge-made law. "Common law," writes Hannan, "is thus empirical rather than conceptual: it concerns itself with actual judgments that have been handed down in real cases, and then asks whether they need to be modified in the light of different circumstances in a new case."[18] And English common law recognized the rights of all Englishmen, which made all the difference.

I don't want to get bogged down in the history of the Magna Carta, but it's worth noting that the Magna Carta (the Brits don't say "the" as we do, by the way; they simply say "Magna Carta") came after the development of formal institutions of common law. In the late twelfth century, Henry II created a system of circuit courts and even a central court of appeals. When the Magna Carta was struck a half century later, it recognized this development, creating a written precedent for the future. Likewise, the Magna Carta's requirement that the king rule in consultation in "common counsel of the realm" was a nod to more ancient traditions while at the same time a new, incalculably valuable precedent for the creation of a formal parliamentary system.

There are numerous other cultural idiosyncrasies that define English weirdness—or, if you prefer, exceptionalism. The right to petition authorities for redress, the rights of the individual, an almost obsessive concern with just taxation, and numerous other concepts we tend to think of in high-flown philosophical or legal terms have deep roots in English custom. They emerged not as formal deductive law but through local trial and error over countless generations.

In subsequent chapters, I will refer often to the "Lockean Revolution" to describe the gift we inherited from the Founding era of both England's Glorious Revolution and the American Revolution. But as I will explain, the problem with the term "Lockean Revolution" is that it makes it sound like the extended order of liberty was purely a kind of legalistic creation crafted by lawyers and philosophers like Locke. The truth is it developed and evolved organically over a millennium before Locke did us all the great service of writing some of it down. Just as the Magna Carta locked in certain principles in 1215, Locke and the American founders did something very similar.

The colonists at the time of the American founding saw themselves for the most part as English. They brought their weird cultural biases with them, and their argument with the crown was an extension of the Whiggish fight for liberty that defined English history for a thousand years. As Winston Churchill observed in his *History of the English-Speaking Peoples*, "The Declaration [of Independence] was in the main a restatement of the principles which had animated the Whig struggle against the later Stuarts and the English Revolution of 1688."[19]

Just as Martin Luther King Jr. used America's best ideals to make the case for a richer liberty in America, the Founders invoked England's highest principles to make the case for their liberties in the New World. Jefferson's rough draft of the Declaration included the line "We might have been a free and great people together," but it was cut from the final version.[20] Still, the Declaration drips with a sense of familial betrayal:

> We have warned them from time to time of attempts by their legislature to extend an unwarrantable jurisdiction over us. We have reminded them of the circumstances of our emigration and settlement here. We have appealed to their native justice and magnanimity, and we have conjured them by the ties of our common kindred to disavow these usurpations, which would inevitably interrupt our connections and correspondence.[21]

That line about the "circumstances of our emigration and settlement here" is a reference to the fact that so many of the original colonists crossed the ocean in search of religious liberties that had been denied to them at home. Indeed, as important as the issue of unjust taxation was to the Founders, the cause of religious liberty served as a vital motivation as well. The Church of England had in the years leading up to the Revolution tried to impose an official faith in the colonies and even install American bishops, arousing a wellspring of vestigial Puritan rage. "The American Revolution was, at least in part, the result of a spasm of religious intolerance," writes Hannan. "That this spasm should have engendered the first truly secular state on earth, one in which all religions might compete on even terms, is close to miraculous."[22]

The reason I bring this up is that I think we often fail to see the Constitution in the proper light. The profound (though at times insufficient) legal authority we invest in it tends to obscure the cultural authority of the document. And so we talk about it in formalistic terms. Section one says this, section two says that, and so on. The Whiggish legal historians, naturally, see history as a book in which each page is filled with new legal documents. But these documents almost always are lagging indicators, validations of cultural advances.

And it is fine for historians, lawyers, and lawmakers to see the past through the legal prism of the present. It is, in fact, essential for lawyers and lawmakers to look at the text and textual history of the Constitution. But the Constitution is not simply a machine on parchment or an instruction manual for the government. It is an expression of a specific culture at a specific time. And that culture comes from somewhere. Specifically, it comes from England. Patrick Henry at the Virginia ratifying convention of 1788 spoke glowing of their "glorious forefathers of Great Britain" who "made liberty the foundation of every thing."[23]

Numerous Latin American countries have constitutions based on the American model, but they have struggled to re-create America's political and economic successes because culture matters—a lot. Not for nothing did Alexis de Tocqueville describe the American as "the Englishman left to himself."[24]

For a certain group of intellectuals on the right and, to a lesser extent, on the left, the Constitution is the wellspring of the American order. From one perspective, this is undoubtedly true. The Constitution provides guardrails for our society in all the formal and legal ways you can think of (even if those guardrails have, over time, succumbed to entropy, thanks to a lack of care in their upkeep). But the Constitution is a cultural and psychological artifact as well. It informs the way we *think* about government, rights, and civil society. Our tendency to take things for granted rusts all that glitters eventually. So when we say, "I can do this because the Constitution gives me the right to do this," it seems perfectly natural, but it is actually one of the most radical things a human can say.

Like the Magna Carta that came before it, one of the greatest services the Constitution provides is that it is simply *written down.* As

Ernest Gellner has noted, humans have a tendency to sacralize texts. That is precisely what Americans have done with the Constitution, thank goodness.

Barack Obama said in his Farewell Address:

> Our Constitution is a remarkable, beautiful gift. But it's really just a piece of parchment. It has no power on its own. We, the people, give it power—with our participation, and the choices we make. Whether or not we stand up for our freedoms. Whether or not we respect and enforce the rule of law. America is no fragile thing. But the gains of our long journey to freedom are not assured.[25]

Many of my fellow conservatives were angered by this, and given Barack Obama's remarkable, yoga master–like flexibility in interpreting constitutional text, I can understand why. But on its face, Obama's claim was right. The Constitution only has real power if the people give it power. James Madison noted as much when he fretted that "parchment barriers" are often inadequate against "the encroaching spirit of power."[26] The real power of the Constitution is to be found not in it but in *us*. The Constitution is a paper manifestation of a deeper cultural commitment to liberty and limited government, in the same way a marriage certificate is a physical and legalistic representation of something far deeper, mysterious, and complicated. When the marriage fails, the marriage certificate won't save it. And when the American people lose their love of liberty, the Constitution will not save us either.

What made the American founding such an amazing one-of-a-kind event was that it took the weirdness of one obscure successful tribe, culled from its cultural peculiarities universal principles, and *then wrote them down*. The Founders had enormous help from John Locke, who did much of the intellectual groundwork in support of the Glorious Revolution a hundred years earlier. And they also had help from Montesquieu and the Philosophes and many others, including Cicero. The text needed to be amended over time to make those principles more universal, but the basic cultural inheritance was amplified by the intellectuals and statesmen, and their work in turn reinforced the culture.

HAVING MADE THE CASE, however briefly (or tediously) that America's love of liberty is in fact a cultural artifact bequeathed to us from England, let me now claw it back—at least somewhat. The problem with this tale, and many like it, is that it is what Rudyard Kipling would call a "just-so" story. A just-so story in anthropology is a form of post hoc fallacy that says because B follows A and C follows B, therefore A caused B and B caused C.

Though he tries to deny it, Hannan is offering an updated—and often compelling—version of the Whig interpretation of history, as famously formulated by the historian Herbert Butterfield in his conveniently titled 1931 book, *The Whig Interpretation of History*. Butterfield criticized previous generations of British historians who described world history as if it were an unfolding novel whose plot and conclusion were knowable to all. The heroes of the tale were lovers of liberty, the villains the forces of absolutism and arbitrary power. Their story was the tale of the inevitable victory of British liberal values.

As Butterfield put it, there is a lamentable "tendency in many historians to write on the side of Protestants and Whigs, to praise revolutions provided they have been successful, to emphasize certain principles of progress in the past and to produce a story which is the ratification if not the glorification of the present." He adds:

> The whig historian can draw lines through certain events . . . and if he is not careful he begins to forget that this line is merely a mental trick of his; he comes to imagine that it represents something like a line of causation. The total result of this method is to impose a certain form upon the whole historical story, and to produce a scheme of general history which is bound to converge beautifully upon the present—all demonstrating throughout the ages the workings of an obvious principle of progress.[27]

Teleology, the great sin of historians, is the idea that there is a purpose to things and events—a grand plan that we are all working under. Providence is, of course, the most famous teleological claim: "It's all God's plan." Prior to the Enlightenment, this was pretty much every Westerner's theory of everything. The great Enlightenment thinkers threw out religion as the driver of history, but they thought they spied a different prime mover: progress, and later History with a capital *H*. Mankind was ineluctably getting freer and better. Different philosophers debated how this "progress" worked and why it was inevitable.

Ultimately, teleology is an antidote to despair and nihilism. Just as we as individual humans want to believe there's a point to our own personal lives, we also want to believe there's a point to everyone else's. Indeed, unless you fancy yourself a messiah or prophet of some kind, you pretty much have to believe that there's an external, metaphysical purpose to life for everyone if you believe in such a thing for yourself.

The reason I raise the issue of teleology is to illuminate the fact that *if there is a purpose to economic and political evolution, we can no more prove its existence than we can prove God's.* It requires a leap of faith. Maybe this is all God's plan. Or maybe the universe has a purpose.

Or, maybe, history, like life, is just one damn thing after another.*

At countless moments in English history things could have gone very differently. The fact that the "good" forces won does not mean they were destined to. The Gunpowder Plot, in which a group of English Catholics tried to assassinate King James I by blowing up the House of Lords during a royal address, failed, thus saving England from a very different fate. But it didn't fail because of the English love of liberty. It failed because one person with knowledge of the scheme to reduce Parliament to rubble and return Catholicism to England sent a letter exposing the plot.[28] Whether Henry VIII broke with the Catholic Church so he could bed Anne Boleyn or because he wanted a wife to produce a male heir, the fact is that if Catherine of Aragon, his first wife, had been able to provide Henry VIII with a son, or perhaps even if Anne Boleyn had had lower standards and agreed to be his mistress, England might have stayed a Catholic nation.

It is fine and dandy to pan the river of "Germanic" history to sift out the republican and democratic nuggets as proof England was destined to usher in the era of liberty. But I don't think it is a gross overstatement to suggest that one can find counterexamples in the historical record.[29]

---

* This phrase is often attributed to Arnold Toynbee, but in no way do I believe that to be the case. The original source is apparently Max Plowman. See "History Is Just One Damn Thing After Another," Quote Investigator. http://quoteinvestigator .com/2015/09/16/history/

None of this is to say that Hannan—a friend of mine—is wrong. It is to say that he was right when he said the English "stumbled" into modernity. The tradition of English liberty was a flame that could have been extinguished if the winds of history had shifted slightly at any one of a thousand different moments. We are fortunate that circumstances worked out the way they did. But at the most fundamental level, if you take providence or some other teleological theory of the purpose of history out of the equation, modernity happened in England by accident.

The ingredients for liberty and prosperity have existed on earth for thousands of years, sloshing around, occasionally bumping into each other, and offering a glimpse to a better path. Religious toleration, restraints on monarchy, private property, the sovereignty of the individual, pluralistic institutions, scientific innovation, the rule of law—all of these things can be found, piecemeal, across the ages. The Chinese were pathbreaking scientific (and bureaucratic) innovators, but they couldn't relinquish their political monopoly and eventually snuffed out technological progress in the name of imperial hegemony.[30] Private property, likewise, existed in one form or another in countless societies,[31] but it alone was not enough absent the other necessary ingredients, and without those ingredients private property was often snuffed out. Prosperity itself wasn't unknown before the Miracle. But it was always a short-lived and local phenomenon.

To understand how miraculous the Miracle really is, we should take a moment and look more closely at some of the more well-known competing theories about why the Great Enrichment happened, including the complicated role of Protestantism—real and imagined—as well as the scientific revolution, slavery, imperialism, and other materialist factors.

THE PROTESTANT ORIGIN STORY of the Miracle takes several forms on its own and informs other theories as well.

The first and most straightforward theory, famously introduced by the sociologist Max Weber in his *Protestant Ethic and the Spirit of Capitalism*, published in Germany in 1905 (and in English in 1930), holds that Protestantism, particularly certain Puritan sects like the Calvinists, created new habits of the heart that gave birth to capitalism. The simple version of this story goes like this: The "other-worldly" Catholic cared little about material things in this life and was content to live a materially impoverished life, working as little as he or she needed to. Meanwhile, Weber argued, Protestants believed in accumulating wealth.[32] The Puritan, powered by the doctrine of predestination, moved his sights to this world, believing that material success was proof of virtue and a sign that one had been selected for reward in the next life. Hard work was a way to give glory to God. But economic success was achieved not just through hard work but by demonstrating honest dealings, piety (of course), and thriftiness ("The *summum bonum* of this ethic [is] the earning of more and more money . . . Acquisition . . . [is] the ultimate purpose of life," explained Weber, in a passage casting Benjamin Franklin as the poster boy for Protestant industriousness).[33] As Joyce Appleby summarizes Weber's argument, "Protestant preachers produced great personal anxiety by emphasizing everyone's tenuous grip on salvation."[34] In turn, this "promoted an interest in Providence in which believers scrutinized [economic] events for clues to divine intentions . . . [which] turned prosperity into evidence of God's favor."[35] In other words, acting as if you're blessed might actually be a sign you're blessed—the theological version of "fake it until you make it."

Let's put a pin in this theory and what it actually means for a moment. While Weber published his theory in the first decade of the twentieth century, the idea that capitalism depends on "thrift" or the accumulation of capital through savings was central to the bulk of Marxist thought in the nineteenth century. Marx believed that capitalism was, at its core, simply the exploitation of labor. All wealth and value, according to Marx, is created by the workers. All profit that does not go to the workers is essentially theft. Since all value is captured by labor, any "surplus value" collected by the owners of capital is, by definition, exploitative. The businessman or inventor who risks his own money to build and staff a factory is not adding value; he is subtracting value from the workers. Indeed, the money he used to buy the land and the materials is really just "dead labor."

Marx is still seen by many as a forward-thinking visionary. But the truth is Marx was a romantic popularizer of ancient biases against money and finance, or "usury" (and, to a very large extent, Jews). "To a degree rarely appreciated, [Marx] merely recast the traditional Christian stigmatization of moneymaking into a new vocabulary and reiterated the ancient suspicion against those who used money to make money," writes historian Jerry Z. Muller. "In his concept of capitalism as 'exploitation' Marx returned to the very old idea that money is fundamentally unproductive, that only those who live by the sweat of their brow truly produce, and that therefore not only interest, but profit itself, is always ill-gotten."[36]

This idea that excess capital or "surplus value" fueled capitalism is essential for numerous Marxist—and Marxish—explanations for its triumph. They all rest on a psychological desire among the enemies of capitalism, starting with Jean-Jacques Rousseau, to claim that capitalism was born in some kind of original sin. Some writers want slavery to be capitalism's original sin in order to exaggerate the crime of slavery (and to justify calls for reparations) and/or to delegitimize capitalism. But slavery requires no such exaggeration. Its evil stands on its own right. Similarly, claims that the West got rich by pillaging foreign lands amount to an effort to pad the indictment against imperialism. These theories all share the psychological assumption that capitalism marked a wrong turn in humanity's past. And they often drive people to make patently ridiculous claims. "Without slavery you have no cotton, without cotton you cannot have modern industry," Marx wrote. "It is slavery which has given their value to the colonies, it is the colonies which have created the commerce of the world, it is the commerce of the world which is the essential condition of the great industry."[37] Never mind that the Japanese dependence on silk from China was at least as great as England's demand for cotton, yet Japan did not become a capitalist country until after World War II. The idea that the cheap cotton made possible by slavery jump-started capitalism, most recently revived by Harvard's Sven Beckert, overlooks the fact that the price of cotton didn't increase appreciably after slavery in the United States was abolished. In fact, in the 1870s, it was 42 percent lower than the pre–Civil War price.[38]

Deirdre McCloskey surveys the research and finds the evidence to support such claims somewhere between nonexistent and meager. Yes, of course enormous profits were made from both slavery and

empire, but neither "created" capitalism, and the profits were ultimately incidental in the grand scheme of things. Moreover, if capitalism is dependent on the sort of mass-scale exploitation implicit
in slavery and imperialism, why did capitalism take so long to materialize? The ancient Chinese, Persians, Romans, and Aztecs all had
empires and slaves, yet none were capitalist. Why has capitalism survived the demise of slavery and the age of empire? Why are traditional
and anti-capitalist societies more likely to maintain the institution of
slavery in one form or another? If capitalism relies on exploitation,
why have Westerners gotten so much richer and enjoy such an abundance of leisure time?

The claim that thrift—i.e., increased savings from profit creating the capital necessary for industrial investment—led to the rise
of capitalism falls apart once you realize that it gets the causality
backward: Capital accumulation is not the engine of capitalism, it is
the by-product of it. Indeed, thrift is hardly a Western or Christian
invention, never mind a Protestant one. People have saved or otherwise been careful with their money since money was invented.[39] But
absent a market system, what someone could do with their money is
extremely limited.

Other materialist theories about the origins of capitalism, some
quite interesting and important, ultimately fail to satisfy the question
"Where does the Miracle come from?" The relative autonomy of European city-states and principalities surely encouraged freedom and
served as tributaries that led to eventual dam breaking. Sure, British
and European geography was no doubt essential to Europe's political
development, but the idea that capitalism was inevitable because of
Europe's rivers and temperate climate is the ultimate just-so story.

The scientific revolution, a miracle in its own right, is obviously a
hugely important part of the story. Would the Miracle have happened
without Isaac Newton, Francis Bacon, Thomas Edison, and other
great scientists and innovators? I'm inclined to say probably not. But
that does not mean that the scientific revolution created capitalism.
The deeper you look at this argument, the more you can see the cart
overtaking the horse. The Islamic world and China had their turns
at being at the forefront of science for centuries, and yet the Miracle
never materialized in either place. Indeed, for a millennium, England

certainly, and arguably the entirety of Western Europe, were backwaters. An alien visiting Earth a thousand years ago would not assume that the peoples of Europe were destined to achieve escape velocity from the norm of human existence.

So what did create it? In order to answer that, we need to circle back to another theory of Protestantism's role in Western development. This theory holds that Protestantism unleashed the spirit of innovation and liberty. My *National Review* colleague Charles C. W. Cooke, a Whig imported to our shores from England to do the hard work too few American-born writers will do, argues that Protestantism plays exactly this role. "I have long argued in vague terms that America is a fundamentally 'Protestant' society," he writes, "by which I have absolutely not meant that only Protestants can be good citizens, but rather that the Founders were the product of not just a religiously Protestant inheritance but also of a politically Protestant worldview—and, too, that the two are historically inextricable.

"This is to say," he continues, "that once a people becomes accustomed to cutting out the middlemen from their path to God, absolution, and salvation, it becomes easier for them to countenance cutting out the middlemen from their path to liberty and the pursuit of happiness as well."[40]

To be sure, there's something to this. Protestantism wouldn't have spread without the printing press, an innovation that disrupted the Catholic Church's theological monopoly. Protestantism also breathed new life into the idea that the individual is sovereign. But this overlooks the fact that while Protestantism eliminated the middleman theologically, politically Protestants were just as capable of crushing any deviation from orthodoxy as the most zealous Catholics. After all, early Protestants were not political "moderates." They did more than their share of witch-hunting. In England in the 1650s and 1660s, the Quakers were horribly brutalized by Anglicans. The Puritans of Salem weren't exactly a live-and-let-live bunch. In Europe, Lutherans and Calvinists adapted political—i.e., monarchical—absolutism to their theology quite easily, as did the Anglicans of Henry VIII's England. Frederick the Great was the most gifted absolute monarch of the nineteenth century, and he was raised in Calvinism.

NOW LET ME BACKPEDAL a bit. My point here is not to say that the various theories of where the Miracle came from are entirely wrong. My objection is to any argument that singles out one factor and says, "This—and only this—is why it happened." Nearly all truly complex and important phenomena have multiple mutually dependent factors that lead to their creation. Why did World War II happen? Why are you the way you are? Any attempt to focus on a single discrete mono-causal explanation is folly.

And capitalism is far, far more complicated. The reason I call the emergence of the Miracle a *miracle* is simply this: No one intended it. No single thing made it happen. It was an unplanned and glorious accident.

Again, consider the crude version of the Weberian thesis. Even if you grant that Protestantism "created" capitalism, you must also acknowledge that this isn't what Protestants, starting with Luther, had in mind. Martin Luther despised usury in all its forms (no doubt in part because of his virulent anti-Semitism). No seventeenth-century Puritan preacher said, "If you get rich you'll get into Heaven." They said, "Behave this way, and it's more likely that God will find you worthy." The changes in behavior elicited by this stern and pious instruction were never intended to be a get-rich-quick scheme. That would be the so-called prosperity theology, a very recent creation closely associated with televangelism. (Donald Trump's "spiritual advisor" Paula White is of this sect.)[41]

Similarly, the pluralism that made capitalism possible wasn't a product of some high-minded ideal about how to structure society. The religious tolerance that starts to emerge in Europe after the Peace of Westphalia in 1648 was far less a product of theological changes than it was of political and military exhaustion. The Treaty of West-phalia ended the "wars of religion" in Europe. Those wars, running off and on for more than a century, took an enormous toll on Protestants and Catholics alike. In their wake, as historian C. V. Wedgwood put it, the West began to understand "the essential futility of putting the beliefs of the mind to the judgment of the sword."[42] In other words,

Protestants and Catholics alike settled on a modicum of tolerance as "the last policy that remained when it had proved impossible to go on fighting any longer," in the words of Herbert Butterfield.[43] The social space created was an advance in liberty, but that was nobody's first choice. Rather, it was an accidental by-product of military futility.

If I have to offer my own explanation for where the Miracle comes from, I will second the argument put forth by Deirdre McCloskey in her awe-inspiring multivolume work on the birth of capitalism. Her answer, in brief: The Miracle is an attitude, expressed in new ideas and the rhetoric that accompanies them. "The North Sea economy, and then the Atlantic economy, and then the world economy grew because of changing forms of speech about markets and enterprise and innovation."[44] These new forms of speech made innovation possible by recognizing innovation as a good thing. Innovation dies on the drawing board without a climate that welcomes and rewards it. The Chinese and Arab advantages in technology amounted to little in the long run, because the political and religious climate proved inhospitable to sustain innovation, because innovation disrupts the status quo and undermines the powers that be. The Chinese inventor Bi Sheng, after all, invented printing centuries before Gutenberg.[45] The Japanese had guns, but then banned them because they recognized the threat they posed to the aristocracy of the sword-wielding warrior class of the samurai.[46]

For centuries, Christian—and Protestant!—rulers alike were hostile to innovation for the same reason. For instance, in 1548, Edward VI, Henry VIII's successor, issued *A proclamation against those that doeth innovate* . . . In her paper "'Meddle Not with Them That Are Given to Change': Innovation as Evil," Benoît Godin recounts the story of Henry Burton, a Puritan Church of England minister. Burton accused the Church of innovating doctrine against the king's wishes in two pamphlets in 1636. He was called before the court to defend himself. The court found that Burton, not the Church, was guilty of innovation. They sentenced Burton to prison for life—after cutting off his ears.[47] And this was *Protestant* England, the supposed ancestral homeland of liberty.

But then something happened. "About the end of the seventeenth century," Joseph Schumpeter writes in *Business Cycles: A Theoreti-*

cal, Historical, and Statistical Analysis of the Capitalist Process, the English political establishment "dropped all systematic hostility to invention. So did public opinion and the scribes." It was this remarkable, unprecedented, *miraculous* change in attitudes that made the Miracle possible. The way people talked and thought about how the world worked changed. "The economy is nothing without the words supporting it," McCloskey writes, "whether conventional wisdom or creative entrepreneurial projects."[48]

I am almost wholly convinced by this. For 100,000 years, the great mass of humanity languished in poverty. This great flat line of material misery plodded along unchanged until attitudes changed in England and Holland, not just among intellectuals or aristocrats, but among the common people, particularly the bourgeois—the mostly urban middle and upper middle class of professionals, artisans, craftsmen, merchants, and other laborers who did not till the soil. Prior to that, notions of betterment, innovation, and improvement were seen, literally, as heresy. *"Curiositas,"* or curiosity, was a sin, and the innovator a heretic.

For millennia vested interests—bureaucrats, aristocrats, guilds, and priests alike—formed coalitions of common interest to stifle innovations. A few examples from Joel Mokyr (by way of McCloskey):

- In 1299, Florence banned bankers from adopting Arabic numerals.
- At the end of the fifteenth century, scribe guilds of Paris managed to fight off the adoption of the printing press for two decades.
- In 1397, pin manufacturers in Cologne outlawed the use of pin presses.
- In 1561, the city council of Nuremburg made the manufacture and selling of lathes punishable with imprisonment.
- In 1579, the city council of Danzig ordered the secret assassination of the inventor of a ribbon loom—by drowning.
- In the late 1770s, the Strasbourg council barred a local cotton mill from selling its wares in town because it would disrupt the business model of the cloth importers.[49]

This is an ancient and universal story of elites seeking to protect their privileges and incomes from the gales of change. It is why the emperor of China burned his oceangoing vessels in 1525 and the Turkish caliph banned the printing press in 1729.[50] The merchant guilds that dominated much of Europe and the world for the better part of a thousand years endured not because they met economic demand but because they—with the help of the crown and the church—*restricted it*. They "limited competition and reduced exchange by excluding craftsmen, peasants, women, Jews, foreigners, and the urban proletariat from most profitable branches of commerce," writes Sheilagh Ogilvie. "Merchant guilds and associations were so widespread and so tenacious not because they efficiently solved economic problems, making everyone better off, but because they efficiently distributed resources to a powerful urban elite, with side benefits for rulers."[51]

Hostility to innovation and free trade was grounded in a broader worldview that saw money itself as the root of all evil. From the time of antiquity until the Enlightenment, trade and the pursuit of wealth were considered sinful. "In the city that is most finely governed," Aristotle wrote, "the citizens should not live a vulgar or a merchant's way of life, for this sort of way of life is ignoble and contrary to virtue."[52] In his *Republic*, Plato laid out one vision of an ideal society in which the ruling "guardians" would own no property to avoid tearing "the city in pieces by differing about 'mine' and 'not mine.'" He added that "all the classes engaged in retail and wholesale trade ... are disparaged and subjected to contempt and insults." Furthermore in his hypothetical utopian state, only non-citizens would be allowed to indulge in commerce. A citizen who defies the natural order and becomes a merchant should be thrown in jail for "shaming his family."[53]

In ancient Rome, "all trade was stigmatized as undignified ... the word *mercator* [merchant] appears as almost a term of abuse," writes Professor D. C. Earl of the University of Leeds. Cicero noted in the first century B.C. that retail commerce is *sordidus* [vile] because merchants "would not make any profit unless they lied constantly."[54]

Early Christianity expanded this point of view. Jesus himself was clearly hostile to the pursuit of riches. "For where your treasure is," he proclaimed in his Sermon on the Mount, "there will your heart be also." And of course he insisted that "it is easier for a camel to go through the eye of a needle than for a rich man to enter the kingdom of God."

The official teaching of the Catholic Church echoed these sentiments for centuries, holding that economics was zero-sum. "The Fathers of the Church adhered to the classical assumption that, since the material wealth of humanity was more or less fixed, the gain of some could only come at a loss to others," Jerry Z. Muller explains.[55] As Saint Augustine put it, "*Si unus non perdit, alter non acquirit*"—"If one does not lose, the other does not gain."[56]

The most evil form of wealth accumulation was the use of money to make money, i.e., usury. Lending money at interest was unnatural, and therefore invidious. "While expertise in exchange is justly blamed since it is not according to nature but involves taking from others," Aristotle insisted, "usury is most reasonably hated because one's possessions derive from money itself and not from that for which it was supplied. . . . So of the sorts of business this is the most contrary to nature."[57] Aristotle was right that finance is contrary to the natural order; it is also the driver of incredible prosperity and human betterment.

Despite all this, the case is often made that Christianity gets the credit for the Miracle. And, in broad strokes, I am open to the idea that without Christianity, the Miracle may never have happened. But that is not quite the same argument as Christianity caused the Miracle (and it certainly did not intend it). However, the lesser claim, that Christianity was a necessary ingredient, certainly seems likely.

Jesus said that his followers should render unto Caesar what is Caesar's, establishing that there were in fact two realms, which Saint Augustine called the "City of Man" and the "City of God." The City of Man was for temporal rulers, the City of God for ecclesiastical ones. When the Western Roman Empire fell, the Church remained in Rome as a religious authority. This established the principle that the Church would serve as the conscience for the realm. This really was a significant advance, creating one of the first and most important mental divisions of labor in the Western mind. Jesus's admonition of separating the realm of faith and the realm of rulers was an imperfect arrangement, to be sure, but this distinction served as an important check on the arbitrary rule of kings by introducing the idea that even rulers were answerable to a higher law. This was in marked contrast with Chinese emperors and Islamic sultans. While Christians had to render unto Caesars, Muhammad played the role of both Caesar and Jesus, and the political system he left behind recognized no space between secular and religious authority. Without that space, institutional pluralism and the division of meaning are impossible.

Also, some insist that Christianity—I would argue borrowing from Judaism—invented, or introduced, the idea of individual rights. Larry Siedentop, in his *Inventing the Individual: The Origins of Western Liberalism*, argues that by the fifteenth century the internal logic of Christianity's emphasis on the individual conscience had made the Enlightenment all but inevitable.[58]

Again, maybe. Then again, maybe not. It is quite simply impossible to know. There were certainly countless Christian regimes and movements that were hostile to innovation, individual liberty, and pluralism. Would the Miracle have happened if they had won their battles?

But, again, my aim here is not actually to discredit or rebut any of the serious arguments for why the Miracle happened, because I think many have merit. But all of the material factors are meaningless absent the broader context of culture. Biologists can grow just about anything in a lab, but they can't grow anything without the right medium.

At the end of the day, it is impossible to authoritatively answer the question of *why* beyond simply documenting *that* it happened. Why do certain ideas take hold and others do not? Why did the ideas of a Jewish carpenter in a backwater province of the Roman Empire capture the minds of millions and ultimately conquer the empire itself? The devout Christian can argue because they were true. But, as a sociological question, the only answer is that they just did.

The more important question is: Will it last?

MCCLOSKEY IS A GREAT optimist about the Miracle's prospects. I hope that optimism is warranted. But it seems to me axiomatic that an explanation of capitalism's birth grounded entirely in the power of ideas and words opens itself to a depressing rejoinder: What words and ideas can create, words and ideas can destroy. Whatever we can think ourselves into, we can unthink our way out of. And here we must consider what I believe is the most persuasive theory of why capitalism might be fated to vanish either from the earth or at least from America and the West. To do so, we must first look at the most influential and famous prophecy of capitalism's demise, made by Karl Marx.

According to Marx the working classes—the "proletariat"—were the sole source of all economic value. The "real" value of any good or service is derived not from the price it fetches in the market, but from the amount of time and effort put into it by the laborer. Hence, under Marx's "labor theory of value," when a factory owner sells that product at a profit, that profit is "surplus value" and by its nature exploitative and unjust. Indeed, for Marx, the economic ruling classes were akin to vampires, and his writing is full of bloodsucking imagery (which at the time was often a thinly veiled and occasionally explicit anti-Semitic reference to greedy Jewish moneylenders).

In Marx's futuristic fairy tale, the workers of the world would one day in the near future recognize that they were merely wage slaves and, having attained class consciousness, would overthrow their masters, seize the means of production, and live in a new utopian world where they would live very much like modern noble savages, working as much or as little as they wanted in a state of blissful harmony.

There are three things that need to be said about Marx's romantic vision. First, it truly was *romantic*, grounded in profound alienation and paranoia about the society he lived in. Second, for all of its pseudo-scientific jargon, Marxism was not a modern, forward-thinking project. Rather, it was a modern-sounding rehabilitation of ancient ideas and sentiments.[59] For the Christian, the meek would inherit the earth; for the Marxist, the workers would.

And, third, Marx's vision was entirely wrong. The idea that the inventor or the entrepreneur creates no value by bringing an idea into the world is ridiculous. According to Marx's economic analysis, the inventor of a better mousetrap doesn't create any value; only the workers who put it together do.

But it was Marx's political or sociological analysis that really missed the mark. To understand why, we need to look to Joseph Schumpeter, one of the great economists of the twentieth century. In *Capitalism,*

Socialism and Democracy (1942), Schumpeter argued that capitalism was ultimately doomed. But not remotely for the reasons Marx had predicted.

"Schumpeter turned Karl Marx on his head," writes biographer Thomas K. McCraw. "Hateful gangs of parasitic capitalists become, in Schumpeter's hands, innovative and beneficent entrepreneurs."[60] Schumpeter saw—and explained—earlier than almost anyone that the power of capitalism stemmed in large part from the liberation of, and tolerance for, entrepreneurs. The entrepreneur is the engine of innovation, and innovation is what drives economic growth by finding new opportunities for wealth where mere investors and managers saw only the way we've always done things.[61]

One of Schumpeter's key insights—and quite radical at the time—was to look at economic actors as entities over time, and economics generally as an evolutionary process. The market is constantly changing, and companies that are monopolies one minute fall prey to innovative firms that render them obsolete the next minute. The driver of that process was what Schumpeter famously called "creative destruction." Schumpeter applied the same insight to capitalism itself, and concluded that capitalism itself would fall prey to a kind of social analogue to creative destruction.

His analysis is rich and complicated, but I will highlight the three essential components as they relate to my argument.

First, capitalism is relentlessly and unsentimentally rational and efficient. The free market tends to wipe away tradition and ritual in the name of profit. This is a wonderful thing when the traditions and rituals it is corroding are based in bigotry and oppression. But like water seeking its own level, the capitalist tide doesn't stop at clearing away bad forms of tradition, custom, and sentiment. It carves a path through the social landscape heedless of the social value certain institutions and customs provide. Or, as Schumpeter puts it, capitalism "creates a critical frame of mind which, after having destroyed the moral authority of so many other institutions, in the end turns against its own; the bourgeois finds to his amazement that the rationalist attitude does not stop at the credentials of kings and popes but goes on to attack private property and the whole scheme of bourgeois values."[62]

Anyone who has bemoaned the demise of a beloved bookstore or bakery because it was more profitable to build a bank branch under-stands the point. To the mind of the pure profit maximizer a public park is a waste of space compared to a lucrative parking lot. The ratio-nalist who only seeks perfect economic efficiency sees no reason not to use a church as a stable. Schumpeter called the moral and senti-mental attachments that tell us there are more important things than simple efficiency and profit maximization "extra-rational" or "extra-capitalist" commitments. The "extra-" here means outside or above or apart from.

The problem is that, as we've seen, the free market needs "extra-rational" customs and traditions to survive. The "capitalist order," Schumpeter explains, "not only rests on props made of extra-capitalist material but also derives its energy from extra-capitalist patterns of behavior which at the same time it is bound to destroy."[63] As we've seen, capitalism emerged from a specific culture and it depends on the habits of the heart that made it possible. Thrift, delayed gratification, and honesty, not to mention the sovereignty of the individual, aren't solely products of mere reason; they are also extra-rational commit-ments derived, in the Western context, from Christianity, custom, history, family, patriotism, language, and all of the other ingredients that make up culture and faith. "No institution or practice or belief stands or falls with the theory that is at any time offered in its sup-port," Schumpeter writes. "Democracy is no exception."[64] Schumpeter is making the same point I made earlier about the Constitution. What sustains the constitutional order is our faith in it—not merely the arguments for it.

Think of it this way: No one is loyal to their family based solely on some *theory* of family loyalty. The "theory" is downstream of the more important and powerful emotional and instinctual commitments. The same dynamic applies to the political and religious systems we live under.

The second component of Schumpeter's theory is that capitalism's relentless assault on tradition and custom creates a market opportu-nity for intellectuals, lawyers, writers, artists, bureaucrats and other professionals who work with ideas to undermine and ridicule the existing system. They do so for a host of reasons. Some have a largely frivolous, even funny desire to "shock the bourgeoisie!"[65] Others, like

Marx, have a passionate and radical anger at the real or perceived injustices of modern society.

But there is another, more cynical explanation for why the peddlers of words, symbols, and ideas declare war on the existing system: They have a *class interest* in doing so. As Joel Mokyr puts it in *The Gifts of Athena: Historical Origins of the Knowledge Economy,* "Sooner or later in any society the progress of technology will grind to a halt because the forces that used to support innovation become vested interests." He adds, "In a purely dialectical fashion, technological progress creates the very forces that eventually destroy it."[66]

But the reason groups become "vested interests" isn't solely economic. When I use the term "class interest," I do not mean the simple pursuit of economic gain, as the Marxist does, or as the *public choice* economist does. Man lives by more than bread—or profit—alone.

Intellectuals surely have a financial motive in arguing for a system in which intellectuals would run things, but they also have a psychological one. That desire is often the more important one. Marx wanted to be the high priest of a new world order, but he didn't necessarily want to be rich. We are wired to want to have higher status than others. We are also wired to resent those who we believe have undeservedly higher status than we do. Intellectuals and artistic elites have heaped scorn on other elites—the wealthy, the military, the bourgeois, the Church—for centuries.

Schumpeter's analysis was deeply influenced by Friedrich Nietzsche's concept of *ressentiment,* laid out in his *On the Genealogy of Morals. Ressentiment,* in Nietzsche's highly literary telling, is the process by which priests use their skills to redefine the culture's idea of what is virtuous in order to undermine the power of knights, i.e., the ruling nobility. The knights are non-intellectual men of action who hold more power than the priests, and the priests hate them for it.[67] Thus, according to Nietzsche, Christianity elevated the meek and denigrated the powerful (just as Marx lionized labor and demonized entrepreneurs). It's much more complicated than that—Nietzsche always is—but Schumpeter took this framework and applied it to capitalism over time.

There is one very common—if not quite universal—thing that

unites these different kinds of "priests": They tend to come from the ranks of the bourgeois and the very wealthy themselves. There's something about growing up prosperous that causes people not only to take prosperity for granted but to resent the prosperous. "It wasn't the children of auto workers who pulled up the paving stones on the Left Bank in 1968," writes Deirdre McCloskey. "The most radical environmentalists and anti-globalists nowadays are socialist children of capitalist parents."[68]

The third component of Schumpeter's theory is that, as capitalism creates more and more mass affluence, it creates more and more intellectuals, until they actually become a "new class." There have always been court intellectuals and artists. But until very recently they made a living by working for the ruling class (which is why so much classical philosophical writing is esoteric; criticism of the rulers had to be in code). As capitalism makes mass education possible, it creates a mass audience, a whole market, for what the intellectuals are selling. And what the intellectuals are selling is resentment of the way things are. This creates a much broader climate of hostility to the social order itself. "For such an atmosphere to develop," Schumpeter writes, "it is necessary that there be groups whose interest it is to work up and organize resentment, to nurse it, to voice it and to lead it."[69] One cannot watch cable television news, listen to talk radio, read a campus bulletin board about upcoming speakers, or listen to the preening speechifying that comes with every Oscar and Emmy award ceremony and not see that denigrating and undermining the established order is now not only a lucrative calling but a major part of the culture.

James Burnham, the former Communist turned cold-eyed conservative, came to many of the same conclusions in his *Managerial Revolution: What Is Happening in the World*, published in 1941, a year before Schumpeter's *Capitalism, Socialism and Democracy*, albeit from a different perspective. By the time Burnham released *Suicide of the West: An Essay on the Meaning and Destiny of Liberalism* in 1964, the "New Class" thesis was widely debated across the ideological spectrum. Burnham argued that the overwhelmingly "liberal" (in the progressive sense) New Class intellectuals weren't simply interested in power but that they were motivated by guilt:

For Western civilization in the present condition of the world, the most important practical consequence of the guilt encysted in the liberal ideology and psyche is this: that the liberal, and the group, nation, or civilization infected by liberal doctrine and values, are morally disarmed before those whom the liberal regards as less well off than himself.[70]

I think guilt still plays an important role for some people. But I think, a half century later, guilt has mostly given way to anger. Many academics and writers no longer feel guilty about what Western civilization or America has done, because they no longer feel like they belong to it. Many members of the new class today—particularly those called "globalists"—have a post-national attachment to their cosmopolitan class. They see themselves as citizens of the world, sharing more in common with their compatriots in London and Paris than with the fellow citizens who sweep their floors, create small businesses, or simply feel a patriotic attachment to their own nation and culture.

Both Schumpeter and especially Burnham were overly invested in their theory of capitalism's demise. George Orwell was deeply influenced by Burnham's writing on the New Class and that fascination was a major inspiration for his novel *1984*. But Orwell rightly rejected the idea that a managerial dystopia was inevitable. He astutely identified the problem in Burnham's worldview. Burnham was in many ways the kind of rationalist Schumpeter had identified. The moral and idealistic commitments that make liberal democracy possible were, for Burnham, an illusion. Everything boiled down to mere contests of power. Burnham, according to Orwell, believed that "power can never be restrained by any ethical or religious code, but only by other power. The nearest possible approach to altruistic behaviour is the perception by a ruling group that it will probably stay in power longer if it behaves decently."

This obsession with power distorted Burnham's analysis of politics. Because power was everything, those in power would always remain in power. "It will be seen," Orwell writes, "that at each point Burnham is predicting *a continuation of the thing that is happening*. Now the tendency to do this is not simply a bad habit, like inaccuracy or exaggeration, which one can correct by taking thought. It is a major mental disease, and its roots lie partly in cowardice and partly in the worship of power, which is not fully separable from cowardice."[71]

Orwell might be a bit too harsh, but he is ultimately correct. If those in power always win, then the Miracle would never have happened. The kings of Europe would have crushed the bourgeois upstarts. Burnham was incredibly insightful about the way power really works in every society, but he failed to appreciate the way the Founders had created a system that recognized the dangers of concentrated power.

Schumpeter's analysis of social evolution is more subtle and dynamic than Burnham's, taking into account the complex role psychology plays in every society. But Schumpeter suffered from the same conviction that events were evolving in an inevitable direction in accordance with a process ultimately beyond our control to stop.

If Schumpeter and Burnham were right, the only intelligent course of action would be to surrender to the inevitably of it all and scurry to the "right side of history." But as I argue in the first pages of this book, I reject that view. Fatalism, not Burnham's "liberalism," is the real force driving the suicide of the West. Folding your hands in your lap and saying "Let History take the wheel!" is the fastest route to self-destruction. In other words, Schumpeter and Burnham might be right about capitalism's doom, but what will make that doom inevitable is taking their word for it. What they offer is not a prophecy but a warning. And that warning is worth heeding.

TAKEN AS A WARNING, their analysis is incredibly valuable. It is true that a free society will create wealthy and influential classes or interests. And they are right that some of these groups will try to undermine a free society for their own benefit. The way those vested interests sabotage the engine of innovation is with *words and ideas*. And while they may not be succeeding as much as they would like, no observer of the current political and cultural scene can deny that they are constantly trying. But their victory is not inevitable. If it is true that the Miracle was created by words, that means it can be destroyed by words. But it is also true that the Miracle can be sustained by words. Our civilization, like every civilization, is a conversation. Therefore the demise of our civilization is only inevitable if the people saying and arguing the right things *stop talking.*

This works both ways. Every conflict ends when one side stops fighting. Usually we think of the loser as the one who accepts defeat. But the truth is that the battle can just as easily be lost if one side *declares premature victory.*

In our own time, the most famous writer to be accused of that sin is the brilliant scholar Francis Fukuyama. As a young State Department intellectual, Fukuyama wrote a short essay for *The National Interest* titled "The End of History?" in which he argued that the fall of communism meant the debate over human organization had essentially been settled:

> What we may be witnessing is not just the end of the Cold War, or the passing of a particular period of post-war history, but the end of history as such: that is, the end point of mankind's ideological evolution and the universalization of Western liberal democracy as the final form of human government.[72]

Fukuyama's argument has been widely misunderstood and caricatured. Despite his reliance on Hegelian philosophy, Fukuyama is less committed to teleology than he is to old-fashioned social science and history. He believed (and still believes) that liberal democratic capitalism is the best possible system for organizing society. The problem is that he took it for granted that the battle was over. His argument was much more plausible in 1989 than it is in 2018, as he has since conceded.

The point here is that the defenders of the Miracle can never get cocky. They can never lay down their rhetorical swords and retreat to their farms. All we can do is defend the principles and ideals that the Miracle made possible in our lifetimes and hand off the project to our children. When we fail to do that, when we do not fill our children with gratitude for their inheritance, they will remain childish in their expectations of what politics and economics can accomplish.

Simply put, cultures that do not cherish their best selves die by their own hand. We protect what we are grateful for. That which we resent, we leave out for the trash man or let rot and decay in the elements, as the termites of human nature gnaw away at it. Ingratitude is the spirit that inebriates us with despair and, in our dark moments, makes suicide seem heroic.

"From whence shall we expect the approach of danger?" asked Abraham Lincoln. "Shall some trans-Atlantic military giant step the earth and crush us at a blow? Never. All the armies of Europe and Asia . . . could not by force take a drink from the Ohio River or make a track on the Blue Ridge in the trial of a thousand years. No, if destruction be our lot we must ourselves be its author and finisher. As a nation of free men we will live forever or die by suicide."[73]

5

THE ETERNAL BATTLE
Reason Versus the Search for Meaning

THE HISTORY OF POLITICAL PHILOSOPHY IS REALLY THE history of the stories we tell ourselves about ourselves. The two most important creation myths of the modern West were told by Locke and Rousseau. They are in constant battle with each other to this very day, and as of this writing, Rousseau is winning.

In fact, for years I've argued that almost every political argument boils down to Locke versus Rousseau. It's a staple riff of mine when I talk to college students. It goes something like this: Locke believed in the sovereignty of the individual and that we are "captains of ourselves." Rousseau argued that the group was more important than the individual and the "general will" was superior to the solitary conscience. Man is sinful according to Locke, a noble savage according to Rousseau. Our rights come from God, not from government, declares Locke. No, we surrender our individual rights to the judgment of the sovereign, replies Rousseau. Locke says that the right to property and to the fruits of our labors is the keystone of a free and just order. Rousseau says property is the original sin of civilization and, in a just society, property must be managed by the sovereign for the good of the whole community. Locke believes in equality before the law, but tolerates or celebrates inequality of wealth, merit, and virtue in civil society.[1] Rousseau believes economic inequality is the source of all social ills, and that "one of the most important tasks of government [is] to prevent extreme inequality of fortunes."[2] Locke sees the formation of liberal governance as the greatest advance for mankind. Rousseau, in the words of Michael Locke McLendon, sees the opposite: "For Rousseau, Lockean freedoms secured through the social contract are nothing more than a ruse, a confidence trick the rich play on the poor to consolidate their power. Thus, modern humans are enslaved socially, economically, and politically."[3]

Look at almost any contemporary debate between the left and the right and you will find echoes of this divide. Progressives take after Rousseau. Leftists insist, with varying degrees of intensity, that the rules of the game are nothing more than a rigged system of exploitative capitalism: "white privilege," "the patriarchy," etc. A unifying idea across the left is the Rousseauian idea that income inequality is a great evil, the "defining challenge of our time," in the words of Barack Obama.[4]

The right argues for the other side of the coin. Donald Trump, and some of a Randian bent, cartoonishly insist that great wealth is a virtue unto itself. Conventional conservatives make a more sophisticated argument, emphasizing that freedom and merit will inevitably lead to economic inequality and there's nothing wrong with that. The job of government, Speaker Paul Ryan likes to say, is to create opportunity for upward mobility, not to tell people you're stuck in your station, so here's a check to make life a little less miserable.

I think this Locke-versus-Rousseau comparison illuminates a great deal. But it should be gripped lightly. There is a temptation, common among intellectual historians and others who believe in the power of ideas, to play a game of connect-the-dots (a tendency I definitely suffer from). A philosopher says X in 1800. Then in 1900 a writer says something very similar to X. Ergo, the intellectuals conclude the philosopher's influence spanned a century. This obviously does happen—a lot—but almost surely not nearly as much as intellectuals would like to believe.[5]

But the relationship between ideas, culture, and politics isn't incremental or linear but catalytic and interactive. Westerners have wanted the Middle East to become, variously, Christian or liberal or democratic for centuries. If ideas alone had the power we sometimes ascribe to them, we could have just air-dropped copies of the *Federalist Papers*—or the Bible—over Baghdad and Riyadh and waited for them to have the desired effect. The two most popular and closely related metaphors for ideas and their role in the world are "light" and "flame." The Enlightenment, that great awakening of liberal political philosophy and scientific exploration, "shed light" on the world. Sometimes an idea is a spark that ignites some great fire or sets off a bomb. That's all fine. But no great fire can endure without the right fuel. No bomb can detonate if it's not made from the right materials. Ideas take root (another metaphor) only when the soil is right. And the nature of the soil changes the way an idea grows.

Rousseau's psychological response to the Enlightenment led him to articulate a certain argument. But what links Rousseau to Bernie Sanders or Occupy Wall Street isn't primarily an *intellectual* lineage but a *psychological* tendency. How many members of Occupy Wall Street or MSNBC pundits have read Rousseau's *Discourse on Inequality*? Of the fraction who read it, probably in college, how many of them can attribute their opposition to tax cuts or the Koch brothers to that text? The answer must be very close to zero. Likewise, how many Tea Partiers or Fox News contributors consult John Locke for their positions? The answer is the same.

We tend to give too much credit to intellectuals for creating ideas. More often, they give voice to ideas or impulses that already exist as pre-rational commitments or attitudes. Other times they distill opinions, sentiments, aspirations, and passions that already exist on the ground, and the distilled spirit is fed back to the people and they become intoxicated by it. Revolutions die in the crib when the people are not inclined to be revolutionary.

So, just as the state is a myth agreed upon, most civilizational creation stories are just that: stories. That doesn't mean they are untrue. But the truth's significance is on a separate track from the significance of the story itself.

It would be fair to say that John Locke was a storyteller who, more than anyone, created the Miracle. But a more accurate way of saying it would be "the story we tell about Locke" helped create the Miracle.

Born in 1632 in the small English village of Wrington, Locke spent his childhood in the nearby market town of Pensford.[6] His father (also John), a former soldier in the English Civil War, worked as a lawyer and clerk to a justice of the peace in a nearby village. The Lockes, devout Puritans, were prosperous but not particularly prominent. Thanks to his father's former commander, who was a member of Parliament, John received a scholarship to the Westminster school in

London, where he excelled, winning placement at Christ Church in Oxford. He studied scholastic philosophy there but was not particularly enamored with it. He spent more time studying medicine and science (then called "natural philosophy"). He stayed at Oxford for fifteen years, from 1652 to 1667, in various administrative and teaching positions. In 1667 he moved to London, where he worked as a tutor and physician in the household of Anthony Ashley Cooper, who would become the first Earl of Shaftesbury. Cooper was a member of the "Cabal" that largely governed in England at the time for King Charles II.* Through Shaftesbury, Locke procured several important administrative jobs in His Majesty's government.

Shaftesbury, a leader of the Whigs, was one of the central political figures of his time, first siding with Royalists in the English Civil War but later switching to the Parliamentary side. Whigs were united by three ideas: Parliament was supreme, Protestant minorities should be respected, and Catholicism was a threat to English liberty and sovereignty. (The Whigs' anti-Catholicism, while regrettable, should not be viewed through the prism of the present day. In the 1600s—and well after, in some quarters—Catholicism was deeply enmeshed with the power politics of the age.)

If Locke was a tutor to Shaftesbury's son, Shaftesbury was a father-like tutor to Locke in the realm of politics. (It was during this time that Locke probably cowrote with Shaftesbury the Fundamental Constitution of Carolina, the charter for colonial lands consisting of most of the territory between Virginia and Florida, of which Shaftesbury was one of the proprietors.)

In 1675, Locke moved to France for several years. When he returned, the politics of England were very different. Shaftesbury was now persona non grata with the crown, a leader in the effort to bar Catholics from the throne. This is relevant because Charles II, while not Catholic, was sympathetic to Catholicism. Indeed, Charles had once secretly promised the king of France to convert in exchange for support in his war against the Dutch. Worse, Charles's brother, James, was Catholic,

<hr>

* The term "cabal" has special meaning here. Normally, the king selected a single "favorite" counselor to advise and manage his rule. The so-called Cabal ministry, instead, was made up of five privy counselors whose names (Clifford, Arlington, Buckingham, Ashley-Cooper, and Lauderdale) spelled out the acronym "CABAL."

and because the king had no legitimate sons (though plenty of illegiti-mate ones), James was next in line to the throne. That fact, combined with rumors of his dealings with the French, aroused a fierce back-lash in Parliament amidst something of a national anti-Catholic panic in England, prompting the Exclusion Crisis from 1679 to 1681. Lord Shaftesbury led the "Country Party" (later called the Whigs) in the fight to legally ban a Catholic from wearing the crown. Charles repeat-edly dissolved Parliament to fend off the effort. In 1681, Charles dis-solved Parliament permanently until his death four years later. While Charles was still alive, however, Shaftesbury had been arrested and imprisoned in the Tower of London for high treason. Shaftesbury was acquitted by a grand jury, thanks to a weak case by the government and a jury handpicked by a Whig sheriff. He tried, unsuccessfully, to organize an outright rebellion against the crown, but when that failed, he fled to exile in the Netherlands in the fall of 1682, lest he not be so lucky a second time. In January 1683, he died in Amsterdam.

It was against this backdrop that Locke wrote his *Two Treatises of Government*. But he would not dare publish them for nearly a decade, lest he be put to death. In 1683, Locke also fled to the Netherlands. He did not return until after the Glorious Revolution of 1688.

Recounting the story of the Glorious Revolution in detail would take us too far afield for our purposes. But a very brief summary is necessary.[7] When Charles II died, his Catholic brother James inher-ited the throne. Again, English Protestants were convinced that Catholicism was a tyrannical creed that put the interests of foreign powers ahead of the interests of the English people. James set out to lift all of the legal prohibitions on Catholics in government. Worse, he attempted to transform Parliament—the seat of popular sovereignty—into a body of lackeys, lickspittles, and yes-men, reversing the progress of liberty in England and seeming to confirm the worst fears about Catholic absolutism. After all, France's king, Louis XIV, had spent much of the 1680s persecuting French Protestants, dismantling popu-lar assemblies, and attempting to expand Catholic hegemony on the Continent. There's a rough parallel between the 1680s and the 1930s in that during both periods it seemed tyranny (by whatever label you want to put on it) was the wave of the future, not just in France but in the Hapsburg Empire and throughout much of Europe.[8]

Things came to a boil when James had a son with his second, Catholic wife. This meant that the heir to the throne was no longer James's Protestant older daughter, Mary, but another Catholic. Mary's husband William of Orange, the stadtholder (or chief magistrate) of the Netherlands—and James's nephew—organized an invasion for the purpose of regime change. He orchestrated an invitation from seven English Lords to come to England. William put together an army of 25,000 men and an armada of five hundred ships. His agents disseminated some 50,000 copies of a pamphlet vowing to seek a "free Parliament"—i.e., one properly elected, and not a tool of the king, the Catholics, or the French. After a daunting November channel crossing, William's forces landed in Torbay, in southwest England.

There were two minor skirmishes, but James was inadequate to the task of rallying popular support, particularly at a time when anti-Catholic sentiment in England was so high. His foremost general, John Churchill—an ancestor of the twentieth-century prime minister—switched sides, at enormous risk. Isolated and inept, James ordered his troops not to fight the invading army. He fled to France instead. But first he did something remarkable and hugely significant. He took a sheaf of writs establishing a new Parliament and burnt them. He then took the king's seal and hurled it into the Thames. This was not simply an act of spite. James believed, with some good reason, that if the official documents authorizing a Parliament, and the seal which legitimized that authority, were disposed of, then no new government could be formed.

"We may think of official documents as readily fungible; if there is an original somewhere, of an act of Congress or a Supreme Court decision, it is readily replicable, and its validity is not expunged if, by some unhappy accident, the original is consumed by fire or vermin. But in the seventeenth century the document *was* the law," writes Michael Barone in *Our First Revolution: The Remarkable British Upheaval That Inspired America's Founding Fathers.*[9] To the modern mind, this may seem almost comical. One can imagine the plot of some action movie in which the dastardly villains endeavor to find and destroy all the original copies of the U.S. Constitution, thus in one fell swoop eliminating the Bill of Rights and our system of government. But that's not how it works. That wasn't clear to James at the time.

William marched into and occupied London. But he did not declare himself king. Rather, he called for new parliamentary elections and theatrically made no effort to sway them. The new Parliament debated whether James was still king, decided that he was not, and named William and Mary the king and queen. The immediate political significance was obvious. There would never again be a Catholic on the throne. French influence on England was thwarted. A new Anglo-Dutch alliance was formed.

But the lasting significance was far greater. *Parliament*—not God—had made William king. Moreover, it had established that Parliament was the ultimate authority in England and that the king was not above the law. This was a watershed moment. The idea of parliamentary supremacy—and hence the ultimate sovereignty of the people—had been around in some form since at least the days of the Magna Carta. Now the idea was manifested in the real world. The new Parliament passed the English Bill of Rights, which cemented for all time the rights of Parliament (never to be permanently dissolved again), the English people, and the limits on royal authority. No longer could the king (or queen) suspend laws, levy taxes, raise standing armies, and the like without the consent of Parliament. The right to free speech in Parliament was now beyond the power of the king to abrogate as well.

It's crucial to understand how ideas and culture were intertwined in the Glorious Revolution. The new order was understood and ratified not as a radical departure from tradition and custom but as a *reassertion of it*. In the text of the Bill of Rights itself, Parliament insisted that it was merely asserting and vindicating the "ancient rights and liberties" of the English people. In William's "Declaration of Reasons" for the invasion, he hammered the point that he was merely trying to restore the English tradition of liberty and defeat the forces of tyranny and absolutism. He claimed to be unable to "excuse ourself from espousing their interest in a matter of so high consequence, and from contributing all that lies in us for the maintaining both the Protestant religion and the laws and liberties of these Kingdoms, and for the securing to them the continual employment of all their right" and to come "for no other design, but to have a free and lawful parliament assembled as soon as possible." He was "appearing upon this occasion in arms" to rescue the Church of England and the "ancient constitution."[10] In other words, the English culled from their past a story of themselves and ratified it in a legal principle. The story, not the principle, was what mattered most. But, once committed to the story, new principles—or ideas—emerged that would eventually drive the story in new directions.

Historians debate how sincere William was. To be sure, William had his own ambitions in mind, as did all of those Whigs and other members of Parliament piously invoking the ancient customs of liberty as validation for a coup. Similarly, there was no end of realpolitik motivating the Dutch to pull off one of the greatest regime changes in human history.

But what stuck was the story. Just as the Magna Carta became something more than a fairly mercenary, even grubby truce between the king and the nobles, the relatively bloodless Glorious Revolution reinforced the story the English told themselves about themselves. As Edmund Burke would put it a century later, "The Revolution was made to preserve our *ancient,* indisputable laws and liberties, and that *ancient* constitution of government which is our only security for law and liberty."[11] The Glorious Revolution simultaneously severed England from its feudal past while at the same time grounding its new embryonic democratic society, not in grand abstractions, but in a nationalistic, essentially tribal story of Englishness. The abstractions came later. And that is where John Locke came in.

John Locke's *Second Treatise,* published in 1689, provided a philosophical binding for the pages of the story of English liberty. But it also contained within it a radical departure from English particularism. In tone and ambition, it spoke to the English heart and mind, but within it lay a universal worldview. I will offer a brief and somewhat selective summary, even though—spoiler alert—I will go on to argue that the precise details do not matter as much as some like to think.

The *Second Treatise on Government* contains its own creation myth: "Thus in the beginning," Locke declared, "all the world was America ..." What Locke meant is that in our original tribal state everyone lived like the Indians across the Atlantic. Why? Because "no such thing as money was any where known."[12]

What Locke means by money here is *property.* And Locke's understanding of property is the key to his entire political worldview. Locke argues that, in the state of nature, men exist in "a State of perfect Free-dom to order their Actions, and dispose of their Possessions, and Per-sons as they think fit, within the bounds of the Law of Nature, without asking leave, or depending Upon the Will of any other man . . ."[13] Locke's state of nature is remarkably similar to Rousseau's in many respects. Locke says in the state of nature is "a State also of Equal-ity, wherein all the Power and Jurisdiction is reciprocal, no one hav-ing more than another; there being nothing more evident, than that Creatures of the same species and rank, promiscuously born to all the same advantages of Nature, and the use of the same faculties, should also be equal one amongst another without Subordination or Subjec-tion, unless the Lord and Master of them all should, by any manifest Declaration of his Will set one above another, and confer on him by an evident and clear appointment an undoubted right to Dominion and Sovereignty."[14]

For Locke, the problem with the state of nature is that it is unstable. It invites a "state of war" in which one man—or group of men—may use force to impose their will on another. Because the state of nature lacks "a common judge with authority"[15] to settle disputes, disputes are therefore settled by force. The loser of such contests, if he survives but remains involuntarily under the control of the "conqueror," is now in "the perfect condition of slavery."[16] This is an illegitimate, or arbi-trary, use of force, for no man has the right to exert his will against another's will.

That is because *the first property right is the right to own yourself*—and all other rights derive from this one. Thus, government is a neces-sary tool, created collectively to protect property, which is another way of saying protecting life. Men, according to Locke, voluntarily com-bine to create government to do limited and specific things, because our rights are prior to government. As we've seen, Locke was wrong about this in terms of history or anthropology. But Locke recognized what Mancur Olson meant when he said that order is "the first bless-ing of the invisible hand."[17]

Long before Marx, Locke offered his own labor theory of value—or, in Locke's case, a labor theory of property. For every man, Locke writes, "the *Labour* of his Body, and the *Work* of his Hands, we may say, are properly his. Whatsoever then he removes out of the State that

Nature hath provided, and left it in, he hath mixed his *Labour* with, and joyned to it something that is his own, and thereby makes it his property."[18] God gives us trees, but when a person chops down a tree and turns it into a table, it becomes *property*.

Locke believed that property was the route to *improvement*; it was literally the vehicle of progress. The tribes of America might be exotic and fascinating but it was nonetheless the case that a "King of a large and fruitful territory there feeds, lodges, and is clad worse than a day labourer in *England*."[19] In other words, Locke understood that human ingenuity *creates* wealth.

For Locke, our inalienable rights were life, liberty, and property. The Declaration of Independence changed this to Life, Liberty, and the Pursuit of Happiness, but there is no insurmountable contradiction here, because Locke believed that property was the route to happiness. When the first man put a fence around a piece of land to cultivate it, he was beginning the process of human advancement, of culture. As we will see, this is the exact opposite of Rousseau's vision.

Locke was interested not in material equality but in equality in the eyes of God, and therefore in the eyes of government. People may have different perspectives and opinions, but that is because they have different experiences. And therefore tolerance for differences should be maximized.

This is where Locke's doctrine of the "blank slate" (or in his case blank paper) proved so useful:

> Let us then suppose the mind to be, as we say, white paper void of all characters, without any ideas. How comes it to be furnished? Whence comes it by that vast store which the busy and boundless fancy of man has painted on it with an almost endless variety? Whence has it all the materials of reason and knowledge? To this I answer, in one word, from EXPERIENCE.[20]

This idea, which comes from Locke's work as one of the founders of empiricism, arguably did more to transform the world than anything he wrote on government and politics. As a matter of science, Locke was wrong. Obviously, experience informs and shapes how we see and understand the world, but we also come preloaded with all manner of genetic software that processes the data in various ways. But as a matter of politics and philosophy, Locke's rejection of original sin, innate ideas, and the natural—i.e., divine—authority of kings moved politics from a God-centered universe to a man-centered universe. God was the only master of mankind, according to Locke, and no man could appropriate God's power. This meant that, in this world, each man was the master of himself and just power had to be rooted in his consent.

As Steven Pinker notes, one of Locke's targets was the then dominant medieval understanding of human nature. "Locke opposed dogmatic justifications for the political status quo, such as the authority of the church and the divine right of kings, which had been touted as self-evident truths," Pinker writes. The blank slate "also undermined a hereditary royalty and aristocracy, whose members could claim no innate wisdom or merit if their minds had started out as blank as everyone else's. It also spoke against the institution of slavery, because slaves could no longer be thought of as innately inferior or subservient."[21] Locke's blank slate, in other words, was a part of a larger argument for pluralism, meritocracy, and tolerance.

Locke elevated reason above revelation. He believed that man could reason his way through this world and create political structures based upon universal equality and consent. Since every person is "furnished with like Faculties," he wrote, and "shar[ed] all in one Community of Nature, there cannot be supposed any such Subordination among us, that may Authorize us to destroy one another, as if we were made for one another's uses, as the inferior ranks of Creatures are for ours."[22] This idea was essentially a time bomb, placed at the foundations of hereditary aristocracy, slavery, and the divine right of kings. "Locke explicitly challenged the fixed hierarchical arrangements taken for granted almost everywhere seventeenth-century Europeans lived," writes James T. Kloppenberg.[23]

Locke wanted the same rules applied to everyone: "promulgated, establish'd Laws, not to be varied in particular Cases, but to have one Rule for Rich and Poor, for the Favourite at Court, and the Country Man at Plough."[24] The rule of law that pays no heed to notions of inherited superiority was the ideal means to achieve "the Peace, Safety, and publick good of the People."[25] This idea is the whole ball game. We cannot police what is in the human heart, but only how people act on it. "But Freedom of Men under Government is having a standing Rule to live by, common to every one in the Society in question, and made by the legislative power erected in it. . . ." Locke writes. "A Liberty to follow my own Will in all things, where the Rule prescribes not; and not to be subject to the inconstant, uncertain, unknown, Arbitrary Will of another man . . ."[26]

Many historians once argued that Locke's *Second Treatise* is less a stand-alone work of political philosophy and more a political document intended to justify the Glorious Revolution. But it's clear that Locke wrote most of it well before the Glorious Revolution unfolded, and when doing so was an act of high treason. "In the 1680s, even entertaining the idea that sovereign power resided in the English people rather than the king-in-Parliament put dissidents' lives in danger," writes Kloppenberg.[27] Again, the causality here is important. The facts on the ground changed before the idea that legitimized the facts. The debate over whether the *Second Treatise* was primarily a political document or a philosophical one misses the key point: It was a cultural document, reflecting an idea whose time had come.

JOHN LOCKE SAW THE past as a pit humanity must labor to escape from. Jean-Jacques Rousseau, on the other hand, believed it was a shame we built the ladder at all. Whereas Locke saw the emergence of modern society as a story of liberation, not just of people but of the mind, Rousseau saw modernity as a form of oppression.

Rousseau was born in Geneva, Switzerland, the only society that rivaled ancient Sparta in Rousseau's mind as an ideal form of political organization. Rousseau's mother died shortly after giving birth to him. His father, Isaac, a grandiose and overeducated watchmaker who had married above his station, raised Jean-Jacques in Geneva until trouble with the law prompted the father to abandon his son, leaving Jean-Jacques to be raised by relatives who treated him poorly.

At sixteen, the precocious Rousseau left for a life of adventure. In Savoy, Rousseau was taken in as steward to a rich, eccentric woman, the Baroness de Warens. The fairly young baroness had left her husband, taking much of his money with her, and became a kind of eccentric adventurer herself. One of her vocations was as a Catholic missionary of sorts, specializing in converting young Protestant men. She served as Rousseau's patron and, eventually, his lover. By the time he left her employ, Rousseau—who had never been formally educated—was a full-blown man of letters and burgeoning philosopher. Eventually he set off for Paris to make his mark, expecting to be recognized as a unique talent.

When Rousseau arrived in Paris at the age of thirty, the city was the intellectual capital of the world. He met Denis Diderot, another ambitious young intellectual, who would go on to cofound and edit the *Encyclopédie*—the great compendium of the arts and sciences, and the most important publication of the French Enlightenment. The two were the most prominent of the *philosophes*, the radical, anticlerical, democratic intellectuals who laid much of the groundwork for the Age of Reason.

Rousseau would go on to become more famous than Diderot and all the other philosophes. He was a true celebrity intellectual, admired by the royal court (for a time) as much for his brilliant writing as for his musical compositions and operas. "Yet he never seemed at home in Paris and eventually succumbed to severe feelings of alienation and self-loathing," writes Michael Locke McLendon.[28]

There's a reason for that. Rousseau was, to put a fine point on it, a miserable bastard. Rousseau was a cad, a showman, and a staggering and often heartless hypocrite. If you've seen the film *Amadeus*, he was surely less of a fool than Tom Hulce's Mozart, but he was just as contemptuous of social mores. He had numerous mistresses. In his own *Confessions*, he admits that he had multiple children with one of them, a former scullery maid named Thérèse Levasseur. The man who said "I know nothing which exercises a more powerful influence upon my heart than an act of courage, performed at an opportune moment, on behalf of the weak who are unjustly oppressed"[29] nevertheless forced his mistress to give each of the children to an orphanage immediately upon birth. The man who wrote some of the most influential and famous work on how to raise children properly abandoned his own children.[30]

Rousseau seems a familiar type today. Indeed, he created the type: a celebrity intellectual who simultaneously yearned for ever more

fame and controversy while heaping scorn on other intellectuals for
their lack of integrity and concern with petty things. It should be no
wonder that he was very much despised by many of the other leading
thinkers of his age. "I have received your new book against the human
race, and thank you for it," Voltaire wrote to him about Rousseau's
Social Contract. "[N]o one has ever been so witty as you are in trying
to turn us into brutes," he said. "To read your book makes one long
to go on all fours."[31] Rousseau's feud with the English philosopher
David Hume became an international drama. (Hume had endeavored
to help Rousseau find safety in exile in England; Rousseau repaid the
kindness with bizarre accusations that Hume was the ringleader of
some kind of elaborate plot against him.)[32] In a letter to his friend
Adam Smith, Hume wrote of Rousseau:

> Thus you see, he is a Composition of Whim, Affectation, Wicked-
> ness, Vanity, and Inquietude, with a very small, if any Ingredient of
> Madness.... The ruling Qualities abovementioned, together with
> Ingratitude, Ferocity, and Lying, I need not mention, Eloquence
> and Invention, form the whole of the Composition.[33]

Rousseau had such a gift for personal ingratitude and public score
settling that his life was a kind of literary reality show. In fact, that
was probably the point. Rousseau, not constrained by conventional
notions of honesty or integrity, would simply invent scandals and
conflicts to stay in the public eye, a fact Denis Diderot had warned
Hume about. Meanwhile, Diderot never took Rousseau's bait. In a letter to a friend seeking guidance about how to handle public scandal,
Diderot wrote: "I am in control of my own happiness and I challenge
all the ingrates, scandalmongers, slanderers, envy-ridden scoundrels
of the world to try taking it away from me."[34] He was almost surely
referring to Rousseau. In another letter, Diderot said of Rousseau:

> I despise and I pity him. He is remorseful and shame pursues him.
> He is alone with himself.... I am loved, esteemed, I'll even say
> honored, by my fellow-citizens and by strangers.... The benefits
> held out by the great empress extend far and wide her renown, the
> praise of her actions and of my own. The news come to the traitor's

ears: he bites his tongue with rage. His days are filled with sadness; his nights are restless. I sleep peacefully, while he grieves, perhaps he cries, tortures himself and wastes away.[35]

In the debates about Rousseau, it is somewhat standard to reply that this amounts to *argumentum ad hominem*, an attempt to discredit an argument by attacking the person making it. But that's not my aim here. Rather, I think there is a deep connection between Rousseau's immoral behavior and his philosophy. I am not saying that his philosophy is simply a rationalization of his morality (though there is much of that in his *Confessions*). Rather, I think Rousseau's feelings of alienation from society—both fashionable and bourgeois—gave him a powerful visitor-from-Mars insight into the hypocrisies of the age.

They also opened a hole in his soul, a hunger of the spirit. He believed that a disordered society created disordered souls. This disorder required a new society that harmonized the inner life of the soul with all social arrangements. It's as if Rousseau rejected the chastity and uprightness of his youthful Puritanism but retained many of its theological assumptions: The world as we know it is corrupt. All "middlemen" between the individual and God distract us from the truth and the divine.

Fittingly, Rousseau's conversion story to the new faith rivals Paul's story about finding God on the road to Damascus. At the age of thirty-seven, while walking to Vincennes to visit Diderot, in prison for criticizing the government—he couldn't afford the fare for a carriage—Rousseau stumbled upon a flier for an essay competition sponsored by the Academy of Dijon. The topic: "Has the progress of the sciences and arts done more to corrupt morals or improve them?"

"The moment I had read this," he later recalled, "I seemed to behold another world and became another man." The romantic spirit inhabited Rousseau. "I felt my mind dazzled by a thousand lights. . . . I felt my head seized by a dizziness that resembled intoxication." Rousseau claimed that he crumpled to the ground and fell into a kind of transcendent state. He awoke to find his coat drenched in tears.

"The reason for this effusion," writes Tim Blanning, "was Rousseau's sudden insight that the Dijon Academy's question was not rhetorical."[36] I suspect the rectors of the academy would have disagreed.

The question almost surely was intended to be rhetorical in the same way the organizers of an essay competition at Oberlin asking "Has diversity made us stronger?" would simply assume the contest was over who would most creatively—or loyally—answer "Yes."

Rousseau's essay, *A Discourse on the Moral Effects of the Arts and Sciences*—which won the contest!—is the keystone for the entire cathedral of his thought. Rousseau turned the story of civilization on its head. All progress was really decay. All refinement was just a pleasant coat of paint hiding the corruption underneath. Civilization didn't liberate; it enslaved. "Man is born free and everywhere he is in chains," as he would famously put it in *The Social Contract*.[37] But the idea was already there in his *Discourse on the Moral Effects of the Arts and Sciences*:

> So long as government and law provide for the security and well-being of men in their common life, the arts, literature and the sciences, less despotic though perhaps more powerful, fling garlands of flowers over the chains which weigh them down. They stifle in men's breasts that sense of original liberty, for which they seem to have been born; cause them to love their own slavery, and so make of them what is called a civilised people.[38]

The writings of Rousseau were all, in a sense, variations on the first sentence of his novel *Emile, or On Education*: "Everything is good as it leaves the hands of the Author of things, everything degenerates in the hands of man."[39] *Emile*, he insisted, was "nothing but a treatise on the original goodness of mankind."[40]

Like Locke, Rousseau bases his entire political philosophy on a fictional origin story of mankind, grounded in his doctrine of the noble savage (even though he never used the term), which we've already discussed. Man is good. Man is solitary. (Rousseau makes little mention of women.) Man's biggest mistake was leaving the world of solitary self-sufficiency (and selfishness) and forming a society, because society is corrupt and takes us away from nature and man's natural state.

Locke had complicated views on original sin, rejecting the view that Adam's fall carried to all mankind for all time. Like Rousseau, he believed that there was no sin in a state of nature. But that was because the state of nature was lawless in the broadest conception possible. First with the Jews and then Christians, man was blessed to receive moral laws from God, and thus defiance of those laws constituted sin. Rousseau sees it exactly the other way around. Recall what he wrote in *Emile*: "Everything is good as it leaves the hands of the Author of things, everything degenerates in the hands of man." Locke sees man's ability to apply reason and labor to create artificial things—i.e., wealth and property—with his own hands as the heart of human progress; Rousseau sees all artificiality as corrupting. Locke sees God's moral instruction as a blessing; Rousseau sees it as a corrupting curse. Indeed, Rousseau held that the moment man started down this path, the process of corruption had begun. In the most famous passage from the *Discourse on Equality*, Rousseau writes:

> The first man who, having enclosed a piece of ground, bethought himself of saying *This is mine*, and found people simple enough to believe him, was the real founder of civil society. From how many crimes, wars, and murders, from how many horrors and misfortunes might not any one have saved mankind by pulling up the stakes, or filling up the ditch, and crying to his fellows, "Beware of listening to this imposter, you are undone if you once forget that the fruits of the earth belong to us all, and the earth itself to nobody."[41]

"All subsequent advances have been apparently so many steps towards the perfection of the individual," Rousseau wrote, "but in reality so many steps towards the decrepitude of the species."[42] He brilliantly identifies that private property and the division of labor are among the chief drivers of civilizational and economic advance. He just hates them:

> In a word, so long as [men] undertook only what a single person could accomplish, and confined themselves to such arts as did not require the joint labour of several hands, they lived free, healthy, honest and happy lives, so long as their nature allowed, and as they continued to enjoy the pleasures of mutual and independent intercourse. But from the moment one man began to stand in need of

the help of another; from the moment it appeared advantageous to any one man to have enough provisions for two, equality disappeared, property was introduced, work became indispensable, and vast forests became smiling fields, which man had to water with the sweat of his brow, and where slavery and misery were soon seen to germinate and grow up with the crops. Metallurgy and agriculture were the two arts which produced this great revolution. The poets tell us it was gold and silver, but, for the philosophers, it was iron and corn, which first civilised men, and ruined humanity . . .[43]

I am quite hard on Rousseau here, but I must confess that I've grown to have a greater appreciation of his writings. His personal behavior was repugnant. His inconsistencies and conclusions are often infuriating. But his eye for the false pieties, hypocrisies, and corruptions of others was as remarkable as his skill at describing them. Long before neuroscience confirmed it, Rousseau recognized that we all crave social recognition as special, unique, or important. Rousseau calls this *amour-propre*—or self-love—which is often translated into English as "vanity" or "pride" or "esteem." He contrasts it with *amour de soi,* which, annoyingly, also means self-love. *Amour de soi,* according to Rousseau, is the natural self-interestedness primitive man shared with the animals before he was corrupted by society. *Amour de soi* is always noble and good, because in Rousseau's state of nature, man's self-interest never came at the expense of another. This is, of course, nonsense. Animals, particularly predators, pursue their self-interest in ways that harm others—and primitive humans are certainly no exception.

Rousseau even recognized that *amour-propre* has its roots in sexual competition and status seeking in small tribes or bands. Rousseau believed that the social ills of modernity stemmed from an inflammation of *amour-propre,* in part because the market system enthrones wealth as the measure of social status. In other words, by Rousseau's own often brilliant analysis, ideology is secondary to what he calls passions—and he's right.

As the author of the first modern autobiography, Rousseau was honest about his quest to find his real self and stay true to it. He was more dishonest about his contempt for the concerns of polite society.

He loved its attention. He may have believed that the desire for status and the respect of others—*amore-propre*—was the source of so much evil in the world, but he craved status and recognition himself. There was a Trumpian quality to Rousseau in that he seemed to believe it was better to be talked about negatively than not at all.

Near the end of his *Discourse on the Moral Effects of the Arts and Sciences*, Rousseau makes a prediction. Mankind will one day recognize the horrible mistake he has made and offer up a prayer to the Lord: "Almighty God! thou who holdest in Thy hand the minds of men, deliver us from the fatal arts and sciences of our forefathers; give us back ignorance, innocence and poverty, which alone can make us happy and are precious in Thy sight."[44] (You can't get less Lockean than that!)

Rousseau is called the father of romanticism for a reason. The romantic eye sees the modern world as alien and alienating, amputating the soul and at war with nature. "The system is rigged"—as so many people say today—is, in its most intense forms, a romantic battle cry.

Indeed, radicalism in all its forms is fundamentally romantic whether it comes from the right or the left. The ambition to "tear it all down" should be seen first as a psychological response to the status quo. Different ideologies color that ambition in different ways, but the substance beneath is not ideological but instinctual. Lenin, Hitler, and all of their petty imitators begin with the assumption that the current edifice of civilization is corrupt and must be torn down. Radicalism is romanticism taken to its extreme. Get rid of it all and start over!

Another way to look at Rousseau, however, is that he was the father of the modern idea of alienation. People no doubt felt alienated prior to the Enlightenment, but, like so many other passions and ideas, such feelings were seen through the prism of religion. One solved feelings of alienation (never mind undeserved status) by getting right with God.

But the Enlightenment had dethroned God and made man the measure of man. And it was Rousseau who first argued for *getting right with yourself,* because *you,* your conscience, your inner lantern of truth, lit the path in this world. He believed there was, or had been, an authentic, real noble savage deep down inside every one of us and that civilization had corrupted it by making us care more about status, wealth, respect, fame, and other artificial concerns.

In pre-Enlightenment society, according to Rousseau, the Church was a kind of corrupt guild, using its power for its own benefit and not for the needs of the faithful or the citizens in general. He said the new princes of the Enlightenment were no better than the princes and priests they had dethroned. The same ambitious intellectuals casting themselves as freethinkers and philosophers, Rousseau wrote, "would have been for the very same reason nothing more than a fanatic" of the Church in an earlier era.[45]

Rousseau was prescient about the role intellectuals would play in modern societies and how ideologues—not just intellectuals, but also artists, educators, and every other profession that works with ideas and concepts—have replaced priests as the definers of meaning. For Rousseau, the so-called Age of Reason was simply a new age of oppression by another name. The Enlightenment theories of democracy and limited government as developed by Locke, Montesquieu, and the Founders were, to him, no better than what they sought to replace.

Here we can see why I think Rousseau's personal character informs his philosophy. The Scottish writer James Boswell recounted a conversation he had with Rousseau. "Sir, I have no liking for the world," Rousseau told him. "I live here in a world of fantasies and I cannot tolerate the world as it is. . . . Mankind disgusts me. And my housekeeper tells me that I am in far better humors on a day when I have been alone than on those I have been in company."[46]

This dual indictment of the Enlightenment and the old system of absolutism might sound a bit like anarchism or libertarianism: The system is rigged, the rulers are in it for themselves, don't trust the Man. But Rousseau's solution wasn't to reject statist coercion and manipulation. It was to employ them for ostensibly purer ends.

For Rousseau, man and society alike were disordered, unnatural, broken—*alienated*. Individuals were out of harmony with their nature, and that meant society was too. The only way to fix people was to create a new society empowered to fill the holes in our souls. Salvation was a collective endeavor. Mankind could not go back to being a solitary noble savage; mankind must find new meaning in the group, governed by the "general will," a kind of collective consciousness that outranked the individual conscience.

This was a brilliant intellectual updating of the tribal instinct.

Every citizen in Rousseau's ideal society would have meaning through the group and only through the group. The group itself would be the object of a new religious faith that defined one's purpose in relation to service to the whole. Tellingly, Rousseau looked to the militarized state of Sparta for a new model of social organization in which social planners would apply the ancient Roman and Greek concept of a civil religion to a modern society. This civil religion would emotionally bind the citizen to the general will and the community.

Rousseau's civil religion is a thoroughly totalitarian affair. If you refuse to subscribe to the dogmas of the new civil religion, you should be banished. He who publicly accepts the law of the general will and then violates it, "let him be punished with death: he has committed the worst of all crimes, that of lying before the law."[47] Rousseau explains: "Those who distinguish civil from theological intolerance are, to my mind, mistaken. The two forms are inseparable. It is impossible to live at peace with those we regard as damned; to love them would be to hate God who punishes them: we positively must either claim or torment them."[48] To this end, public "censors" and other magistrates would mold and define public opinion and identify "unbelievers" in need of extermination. The state, in other words, had complete authority to improve men's souls for the greater good. Thus Rousseau sought to eliminate the original division of labor that Christianity had introduced into the West through Saint Augustine. He wanted a new theocracy that closed the space between the religious and the secular. This idea amounts to what the great sociologist Robert Nisbet called, with perhaps only modest exaggeration, "the most powerful state to be found anywhere in political philosophy."[49]

Nationalism served as the framework for this new imagined community. The most obvious illustration of Rousseau's ideas at work can be found in the horrors of the Reign of Terror at the end of the French Revolution, in which the Committee of Public Safety became a real-world example of Rousseau's boards of censors, sentencing unbelievers to death in the name of the great new French nation they were building. The Revolutionaries believed they were creating a nation from scratch in Year Zero. Rousseau's social contract was hailed as "the beacon of legislators."[50]

Maximilien Robespierre, the chief architect of the Jacobin Reign of

Terror, and thus the first modern totalitarian mass murderer, report-
edly read Rousseau every day like a daily devotional.[51] Robespierre
used Rousseau's ideas to justify his authority in a higher ideal. "For us,
we are not of any party, we serve no faction, you know it, brothers and
friends, our will is the General Will," he proclaimed in a 1792 address
to leaders of the various French départements.[52]

Even after the Thermidorian Reaction, when Robespierre was
killed in a coup by a faction appalled by his excesses, the French Revolutionaries did not abandon Rousseau. They believed that Robespierre
had betrayed the true spirit of Rousseau. In 1794 the revolutionary
government called for Rousseau's remains to be exhumed and brought
to Paris to be reinterred at the Panthéon. A copy of the *Social Contract*
was carried on a velvet cushion while a twelve-horse carriage pulled a
statue of Rousseau.[53]

The stories Rousseau and Locke told, as well as the stories we tell
of Rousseau and Locke, represent the two main currents in Western
civilization and, increasingly, in modernity itself. It is a fight between
the idea that our escape from the past has been a glorious improvement over mankind's natural state and the idea that the world we have
created is corrupting because it is artificial. One side says that external
moral codes and representative government are a liberating blessing.
The other says that the truth is found not outside of ourselves in the
form of universal rules and tolerance for others but in our own feelings and the meaning we get from belonging to a group.

Locke and Rousseau may stand as useful markers between the left
and the right, but the divide is more fundamental than that, for it runs
straight through the human heart. There are people of the left who are
more Lockean than they realize, and there are people of the right who
are far more Rousseauian than they would care to admit. Locke represents the idea that we can conquer not just nature but human nature.
Rousseau is a stand-in for the notion that such conquest is oppressive.
This tension is not permanently resolvable because the Lockean world
is an imposition on human nature, and human nature doesn't change.
Each of us starts our journey as an ignoble savage. Nobility must be
taught—and *earned*. It is not inherited.

6

THE AMERICAN MIRACLE
They Put It in Writing

"We hold these Truths to be self-evident, that all Men are created equal, that they are endowed by their Creator with certain unalienable Rights, that among these are Life, Liberty, and the Pursuit of Happiness. . . ."

—THOMAS JEFFERSON ET AL., THE DECLARATION OF
INDEPENDENCE

T HE FOUNDING FATHERS WERE WRONG.

It is not self-evident that man is endowed by his Creator with certain unalienable rights. Colloquially, "self-evident" simply means obvious. Something that is self-evident, according to the dictionary, is something that does not require demonstration. The existence of gravity is self-evident and that is a very easy thing to prove. It is obvious that fire burns, and if you need a demonstration, I can provide one on request.

Meanwhile, how does one demonstrate that we are endowed by our Creator with unalienable rights? People have been trying to demonstrate that our Creator exists for thousands of years. If that cannot be done to everyone's satisfaction, it seems a daunting task to prove He created unalienable rights. The simple fact is that the existence of natural rights, like the existence of God Himself, requires a leap of faith. Meanwhile, the vast history of mankind provides one endlessly dreary demonstration after another that people can be alienated from their rights quite easily, starting with their right to life.

The first and most glorious achievement of the American founding was to assert in writing—not argue for, claim, or suggest—that all men are created equal and endowed by our Creator with unalienable rights. It's a bit of a strained analogy, but in the context of the Miracle, one can think of the English people as the Jews. The Jews introduced a moral monotheistic framework into the world. But in ancient times, it only applied to Jews. Christianity took those precepts and universalized them. Similarly, the English introduced an understanding of rights and liberty into the world—and made it work. But initially it only applied to the English. America universalized these English ideas.

It is a common response to such claims to point out that the Founders didn't mean it. They were hypocrites who denied the rights of slaves, women, and, to a lesser but still significant extent, the propertyless. But this is an exercise in looking through the wrong end of the telescope, which robs the heroism of every soul who made the world a better place. We judge the strides we make in the present by the extent of our improvement over the past. But we have an annoying tendency to judge the past by the standards of the present. "The study of the past with one eye, so to speak, upon the present is the source of all sins and sophistries in history, starting with the simplest of them, the anachronism. It is the fallacy into which we slip when we are giving the judgments that seem most assuredly self-evident," Herbert Butterfield observed. "And it is the essence of what we mean by the word 'unhistorical.'"[1]

The Founders advanced the "wheel of history" as none had before. They started a revolutionary new chapter in the story of humanity by broadening the principles laid out by Locke and the English people generally. Consider the evolution of the Declaration of Independence.

Some ninety years before Jefferson put pen to paper, the Glorious Revolution had cemented the English commitment to ancient *English rights*. That revolution had a huge impact on the politics and popular attitudes in the American colonies. Just as the threat of absolutism in the mother country had been thwarted, it was curtailed in the New World as well, allowing for representative institutions to develop organically.[2] That English notions of rights and liberties would intensify only makes sense, given that the yoke of the crown felt tighter, or at least more unjust, across the Atlantic. As the case for independence grew in the hearts and minds of the colonists, the argument inevitably shifted from the rights and liberties of Englishmen to the rights and liberties of men generally. Events, in other words, forced the Americans to shed allegiance not only to the English crown but also to the idea of English particularism.

A good illustration of this evolutionary process is the expression "A man's home is his castle." The original saying was "An Englishman's home is his castle," and it was more than just a slogan for husbands trying to get out of doing chores. The idea that even the king himself could not enter a man's home without an invitation is precisely one of those ancient English rights and liberties. It was a common understanding centuries before the Glorious Revolution. Sir Edward Coke wrote the cultural custom into the common law 1628: "For a man's house is his castle, *et domus sua cuique est tutissimum refugium* [and each man's home is his safest refuge]." In 1763, William Pitt clarified the meaning of "castle": "The poorest man may in his cottage bid defiance to all the forces of the crown. It may be frail—its roof may shake—the wind may blow through it—the storm may enter—the rain may enter—but the King of England cannot enter."

Now, in practice, this did not mean that the home was an inviolable sanctuary in which one could break the law or escape from its reach. What it meant was that the state needed a good reason to enter a home. And the state needed to make its case to a judge, who would issue a writ or later a warrant. This, in short, is where the Fourth Amendment right "of the people to be secure in their persons, houses, papers, and effects, against unreasonable searches and seizures" comes from. What began as English custom over time became an inalienable right.[3]

The Declaration of Independence follows a similar pattern. It is chockablock with echoes of Locke, from the "life, liberty and happiness" line to the talk of unalienable rights. But the Declaration is less indebted to Locke than it is to the American people, who, at the time, had only recently stopped thinking of themselves as Englishmen. Years later Jefferson would write that, "neither aiming at originality or principles or sentiments, nor yet copied from any particular and previous writing, it was intended to be an expression of the American Mind."[4] Proof of this can be found in the fact that the Declaration was not quite as original a document as we've come to be taught. Pauline Maier found that there were in fact some *ninety* Declarations of Independence written up by various groups, from county conventions to New York mechanics' guilds and Massachusetts town halls. Jefferson wasn't *inventing* anything in the Declaration. Rather, a brilliant writer on deadline, he contented himself with eloquently summarizing what was little more than American conventional wisdom.[5]

As Gordon S. Wood has observed, when the Declaration was issued, the important part was the conclusion: the break with England. Only later did the beginning "all men are created equal" take on philosophical and metaphysical significance. "Certainly no one initially saw the Declaration as a classic statement of political principles," Wood writes. "Only in the 1790s, with the emergence of the bitter partisan politics between the Federalists and the Jefferson-led Republicans, did the Declaration begin to be celebrated as a great founding document."[6] And that celebration evolved into sacredness.

"Let us revere the Declaration of Independence," Abraham Lincoln insisted.[7] "Let us readopt the Declaration of Independence, and with it the practices and policy which harmonize with it."[8] That is what he did in the Gettysburg Address when he proclaimed, "Four score and seven years ago, our fathers brought forth, on this continent, a new nation, conceived in Liberty, and dedicated to the proposition that all men are created equal."[9] Lincoln essentially rewrote the meaning of the Founding and consecrated it with the blood of Americans. It didn't matter that Southerners had a plausible argument that they understood the Declaration better. What mattered was the new meaning breathed into it. The Founders may well have believed in the Lockean notion of natural rights, but it is not news that they didn't apply it consistently. They risked their lives and sacred honor for more worldly reasons. But Lincoln sifted a golden idea from the currents of our story and molded it into an icon. That idea of human equality took deeper root in American life because of it. A century later, Martin Luther King Jr. did the same thing once again. In 1963, in his "I Have a Dream Speech," he said:

> In a sense we've come to our nation's capital to cash a check. When the architects of our republic wrote the magnificent words of the

Constitution and the Declaration of Independence, they were signing a promissory note to which every American was to fall heir. This note was a promise that all men, yes, black men as well as white men, would be guaranteed the "unalienable Rights" of "Life, Liberty and the pursuit of Happiness."[10]

Both Lincoln and King were appealing to the story—the best story—we tell about ourselves. That our story begins with Americans falling short of the ideals embedded in the Founding is not an indictment of the ideals; it is testament to the nobility of America's story arc. Without even considering the material prosperity that the American miracle created not just for its own citizens but for billions of people around the world, if America had done nothing else but this, it would be a glorious leap forward for humanity.

Let us now look more closely at how the story begins.

IT IS SOMETHING OF an article of faith, particularly among some American conservatives, that the Founding Fathers were deeply influenced by John Locke. For generations, this was the consensus opinion of most leading historians as well.[11] Some recent scholarship is more skeptical. The skeptics have a much better argument than I thought when I set out to write this book. For instance, I searched the National Archives' wonderful online database of writings from the Founding, thinking it would be a simple task to find one encomium after another to the man often described as the father of the English Enlightenment, the "philosopher of freedom" and the "founder of liberalism." There are some, to be sure, but far fewer than you might think.

Perhaps most shocking: There are no references to Locke in the *Federalist Papers* (though he does have a brief cameo in the *Anti-Federalist Papers*). Oscar and Lilian Handlin note that, even though Locke dedicates an entire chapter to slavery, there's no record of any Founder invoking his work in the many debates about the subject during the period.[12]

One of the few unequivocal accolades from a signatory of the Declaration of Independence comes from James Wilson, a prominent drafter of the Constitution and one of the first (six) Supreme Court

Justices. At the ratifying convention Wilson said that "the truth is, that the supreme, absolute, and uncontrollable authority remains with the people . . . [T]he practical recognition of this truth was reserved for the honor of this country. I recollect no constitution founded on this principle; but we have witnessed the improvement, and enjoy the happiness of seeing it carried into practice. The great and penetrating mind of Locke seems to be the only one that pointed towards even the theory of this great truth."[13]

We do know that Thomas Jefferson was a great admirer of Locke. Indeed, in a letter to Benjamin Rush, Jefferson tells a story of Hamilton's visit to his home. On Jefferson's walls hung portraits of John Locke, Isaac Newton, and Francis Bacon. Hamilton asked who they were. Jefferson replied that they were his "trinity of the greatest men who ever lived."[14] Still, there's not much evidence in his papers that he read Locke's *Two Treatises*. Nor was there a copy in the book collection he bequeathed to the Library of Congress.

On the other hand, Jefferson took copious notes from Locke's *Letter Concerning Toleration*, which served as the inspiration for his own Virginia Statute for Religious Freedom.

The statute is another good example of how ideas drive a story on the ground and how the unfolding story refines those ideas to the point of creating new ones. Locke had argued that Catholics and atheists could not be loyal subjects or citizens. "All those who enter into [the Catholic faith] do thereby *ipso facto* deliver themselves up to the protection and service of another prince." Atheists could not be trusted because "promises, covenants, and oaths, which are the bonds of human society, can have no hold upon an atheist."[15]

Jefferson, meanwhile, took the internal logic of Locke and extended it to its final conclusion. The statute begins:

> An Act for establishing religious Freedom. Whereas, Almighty God hath created the mind free; that all attempts to influence it by temporal punishments or burthens, or by civil incapacitations tend only to beget habits of hypocrisy and meanness, and are a departure from the plan of the holy author of our religion, who being Lord, both of body and mind yet chose not to propagate it by coercions on either, as was in his Almighty power to do . . .[16]

The statute not only disestablished the Church of England as the official faith of Virginia but also guaranteed religious liberty for Protestants, Catholics, Muslims, Jews, Hindus, and even pagans.

This is just one facet of the transformation wrought less by Locke himself than by what I call the Lockean Revolution. The intellectual historians who want to play connect-the-dots miss the broader revolution in rhetoric that transformed the world. As the Enlightenment unfolded across the landscape of Europe and America, Locke's name became a kind of shorthand for liberty and natural rights, even among people who never read or fully understood him.

What's indisputable is that Locke was routinely invoked in sermons by pro-revolution pastors, which were often turned into pamphlets. (Sermons were at least 10 percent of all the pamphlets published at the time.)[17] So great was Locke's influence among pastors, and so great was the influence of the pastors with the people, that the historian Clinton Rossiter concluded: "Had ministers been the only spokesmen of the American Cause, had Jefferson, Adams and Otis never appeared in print, the political thought of the Revolution would have followed almost exactly the same line—with perhaps a little more mention of God, but certainly no less of John Locke."[18]

As counterintuitive as it might seem, the Founders' intellectual debt to Locke may have had more to do with his philosophical (then considered scientific) writings on empiricism than with his political work in the *Second Treatise*. In 1760, John Adams remarked of Locke's epistemological writings that he "steered his Course into the unenlightened Regions of the human Mind, and like Columbus has discovered a new World."[19]

As discussed earlier, Locke's argument for the blank slate helped to undermine the case for hereditary power by arguing that all men were born equally free with the same natural rights. The American founders carried the Lockean argument even further (though not far enough). They declared unremitting war on hereditary aristocracy in all its unnatural or unjust forms (hereditary slavery excepted, unfortunately). Just as Locke and the Glorious Revolution overturned the divine right of kings, the Founders—particularly Thomas Jefferson—took dead aim at the divine rights of nobles and aristocrats. If all men are created equal, and if government is established by the people, not by God, then the government cannot recognize rankings of men. As Thomas Paine put it, "Virtue is not hereditary."[20]

The Founders understood all too well that mediocre men were capable of being born to high stations and exceptional men were often born to low ones. But even then, just because some men proved themselves to be superior to other men, that does not mean they have any special privileges or authority under the law. As Thomas Jefferson explained, just "because Sir Isaac Newton was superior to others in understanding he was not therefore lord of the person or property of others."[21] A man entering a courtroom in the newly formed United States of America may have had some piece of paper saying he was a baron or duke, and he'd be free to brag about it at a local tavern. But the judge would give that no weight in his dispute with a bricklayer.

THE PROJECT WAS MORE Lockean than anything Locke imagined could happen in England.

Strictly speaking, aristocracy doesn't mean "rule of the nobility" but "rule of the best," which is how the Greeks first conceived of the term. It was only later, when the corrupting influence of human nature worked its will and aristocrats tried to lock in their power for posterity, that this notion became infused with notions of hereditary status. What the Founders wanted was a return to the original Greek conception, which Jefferson called a "natural aristocracy." He wanted to rake "from the rubbish annually" in search of the "best geniuses."[22]

Public education, the founder of the University of Virginia argued, elevates "those persons, whom nature hath endowed with genius and virtue, should be rendered by liberal education worthy to receive, and able to guard the sacred deposit of the rights of their fellow citizens, and . . . should be called to that charge without regard to wealth, birth, or other accidental condition or circumstance."[23] (This is what the "liberal" in "liberal arts" is supposed to mean.)

After the Revolution, Jefferson fought to rid America of entail (the system of irrevocable trusts that barred the sale or division of landholdings) and primogeniture (requiring all property to be left to the oldest son), which tended to concentrate landed estates, elevating some families and their offspring beyond their merit. Jefferson considered his successful effort to abolish entail and primogeniture to be among his greatest accomplishments as a legislator. He saw these efforts as essential to eradicating "every fibre . . . of ancient or future aristocracy" and to lay "a foundation . . . for a government truly republican."[24]

Identity politics will be a recurring theme in the pages that follow. But, for now, it's worth making this simple observation: Notions of inherited nobility are an ancient form of identity politics. Identitarianism holds that a person has special status based upon criteria not of his or her own making. The Founders didn't follow through on this logic when it came to slavery—though many wanted to—but they lit the fuse on the bomb that would demolish such thinking, at least for a time.

It's difficult to appreciate today how radical a departure all of this was from the way the world had worked until that moment. George Washington could have been a king. He declined. He even had to be persuaded to be president. When King George III asked his American portraitist, Benjamin West, what Washington would do after winning independence, West replied, "They say he will return to his farm."

"If he does that," the gobsmacked king replied, Washington "will be the greatest man in the world."[25]

But even though the Founders were creating something new in the world, they did not believe that they could repeal the laws of human nature. The Founders knew that one could not eliminate the natural human tendency to form factions, including aristocracies of wealth, status, and power. But the system of government they established, they hoped, would make it impossible for any faction to attain lasting concentrated power.

The structure of the federal government itself was designed to divide power in all the ways we learned in civics class: checks and balances, divided government, separation of powers. In one of the most famous passages in the *Federalist Papers*, James Madison writes:

> But the great security against a gradual concentration of the several powers in the same department, consists in giving to those who administer each department the necessary constitutional means and personal motives to resist encroachments of the others. The

provision for defense must in this, as in all other cases, be made commensurate to the danger of attack. Ambition must be made to counteract ambition. The interest of the man must be connected with the constitutional rights of the place. It may be a reflection on human nature, that such devices should be necessary to control the abuses of government. But what is government itself, but the greatest of all reflections on human nature? If men were angels, no government would be necessary. If angels were to govern men, neither external nor internal controls on government would be necessary. In framing a government which is to be administered by men over men, the great difficulty lies in this: you must first enable the government to control the governed; and in the next place oblige it to control itself. A dependence on the people is, no doubt, the primary control on the government; but experience has taught mankind the necessity of auxiliary precautions.[26]

This was a great advance on Locke, who never gave a persuasive and cogent explanation for why majority rule could not be tyrannical.[27] Meanwhile, the Founders understood that the *majority* could be a threat to liberty too. Obviously they couldn't see Napoleon coming, but they understood the threat of Bonapartism entirely.[28] Close students of history, they appreciated how a conquering general, like a Caesar or Cromwell (two names that appear often in the *Federalist Papers*), with the masses on his side, could take over the republican government. "Brutus," one of the anonymous writers in the *Anti-Federalist Papers*, put it this way:[29]

> In the first, the liberties of the commonwealth were destroyed, and
> the constitution over-turned, by an army, led by Julius Caesar, who
> was appointed to the command by the constitutional authority of
> that commonwealth. He changed it from a free republic, whose
> fame . . . is still celebrated by all the world, into that of the most
> absolute despotism.[30]

The Constitution, particularly the Bill of Rights, took certain vexatious political questions and made them off-limits (at least in theory) from the politicians. Free speech, freedom of worship, freedom of assembly, the right to bear arms, the right to property (including intellectual property)—these are all massive bulwarks against despotic power. Even the phrasing of the key amendments is essential. "Congress shall make no law" [abridging this right or that]. In other words, the restrictions are all on the power of the state. The rights of the people, collectively and individually, are upstream of the powers of the government.

This, in short, is the difference between Lockeanism and Rousseauism. For Locke, the individual is prior to the state. For Rousseau, the state—or the general will—is prior to the people. For the Lockeans, our rights come from God, not from government. For the disciples of Rousseau, our rights are indistinguishable, or at least inseparable, from our duties to the state.

Perhaps the Constitution's most important contribution is its most prosaic quality: It's written down and very hard to change. Being written down for all to read gives ownership to everyone and creates what economists call "path dependence" for how political disputes are resolved. It reminds us that our fundamental laws are outside the authority of men. It creates the space necessary for institutional pluralism to flourish. The fact that the Constitution is hard to change—a great frustration to passionate political movements of every stripe—automatically confers deep democratic legitimacy to any successful alterations and provides assurance that we will not sacrifice some fundamental liberty in the heat of a given moment. We may, in such moments, ignore the Constitution, but it sits there, outside the time and space of any political moment, as a national conscience, reminding us that such transgressions must be rectified.

There is a decidedly deist flavor to the American founding. Deism holds that God or, "the Creator," is like a watchmaker who makes his creation, winds it up, and then interferes no more. Some of the Founders were indeed deists, and many more were influenced by deism. And, in a sense, they did set up the machinery of liberty and then got out of the way.

But I think there is a better way to understand the Founders' vision and how it differed from other Enlightenment projects, specifically those of Revolutionary France. America borrowed a great deal from French thought, but we cherry-picked the best bits without subscribing to their entire worldview. The philosophes and revolutionaries of Paris were far more ambitious than their counterparts in America. Partially thanks to the influence of Rousseau, they wanted to create, guide, and direct a whole new path for humanity. For all their hatred of religion, they nonetheless set out to create a new religion, a whole system of meaning for the French people.[31] Taking after Rousseau, the French believed in the perfectibility of man. The scientific revolution had granted the new intellectuals the power to create perfect societies and perfect men. As Nicolas de Condorcet put it, there is "a science that can foresee the progress of humankind, direct it, and accelerate it."[32]

The Americans rejected the perfectibility of man, believing the best government could do was take man's nature into account and channel it toward productive ends.

Yuval Levin argues that you can see the differences in these two worldviews in the metaphors the two camps used in explaining what the state should do. The French strain emphasizes movement. The state is there to deliver the people somewhere, advance the "wheel of history," etc. In the English version, the state is there to create a zone of liberty for people to choose their own direction.[33]

One of my favorite illustrations of how this is as much a cultural disagreement as a philosophical one can be found in the differences between French and English gardens. For instance, the French gardens at Versailles, with their ornate, geometric, nature-defying designs, illustrate how the gardener imposes his vision on nature. Nature is brought to heel by reason. The classic English garden, on the other hand, was intended to let nature take its course, to let each bush, tree, and vegetable achieve its own ideal nature. The role of the English gardener was to protect his garden by weeding it, maintaining fences, and being ever watchful for predators and poachers.

The American founders were gardeners, not engineers. The government of the Founders' Constitution is more than merely a "night watchman state," but not very much more. It creates the rules of the garden and the gardeners and little more. This does not mean the government cannot intervene in the society or the economy. It means that, when it does so, it should be to protect liberty, which Madison defined in *Federalist* No. 10 as "the first object of government."[34]

As that quintessential Scottish Enlightenment thinker, Adam Smith, wrote in 1755:

> Little else is requisite to carry a state to the highest degree of opulence from the lowest barbarism, but peace, easy taxes and a tolerable administration of justice; all the rest being brought by the natural course of things. All governments which thwart this natural course, which force things into another channel or which endeavor to arrest the progress of society at a particular point, are unnatural, and to support themselves are obliged to be oppressive and tyrannical.[35]

I think the garden metaphor works better than the watchmaker image, because so many of the Founders were active participants in the unfolding American experiment, as George Washington called it. From Shays' Rebellion to the First Bank of the United States, the Louisiana Purchase, and the War of 1812, the Founders were attentive gardeners in this new nation, creating the conditions for prosperity, fending off predators, and even expanding the garden itself.

WE SHOULD TURN NOW from the Founders to the inhabitants of the garden itself, for the architects of the Constitution were ultimately their servants, both reflecting and guided by their spirit. Although the American colonists were culturally indebted to Britain, by the time of the Revolution, a new, distinct American character and culture began to manifest itself.

One reason the Founding generation could sift the gold from the dross of the English tradition was that they were alienated from it, literally and figuratively. Living thousands of miles across an ocean from their ancestral home, many of the cultural assumptions that seemed live and immediate when living in London or Manchester felt dead or distant in Boston or New York. Just as Texans don't immediately look to Washington to solve their problems, the idea of looking across the Atlantic seemed increasingly irrational and cumbersome.

This alienation from the mother country had an added psychological component. As discussed, British primogeniture laws required that the firstborn son of an aristocratic family get everything: the titles, the lands, etc. But what about the other kids? They were required to make their way in the world. To be sure, they had advantages—educational, financial, and social—over the children of the lower classes, but they still needed to pursue a career. "The grander families of Virginia—including the Washingtons—were known as the 'Second Sons,'" writes Daniel Hannan.

"Many of the younger brothers who had founded their lines in the New World had borne with them a sense of injustice that they had been denied any share of their ancestral lands through an accident of timing," Hannan adds. This idea that primogeniture was a violation of natural justice was expressed by Edmund in *King Lear*:

> *Thou, nature, art my goddess; to thy law*
> *My services are bound. Wherefore should I*
> *Stand in the plague of custom and permit*
> *The curiosity of nations to deprive me,*
> *For that I am some twelve or fourteen moon-shines*
> *Lag of a brother? . . .*[36]

In fact, Hannan and Matt Ridley suggest that much of the prosperity and expansion of the British Empire in the eighteenth century can be ascribed to an intriguing historical accident. At the dawn of the Industrial Revolution, the children of the affluent nobility had a much lower mortality rate, for all the obvious reasons. They had more access to medicine, rudimentary as it was, but also better nutrition and vastly superior living and working conditions than the general population. As a result, the nobility were dramatically more fecund than the lower classes. Consequently, a large cohort of educated and ambitious young men who were not firstborn were set free to make their way in the world. If you have five boys, only one gets to be the duke. The rest must become officers, priests, doctors, lawyers, academics, and businessmen.

This is not an abstract point but a vital cultural and sociological one. European and English societies were drenched in notions of class. The English who valued that system often returned home to England or moved to Canada. The Americans who stayed kept the English attachment to natural rights and popular sovereignty, but they also rejected the cultural obsession with rank and status—and had a powerful attachment to liberty.

Seymour Martin Lipset, the great political sociologist and probably the greatest student of American exceptionalism since James Bryce or Tocqueville, had a wonderful observation about America. (I heard him share it many times.) At the time of the Founding, if you were a loyalist or royalist with no interest in severing ties with the British crown, you often moved to or stayed in Canada. If you believed in the principles of the Founding, you either stayed in America or moved there. This was one of the greatest natural experiments in political history. These were two populations with the same basic ethnic makeup, the same religious beliefs, and, for the most part, the same language. And yet these two nations produced two very different political cultures. Lipset loved to point out that, two centuries later, both the U.S. government and the Canadian government mandated that all of their citizens switch to the metric system. The Canadians, with their deeply ingrained deference to political authority, obliged almost instantly. "Drive around Canada," he'd chuckle, "and everything is kilometers." Not so in America. The U.S. government asked, but the answer was "No."

This points to the revolution in culture the American founding represents. I think Gordon Wood is surely right that the significance of the Declaration of Independence at the time lay largely in the conclusion—independence!—rather than the introduction. But that does not mean the American Revolution was seen as just another conflict between empire and colony, or that America's founding did not represent an earthquake in Western thinking even at the time. Europe's monarchs and emperors recognized the American war for independence was not just another grubby revolt—though they often said it was, for propaganda purposes. "The rulers feared that their subjects would see the American action not as a rebellion against a rightful monarch in his own territories—there had been plenty of rebellions against European sovereigns—but as the proclamation of a revolutionary doctrine of universal application, as the Declaration indeed announced it to be," wrote the late, great journalist Henry Fairlie.[37] "Any notion that the War of Independence was only a rebellion falls to the ground. Both rulers and their subjects saw it as a revolution of universal appeal."[38]

And the Revolution was not merely political. It also had economic motivations and consequences. "What the rebellious Americans wanted," writes economic historian Robert E. Wright, "and with ratification of the Constitution obtained, was what today we call 'economic freedom.' In other words, they wanted to engage in entrepreneurial activities, subject only to necessary regulations and taxes, and credible assurances that they could keep whatever wealth those activities generated."[39]

This is why, for the young Americans, economic and political liberties were indivisible. This was a radical expansion of even the British understanding of liberty, which, in practice, always tended to take the economic rights of nobles more seriously. Meanwhile, the rulers of Europe were aghast at the idea that merchants and strivers should undermine their sovereignty, which is why King George III lamented that his rule was being threatened by a bunch of "grocers."[40] Even Karl Marx declared that "the American war of independence sounded the tocsin for the European middle class."[41]

"The public here is extremely occupied with the rebels [in America]," the Danish foreign minister A. P. Bernstorff wrote to a friend in October of 1776, "not because they know the cause, but because the mania of independence in reality has infected all the spirits, and the poison has spread imperceptibly from the works of the philosophes all the way out to the village schools."[42]

America had created a culture of liberty and equality never before seen. Paris, London, and Vienna each had their claims to financial, intellectual, or artistic freedom. But that freedom was often the freedom of the elites—of intellectuals, artists, writers, and aristocrats. In America, cultural freedom had been democratized. (This probably explains many of the differences between the French Revolutionary project and the American one. The French, accustomed to absolutism, were more inclined to replace one form of absolutism with another. In America, the people acquired a taste for liberty and demanded more of it than the English were willing to provide.)

In the Old World, your clothes, your accent—even your last name—were freighted with notions of superiority and inferiority. Sumptuary laws—codes for what garments people could wear and what products they could use—were largely repealed by the eighteenth century, but they endured as a kind of cultural and social uniform. Even in Britain's comparatively democratic culture, people were still expected to dress in accordance with their station.

Not so in the United States. Thomas Colley Grattan, the British consul in Boston in the 1840s, disdained the peculiar culture of equality in the former colonies. Servant girls, he complained, were "strongly infected with the national bad taste for being over-dressed, they are, when walking the streets, scarcely to be distinguished from their employers . . ."[43] Ferenc Pulszky, a Hungarian politician touring America in 1852, was dismayed to discover that Americans rejected the unofficial uniforms of class. In Europe, there was "the peasant girl with the gaudy ribbons interlaced in her long tresses, her bright corset, and her richly-folded petticoat; there the Hungarian peasant with his white linen shirt, and his stately sheepskin; the Slovak in the closely fitting jacket and the bright yellow buttons; the farmer with the high boots and the Hungarian coat; the old women with the black lace cap in the ancient national style, and none but the young ladies appareled in French bonnets and modern dresses." But in New York, he complained, "no characteristical costumes mark here the different grades of society, which, in Eastern Europe, impress the foreigner at once with the varied occupations and habits of an old country."[44]

"Before the end of the nineteenth century," Daniel J. Boorstin writes, "the American democracy of clothing would become still more astonishing to foreign eyes, for by then the mere wearing of clothes would be an instrument of community, a way of drawing immigrants into a new life. Men whose ancestors had been accustomed to the peasant's tatters or the craftsman's leather apron could show by a democratic costume that they were as good as, or not very different from, the next man. If, as the Old World proverb went, 'Clothes make the man,' the New World's[45] new way of clothing would help make new men."[46]

Boorstin chronicles how the very idea of income was reinvented in the New World. "Before the nineteenth century the concept of 'income' had very little importance in the Old World; it was used indirectly to measure property ownership or stake-in-the-community or as a basis for election reform."[47] In Europe—and virtually everywhere else—the important metric was property ownership, specifically land, because that was the measure by which the state and the society assigned status.

In America, where nearly everyone was an immigrant or the recent descendant of an immigrant, wealth had become disassociated with inherited status or nobility. "Among mobile Americans, a nation of recent immigrants moving from one place to another up and down the social scale, 'income' was a more convenient and more universally applicable standard of measurement than wealth or property. Income was as close as one could come to quantifying the standard of living, and it provided a simple way of telling who was above or below the standard."[48] Even the concept of "standard of living" took on new meaning in America, because that standard was constantly and rapidly improving for nearly everyone.

This explosive growth owed much to plentiful natural resources, especially land. But the indispensable ingredient was, and always has been, people. In this case, a certain kind of individual and specific class of people: the entrepreneur and the bourgeoisie. In Europe, the entrepreneur aroused fear and distrust. Again, innovation had a negative connotation throughout Europe—and much of the world—until the late eighteenth and early nineteenth centuries. In England and Holland, business innovators, like scientific ones, were more honored than anywhere else in the Old World, but in the New World the inventor became a hero. Likewise, in England and Holland, the middle-class merchant was more respected than anywhere else on the Continent, but in America the whole country was being built around a fundamentally bourgeois worldview. The middle class, and those who strived to be in it, for the first time had a government that reflected their interests and aspirations.

In the Old World, the right to form a legal corporation was entrenched in politics and status. It was a special privilege, akin to being granted a title to land. In America "the corporation was democratized by being made a standardized product, available to anyone who followed the simple steps prescribed and paid a small registration fee." Now, as Boorstin notes, "instead of businessmen anxiously seeking the special privilege of incorporation, the states competed for the favors of businessmen. The enticements offered by land speculators, city boosters, and railroad promoters to natural persons and their families were matched by enticements to these artificial persons."⁴⁹

The old iron triumvirate of class, guild, and throne that made economic advancement an act of rebellion against the status quo had been overthrown.

It is a testament to how largely the legacy of slavery hangs over our thinking today that it is difficult to write any of this without constantly offering the balefully accurate caveat "except for blacks" and, to a lesser extent "except for women." It is an entirely accurate point. But, as discussed earlier, slavery was a nearly universal human institution across the world and throughout the ages. Against the yardstick of the present—at least in the democratic, liberal West—every advance in human liberty fails to measure up.

My point here is not to justify or diminish the evil of slavery or Jim Crow. It is simply to argue that we should read the chapters in human history in their correct order. The American Revolution, as Barack Obama has argued, unleashed a new argument for new principles that, when carried to their moral and logical conclusion, commanded the end of slavery and Jim Crow. No one can argue that it shouldn't have happened sooner—or not have been necessary in the first place. But the principles we invoke to condemn the past for its misdeeds are the very principles that the past bequeathed to us.

IN THE CENTURY AND a half following the Revolution, America experienced the greatest run-up in material prosperity of any nation in human history. In the four decades from 1860 to 1900, our population more than doubled, from 31 million to 76 million. When Daniel Webster died in 1852, America was a third as wealthy as Great Britain. Five decades later, it had grown fivefold, with America one and a quarter times richer than the British.⁵⁰ From 1890 to 1910, the U.S. GNP grew at 6 percent a year. According to historian Burton W. Folsom Jr., in 1870 America was creating 23 percent of the world's industrial goods, while Britain and Germany produced 30 and 13 percent, respectively. By 1900, America was in first place with 30 percent; Britain fell to 20 percent, and Germany rose to 20 percent. In 1870, Britain was the world's chief steel producer; by 1900, Andrew Carnegie alone made more steel than all of Great Britain.[51]

In 1775, real GDP per capita was \$1,968.24; by 1820, it was \$2,173.78. By 1929, it was \$11,020.48.[52] Life expectancy rose by leaps and bounds. Workweeks became shorter. Diets improved. "In the Old World, beef was the diet of lords and men of wealth. For others it was a holiday prize. But American millions would eat like lords," writes Daniel Boorstin.[53]

America defied the Malthusian curse that bedeviled societies for all of human history: Even as its population exploded, it got richer even faster. (I wrote an appendix on human progress so I would not have to clutter up later pages with economic statistics. You can refer to it to get a greater appreciation of the explosion of wealth, prosperity, and health that came with this unprecedented experiment in human affairs.)

But while the Miracle repealed Malthus's Law of Population, it did not repeal human nature. The natural tendency of man to form coalitions, factions, guilds, and aristocracies manifested itself continually throughout American history. But the combined power of the constitutional order and sheer economic growth tended to keep it at bay. We'll return to that later.

One last point needs to be made here. The triumph of the Miracle in America isn't simply a story about economics or law. The economics are important because that is the measurement of human material improvement. It is also the chief metric that many of those who despise and revile capitalism invest with the most moral authority. It must be said again and again: The free market is the greatest anti-poverty program in all of human history. In a very real sense, it is the only anti-poverty program in all of human history. The legal system is important because it provides the guardrails for continuing human improvement.

But focusing on economics gives short shrift to another kind of entrepreneurialism that America unleashed upon the world more than any other nation: the entrepreneurialism of the self. The pursuit of happiness is not an inherently or exclusively an economic concept. It is much bigger than that. America's culture of liberty, its legal doctrines of natural rights, and perhaps most of all its staggering material prosperity made it possible for the masses to define happiness on personal and individual terms, to earn their own success as they defined it. This fact is a double-edged sword, for by removing the idea of external authority like never before and exalting the sovereignty of the personal, we have opened a door for human nature to come rushing back in.

PART III

7

The Elites
Aristocrats Unchained

A S WE'VE SEEN, THE AMERICAN FOUNDERS BELIEVED THAT the enemy of liberty was arbitrary power. They rejected a line of thought that stretches from Plato's *Republic* through Rousseau's social contract to any number of modern ideologies that men—the right men, disinterested men—could be trusted with unchecked power.

George Washington was the most admired man in America at the time of the Founding, and the office of the presidency was in many ways molded around the granite edifice of his reputation for honor and good character. And yet the Founders still placed enormous checks on the president's power because they knew that a George Washington would not always be on the ballot.

In theory, the threat of concentrated power falling into the hands of a few people or a single person—be it an aristocracy, caste, guild, star chamber, priesthood, or even some "elective despotism"—was foreclosed with the ratification of the Constitution. But not all of the Founders were entirely optimistic that the experiment would work. First, they believed the system could work only if the public remained virtuous, for the good character of the people is the best guarantor of fidelity to the law. John Adams worried that the people themselves might, in some populist fervor, seek to overthrow limited government. This would be made even more likely if the people turned away from virtue and, in turn, liberty. As Washington said, "Arbitrary power is most easily established on the ruins of liberty abused to licentiousness."[1]

More than any other Founder, Adams was worried about the possibility that aristocracy—perhaps under some other name—could return. Establishing a nation where ambition is set against ambition almost by definition invites people to strain against any external impediments to their objectives. Men naturally form coalitions—or "factions"—and who is to say some coalition couldn't get enough power to overwhelm the constitutional order? Jefferson wanted a "natural aristocracy" of merit. But was it not possible, if not inevitable, that, after having climbed the ladder of merit to the heights of power, that same natural aristocracy would then pull the ladder up behind them?

This is precisely what John Adams feared. A "natural aristocracy" may yield "a body of men which contains the greatest collection of virtues and abilities in a free government, is the brightest ornament and glory of the nation, and may always be made the greatest blessing of society." But, he noted, it must "be judiciously managed in the constitution." Because when such constitutional management fails, "it is always the most dangerous; nay, it may be added, it never fails to be the destruction of the commonwealth."[2]

"Every government is an aristocracy in fact," Adams argued in a letter to Benjamin Rush, and it may contain men of great but dark talents. The solution lay in recognizing and planning for this reality. "The great Secret of Liberty is to find means to limit [the aristocrats'] Power and controul [sic] their Passions."[3]

"I can never too often repeat that aristocracy is the monster to be chained," he said. "Yet so chained as not to be hurt, for he is a most useful and necessary animal in his place. Nothing can be done without him. . . . Bind aristocracy then with a double cord, shut him up in a cage from which, however, he may be let out to do good but never to do mischief."[4]

If you like the idea of putting the aristocrats in a dungeon of some kind, you will be disappointed. The "cage" Adams had in mind was the United States Senate. He had as his guide the practices of Britain and ancient Rome, each of which had a higher legislative body of nobles whose role and power were clearly delineated in a mixed regime. He did not want to have a House of Lords comprising hereditary nobles, but did not rule out the possibility that it might be necessary.

Fortunately, we never felt the need to formally restore hereditary aristocracy. But it is clear that Adams and others were deeply concerned about the possibility, if not the inevitability, of a return to aristocracy. Theoretically, it wouldn't be impossible, but the Founders thought that this liberty-loving people might one day re-embrace aristocracy despite its being entirely prohibited by the Constitution and totally discredited in the hearts and minds of the people. Why?

A simple answer: They were right. *Aristocracies are natural.*

To understand this, we need to get past the word "aristocracy." It clangs off the modern ear precisely because we so completely associate it with earlier times. And while lords and earls are fit for medieval history and *Game of Thrones* fans, those are not the only form of aristocracy. It might be better to simply refer to elites or ruling classes. The terms aren't all completely synonymous, of course. But they can come far closer to being interchangeable than people often realize. In North Korea, the party elite would be instantly recognizable as aristocrats or nobles to a time traveler or alien visitor. They have special rights and privileges and live in special areas reserved for the ruling class. Indeed, in any communist country, members of the Party are simply a modern form of an aristocratic caste class.

Things are better in free countries, where equality before the law is a more enshrined and valued concept. But can anyone dispute that wealth, power, influence, race, and, perhaps most of all, celebrity can contribute to a kind of informal aristocracy or nobility? Certainly everyone can see the disparities. There may be nothing on the books that says the police should cut a Kennedy or a Kardashian a break. But that doesn't mean that they don't get one.

There's also the simple fact that there's a natural human tendency to defer to people with higher status—whether it is earned or unearned. This is neither good nor bad. What matters is why the person being deferred to *has* status.

In other words, it is natural and normal to have elites. And, contrary to the populist mood in America and much of the West right now, there is nothing inherently bad about an elite. Like Jefferson's natural aristocracy, most of us respect people who achieve great things in their pursuit of excellence. We admire elite athletes and elite soldiers. No one wants to be operated on by a particularly average heart surgeon. Culturally, it is only when elites become synonymous with people who practice "elitism"—i.e., snobbery—that America's rebellious DNA kicks in. Similarly, in politics and economics, our problem with elitism stems from a suspicion that the ruling classes are operating in their own self-interest, not ours. This healthy suspicion can always grow unhealthy and conspiratorial, and both the left and the right have their own versions of anti-ruling class paranoia.

But it remains the case that every large or complex society has elites. Indeed, every organization of even modest size does as well. The German sociologist Robert Michels coined the term "the Iron Law of Oligarchy," which holds that all organizations, including those expressly committed to advancing democracy, inevitably become ruled by an elite few.[5] A small organization—a business, a political party, or even a society like a tribe or band—can make decisions largely by consensus. But as organizations grow in size, it becomes increasingly difficult to manage decision making inclusively (thus the irony of the iron law: It only kicks in when the cause is sufficiently attractive to large numbers of people). A fire team in the U.S. Army can largely work without much hierarchy, but an army cannot.

Members of the group specialize in all sorts of ways, including in the realm of leadership and management. These leaders and managers, i.e., elites, emerge within even the most collaborative or consensual organizations—or the organizations simply fall apart under their own weight. The elites take on more responsibilities and, in the process, gain power and expand their access to special knowledge about how the organization works (what Michels calls "administrative secrets"). They can use these "secrets" to elevate their status and consolidate their power even further by allocating resources to reward allies and punish foes.

Michels's study focused on, of all things, democratic socialist labor unions, drawing on his own experience in the German Socialist Party. But his insight is applicable to every sphere of human activity that requires a division of labor. Have you ever belonged to an even modest-sized voluntary organization or club where the bulk of the responsibilities didn't end up falling to a handful of people? What is true for charity drives, high school yearbooks, and peewee soccer leagues is also true of civilizations. The moment we moved from small bands or troops of hunter-gatherers to large agricultural societies, elites in the form of ruling classes were inevitable.

If elites are inevitable in every society and organization, it becomes silly to fret over the existence of elites. This is particularly true in free societies, where people are permitted to pursue happiness as they define it. Not everyone wants to be rich or a politician or a military leader. But some people do. And those who want something the most are always more likely to get it than people who do not want that thing at all. To fret about political, social, or economic inequality in a free society is to fret about the problem of freedom itself, for in the presence of freedom there will always be inequality of some kind.

So the relevant question is not "How can we avoid elites?" but "What kind of elites shall we have?" Following that: "How do we keep them accountable to the rule of law and prevent them from acting in their self-interest in a way that is contrary to law, liberty, or the common good?"

The last three hundred years offer plenty of examples of countries that transitioned to formal democracy only to see it eroded away by a populist tide or yanked out by ambitious elites. But the Founders had other examples in mind. England under Cromwell and the dissolution of the Roman Republic loomed large in their historical memory. And so did the great commercial republic of Venice.

In 1171, Venice established the Great Council, which was made up of aristocrats but also prominent businessmen, magistrates, and other state officials. The Great Council was remarkable in its time for several reasons. It was republican, i.e., the leaders were representative of the people. Every year, one hundred people were nominated to join the council. The members of the nominating committee were chosen by lot to avoid corruption of the process. This not only helped bring in fresh blood to the council but also created legitimacy among newly wealthy merchants. The Great Council, through various mechanisms, also created one of the first systems of checks and balances and divided government. It chose the doge, or chief magistrate of Venice, and required the doge to accept limits to his authority.

"These political reforms led to a further series of institutional innovations: in law, the creation of independent magistrates, courts, a court of appeals, and new private contract and bankruptcy laws," write Daron Acemoglu and James A. Robinson in their book *Why Nations Fail: The Origins of Power, Prosperity, and Poverty*. "These new Venetian economic institutions allowed the creation of new legal business forms and new types of contracts. There was rapid financial innovation, and we see the beginnings of modern banking around this time in Venice. The dynamic moving Venice toward fully inclusive institutions looked unstoppable."[6]

Until it stopped. Venice's economic boom, "supported by the inclusive Venetian institutions," was also "accompanied by creative destruction. Each new wave of enterprising young men who became rich via the *commenda* [an early form of joint stock company] or other similar economic institutions tended to reduce the profits and economic success of established elites. And they did not just reduce their profits; they also challenged their political power."[7]

By 1286 the existing elites had had enough. They implemented a law that membership in the council would henceforth be hereditary. By 1297 the council had effectively rendered itself closed to outsiders. The council soon created the *Libro d'Oro*, or Gold Book, which listed the recognized members of the Venetian nobility. If you weren't in the book, you could not be a member of the council. If you, or your parents or grandparents, were in the book and had been a member of the council, you were automatically in. Term limits on service were eliminated as well. In short, the council became a permanent and hereditary aristocracy, whereas it had once been an institution advancing republicanism and merit.

This was the *Serrata*, meaning closure or lockout. Having closed off politics from upstarts, the council soon set off to close off the economy from upstarts as well. They banned the *commenda* and other economic innovations that made it possible for entrepreneurs of low birth to get rich. By 1314 the Venetian state began nationalizing—-i.e., socializing—trade for the benefit of the elites. Trade was heavily taxed. "Long-distance trade became the preserve of the nobility. This was the beginning of the end of Venetian prosperity," write Acemoglu and Robinson. "With the main lines of business monopolized by the increasingly narrow elite, the decline was under way. Venice appeared to have been on the brink of becoming the world's first inclusive society, but it fell to a coup."[8]

The Founders knew this history well. They understood that people were always going to form factions and that there will always be elites. The trick was to prevent any faction, including a majority of the people, from commandeering the state for its own ambitions. "The only remedy" to the problem of majoritarian factions taking over the government and bending it to its will, James Madison wrote, "is to enlarge the sphere, and thereby divide the community into so great a number of interests and parties, that, in the first place, a majority will not be likely, at the same moment, to have a common interest separate from that of the whole, or of the minority; and in the second place, that in case they should have such an interest, they may not be so apt to unite in the pursuit of it."[9]

Madison's confidence in "enlarging the sphere" was rewarded throughout the nineteenth century. The U.S. population went from just over five million in 1800 to over 76 million in 1900,[10] and even as the population grew fivefold, per capita GDP more than tripled.[11] Physically, America had conquered the entire territory that would become the "lower 48" (though a few territories would have to wait until the early twentieth century to become states). Whole cities— Chicago, Denver, St. Louis—grew from trading posts at best into teeming metropolises. Hundreds of new colleges sprung up, most of them outside the Atlantic coast. And the American idea expanded too. The slaves were freed. The franchise expanded, even to women, in a few western upstarts like the Wyoming Territory (in 1869) and Utah (where it was passed in the Utah Territory in 1870, repealed by Congress in 1887, and restored upon achieving statehood in 1895-96).

Material prosperity, combined with political liberty, fostered and deepened America's culture of freedom. And in such an environment, it was inevitable that great fortunes would be made. Men with names like Getty, Rockefeller, Vanderbilt, and Gould built businesses from scratch. These economic titans were not investors but entrepreneurs. They created new products and services, or new means of producing old ones, on a massive, cost-reducing scale that made former luxuries into affordable creature comforts.

On the whole, these wealth creators differed from the old aristo-crats of feudal Europe, whose wealth depended on exploitation of the poor. The new magnates made their money by helping the poor. Cotton magnate Edward Atkinson spelled it out. "Through competition among capitalists," he wrote, "capital itself is every year more effective in production, and tends ever to increasing abundance. Under its working the commodities that have been the luxuries of one generation become the comforts of the next and the necessities of the third. . . . The plane of what constitutes a comfortable subsistence is constantly rising, and as the years go by greater and greater numbers attain this plane."

Addressing some workers in 1886, Atkinson tried to explain how everyone gained from a free market. Cornelius Vanderbilt, Atkinson observed, made a profit of 14 cents from every barrel of flour shipped over his railroads. His efficiency lowered the price of flour for consumers. "Did Vanderbilt keep any of you down," challenged Atkinson, "by saving you $2.75 on a barrel of flour, while he was making 14 cents?"[12]

The poor benefited in more direct ways as well. Just drive around the country and count the number of libraries, schools, museums, and parks that would not exist but for the largesse of the supposedly "predatory" wealthy. Without the Morgans, Carnegies, Gettys, Rockefellers, Goulds, and Vanderbilts, few of the truly great cultural institutions we take for granted would be standing today. Carnegie poured millions of dollars into public libraries across the country in the Jeffersonian spirit of providing "ladders within reach upon which the aspiring can rise."[13]

The German sociologist Werner Sombart famously asked: "Why is there no socialism in the United States?" The answer for historians and political theorists has always been: because America has no feudal past. In Europe—and everywhere else—feudal class differences were embedded in notions of wealth and status. The wealthy were aristocrats and the aristocrats were wealthy. The Founders sought to create a new nation where these long-married categories were divorced from one another.

From the time of the Founding until the early twentieth century, the natural tendency of the haves to form new aristocracies and guilds was held largely in check. This tendency was held at bay thanks to a number of factors. First, economic growth was just too robust. Guilds thrive in moribund economies where competing innovators lack access to capital. Second, the nation itself was too large, too mobile, and too diverse. An established widget manufacturer in Pennsylvania might have had the kind of political clout close to home to thwart competition in his own backyard. But he was powerless to reach into Illinois or Colorado or California. A competing widget manufacturer with a better method in, say, Denver had access to local capital, natural resources, and markets all its own.

A third, vital, reason: The Constitution was still functioning largely as designed. Local powers could not establish interstate tariffs or other trade barriers preventing new products from rolling across the borders in train cars. Fourth, and relatedly, the state simply wasn't big enough or intrusive enough to pick winners and losers consistently (although the railroad industry might be a notable exception here). Even if regulators could be captured by established industries, there simply weren't enough of them, nor were they sufficiently powerful, to block start-up industries.

And, finally, American culture itself was simply too powerful. Call it the yeoman spirit, or the Horatio Alger ethic, or the legacy of Puritanism, or the new bourgeois ideology sweeping the world, or simply the American dream, but the American people believed in the nobility of entrepreneurialism. And because Americans believed in it, foreigners who believed in it as well flocked to this country by the millions, carrying with them the expectation that the sky was the limit. Barring one man's ability to make his own fortune was rightly recognized as a threat to every man's right to try for the same thing.

In short, America had a functioning government, but it did not have a state. No doubt this sounds odd. But it's an important distinction. Throughout the nineteenth century and well into the twentieth, historian William Leuchtenburg observes, America "had almost no institutional structure to which Europeans would accord the term 'the State.'"[14] Of course, America had a government, but that is not the same thing as the state.

In political science, the difference between the state and the government is a technical one. The state includes all of the population and its territory and is permanent, while governments may come and go. For instance, France has had five republics, but there has always been the French state. In the U.K., the prime minister is the head of government, but the monarch is the head of state.

However, this is not the distinction that is relevant here.

Among conservatives and some libertarians, the distinction between the government and the state is fairly clear, if rarely articulated. The Constitution creates a government along Lockean lines, an institution designed to protect the liberties of the people. It is the product of a social contract that recognizes that natural rights are prior to the government. The government by this definition has no right to violate the rights of the people or any individual person (save, perhaps, in extreme and extraordinary circumstances). The state, however, is an all-inclusive institution that has rights and interests that must come first. For such thinkers as Albert Jay Nock and Franz Oppenheimer, the state was founded in oppression and conquest—i.e., the stationary bandit model discussed earlier—and is thus a much older phenomenon than government.[15]

For a libertarian like Nock, it was easy to talk about how the state is an enemy but government is a necessary good. "The nature and intention of government . . . are social. Based on the idea of natural rights, government secures those rights to the individual by strictly negative intervention, making justice costless and easy of access; and beyond that it does not go," Nock writes. "The State, on the other hand, both in its genesis and by its primary intention, is purely anti-social. It is not based on the idea of natural rights, but on the idea that the individual has no rights except those that the State may provisionally grant him. It has always made justice costly and difficult of access, and has invariably held itself above justice and common morality whenever it could advantage itself by so doing."[16]

One doesn't have to buy Nock's view that the state is no better than a criminal enterprise, however. That's certainly not how statists themselves see it. Statists—who never go by that term, preferring "progressive" or "liberal" or, in more extreme forms, "Marxist"—subscribe to the French Enlightenment view of the state as an active participant in guiding the direction of society. Government is the stuff of the English garden discussed earlier. The state is a guiding hand of the French garden. Politically, culturally, and philosophically, the idea of a powerful and intrusive state rests on various versions of "the general will" and nationalistic arguments. The state should reflect the values and nature of the people as a whole. So if "the people," collectively, do not want, say, democracy or capitalism or free speech, it's fine for the state to ban such things, because the state is the fullest and most natural expression of the authentic will of the people. Every dictatorship rests on an argument that follows this basic form. But so do plenty of "social democracies," which maintain many liberties while curtailing others, mostly economic ones. The idea that the state should go to great lengths to stamp out income inequality, for example, is wholly consistent with statism in the tradition of Rousseau but antithetical to the idea of government in the tradition of Locke. Throughout Europe, where the monarchy had been both a religious and a civil institution, guiding and directing the people for thousands of years, it seemed only natural that the modern state would continue intervening in the lives of the people. In America, this was a foreign concept. Indeed, it was a concept we fought a revolution to overthrow.

Many, probably most, historians locate the birth of the state in America in the New Deal. And that is largely true in the sense that the New Deal made the state a permanent fixture of American life. "Before the New Deal," observed the late economist Edward M. Bernstein, a prominent member of FDR's Treasury Department, "the only business a citizen had with the government was through the Post Office. No doubt he saw a soldier or a sailor now and then, but the government had nothing to do with the general public. After Roosevelt, the public felt that government was then an active part of everyday life."[17]

But the truth is the birth of the state begins a little earlier, during the Progressive Era, specifically in the Democratic administration immediately prior to FDR's (and one Roosevelt himself served in). In the next chapter, we will look at the rebirth of the state and what should properly be understood as the second American Revolution.

8

THE PROGRESSIVE ERA
The Birth of the Living Constitution and the Death of Liberty

T HE INCREDIBLE EXPLOSION OF WEALTH IN THE UNITED
States, complete with a supposedly new economic ruling class,
aroused profound unease. Millions of Americans had left their rural,
agrarian hometowns and poured into cities. Cut off from traditional communities and let loose in the world of capitalism, they felt
exploited and alienated, cast adrift in a world of strangers. And even
though common people were indeed getting richer and forming new,
vibrant communities, one can only sympathize with the sense of ver-
tigo they must have felt. Capitalism seemed all too chaotic, disorganized, unfulfilling, and, at times, cruel for those lacking in financial
or social capital. Nostalgia, homesickness for an imagined time of
security and spiritual comfort, was in the air. The philosophy of "individualism" was too small to give meaning, or the sense of belonging,
so many yearned for. And while they struggled for security as much as
wealth, the ruling classes seemed to be unjustly rich in both.

A new group of American philosophes emerged, arguing, much as
Rousseau had, that *there has to be a better way*. America needed a new
imagined community, bound together by a new civic religion, which,
like Rousseau's, claimed to be Christian in form but was really nationalistic and Spartan in substance.

The task for these self-anointed philosophes, these new priests
of modernity, was to refound America on new principles that, if put
into action, would create a new society that would fill the holes in the
American soul.

These American philosophes were a diverse lot, but they are best
lumped under the banner of progressivism. And while not all progres-

sives were hostile to every feature of the American order, as a group their goal was to discredit and replace that order with a new one. Princeton historian Thomas C. Leonard identifies two core assumptions of progressive intellectuals: "First, modern government should be guided by science and not politics; and second, an industrialized economy should be supervised, investigated, and regulated by the visible hand of a modern administrative state."[1]

If the original Founders were products of the Scottish Enlightenment, the new founders were products of the new German renaissance, the awakening of German social science. Many of the American sociologists, philosophers, and economists who created their fields and schools of thought in America had attended German universities or studied under those who had. (When the American Economic Association was formed in 1885, five of the first six officers had studied in Germany. At least twenty of its first twenty-six presidents had as well. In 1906 a professor at Yale polled the top 116 economists and social scientists in America; more than half had studied in Germany for at least a year.)[2]

In the nineteenth century, German air was thick with Marx, Hegel, and Herder. All of these thinkers fed into the broader worldview known as the "historical school." Devotees believed that all economic facts are relative and evolutionary, contingent upon their time and place. Descendants of German romanticism, they saw the state as an expression of the spirit of the people (*Volksgemeinschaft*) and, in turn, they believed the state had not only a right but an obligation to forge a new general will.

Richard T. Ely, the first president of the American Economic Association and the founder of the "Wisconsin School" of progressivism (which served as a kind of think tank for the Progressive Era in the first third of twentieth century), earned his PhD at the University of Heidelberg under the historical economist Karl Knies. "The most fundamental things in our minds," he recalled of his generation of intellectuals, "were on the one hand the idea of evolution, and on the other hand, the idea of relativity." And men like Ely would use these ideas to wage unremitting war on capitalism.[3]

Indeed, the most vital ingredient in this German intellectual cocktail was Darwinism. Darwin's theory of evolution injected a new scientific credibility into the old anti-Enlightenment philosophies of nationalism and identity. Darwinism not only made biological racism possible. It also dealt a devastating blow to notions of natural rights while breathing new life into the idea that the state was not just an expression of the people but should also guide the continued "evolution" of society. The idea was that the nation and the state and all of the institutions within it were part of a single organic whole, evolving together, with the state serving as the brain, controlling and regulating all of the other organs. Individuals were little more than cells in the body politic. Herbert Croly, the founder of the *New Republic*, said society was just "an enlarged individual." Edward Alsworth Ross, possibly the most influential sociologist of his day, believed society is "a living thing, actuated, like all the higher creatures, by the instinct for self-preservation."[4] The chaos of capitalism was antithetical to this vision: Organs cannot compete against each other; they must work in harmony.

I do not want to make it sound like American statism began as a mental virus that escaped some German laboratory. American intellectuals made their own original contributions as well. The two most important were the "social gospel," a novel reinterpretation of an ancient interpretation of Christianity, and eugenics, the belief that weeds of the unfit had to be pruned and plucked by the state.

In an echo of Rousseau, the social gospel held that spiritual redemption was—or must now be—a collective enterprise. Saving souls retail was a fool's errand. The state, according to Ely, was "a moral person."[5] But the state was also God's divine instrument. "God works through the State in carrying out His purposes more universally than through any other institution," Ely wrote. It "takes the first place among His instrumentalities."[6] Social gospel preacher Samuel Zane Batten thought that one of the most pressing questions of his time was: Would the state "become the medium through which the people shall co-operate in their search for the kingdom of God and its righteousness?" (He hoped it would.)[7] And the essential task in the pursuit of social righteousness was the war on capitalism and doctrines of individualism. "Our disorganized competitive life must pass into an organic cooperative life," Walter Rauschenbusch, the leading social gospel preacher and intellectual of his time, insisted.[8] "Unless the ideal social order can supply men with food, warmth and comfort more efficiently than our present economic order, back we shall go to Capitalism . . ." Such an eventuality was unthinkable. So he proclaimed, "The God that answereth by low food prices, let him be God."[9]

Without this theological backdrop, eugenics could never have caught on. Telling the full story of eugenics in America would take us too far afield. Suffice it to say that eugenics was seen at the time as cutting-edge science, and there was a large, if not total, consensus that weeding the garden of humanity of the unfit was essential to social progress. In *The Promise of American Life*, the bible of American progressivism, Herbert Croly insisted that the state had an obligation to "interfere on behalf of the really fittest." Richard Ely insisted that progressives must acknowledge the "superiority of man's selection to nature's selection."[10] Letting free people reproduce freely—presumably an integral part of the pursuit of happiness—was folly. Such freedom is just too likely to give us unfit men. But a society guided by the expert hands of science "gives us the ideal man," he explained. "The great word is no longer natural selection but social selection."[11]

While I've focused on the roles of America and Germany, it should be noted that the ideas of the Progressive Era were truly part of a transnational intellectual awakening. For instance, positivism, a widely held philosophy largely invented by the Frenchman Auguste Comte, held that humanity had entered the third stage of history, the Age of Science. Essentially picking up where Condorcet had left off, Comte believed that human society could be directed, guided, and ultimately perfected by enlightened experts. That project, by its nature, would have to be collectivist in outlook. (He called individualism the "disease of the Western World.")[12] Comte coined the term "sociology" and helped create the discipline to achieve this end. Later he created a wholly secular "Religion of Humanity," in which men of science would be the new saints. When Herbert Croly was born in 1869, his parents *literally* baptized him into Comte's "Religion of Humanity."[13]

Still, on a practical level, the influence of Germany, specifically Prussia, was especially significant because it was seen as a real-world example of how politics should work. It helped fuel a deep contempt for traditional notions of democracy. Prussia—where so many progressives had studied—at the end of the nineteenth century (1871-90) had been ruled by Otto von Bismarck, the authoritarian "Iron Chancellor," who introduced what was then called "top-down socialism" run by professional civil servants. Bismarck's Prussia was seen as state-of-the-art in governance by a new generation of American academics. One such academic, who studied under Ely and who was granted one of the first PhDs from the new Johns Hopkins University, the first major German-style research university in America, was Woodrow Wilson. He would later write that Bismarck's Prussia was an "admirable system" and "the most studied and most nearly perfected" in the world.[14]

In the 1880s, Wilson had argued the "most despotic of governments under the control of wise statesmen is preferable to the freest ruled by demagogues." Alas, America was a democracy, and, to counter that, Wilson wanted to limit "the error of trying to do too much by vote" by walling off as much policy making from the court of public opinion as possible. "Let administrative study find the best means for giving public criticism this control and for shutting it out from all other interference."[15] After all, he explained, "self-government does not consist in having a hand in everything, any more than housekeeping consists necessarily in cooking dinner with one's own hands. The cook must be trusted with a large discretion as to the management of the fires and the ovens."[16] "Give us administrative elasticity and discretion," Woodrow Wilson wrote in 1891; "free us from the idea that checks and balances are to be carried down through all stages of organization."[17]

It is difficult to exaggerate Wilson's arrogant and sovereign contempt for the system set up by the Founders. "The reformer is bewildered," he whined, by the need to persuade "a voting majority of several million heads."[18] Elsewhere he scoffed, "No doubt, a lot of nonsense has been talked about the inalienable rights of the individual, and a great deal that was mere vague sentiment and pleasing speculation has been put forward as fundamental principle."[19]

Wilson's views on democracy and the Constitution were relatively tame compared to those of many of his peers. But they capture the essential spirit of the progressive outlook.

Woodrow Wilson depended heavily on Darwin to argue for throwing the Constitution in the dustbin:

The Constitution was founded on the law of gravitation. The government was to exist and move by virtue of the efficacy of "checks and balances." The trouble with the theory is that government is not a machine, but a living thing. It falls, not under the theory of the universe, but under the theory of organic life. It is accountable to Darwin, not to Newton. It is modified by its environment, necessitated by its tasks, shaped to its functions by the sheer pressure of life. No living thing can have its organs offset against each other, as checks, and live.[20]

Thus, for all practical purposes, was the insidious American cult of the "living Constitution" born. "Living political constitutions," Wilson wrote, "must be Darwinian in structure and in practice. Society is a living organism and must obey the laws of life, not of mechanics; it must develop."[21]

Contempt for the Founding became the hallmark of sophistication. The philosopher John Dewey, the most important philosopher of the Progressive Era, argued that the folly of the Founders lay in their belief that their principles would or should outlive their time. The Founders "lacked," he explained in *Liberalism and Social Action* (1935), "historic sense and interest."[22] The Lockean ideal of government merely protecting the rights of the citizens and otherwise leaving the people alone was antiquated codswallop. Even the idea of individual rights was a bygone relic. "Natural rights and natural liberties exist only in the kingdom of mythological social zoology."[23] Rights can only be properly secured through "social control of economic forces in the interest of the great mass of individuals."[24] Humans were "nothing in themselves"[25] for Dewey; the General Will was everything.

"Social expediency, rather than natural right," argued Frank J. Goodnow, the first president of the American Political Science Association and a hugely influential professor of administrative law at Columbia University, must "determine the sphere of individual freedom of action."[26] "Changed conditions," he added, ". . . must bring in their train different conceptions of private rights if society is to be advantageously carried on."[27]

These views were no doubt sincerely held. But the supposedly "disinterested" experts and intellectuals who pushed them had an interest in doing so. They weren't merely arguing in the abstract that experts should guide society forward; they were claiming that they themselves were the experts who should do so. "The period of constitution-making is passed now," Woodrow Wilson huffed. "We have reached a new territory in which we need new guides, the vast territory of *administration*."[28]

As we've seen, the progressives were not the first to advocate the creation of extra-legal administrators licensed by the general will to wield arbitrary power for the greater good. Rather, the progressive desire for a new aristocracy of expertise was yet another example of how the old *reactionary* drives of human nature continually reappear in new forms. As Jefferson warned, "The natural progress of things is for liberty to yield, and government to gain ground."[29] My only quibble with Jefferson here is that he chose the wrong word. The dynamic he was describing was not progress but decay, or corruption.

So what happens when you commit to the notion that there is a special class of administrators allegedly insulated from politics with a providential writ to do good without reference to the law or the voters?

You get the administrative state.

What is the administrative state?

Most directly, it is the fruit of the second American Revolution. As we've seen, the progressives sought to inter the old "Newtonian" constitutional order and replace it with a new "Darwinian" paradigm. This new regime would be run by "disinterested" social scientists, or simply administrators, who drew their legitimacy not from "We the People" but from their superior insight and, in Woodrow Wilson's words, "special knowledge."*

---

* In this, Wilson was fitting heir to the Gnostics identified by Eric Voegelin:

And, finally, with the prodigious advancement of science since the seventeenth century, the new instrument of cognition would become, one is inclined to say inevitably, the symbolic vehicle of Gnostic truth. In the Gnostic speculation of scientism this particular variant reached its extreme when the positivist perfector of science replaced the era of Christ by the era of Comte. Scientism has remained to this day one of the strongest Gnostic movements in Western society; and the immanentist pride in science is so strong that even the special sciences have each left a distinguishable sediment in the variants of salvation through physics, economics, sociology, biology, and psychology.

Eric Voegelin, *The New Science of Politics: An Introduction,* Walgreen Foundation Lectures (Chicago: University of Chicago Press, 1987, Kindle edition), pp. 127-28.

Wilson thought it bewildering that the reformers should have to consult with the wishes of the people. If you have the "scientific" facts on your side, why would you put the question before the voters? Wilson explained that

> the functions of government are in a very real sense independent of legislation, and even constitutions, because [they are] as old as government and inherent in its very nature. The bulk and complex minuteness of our positive law, which covers almost every case that can arise in Administration, obscures for us the fact that *Administration cannot wait upon legislation, but must be given leave, or take it, to proceed without specific warrant in giving effect to the characteristic life of the State.*[30]

This was not Wilson's pet theory. This was a time when science and technology were conquering nature at a breakneck speed. Industry was achieving once unimaginable efficiencies in production. Engineering was a glamorous new vocation as experts in every field revolutionized business, medicine, infrastructure, and food production. Thanks to Darwin, the experts now believed they also understood how the human machine worked. So why not let the new "social engineers" revolutionize government the way technological engineers revolutionized industry and public works? What did the common people know about the science of society, i.e., "social science"?

The public intellectual and journalist Walter Lippmann was among the foremost critics—for a time—of old-fashioned and outdated democracy. "In ordinary circumstances voters cannot be expected to transcend their particular, localized and self-regarding opinions," he wrote. "In their circumstances, which as private persons they cannot readily surmount, the voters are most likely to suppose that whatever seems obviously good to them must be good for the country, and good in the sight of God."[31] Putting faith in the wisdom of the people was simply a colossal error. "The crucial problem of modern democracy," Lippmann wrote, "arises from the fact that this assumption is false."[32]

This widespread conviction was put into action by Woodrow Wilson (for whom Lippmann had worked as an advisor). While Madison believed that self-interest is "sown in the nature of man,"[33] Wilson believed that the science of administration could elevate man above his nature and the people he serves. The old dream of the perfectibility of man would be achieved in, of all types, the bureaucrat! Ronald J. Pestritto adds that "Wilson assumed, just as Hegel had in the *Philosophy of Right*, that a secure position in the bureaucracy, with tenure and good pay, would relieve the civil servant of his natural self-interestedness, thereby freeing him of his particularity and allowing him to focus solely on the objective good of society."[34]

IT IS VITAL TO underscore once again that intellectuals draw their ideas from the times they live in. There is a feedback loop at work in every age. Just as the American founding was an expression of the "American mind," as Jefferson put it, and just as rebelling against the British and romantic nationalism was fueled by a popular backlash against Napoleon and the Enlightenment among the German people, the progressives drew sustenance from a popular backlash against capitalism itself. When confronted with the seeming chaos of capitalism and democracy, the human mind retreats to its tribal programming.

This doesn't mean Americans during the first three decades of the twentieth century dabbed war paint on their faces and fought with spears. We all speak in the language and symbols of the time we live in. Percival Lowell, the turn-of-the-century astronomer who built the telescope that discovered Pluto, lived at a time when large-scale canal building was a sign of technological and industrial advancement. So when he saw straight lines on the surface of Mars, he assumed they were put there by an advanced civilization.[35] During the Progressive Era, industry, engineering, medicine, and science were making incredible breakthroughs. For entirely understandable reasons, progressive intellectuals, and Americans generally, assumed that if science and technology could solve age-old problems in real life, if industrial managers could create amazingly efficient new forms of organization, then surely experts could do the same thing for politics. This was a time when social science was new, the phrase "social engineering" had no negative connotation, and it was assumed that political science was, or could be, every bit as scientific as physics or chemistry.

But enough with the theory and philosophy. What was the administrative state in practical terms? Put most simply, it was the vast enlargement of the government. But this simplification doesn't capture the revolutionary nature of the administrative state, because the new army of regulators and revenuers worked outside the constitutional framework, which is why the administrative state is sometimes called the "fourth branch" of government. (For reasons I'll discuss in the next chapter, I think this label misses the mark.) Congress is responsible for making policy, also known as legislation. The president, the head of the executive branch, is responsible for executing that policy. But with the rise of the administrative state, bureaucrats began driving the policy-making process.

By the end of Wilson's first term, the administrative state had been created. Personal income was now taxed directly by the federal government, as were corporations and estates. Big industries were broken up. The newly minted Federal Reserve regulated money, credit, and banking. The Federal Trade Commission supervised domestic industry, and its new Tariff Commission regulated international trade. State and federal labor legislation mandated workmen's compensation; banned child labor; compelled schooling of children; established minimum wages and maximum hours; and established pensions for single mothers with young children. Armies of regulators inspected factories, intervened in businesses, and demanded all manner of licenses to work in various fields.[36]

One can certainly argue that some of these reforms were valuable and necessary. But that is a different argument. What was revolutionary was the argument that the state should take its own counsel on what society needed. "Social expediency," as Frank J. Goodnow put it, now trumped constitutional fidelity and democratic sovereignty.

And all of this happened *before* Wilson plunged America into World War I. During the war, the American government became vastly more intrusive not only economically but also *politically.*

President Wilson's war to "make the world safe for democracy" obviously had ample support for its expressed foreign policy aims, particularly among the hawkish Teddy Roosevelt wing of the progressive movement, who tended to think Wilson wasn't belligerent enough. But for the social-engineering wing, international affairs were largely incidental. What fascinated them was what John Dewey called "the social possibilities of war." Dewey meant by the phrase that he wanted the war to force Americans "to give up much of our economic freedom." He continued: "We shall have to lay by our good-natured individualism and march in step." He hoped that the war would constrain "the individualistic tradition" and convince Americans of "the supremacy of public need over private possessions." Another progressive put it more succinctly: "Laissez-faire is dead. Long live social control."[37]

(Randolph Bourne, the dissident progressive intellectual who famously declared, "War is the health of the state," was almost alone in noticing the "peculiar congeniality between the war and these men." He added that "it is as if the war and they had been waiting for each other.")[38]

During the war, all of the tribal impulses were given free rein. Woodrow Wilson demonized the "others" in our midst: the so-called hyphenated Americans, i.e., German-Americans, Italian-Americans, and any other ethnicity or group that didn't commit to what many called "100 percent Americanism." "Any man who carries a hyphen about with him carries a dagger that he is ready to plunge into the vitals of this Republic whenever he gets the chance," Wilson proclaimed.[39] Under Wilson's administration, America created the first modern propaganda ministry in the world: the Committee for Public Information.[40] It threw thousands in jail for criminal thoughts and speech.[41] It enlisted the help of an army of quasi-official *fascisti*, the American Protection League, who beat up protestors, interrogated "hyphenated-Americans," and enforced loyalty to the state.[42]

Economically, the government pursued a policy that was widely dubbed "war socialism." Big corporations were essentially enlisted in the war effort and cartelized. The state didn't nationalize every industry outright; instead, it pursued a policy of neo-guildism. The point was that the economy had to be oriented toward the aims of the state in all matters. Over 5,000 "mobilization agencies" were created to make sure all of the oars pulled in the same direction. The state, Robert Higgs adds,

> virtually nationalized the ocean shipping industry. It did nationalize the railroad, telephone, domestic telegraph, and international telegraphic cable industries. It became deeply engaged in manipu-

lating labor-management relations, securities sales, agricultural production and marketing, the distribution of coal and oil, international commerce, and markets for raw materials and manufactured products. Its Liberty Bond drives dominated the financial capital markets. It turned the newly created Federal Reserve System into a powerful engine of monetary inflation to help satisfy the government's voracious appetite for money and credit.[43]

In the 1918 midterm elections, the Republicans took back Congress. Two years later the Republicans reclaimed the White House as well on a platform of a "return to normalcy." The slogan resonated with Americans fed up not just with war but also with domestic authoritarianism. The progressives who saw the war as an exemplary use of state planning were dejected that the American people had turned their backs on them. As a consequence, as I detail at length in *Liberal Fascism: The Secret History of the American Left, from Mussolini to the Politics of Change,* the progressives cast their eyes to "advanced" countries that continued the struggle for social engineering and "scientific" management of society: Fascist Italy and Soviet Russia. The American progressive rallying cry during the Roaring Twenties was a plaintive "We planned in war, why not in peace?"

A dozen years after Wilson left office, Franklin Roosevelt entered office. The lingering Depression of 1929 provided ample ammunition—and popular support—for finding a replacement for laissez-faire capitalism, even though government interference had contributed to the economic problems the country faced. Roosevelt picked up right where Wilson left off, transforming Wilson's war-time agencies into permanent fixtures of the state. The Securities and Exchange Commission was an extension of the Capital Issues Committee of the Federal Reserve Board. The Reconstruction Finance Corporation was an updated version of the War Finance Corporation. FDR's public housing initiative was run by the architect of World War I–era housing policies.

Of course, Roosevelt went much further than Wilson. With Congress's help, and the American people's approval, American government was permanently transformed into a state.

In the next chapter we look at what has become of the administrative state.

9

THE ADMINISTRATIVE STATE
The Shadow Government

I N THE EARLY DAYS OF THE TRUMP ADMINISTRATION, THEN
White House senior advisor Steve Bannon laid out his three priorities. The first was "national security and sovereignty." The second: "economic nationalism." The third was "the deconstruction of
the administrative state."[1] For many journalists and casual political
observers, this third item was a head scratcher. But for intellectual
conservatives, it was cause for celebration.[2]

Sometimes called the regulatory state or the fourth branch of
government, the administrative state is today a vast complex of
bureaucrats and regulators—and the rules they work by—outside the
constitutional order. They make "rulings," often without the slightest feedback from voters or even elected officials. (When rule making
does include a "public comment" period, it is often more ceremonial
than democratic.) And regulators' success has been so complete that
elected officials have been willing accomplices in this travesty. Congress, as an institution, abdicated its sole responsibility to legislate, the
courts have abandoned their obligation to safeguard the separation of
powers, and presidents of both parties have proved unable or unwill-
ing to curtail the bureaucracy.

For the most part, Congress no longer makes laws the way the
Founders intended. They outsource the heavy lifting to the bureaucracy. This was already true when James Burnham published *The
Managerial Revolution*, one of the first seminal works on the subject,
in 1941. "Laws today in the United States, in fact most laws, are not
being made any longer by Congress," Burnham wrote, "but by the
NLRB, SEC, ICC, AAA, TVA, FTC, FCC, the Office of Production

Management (what a revealing title!), and the other leading 'executive agencies.' How well lawyers know this to be the case!"[3]

Consider the Affordable Care Act, or "Obamacare." Journalist Phillip Klein dived into the fine print and found that

> there are more than 2,500 references to the secretary of [Health and Human Services] in the health care law (in most cases she's simply mentioned as "the Secretary"). A further breakdown finds that there are more than 700 instances in which the Secretary is instructed that she "shall" do something, and more than 200 cases in which she "may" take some form of regulatory action if she chooses. On 139 occasions, the law mentions decisions that the "Secretary determines." At times, the frequency of these mentions reaches comic heights. For instance, one section of the law reads: "Each person to whom the Secretary provided information under subsection (d) shall report to the Secretary in such manner as the Secretary determines appropriate."[4]

It is impossible to quantify the discretion—i.e., arbitrary power—Congress bestowed on the HHS secretary. "Either the new powers and responsibilities given to the Secretary are too complicated for even HHS to figure out," Klein writes, "or they're so arbitrary that [then HHS secretary Kathleen] Sebelius can pick and choose how she'll comply with parts of the law."[5]

But this merely scratches the surface of the administrative state. Whole agencies are independent of political control—which is very different from saying they are independent from politics. Consider just one example. According to the Constitution, only Congress can levy a tax. This is not some mere procedural nicety. It is concrete expression of the Founders' core conviction that taxation must be legitimized by representation. That, after all, was the crux of their argument with King George. And that is why Article I of the Constitution requires that "all Bills for raising Revenue shall originate in the House of Representatives," a.k.a. "the people's chamber."

But Congress has grown comfortable relinquishing this power. In 1996 the Federal Communications Commission was granted the authority to raise taxes as it sees fit. The Universal Service Fund started as a tax on long-distance phone calls. Originally set at 3 percent, within a decade the "fee" reached 11 percent, all absent congressional approval.[6] (During the Obama administration, the FCC moved toward imposing a similar tax on broadband Internet services, in part because revenue had fallen off due to people abandoning landlines.)[7] The revenues ostensibly go to pay for expanding access to the Internet in rural areas and providing computers for poor schools and libraries. But there have also been numerous scandals in which the monies were poorly spent, misallocated, and sluiced to politically connected players.[8] As we'll see, this should be expected.

IN 2002, UNDER THE Sarbanes-Oxley Act, the Public Company Accounting Oversight Board was given the power to fund itself with taxes on publicly traded companies as it sees fit. "The Board sets its budget for the year," writes economist Christopher DeMuth, "... divides that amount by the number of U.S. companies weighted by their market capitalizations, and sends each company a bill." In 2004, the budget was $103 million. In 2005, the Accounting Oversight Board unilaterally increased its budget by 33 percent to $137 million.[9] Since then, the budget has nearly doubled, to $268 million as of 2017.[10] In fairness, the Securities and Exchange Commission must approve the board's budgets, but a close reading of the Constitution reveals that "the SEC" is not a nickname for Congress. The power of the purse is the essence of Congress's power and authority, and its members voluntarily abdicated it.

The term "fourth branch of government" is far too pallid a descriptor of what more properly should be called a shadow government, a state within the state, or *imperium in imperio*. There is nothing intrinsically sinister in the idea of a fourth branch of government. The Founders could have divided the federal government's power four ways instead of three if they had wanted to. So long as the doctrine of separated powers was maintained, who would care?

The administrative state is no fourth branch of government. It is a *parallel government,* operating in the shadows, outside the light of democratic transparency. The best indicator of this stems from the fact that members of the administrative state are not subject to the same system of justice as the rest of us. Charles Murray describes this system well:

> If you are prosecuted for violating a regulation issued by the EPA, OSHA, HHS, Department of Energy, or any of the myriad other federal regulatory agencies, you appear before an administrative law judge (ALJ) sitting in an administrative law courtroom. An ALJ is selected by the agency whose cases he will hear, and is subsequently an employee of that agency. The agency gets to choose its preferred candidate from among the three top-rated candidates identified by the Office of Personnel Management. An administrative law judge is exempt from performance reviews and other oversight by the regulatory agency, but may be overruled by the head of the agency.
>
> There's no jury. When appearing in an administrative court, you do not get a lawyer unless you pay for it. Most rules of evidence used in normal courts do not apply. The legal burden of proof placed on the lawyer making the case for the regulatory agency is "a preponderance of the evidence," not "clear and convincing evidence," let alone "evidence beyond a reasonable doubt" that you are guilty. If the administrative judge thinks that it's a 51/49 percent call in favor of the regulatory agency that accused you, you're found guilty. If the administrative court judge's decision is adverse, you may, in most cases, appeal that decision to another body within the agency.[11]

Although it is necessary to describe the administrative state, my deeper aim here is to explain how this sorry state of affairs is an example of the corruption of the Founders' project.

The Constitution is indisputably clear. At the federal level, only Congress can legislate. The executive branch *executes* the law—hence the word "executive." As John Adams said, the president enjoys "the whole executive power, after divesting it of those badges of domination called prerogatives."[12] Defenders of the administrative state today use the same arguments the progressives used: Such unaccountable power is simply the very definition of good, "modern," governance. The truth, however, is that it is a throwback to pre-modern forms of state power.

192 SUICIDE *of the* WEST

The best authority on this subject is the prominent legal historian Philip Hamburger, a professor at Columbia University. In his seminal book *Is Administrative Law Unlawful?*, Hamburger demonstrates that the rise of the administrative state is a reactionary effort to restore the lawlessness of arbitrary power banished by the Founders. Hamburger uses the term "absolute power" much the way I've been using "concentrated power" or "arbitrary power." For our purposes, it is a distinction without a difference in that we both mean the wielding of power without lawful checks or popular consent. I prefer "arbitrary power" because it is more suggestive of the human whim behind it. But Hamburger is arguing in the context of a legal tradition that associated the term "absolute power" with prerogative power of kings.

Hamburger offers three reasons why administrative law is unconstitutional. "First, like the old absolute power, administrative power runs outside the law" because it is not directly answerable to, or derived from, constitutional legislative or judicial authority.[13] Second, administrative law "is not only extralegal but also supralegal." "Supralegal" is a fancy way of saying "above the law." The administrative state is precisely that because judges defer to its authority. In feudal monarchies, the king or queen's rule is above the common law, in effect creating two systems of justice, one for the people and another for the state. That is the arrangement we have under the administrative state. And third: "The administrative regime consolidates in one branch of government the powers that the Constitution allocates to different branches."[14] This blatantly violates the Madisonian architecture of our republic. As Madison says in *Federalist* No. 47: "The accumulation of all powers legislative, executive and judiciary in the same hands . . . may justly be pronounced the very definition of tyranny."[15]

Clarence Thomas, one of the few Supreme Court justices to see this abomination for what it is, has chastised the courts for having "overseen and sanctioned the growth of an administrative system that concentrates the power to make laws and the power to enforce them in the hands of a vast and unaccountable administrative apparatus that finds no comfortable home in our constitutional structure."[16]

The legal origins of the administrative state in America are somewhat disputed by legal scholars, though the conventional explanation is that it began with the Interstate Commerce Commission in 1887 and was then massively expanded first under Wilson and later under the New Deal and the Great Society. But that misses the point. "The history of administrative law," Hamburger writes, ". . . reaches back many centuries. Indeed, this sort of power, which is said to be uniquely modern, *is really just the most recent manifestation of a recurring problem* [emphasis mine]. It thus is not a coincidence that administrative law looks remarkably similar to the sort of governance that thrived long ago in medieval and early modern England under the name of the 'prerogative.' In fact, the executive's administrative power revives many details of king's old prerogative power. Administrative law thus turns out to be not a uniquely modern response to modern circumstances, but the most recent expression of an old and worrisome development. Although the label 'administrative' is more comforting than the old term 'prerogative,' the danger is no less acute."[17]

In the Anglo-American tradition, government officials are supposed to be subject to the same laws as everyone else. But not under the administrative state, which insulates the bureaucrats from the rule of law. If a corporation were found responsible for poisoning a river, not only would the corporation be subject to civil and criminal penalties, but so would—at least in certain cases—the corporate officials responsible. Not so when the EPA did exactly that in 2015 when it accidentally dumped one million tons of toxic waste into the Animas River in Colorado.[18]

One argument that is often made in defense of the permanent bureaucracy in Washington is that it is "virtually" representative in some way. One version of this argument says that because the president is elected, his appointments have democratic legitimacy. And it is true that presidents typically appoint some 4,000 agency heads, commissioners, and the like. That alone should give one pause. We do not have a parliamentary system, and appointing thousands of commissars is a sorry substitute for one. The president, as Hamburger notes, is not a representative body, like Congress or the British Parliament. He is an executive charged with executing laws, not making them.

More to the point, the vast majority of the people who make law through administrative rulings are not picked by a president or any other elected politician. "Far from being elected by the people, let alone elected politicians, they are appointed by other administrators," Hamburger writes. "Their authority thus is not even virtually representative, but is merely that of a self-perpetuating bureaucratic class. Accordingly, the suggestion that their lawmaking comes with virtual representation is illusory."[19] Indeed, the idea that the state is an entity unto itself charged with advancing the wheel of progress isn't merely undemocratic; it is a form of mysticism.

Hamburger comes from a different direction, but as the passage above suggests, he comes to a familiar place for the reader who has been paying attention. The regulatory state represents the elevation of a new class, an aristocracy, of men and women who are above the law. This was the original intent of the progressives who set up the administrative state.

Without checks on the power of the shadow government, the shadow government has, predictably, grown in power, scope, and size. It shouldn't be necessary to document what must be apparent to the average citizen. Still: In 1960 the Code of Federal Regulations had 22,877 pages. It held relatively steady until 1963, the eve of the Great Society. Then, through the end of Lyndon Johnson's term, the code increased by an average of 5,537 pages per year.[20] In 2012 there were 174,545 pages.[21]

I could go on describing the byzantine bureaucracies within bureaucracies within bureaucracies that spider-web across the nation. But, again, no one disputes the growth in the size of the bureaucracy because it is indisputable. The point here is to see it for what it is, shorn of modern labels. It is a class, an aristocracy, a virtual tribe, that protects its parasitic interests. "Parasitic" is a loaded word, of course, but an appropriate one. One can even stipulate that the permanent bureaucracy does many good things. Our bodies are full of beneficial parasites we literally could not live without. But that doesn't change the fact that the parasites pursue their ends not out of altruism but out of self-interest.

One can also concede that various civil service reforms in the nineteenth and twentieth centuries addressed some of the very real problems with graft in American government by awarding government jobs based on merit instead of political contacts. But, by doing so, they basically enshrined a kind of gnostic moat around government. The bureaucracy behaved like a guild, rigging not just the rules for entry but for, in effect, lifetime tenure in their favor. As Hamburger puts it, "Civil service reform ensured that only the right sort of persons would be allowed into government, and it simultaneously secured them against being removed by those who were politically accountable to the people."[22] The progressives' ambitions were much greater than simply sweeping the broom of reform. And by protecting the civil service from the meddling of corrupt politicians, in theory progressives also protected them from honest and responsive politicians who want to make the government accountable.

Moreover, it is simply a fantasy that the administrative priesthood can be walled off from the seductions of human nature. The Turks and Chinese castrated their civil servants and still couldn't accomplish that. By comparison, a generous salary and a nice pension seem wholly inadequate to the task. No doubt, vast numbers of bureaucrats are decent and committed professionals. But the long history of humanity teaches us that any group of people walled off from accountability can become corrupted.[23] The scandals at the Department of Veterans Affairs are sufficient proof of that. You can falsify records and kill patients through bureaucratic subterfuge without getting fired, but if you call attention to such atrocities, that will get you terminated. "Our concern is really about the pattern that we're seeing, where whistleblowers who disclose wrongdoing are facing trumped-up punishment, but the employees who put veterans' health at risk are going unpunished," Carolyn Lerner of the U.S. Office of Special Counsel explained.[24]

Whether it was the goal or just the unintended consequence of progressives' actions, the result has been to create a new class of social engineers. The permanent bureaucracy is in reality a kind of permanent legislative, executive, and judicial branch, immune from the priorities of the people it allegedly serves. As John Locke noted, "Where the Legislative is in one lasting assembly always in being" there is always the threat that "they will think themselves to have a distinct interest, from the rest of the Community." While Locke acknowledged that the class interests of permanent legislatures could lead them to seek "to increase their own riches and power,"[25] his chief concern was that they would come to place their own interests and priorities over those of the people.

This is no small concern. Government officials are the only citizens—and they are citizens, not feudal lords—who are allowed by law to use violence for reasons other than self-defense. In this, a flunky from the IRS or the EPA is vastly more powerful than the Koch brothers. "The power which a multiple millionaire, who may be my neighbour and perhaps my employer, has over me is very much less than that which the smallest *functionaire* possesses who wields the coercive power of the state, and on whose discretion it depends whether and how I am to be allowed to live or to work," Friedrich Hayek observed.[26]

The bureaucratic wing of the new class has other special rights and privileges as well. For starters, its members are virtually unfireable. "Death—rather than poor performance, misconduct or layoffs—is the primary threat to job security at the Environmental Protection Agency, the Small Business Administration, the Department of Housing and Urban Development, the Office of Management and Budget and a dozen other federal operations," a study by *USA Today* found. In 2010, the 168,000 federal workers in Washington, D.C.—who are quite well compensated—had a job security rate of 99.74 percent. A HUD spokesman told *USA Today* that "his department's low dismissal rate—providing a 99.85 percent job security rate for employees—shows a skilled and committed workforce."[27]

Not to overly strain the analogy, but if the bureaucrats are a priesthood, the public sector unions are its Jesuits. Unions by their nature are first and foremost concerned with their own members' interests. Private sector unions often do not put the consumer's, never mind the employer's, well-being above their own, and public sector workers do not put the citizenry's interests first either. Many individual members of teachers' unions no doubt care about the plight of students, but there is remarkably little empirical evidence that they, institutionally, put the interests of children ahead of their own.

I've tried to avoid making explicitly partisan arguments, but attention must be paid to the insidious and incestuous relationship between the Democratic Party and government unions. It is no accident that the National Treasury Employees Union, which represents the IRS, gave about 96 percent of its political donations during the 2016 election cycle to Democratic candidates.[28] In 2016, the American Federation of Government Employees contributed about 93 percent of its political donations to Democratic candidates.[29] It is fine to argue that the wealthy support the Republican Party out of economic self-interest—even if the evidence for this is disputable—but is it really so ridiculous to imagine that a class of workers might be seduced by the same impulses? The new class is economically, ideologically, and psychologically invested in the primacy of government. It should not surprise us that its members would seek to protect that investment by supporting the party of government, particularly the shadow government.

Milovan Djilas, writing about the new class in communist countries, observed that "this new class, the bureaucracy, did not come to power to complete a new economic order but to establish its own and, in so doing, to establish its power over society."[30] There are obvious differences between the new class of, say, the Soviet Union and the United States of America. But beneath the ideological and culture distinctions, no matter how important, lies the unchanging fact of human nature. There is no limiting principle inherent to the idea that a caste of experts should be empowered to do whatever they think is right. The one idea even the most pragmatic bureaucrat will never contemplate is the suggestion that maybe we would be better off if he did not have a job anymore.

One more point must be made, or remade but emphasized. In its best and most sincere form, the argument for a "disinterested" permanent bureaucracy walled off from elected politicians hinges upon the claim that this is the only way to advance the public interest against private interests. The problem with this claim is that it is patently false on its face.

The branch of economics called "public choice" has demonstrated at length that in a system in which you have concentrated benefits and dispersed costs, a small number of agents with a lot to gain often, maybe even routinely, overpower the interests of the majority.[31] Democracies naturally tend to give special benefits to certain groups or constituencies. The groups care a great deal about these benefits, but the general public does not. The beneficiaries come to expect and depend on these "rents" and will fight with a passion to keep them, but there are few constituencies nearly as committed to getting rid of them. Over time, the special interests proliferate. The more they proliferate, the more the government sector grows but also becomes a kind of virtual tragedy of the commons, as it becomes clear to all others that they, too, must press for their own special benefits. (This is one reason for the incredible explosion of lobbying over the last forty years.)[32] Eventually, more and more of the government becomes dedicated to servicing special interests, and the ability of the government to deal with new or simply more pressing challenges narrows. Rather, the government gets better and more efficient at servicing the needs of clients while becoming clumsy and unresponsive to more important public problems. In short, the government becomes "sclerotic," hence the "sclerosis" in "Demosclerosis," a term coined by Jonathan Rauch in his 1994 book by the same name. Rauch defined "demosclerosis" as "government's progressive loss of the ability to adapt." This process has been identified in virtually every advanced democratic country.

The favor seekers "are acting not out of greed or depravity," Rauch writes, "but out of the impulse to survive in the world as they find it. Good intentions, or at least honest intentions, breed collective ruin."[33] Responding to complaints from lawmakers that so many businessmen and politicians were lobbying the Federal Communications Commission, the economist Ronald Coase replied, "That this should be happening is hardly surprising." He added that "when rights, worth millions of dollars, are awarded to one businessman and denied to others, it is no wonder if some applicants become overanxious and attempt to use whatever influence they have (political and otherwise), particularly as they can never be sure what pressure the other applicants may be exerting."[34]

One of the most famous examples is the mohair subsidy. Virtually nobody benefits from the mohair subsidy—implemented over sixty years ago—save producers of mohair, and yet it survives. It survives because the mohair lobby cares only about one thing, while the public cares about many, much more important things.

In fairness, the mohair subsidy—like the sugar subsidy and countless others—is primarily an indictment of Congress. But at least Congress is elected. The bureaucracy, which on its own terms is supposed to be walled off from special interests, is even more susceptible to special pleading, *precisely because* it is shielded from voters. A congressman who relentlessly provides earmarks or other favors for donors can be booted from office. But what of a bureaucrat?

Yes, a government official who takes a bribe can be fired, and it even occasionally happens. But that kind of corruption is trivial. The real corruption, the corruption that more directly stems from human nature, is when the regulator becomes so parasitically connected to that which he regulates that he cannot break the connection. Most public choice economists tend to call this "regulatory capture." There are many different kinds of regulatory capture, and it goes by many different names in the fields of economics and political science. The late, great political scientist James Q. Wilson, who preferred the term "client politics," argued in *Bureaucracy: What Government Agencies Do and Why They Do It* that it "occurs when most or all of the benefits of a program go to some single, reasonably small interest (and industry, profession, or locality) but most or all of the costs will be borne by a large number of people (for example, all taxpayers)."[35]

I have no objection to the term "regulatory capture," but I think the term "guild economics" is the most apt to highlight the true nature of what most concerns me. In medieval economies, as we've seen, political and economic interests were invested in existing economic arrangements. Innovation was an enemy because it unsettled not just the economic order but the social order as well. The key instrument undergirding guild economics was the granting of special rights or privileges by the crown. Now, as then, these grants often go by the term "license."

Rulers, in Europe, Asia, and the Middle East, granted licenses to virtually every kind of manufacture, trade, and craft. It was one of the king's (and queen's, emperor's, czar's, sultan's . . .) many prerogative powers. Sometimes these licenses were as much cultural or even theological. "Licensure is a special case of a much more general and exceedingly widespread phenomenon, namely, edicts that individuals may not engage in particular economic activities except under conditions laid down by a constituted authority of the state," writes Milton Friedman. "Medieval guilds were a particular example of an explicit system for specifying which individuals should be permitted to follow particular pursuits. The Indian caste system is another example. To a considerable extent in the caste system, to a lesser extent in the guilds, the restrictions were enforced by general social customs rather than explicitly by government."[36]

In Europe, guilds formed around these rights and privileges, and entrepreneurs could face a wide range of punishments, including death, for violating them. Guilds and the ruling nobility both benefited from this system and worked together for its perpetuation. The growth of "modern" commercial baking and ale brewing in England led to the ale and bread "assizes": statutes and roving courts assigned with enforcing them. From a progressive perspective, this was the beginning of the noble government tradition of assuring minimal safety and quality standards for food.

But as medieval historian James Davis shows, they were in reality a "*de facto* licensing system. In effect, the lords or corporations were exacting a percentage of the traders' profits." Many saw this as a "customary right," or what the Mafia would call "a piece of the action." The thirteenth-century "Seneschaucy"—office of the steward—advised that "without warrant from the lord no baking or brewing ought to take place on any manor," and in many places, particularly in the thirteenth and fourteenth centuries, lords explicitly gave actual licenses or imposed tolls for brewing.[37]

"During the fourteenth and fifteenth centuries in Germany even the urban poets of each little town were organized into guilds," notes Deirdre McCloskey. "Even in Scotland the corporation of Glasgow, to avoid competition, denied a young James Watt license to set up a workshop—he was driven, happily, to apply to the university, and there invented the separate condenser.

"Without permission from the guild you could not innovate in producing cloth and were unlikely to evade the monopoly unless you could set up your factory, as in England, out in the countryside," she continues. "If you wish nowadays to set up a new pharmacy in Holland you must apply to a town committee—composed of other, local pharmacists. Guess how many pharmacies there are in Holland."[38]

This is the purest form of regulatory capture and guild economics: when the members of the industry themselves become the regulator.

Such systems are ubiquitous and continuous from at least the thirteenth century straight through to today. The acclaimed legal scholar Walter Gellhorn pioneered the study of occupational licensing in his book *Individual Freedom and Governmental Restraints*. "Seventy-five per cent of the occupational licensing boards at work in this country today are composed exclusively of licensed practitioners in the respective occupations," he wrote . . . in 1956.[39]

The problem has only gotten worse in recent years. In the 1950s, less than 5 percent of workers were required to obtain official permission from the government, i.e., a license, to work. Today, 29 percent of U.S. workers need a license to earn a paycheck in their desired fields.[40] A government study conducted by the Obama administration found that the surge in occupational licensing "has been one of the more important economic trends of the past few decades. Today, one-quarter of U.S. workers must have a State license to do their jobs, a five-fold increase since the 1950s. Including Federal and local licenses, an even higher share of the workforce now has a license." To the administration's credit, it concluded that "by making it harder to enter a profession, licensing can reduce employment opportunities, lower wages for excluded workers, and increase costs for consumers."[41]

The perniciousness of occupational licensing is most acute in its capacity to keep millions of low-skilled, entry-level, and uneducated workers from entering the workforce. The Institute for Justice has been a heroic champion documenting and fighting this trend. Perhaps the most notorious example it has cast a light on is professional hair braiding for black women. Natural hair braiding requires no special chemicals, no scissors, heat, or any dangerous equipment of any kind. It is a skill that is traditionally passed from mothers to daughters. And yet thirteen states still require a cosmetology license to sell the service. Such a license takes up to 2,100 hours in "coursework" and up to $20,000 dollars in fees. Fourteen other states require a somewhat less onerous license for hair braiding.[42]

But this is just the tip of the iceberg. The Institute for Justice has a massive database of low-income professions that have set up guild protections barring carpenters, barbers, manicurists, makeup artists, milk samplers, fishers, fire-alarm installers, and many other professions that historically reward a good work ethic and provide a path to

202 SUICIDE of the WEST

a middle-class life for low-income workers.[43] One needn't be a liber-tarian purist on the subject to nonetheless be outraged by the general trend. Perhaps it is necessary for exterminators to have some state-sanctioned training, but do they really need four years of education (or two years working under another licensee), as required by the state of Tennessee?[44]

Contrary to the misperceptions of some, most businesses do not see it as in their interest to do bad work. An employer wants skilled employees and in most cases can be trusted to train them as required. Employers understand the importance of word-of-mouth referrals and professional reputation better than most. McDonald's trains inexperienced workers to handle food for millions of customers. Do we really believe that the safety of Big Macs would be dramatically improved by requiring teenagers to take a state-mandated course? Moreover, thanks to the advent of Internet rating systems—Yelp, Google, etc.—not to mention the ubiquity of informal reviews on social media—Facebook, Twitter, etc.—it is easier than ever for consumers to hold businesses accountable.

An industry that depends on the good graces—i.e., the concentrated benefits—of a regulatory agency will inevitably and unavoidably commit itself to parasitically attaching itself to that agency. The guilds supported the king because the king supported them. It can also work the other way around. "A regulatory apparatus is a parasite that can grow larger than its host industry and become in turn a host itself, with the industry reduced to parasitism, dependent on the subsidies and protections of the very government body that initially sapped its strength," George Gilder observed.[45]

Consider the taxi industry. In New York City, the taxicab business was hugely profitable because yellow cabs were granted a monopoly by the government. Yellow cabs even got a very medieval-looking official seal called a medallion. For decades, taxi medallions outperformed the Dow Jones Industrial Average, and even gold.

The reason they were so valuable? The city of New York froze the number of medallions and essentially held it constant as the population of New York—and the number of visiting tourists—exploded. Government-imposed scarcity was an enormous boon to the taxicab guild. In 2013 the total value of taxi medallions and related assets in

New York City was \$16.6 billion. (In Chicago it was \$2.5 billion.)[46] Such cartels—basically another word for guilds—maintained their monopolies in city after city. Then something changed—in a word, Uber. The company, along with other ridesharing innovators like Lyft, challenged the guild, for the most part successfully. For the first time in living memory, the price of a taxicab medallion is steadily declining, with little chance of recovering.

The example is worth sharing for three reasons. First, it's a pristine example of how guild economics is a conspiracy against the public. Second, it's an important example of how innovation, which can create losers, nonetheless is a net benefit for society—not just passengers, but also the thousands of drivers who were needlessly locked out of a profession for no good reason (back to that in a moment). And last, it demonstrates how quickly a parasitic bureaucracy—in this case the New York City Taxi & Limousine Commission—can become a host to a suddenly parasitic industry. Before the introduction of ridesharing, the commissions fed off the taxi industry. But when their host was threatened, the host became the parasite, running to the commissions to protect it from competition. The taxi industry is a notable example, not because this happened, but because it, for the most part, didn't succeed.

While that may offer a glimmer of hope about the beneficial changes that come with the creative destruction of the so-called gig economy, that hope fades when one realizes that such examples are few and far between. For every successful "disrupter" that puts a crack in the façade of the regulatory state, allowing us to see what might lie on the other side, there are a dozen examples of how that façade is getting thicker and more impenetrable.

At least in the medieval guilds it was understood that giving an inexperienced worker an apprenticeship—i.e., a shot at learning a trade—was something of great value. The wage, if there even was one, was trivial compared to the opportunity to learn how to be a blacksmith, mason, or tanner. That was the path to prosperity. First jobs, particularly for unskilled non-college-educated young workers, play the same role. If you work hard and learn the business at, say, McDonald's, you will likely be promoted to assistant manager before the year is out. That is invaluable experience. Raising the minimum wage above what employers can bear or to the level where hiring an iPad makes more sense is immoral, because it is tantamount to taxing entry-level jobs. If there is anything more settled in economics than the proposition that taxing an activity reduces that activity, I don't know what it is. To say that the minimum wage should be a "living wage" is to tell employers they must pay inexperienced workers above their value, and that is unsustainable.

Today the most powerful constituency lobbying for minimum wage hikes is the most obvious modern incarnation of medieval guilds: labor unions. Some unions favor hikes because they have contracts tied to the minimum wage. If it goes up, so do their far more generous wages. But there are more insidious reasons why unions are pushing the minimum wage. In California, for example, the Service Employees International Union and other unions lobbied for, and got, a "carve out" in the minimum wage law that allows union members to get paid less than the minimum wage. As the *Los Angeles Times* recounts, "Critics see such provisions as a cynical collusion between politicians and big-city labor interests. By making unions the 'low-cost option' for businesses seeking to avoid paying better wages, they assert, the exemptions are designed to drive up union membership— and revenue from dues—at the expense of workers."[47] The critics are right. The goal of labor unions has always been to do what is best for their members. But their first priority must be to have members in the first place.

Again, I think unions play an important and legitimate role in society. But, as with any other institution, their role goes from positive to pernicious once they enlist the state to achieve their ends. When that happens, unions become guilds and, in some extreme cases, indistinguishable from hereditary aristocracies. For instance, throughout much of Mexico, either by law, custom, or both, teachers unions enforce the rule that teaching jobs can be inherited (or sold). In Oaxaca, *Dissent* magazine reports, "36 percent of teachers have directly inherited their position from a close family member, as have nearly half the teachers who start their careers each year." This has created a kind of medieval black market where titles can be sold. "The scions of former teachers who do not wish to follow in their parents' footsteps can sell their places to the highest bidder."[48] When the government has tried to reform the practice, the militant teachers' guild has gone on strike, sometimes violently. "Throughout history," one striking teacher told the *Houston Chronicle* in 2008, "the sons of carpenters have become carpenters. Even politicians' children become politicians. Why shouldn't our children have the same right?"[49]

In this context, "sclerosis" is just another word for corruption, rot, decay, or entropy. In a natural environment, sclerosis (and its attendant symptoms) is one of the more natural ways in which humans and other animals die. I am not fond of metaphors that suggest society is an organism, but in this case it is apt. Guild economics is a sign of entropy and decay for the body politic. Such sclerosis has helped hasten the demise of empires from ancient Rome to the Soviet Union.

And the same force is eating away at much of the European Union and the United States. The World Bank tallies statistics on how long it takes to conduct business in various countries. In 2006, it took an average of 819 days to enforce a contract in Greece. In 2016 that number reached 1,580 days. At the beginning of Barack Obama's administration in 2009, it took 59 days in the United States to get a construction permit. In 2016, it took 81. Over the same period, the time it took to enforce a contract climbed from 300 days to 420 days. The cost of registering property (as a percentage of property value) has gone up nearly fivefold, from 0.5 percent to 2.4 percent.[50] New business formation—historically the source of most big job gains— has been cratering.[51] Regulations of the financial industry have served to protect the biggest banks, while the smaller community banks are being drowned in compliance costs they cannot afford.

There are reams of examples, statistics, and horror stories about what is happening to the national economy as corporatism and guild economics take hold. But there's a broader and simpler point to be made about what is happening to our *society*. "Class," explains Daniel Bell, "in the final sense, denotes not a specific group of persons, but a system that has institutionalized the ground rules for acquiring, holding, and transferring differential power and its attendant privileges."[52] James Burnham, one of the pioneers in the study of the new class, argued that there is a "historical law, with no apparent exceptions so far known, that all social and economic groups of any size strive to improve their relative position with respect to power and privilege in society."[53]

Think of the upper middle class and the truly affluent. They have consciously and unconsciously, through both the state and the culture, strived to make society more complex. Charles Murray and Richard J. Herrnstein, in their woefully maligned and misunderstood book *The Bell Curve: Intelligence and Class Structure in American Life*, argued that the Jeffersonian project of creating a meritocratic society where only native ability, virtue, and perseverance determine success has backfired. A "cognitive elite"—an aristocracy of good test takers—has emerged, and they, like any class, were rewriting the rules of the game for their own benefit.[54]

Even if you do not subscribe to their larger argument, this key point seems irrefutable. The upper class in this country is making the rules of the game more complex. And the problem with that can be simply stated: *Complexity is a subsidy.* The more complex government makes society, the more it rewards those with the resources to deal with that complexity, and the more it punishes those who do not. Judge Richard Posner made a remarkable confession upon his retirement from the bench. "About six months ago," Judge Posner told the *New York Times* in September of 2017, "I awoke from a slumber of 35 years." He "suddenly realized," in the words of the *Times*, "that people without lawyers are mistreated by the legal system."[55] He went on to explain that poor and poorly educated people had real grievances but the legal system had erected a system that was attentive to people with expensive lawyers and treated people with no lawyers at all as "trash." Posner is a strange creature, but can anyone not see how this insight speaks to far larger social patterns?

PEOPLE OF GOOD FAITH disagree about which resources or "capital" are key to success in life—political, financial, social, genetic, educational, professional, cognitive, or just plain old luck (which technically isn't capital). Those are all interesting disagreements, but utterly irrelevant to the point at hand. If you are lacking in any, most, or all of these kinds of intangible capital, the more complex the rules get, the more you are left out in the cold. A dumb rich person with good lawyers or social connections will always jump over the hurdles laid down by government more successfully than dumb poor people lacking lawyers or connections. In feudal societies, the dim-witted scion of a great family could negotiate his way around life quite easily, because the rules were set up for him to do so.

Some advantages are impossible to completely overcome. As we've seen, people will always do favors for friends and family over strangers. Attractive people will always have a leg up on unattractive people. One can minimize such advantages, but one cannot eliminate them. And to try would unavoidably lead to tyranny, for the state can never fully straighten the crooked timber of humanity.

"Over the past few decades, upper-middle-class Americans have embraced behavior codes that put cultivating successful children at the center of life," writes David Brooks. "As soon as they get money, they turn it into investments in their kids." That is right and proper. Indeed, that should be the mind-set of all parents. The problem is that we are setting up a system that makes it increasingly difficult for all parents to follow the same strategy. "Since 1996," Brooks notes, "education expenditures among the affluent have increased by almost 300 percent, while education spending among every other group is basically flat."[56] That spending gets results. And while the children of the affluent do get educated in the three R's, they are also being taught how to maneuver in a system rigged for the benefit of their faction, as it were. In other words, we're teaching to the test. I don't mean that upscale high schools have classes in social networking or the correct pronunciation of elite shibboleths. But they are getting that education all the same. They are also learning, as we shall see, a profound and sophisticated ingratitude toward the country they grew up in.

The administrative state, launched by Woodrow Wilson, is deeply invested in this project. And the more success they have, the more the arrogant and condescending elitism of the progressives becomes a kind of self-fulfilling prophecy. If you start from the assumption that people are too stupid to understand what's in their interest, and then you proceed to make society a byzantine maze of hurdles, the more likely it is that you'll be able to claim you're right.

All of the educated liberals who cannot fathom why so many

working-class Americans voted for Donald Trump need to undertake some vigorous moral—and policy—introspection. For modern progressives have not only helped set up a system that millions of Americans believe is dedicated to making their lives more difficult and their path to success more daunting; the progressives also heap scorn on them for complaining about it.

It is easy to point at Donald Trump and say the American body politic is rotting from the head down.

But the real rot is systemic. The shadow government of the new class has fortified itself against democratic accountability and is sawing off the ladder to success beneath it.

10

Tribalism Today
Nationalism, Populism, and
Identity Politics

T HE OLD AMERICAN IDEAL IS THAT ALL MEN ARE CREATED
equal and are masters of their fate, captains of their souls. It was,
in the words of Barack Obama, "a creed written into the founding
documents that declared the destiny of a nation."[1] It took a good deal
of time for that concept to include women, blacks, and other marginalized groups. But one of the reasons why women and blacks succeeded in changing the Constitution and American attitudes is that
they were appealing to that ideal, not rejecting it. It is always easier
to win an argument when you can truthfully tell your adversary he's
right in what he believes, just wrong in how he's applying the principle.

But America has other ideals too. And sometimes these ideals can
be in conflict. The other side of the coin to the conviction that the
individual is the master of his fate is the idea that every American *be
an American*. There is a healthy tension between these two principles.
The German-Americans of the eighteenth and nineteenth centuries
wanted to be Americans, but they did not want to abandon their
culture and language wholesale either. It is the difference between
enforced ghettos and free communities. No one should be barred
from fully participating in the American experiment on account of
ethnicity, race, or religion, but no one should be forced to forsake one's
heritage either.

The key to resolving this tension was twofold: liberty and time.
Giving individuals the freedom to make these trade-offs on their own
terms and giving society time to let the melting pot work its magic.
That magic depended on many things, but none was more important

than simple good manners. America has a culture as deep and rich as any other society, but Americans tend to think otherwise. When they travel abroad, they rub against the other cultures without realizing that the friction comes from the fact they brought their cultural expectations with them. In America, it is simply good manners to take individuals as you find them and not as representatives of some abstract group or classification. Accepting that is part of becoming an American. In other parts of the world, and for most of human history, it has been natural to treat individuals as a member of their tribe. In America, you're supposed to judge people by their character.

This cultural norm is as much a product of the Enlightenment as our Constitution, and arguably just as essential. The whole Enlightenment-derived idea behind the American founding is that America can turn Frenchmen, Italians, Germans, Chinese, Arabs, etc., into Americans—that is to say, a new people dedicated to the principles of the Founding and the culture of liberty it birthed. The appeal of this vision attracted millions of people from around the world eager to escape the deadweight of history, class, and caste in their native countries. My brilliant friend, the late Peter Schramm, liked to tell the story of his family's escape from Hungary in the aftermath of its failed revolution against Russian Communists:

> "But where are we going?" I asked.
> "We are going to America," my father said.
> "Why America?" I prodded.
> "Because, son. We were born Americans, but in the wrong place," he replied.[2]

We were once taught that, when America deviated from this ideal, it was a shameful betrayal of our best selves. When, for instance, the Supreme Court upheld the Chinese Exclusion Act in 1889, it agreed with the government that the Chinese "remained strangers in the land, residing apart by themselves," and that they were unlikely "to assimilate with our own people or to make any change in their habits."[3] I was always taught this was a dark moment in American history.

To be sure, American students are still taught that. We still believe that the government shouldn't exclude some groups based upon arbitrary prejudices. But the rest of the melting-pot formula is breaking down in three ways. First, we are now taught that the government should give special preferences to some groups. Second, as a cultural imperative, we are increasingly told that we should judge people based upon the group they belong to. Assimilation is now considered a dirty word. And last, we are taught that there is no escaping from our group identity.

Multiculturalism and identity politics ideologies contain within them myriad contradictions and inconsistencies, but as a broad generalization it is impossible to deny that our culture is shot through with an obsession with race, gender, and ethnic essentialness. "At a very young age, our children are being encouraged to talk about their individual identities, even before they have them," writes the political theorist Mark Lilla. "By the time they reach college many assume that diversity discourse exhausts political discourse, and have shockingly little to say about such perennial questions as class, war, the economy and the common good."[4]

If you can't see this, you are a rare bird, given that the current debate about the explosion of identity politics isn't whether or not it exists but whether it is good or bad. For that reason I will not drown the reader with page after page of horrible or hilarious stories from American campuses and left-wing media outlets (though the curious reader will find in the endnotes a micro-fractional list of examples that is at least somewhat illustrative of the point).[5] But I will offer a few examples that advance my argument that this turn to the tribalism of identity politics is poisonous to the American miracle.

Before I begin, I should recap the argument of this book: First, the rust of human nature is eating away at the Miracle of Western civilization and the American experiment. Second, this corruption is nothing new; nature is always trying to reclaim what is hers. But this corruption expresses itself in new ways in different times as the romantic spirit takes whatever form it must to creep back in. Third, the corruption can only succeed when we willfully, and ungratefully, turn our backs on the principles that brought us out of the muck of human history in the first place. The last point, which is the subject of the next chapter, is that the corruption has now spread, disastrously, to the right, not just in America but throughout the West.

But for more than a generation now, the best principles of the West have been under assault. Intellectuals are recasting the virtues of our system and making them vices. "Merit," the essence of the Jeffersonian ideal of an anti-aristocratic society, is now code for racism. "Whenever you hear someone (White or Black) oppose affirmative action with the 'merit plea,' you are listening to racism," explains Ibram H. Rogers, author of *The Black Campus Movement: Black Students and the Racial Reconstruction of Higher Education, 1965–1972.*[6] CNN commentator Van Jones has said that Republicans who desire a color-blind meritocracy have a racial "blind spot."[7] His colleague Ana Navaro—a liberal Republican—insists that a merit-based immigration points system is "absolutely racist."[8] Which would mean that Canada and Australia rank high on the list of racist nations.

Color-blindness is in fact a facet of not just meritocracy but also of the principle of universal equality. Perhaps Martin Luther King Jr.'s most famous line was that he dreamed of a world where people would be judged on the content of their character, not the color of their skin. The moral clarity and power of this appeal is what fueled the success of the civil rights movement. But the forces of identity have been trying to topple the idol of color-blindness for decades. "Colorblindness is the New Racism,"[9] proclaims one headline. "Color-Blindness Is Counterproductive," insists another.[10] A third: "When you say you 'don't see race', you're ignoring racism, not helping to solve it."[11] Ta-Nehisi Coates, the most celebrated author on the issue of race in decades, writes that "the [American] Dream thrives on generalizations, on limiting the number of possible questions, on privileging immediate answers. The Dream is the enemy of all art, courageous thinking, and honest writing."[12] The American Dream, he continues, is a "specious hope"[13] constructed out of "the progress of those Americans who believe that they are white."[14] That white progress is exploitation and violence, based, he says, in "plunder."[15] "'White America' is a syndicate arrayed to protect its exclusive power to dominate and control our bodies."[16] Coates's indictment is primarily of white people, not the Constitution or notions of merit, but his indictment of white people is more than broad enough to include a host of American institutions.

Feminists have more diverse and often convoluted arguments about merit, vacillating between appeals to merit and equality and claims of beneficial female uniqueness when convenience dictates. Before joining the Supreme Court, Justice Sonia Sotomayor repeatedly suggested that a "wise Latina" would reach "a better conclusion than a white male."[17] Long before debates about transgenderism became mainstream, female identity became severed from biology. It is perfectly fine to criticize former Alaska governor Sarah Palin as a flawed politician, but one would think it would be fairly easy to form a consensus around the claim that she is a *woman*. And yet, when John McCain picked her as his running mate in 2008, the response from feminists was to insist that ideological conformity negated gender conformity. A spokeswoman for the National Organization for Women proclaimed Palin more of a man than a woman. Wendy Doniger, a feminist academic at the University of Chicago, wrote of Palin: "Her greatest hypocrisy is in her pretense that she is a woman."[18]

Behind every double standard lurks an unstated single standard, and in virtually every identity politics campaign that standard is *power*. Whatever accrues to the net benefit of my group or to allied groups advances social justice. Thus, for example, in arguments over equal pay, feminists insist that statistical disparities are prima facie evidence of institutional prejudice against women. The principle they invoke is correct, but the disparities they cite don't make their case.[19] The claims hinge on statistical light shows that use aggregate disparities between male and female compensation to prove discrimination. There's a similar problem with the argument over women in science. Women tend not to go into the STEM fields in large numbers. A 2016 study found that only 18 percent of computer science majors were female.[20] This disparity, according to many feminists and diversity activists, can only be explained by systemic biases. It's certainly possible that such biases exist. But women are overrepresented in many other fields. Some 60 percent of postdoctoral biology degrees and 75 percent of psychology degrees go to women. Is there some plausible reason to believe those fields successfully purged their ranks of sexism but computer engineers remained a stubborn hotbed of patriarchal bigotry? As psychiatrist and science blogger Scott Alexander writes:

As the feminist movement gradually took hold, women conquered one of these fields after another. 51% of law students are now female. So are 49.8% of medical students, 45% of math majors, 60% of linguistics majors, 60% of journalism majors, 75% of psychology majors, and 60% of biology postdocs. Yet for some reason, engineering remains only about 20% female. And everyone says "Aha! I bet it's because of negative stereotypes!"[21]

As Christine Rosen of *The New Atlantis* puts it:

On the one hand, the argument goes, if there were no discrimination, women and minorities would be perfectly represented in every field proportionate to their numbers in the general population because there are no substantive differences between these groups and the white men who have long dominated certain fields (such as technology and engineering). At the same time, however, diversity ideology insists that women and minorities bring a special viewpoint and unique experiences to their work, and companies need this in order to thrive. In other words, they are especially valuable *because* they are different, and therefore favoring them in hiring is justifiable.[22]

For our purposes, the question of whether those choices have some grounding in biology or culture or both is a distraction. The more simple answer is this: Individual women made individual choices to pursue careers that appealed to them. When large numbers of free people make choices, expecting the aggregate results of those choices to be perfectly representative by gender (or race or ethnicity) is not only ridiculous but also sexist (or racist) because it assumes a uniformity of talent, interest, and drive for whole categories of people.

Unless, that is, you are someone who makes a living from exploiting these disparities. Few feminists complain about the comparative dearth of female sanitation workers, but they are happy to cite disparities at Google or in corporate boardrooms as proof of sexism. And the technique of their argument is consistent with the real aim: power, not policy. As a prominent feminist textbook explains, feminists measure gender equality by "the degree to which men and women have similar kinds or degrees of power, status, autonomy, and authority."[23] Jessica Neuwirth, founder and director of the ERA Coalition, insists that "the entrenched historical inequality between the sexes cannot be erased by the creation of a level playing field because the players themselves are at two different levels."[24] In other words, the state must intervene on behalf of women because merit is an unworkable standard. The intent of the employer or policy maker and the qualifications or character of the individual job seeker are irrelevant. It is the "system" itself that is corrupt and racist (or sexist). And the proposed remedy is almost always to bend the rules, to discard objective standards in favor of selective ones that arbitrarily designate some group to be entitled to special treatment. This is the logic of the state as an instrument of divine justice manifesting itself yet again.

ONE NEED NOT REJECT the entirety of arguments made by the prosecutors to see the problems with this approach. Freed slaves certainly did deserve forty acres and mule (at least!), as many post–Civil War Radical Republicans proposed. Similarly, the early affirmative action programs targeted specifically to blacks in the wake of the Civil Rights Acts have intellectual and moral merit. Of course, notions of merit and color-blindness can serve to mask conscious or unconscious biases on the part of employers, managers, and others. There are indeed structural problems in American law and culture that are worth addressing or discussing. The embryonic left-right consensus on criminal justice reform has a lot of promise, for example. But the argument being made by countless tenured radicals goes much further than a call for practical reforms. They seek to overturn the status of merit and color-blindness as ideals.

Stanley Fish, one of the pioneers of this project, is honest. The literary and legal scholar has made it plain that he considers objective and neutral standards, fair rules of the game, to be a mirage concealing the will to power of whites or the system or the European mind. Even reason is a con. According to Fish, there really is nothing called reason; there is simply argument and other contests of power. Whoever wins the argument gets to claim that reason validates his position. He writes that "like 'fairness,' 'merit,' and 'free speech,' Reason is a politi-

cal entity," an "ideologically charged" product of "a decidedly political agenda."[25] University of Virginia law professor Alex M. Johnson
contends that "the presumed norm of neutrality actually masks the
reality that the Euro-American male's perspective is the background
norm or heuristic governing in the normal evaluative context."[26]

Power politics is as old as politics. Coalitions of interests have vied
with each other for power in every political system ever created. It
would be easy to dismiss the identity politics of race, gender, and ethnicity as simple reinventions of the sort of coalitional squabbles that
defined American politics—and politics generally—forever. Germans
versus Anglos, farmers versus city dwellers, Catholics versus Protestants, everyone versus the Jews. And to be sure, some hucksters, like
Al Sharpton, are less devotees of Stanley Fish and more devotees of the
ward-heeling rabble-rousers common to big-city politics in the nineteenth and early twentieth centuries. But some differences of degree
become sufficiently large to become differences in kind. Racial and
gender identity have been abstracted, converted into a permanent
and immutable ideological category that claims there is no common
ground between groups save perhaps the common effort to overthrow
"white male privilege." Anything associated with the system that
white men created is discredited. Argument, grounded in reason, is
itself now a tool of oppression. And the unshakable faith that those
on the side of "social justice" are right has itself gelled into a kind of
tribal ideology.

The legendary French liberal theorist Raymond Aron commented
in 1957 that "the essentials of liberalism—the respect for individual
liberty and moderate government—are no longer the property of a
single party: they have become the property of all."[27] That is no longer
the case. On the left, and increasingly on the right, large swaths of
tribalists have forfeited their ownership stake in the liberal project.

THIS EFFORT TO DELEGITIMIZE classical liberal standards manifests itself every day on college campuses. When Swarthmore invited
left-wing philosopher Cornel West and conservative philosopher
Robert P. George—close friends and colleagues at Princeton—to
speak, many students were outraged. "What really bothered me is, the

whole idea is that at a liberal arts college, we need to be hearing a diversity of opinion," Erin Ching told the *Daily Gazette*, the school's newspaper. "I don't think we should be tolerating conservative views because that dominant culture embeds these deep inequalities in our society."[28] A student writing in the *Harvard Crimson* bemoans the ideals of "free speech" and "academic" freedom as systems of oppression. "When an academic community observes research promoting or justifying oppression, it should ensure that this research does not continue."[29]

When my *National Review* colleague Kevin D. Williamson and free speech activist Greg Lukianoff spoke on a panel at Yale on the virtues of free speech, many students were livid. The panel was interrupted by a student who shouted: "Stand with your sisters of color. Now, here. Always, everywhere." Some of the participants were spat on.[30]

Again, one could go on not just for pages but at book length documenting these bonfires of asininity at various elite universities.[31] And while it would be too generous to credit many of these individual students with an intellectually sophisticated or thought-through ideology, it's important to recognize that they didn't invent these ideas: They were taught them.

Again, this effort to enthrone liberal ideals is inseparable from a desire for power—power for professors, students, activist groups, Democrats, etc. Some of it is just conventional guild protection stuff: As we've seen, groups of any kind, once organized and established, guard their status jealously. Various professors specializing to the exclusion of almost everything else in the study of race and gender— but also diversity consultants, administrators, and various outside activist groups—have a vested interest in heightening racial and sexual grievances for the simple reason that they make a living from such things. Women's studies departments are not particularly popular, which is one reason women's studies faculty members are eager to create or exploit controversies that make their disciplines relevant. If you are a journalist who only knows how to churn out articles explaining why something is racist, the last thing you want to hear is that racism isn't as big a problem as you claim it is. The Southern Poverty Law Center once did important work identifying bigoted groups and policies around the country. Now it invents new categories of "hate"—so as to sweep conventional conservatives into its demonology—to justify its fund-raising and relevance.[32]

But the pursuit of power isn't merely reducible to careerism and profit. The more important dynamic, the one that makes this such an appealing ideology, is the desire to have authority over others, to control the terms of debate, and to establish yourself as the new authority on what is or is not legitimate. Every society since the agricultural revolution has created a priestly class that defines the scope of right thinking and right action. For millennia that role was played by actual priests. In modern society the new clerisy is increasingly to be found among the self-anointed class of academics, activists, writers, and artists who claim a monopoly on political virtue. They unilaterally get to decide who is to be anathematized or excommunicated for wrong thinking. And college campuses serve as their most formidable monasteries and citadels.

Indeed, free speech isn't merely emotionally painful ("triggering"); it is a threat to ideological hegemony. Identity politics has always been about the politics and psychology of power. By insisting that some questions cannot be asked, some ideas not entertained, the new clerisy is wielding power. The whole notion of creating "safe spaces" should be understood as an effort to control certain battle spaces in the culture war.

The clerisy changes the rules of what is permissible to say—or how to say it—in the same way Mao's Red Guard terrified their elders. The stakes may be lower on the Yale campus, but does anyone doubt that some students would love to march ideologically wayward professors around the quad in dunce caps? According to the Anti-Defamation League, Ben Shapiro, an Orthodox Jewish conservative, came in first on its list of anti-Semitic social media attacks from the alt-right. (I came in sixth.)[33] Nonetheless, when he spoke at Berkeley in 2017, he was widely attacked for being a white supremacist. Tariq Nasheed, a self-described "Anti-Racism Strategist," announced on Twitter: "Suspected white supremacist Ben Shapiro, who tries to mask his racist rhetoric by claiming to be Jewish, is in Berkeley now."[34] Ayaan Hirsi Ali, an atheist classical liberal who was mutilated in her native Somalia, and Maajid Usman Nawaz, a former Liberal Democrat politician in England, are committed opponents of Islamic extremism. But, according to the SPLC, they are now anti-Muslim bigots.[35] They are routinely banned, protested, and disinvited from speaking at college campuses on the grounds that students cannot be exposed to their injurious and dangerous "hate speech."

I was once invited to speak at Williams College by a group that called itself Uncomfortable Learning. The group chose that name because they knew that, if they tipped off students that they might hear conservative or libertarian views, the students would boycott the event. But because "Uncomfortable Learning" sounds so rebellious, and transgressive students assumed they'd be hearing things they already agreed with, the reaction from the audience when I spoke reminded me of my dogs' reaction when they think we're driving to the park, only to discover we're heading to the vet.

THE GREAT IRONY OF all this is that identity politics wins not by making compelling arguments but by exploiting the inherent decency of the American people, including, most ironically, liberal college professors who are terrified of being called racist, even when the accuser is a cynical opportunist, poltroon, or emotionally immature waif.

One needn't be absolutist about such things. The essence of serious thinking is the ability to make meaningful distinctions even when facile analogies can deceive us. Calling someone a "nigger" or "kike" is grotesque, and a campus administrator should have the power to discipline students who do so even if it limits their speech. But using an epithet is not the same thing as "punching someone in the face," as many students increasingly argue.[36] And it is different from making an argument that someone doesn't want to hear. One Yale student, somewhat infamously, argued that the "Master" of her dorm at Yale had oppressed her because he wanted to debate a (ridiculous) controversy about Halloween costumes. "He doesn't get it," she wrote. "And I don't want to debate. I want to talk about my pain."[37] The Master has since lost his job, and Yale has banned the use of the word "Master" to spare students further pain. (After all, slaves had "masters" too.)[38]

To listen to the activists at Yale, you might think the school was a hotbed of white oppression, willy-nilly excluding minorities from participation in campus life. When this "Master" controversy erupted in the fall of 2015, I took a look at the course offerings at Yale that year. By rough count, Yale offered at least twenty-six courses on African-American studies, sixty-four courses on "Ethnicity, Race and Migration," and forty-one courses under the heading "Women's, Gender, and Sexuality Studies." These are conservative estimates and do not include independent study. Meanwhile, I found two courses on the Constitution. A single professor teaches all of the courses on the Founding era: three. As for safe spaces outside the classroom and the dorm, I tallied an Afro-American Cultural Center, a Native American Cultural Center, an Asian American Cultural Center, La Casa Latino Cultural Center, and the Office of LGBTQ Resources. Plus there were nearly eighty organizations dedicated to specific identity groups in one way or another.[39] The same pattern holds at most elite colleges. The moral of the story: Appeasing identity politics demands, like all appeasement, simply leads to more and more demands.

OF COURSE, CAMPUSES ARE simply one front in the larger war. For decades, representatives of various identity groups have asserted authority over how to deal with, or even talk about, certain issues. This effort is ideological, but it is also cynical. "Diversity consultants" and similar specialists have a class interest in perpetuating a constant state of uncertainty about what constitutes racism, because such priestcraft gives them power, status, and income. For instance, it is a settled fact of social science that bilingual education hampers English learning and assimilation.[40] But for a politician to say so is to invite charges of racism or "insensitivity" from the anointed representatives of the "Hispanic community." What better way to prevent assimilation than to foreclose debate on the matter by simply declaring assimilation bigoted? No doubt many advocates believe it, but it's no coincidence that the bureaucrats and educators invested in the business of bilingual education benefit from censoring any competing point of view.

The most redeeming aspect of political correctness stems from the legitimate effort to create a code of good manners for a diverse society. We have a tendency to concentrate on the forms good manners take rather than the purpose of them. From prehistoric times until today, manners—ceremony, custom, etiquette, etc.—have simply been mechanisms for reducing unwanted conflict by showing respect, particularly to strangers. Some believe that the handshake was born by the need to show that one didn't have a weapon in hand. At its best, PC is a way to show respect to people. If black people don't want to be called "Negroes," it is only right and proper to respect that desire. If Asians object to "Oriental," lexicological arguments can't change the fact that it is rude not to oblige them.

The problem is that the ambitions of political correctness go much deeper than that, which is why activists are constantly changing the acceptable vocabulary. The clerisy doesn't own anything other than its monopoly over acceptable words. Clear, universal rules about acceptable terminology—i.e., what constitutes good manners—are a threat to that monopoly. And so the rhetorical ground underneath us is constantly shifting. When I was a trustee of my alma mater, a diversity consultant explained to the board that "tolerance" was no longer kosher, because it implied a certain kind of condescension. "Acceptance" was the new word of the moment. These days, "celebration" seems to be the new "acceptance." But there are enormous differences between "tolerance," "acceptance," and "celebration." "Tolerance" and "acceptance" acknowledge disagreement to one extent or another. The requirement to celebrate, however, is ultimately a form of psychological bullying. It says, "You must abandon your convictions and agree with mine." It is one thing to argue that a free society should accept gay marriage or allow people to define their gender in terms utterly unrecognizable to science. It is another thing to demand that individuals rejoice—or pretend to rejoice—in the lifestyles or decisions of others. But that is precisely what the jihad against "hate speech" demands. Dissent from the orthodoxy is now the equivalent of violence or complicity in it. The war on tolerance has become an effort to make room for a new intolerance.

Even democracy is now seen as a threat to tribal power politics. Support for democracy is eroding across the West, particularly among young people. Much of this has to do with the worldwide populist reaction to "globalism," as we'll see. But the tribal attack on democracy has been under way for a very long time. Consider Lani Guinier, the Harvard professor who briefly achieved celebrity status for her failed bid to run the Civil Rights Division of the Clinton Justice Department. Guinier argues in her book *The Tyranny of the Majority: Fundamental Fairness in Representative Democracy* and in various law review articles that the doctrine of "One man, one vote" needs to be jettisoned in favor a more "authentic" form of democracy. She proposes an idea inspired by her then four-year-old son, Nikolas: "Taking turns."[41] When Nikolas couldn't get a consensus among his friends about what the kids should play, they decided they should take turns deciding. Similarly "authentic minorities" should have a "turn" at representation even if their "authentic leaders" cannot win a majority of the vote.

Guinier places enormous emphasis on the term "authentic"; merely being black is not enough. One must represent the authentic spirit of the people, or what the Germans call *Volksgeist*, of the black community, as determined by those with the deepest investment in a specific definition of authenticity, like Ms. Guinier. "Authenticity reflects the group consciousness, group history, and group perspective"[42] of a specific "social group." "Authentic leadership" is not merely "electorally supported by a majority of black voters." The leader must be "politically, psychologically, and culturally black."[43]

"Authenticity refers to community-based and culturally rooted leadership. The concept also distinguishes between minority-sponsored and white-sponsored black candidates." She clarifies: "Basically, authentic representation describes the psychological value of black representation. The term is suggestive of the essentialist impulse in black political participation." She rejects the principle of color-blindness because it "abstracts the black experience from its historical context" and "ignores the existence of group identity within the black community."[44]

The upshot, as she makes clear at great length in unambiguous prose, is that blacks who are elected with significant shares of the white vote—like then Virginia Democratic governor Douglas Wilder—may not, and often do not, count as authentically black. This is where racial essentialism and political leftism intersect. According to many on the identity politics left, only left-radical politics are authentically black. This is why Justice Clarence Thomas doesn't count as black among so many black activists. Blacks are supposed to think a certain way, and if they do not, they are essentially inauthentic, or "Uncle Toms."

There are countless ominous echoes in these fundamentally romantic, tribalist ideas. Karl Marx believed that the Jew (and the Negro) had authentic natures rooted in psychology, history, and culture (and, in the case of blacks, biology). So did Joseph de Maistre. Needless to say, German nationalists had strong opinions about the essentialism of various groups. German nationalist intellectuals like Johann Gottfried Herder and Johann Fichte wrote at epic length about the essential psychological and cultural uniqueness of the German *Volk*. But perhaps the most interesting parallel is to the great champion of Southern slavery, John C. Calhoun. He argued that a "mere numerical majority" could not overrule a minority if the majority's decision conflicted with the core interests of the minority, i.e., slave-holding whites. Guinier even invokes Calhoun's theory of concurrent majorities as one possible remedy to the problem of "One man, one vote."[45]

Whatever parallel you want to draw, the conclusion is the same: This is not liberalism, rightly understood.

Guinier's views are actually relatively moderate compared to other champions of identity politics on the left. These days, there are whole academic departments dedicated to "Whiteness Studies." But this discipline is not analogous to "Black Studies" or "Hispanic Studies" or "Women's Studies." Those schools of thought are dedicated to the project of building up an identity, celebrating its uniqueness, and cultivating, essentially, a sense of nationhood. Whiteness Studies are dedicated to cataloging the illegitimacy and even the evil of whiteness. The syllabus at one university describes Critical Whiteness Studies as a field "concerned with dismantling white supremacy in part by understanding how whiteness is socially constructed and experienced."[46]

This sort of thinking has spilled out into the mainstream culture. Essentialism for Maistre was all about nationality. Now it is about ethnic or gender categories. As one black journalist recently put it on Twitter: "Yes, ALL white people are racist. Yes, ALL men are sexist. Yes, ALL cis people are transphobic. We have to unpack that. That's the work!"[47]

Again, one need not be categorically opposed to ethnic groups or other minorities flexing their muscles in a diverse society. That's a story as old as the country and is unavoidable in any society. The key distinction, once more, is that some within these groups are not merely fighting for their piece of the pie or for recognition of their legitimate interests. They are seeking to overthrow the ideals that made this country so successful in the first place. They are not merely arguing that the system needs to live up to its own ideals, which was the argument of the suffragettes and the civil rights movement. They are arguing that the ideals themselves are illegitimate.

The tragedy here is that liberalism—in the classic Enlightenment sense—is the only system ever created to help people break out of the oppression of identity politics. For thousands of years, nearly every society on earth divided people up into permanent categories of caste, class, peasant and noble, and, of course, male and female. The Lockean principle of treating every human as equal in the eyes of God and government, heedless of who their parents or ancestors were, broke the chains of tyranny more profoundly and lastingly than any other idea.

Does America fail to live up to that ideal? Of course. Every human and human institution fails to live up to its ideals. That is why we call them ideals. They are something to strive for. Every wife and husband who ever repeated a marriage vow has fallen short of their promise at one point or another. But that is not an argument for not trying to stay true to their oath. The devout Christian is the first to admit that he or she fails to live up to the injunction to be Christlike (1 Corinthians 11:1). But that entirely human failure is not an indictment of the Christian ideal. Even the greatest philanthropists will readily concede that they could be even more charitable. Does that discredit the good they do? Oskar Schindler, the man made famous by Steven Spielberg's *Schindler's List*, was overwhelmed with remorse that he didn't do more to save more Jewish lives during the Holocaust. But he did save more than a thousand of them, at great personal risk. Shall we declare him a villain in that chapter of humanity for doing good while falling short of perfection?

The original argument for diversity was a thoroughly liberal one, in the Lockean sense. Elite universities once discriminated against Jews, blacks, Asians, and women on the grounds that such institutions were a privilege reserved for white Anglo-Saxon Christians.

The argument for diversifying universities was purely an appeal to classic American principles of inclusion and meritocracy. Today, many universities as a matter of core policy and conviction discriminate in admissions against Asians, Jews, and whites on the grounds that the principle of diversity trumps any considerations about merit. When the University of California system was forced, against strenuous objections, to abandon racial preferences, the number of Asians admitted skyrocketed. They now make up a plurality of students, roughly one-third, even though Asians constitute only 15 percent of the state's population. Asian students made up 40 percent of the student population at UC Berkeley in 2012 and 43 percent of the student population at the California Institute of Technology.[48] Meanwhile, in elite universities outside of California, Asians need 140 more points (out of 1600) on the SAT to be admitted (while blacks need 310 points fewer).[49]

In order to defend this institutional discrimination, the clerisy must embrace doctrines of racial essentialism and authenticity. Lee Bollinger, then the president of Columbia University, famously stated:

> Diversity is not merely a desirable addition to a well-rounded education. It is as essential as the study of the Middle Ages, of international politics and of Shakespeare. For our students to better understand the diverse country and world they inhabit, they must be immersed in a campus culture that allows them to study with, argue with and become friends with students who may be different from them. It broadens the mind, and the intellect—essential goals of education.[50]

This is a fine sentiment. But it glosses over the fact that universities subscribe to a very narrow definition of diversity. Intellectual, ideological, and religious diversity take a backseat—sometimes a very distant backseat—to a very specific kind of bean counting. Beside the practical educational problems with racial quotas—promoting students above their ability, making it more likely they will drop out of college, for instance—there is the philosophical and moral problem. It makes racial essentialism into a permanent standard. The original justification for affirmative action policies was that they were a necessary bending of an ideal for special circumstances. "You do not take a person who, for years, has been hobbled by chains and liberate him, bring him up to the starting line of a race and then say, 'you are free to compete with all the others,' and still justly believe that you have been completely fair," Lyndon Johnson famously explained in his 1965 commencement address to Howard University.[51] The argument for bending the ideal of individual merit in 1965 was defensible, given the special history and conditions of African-Americans at the time. The doctrine of "diversity" for its own sake goes past bending to breaking the old ideal.

This highlights the power of words and how the new class intellectuals use them to change or undermine institutions. New class bureaucrats have not only expanded the definition of diversity to include other racial groups that had never been slaves or subjected to Jim Crow but have also arrogated to themselves the arbitrary power to decide what counts as "good" diversity, just as they assert authority over what constitutes acceptable language. When agents of the state and other officials have unilateral authority to change the ideal based upon their own political, aesthetic, or cultural preferences, they are substituting objective standards for their own arbitrary power, their own priestcraft.

ALL POLITICAL PARTIES are coalitional to one extent or another, but the Democratic Party has always been more coalitional than the modern Republican Party, which, since the rise of Goldwater-style conservatism, has been more ideological. To the outside observer, it might seem odd that the FDR coalition contained Klansmen, blacks, and socialist Jews. Even in recent years, it was not intuitively obvious why the party of same-sex marriage should also be the default party of the Teamsters.

Psychologically and ideologically, these alliances are often rationalized by progressive elites on the grounds that they are defending the defenseless victims of social prejudice. This makes some sense if you start from the romantic premise that traditional civilization is retrograde and oppressive and therefore those who want no part of it are oppressed. This kind of argument is routinely voiced in Europe by human rights activists, who have no problem attacking traditional customs and institutions but insist that non-Western religious or cultural minorities must be given the widest possible latitude: "Who are we to judge?" for the practitioners of Sharia, but judgmentalism as far as the eye can see for traditional Christians.

As a broad generalization, the practitioners of identity politics and their coalitional allies have leached off the inherent decency of this country and the constitutional order to press their advantages. To the extent that they have respected the rules while trying to undermine them at the same time, they have done so while living off borrowed capital. You can get away with a lot of illiberal theatrics and demands in a liberal society, and one of the great, eternal challenges for democratic governments is to figure out how much one can tolerate before the forces of illiberalism corrode the liberal order.

But tolerance is a two-way street. In a decent society, the majority owes respect to the minority. And the minority owes the majority respect as well. That bargain has fallen apart, most acutely in Europe, but America is not far behind, as the champions of identity have grown in power. The story has been embellished to the point where the majority are not cast as tolerant and decent citizens trying to figure out how we should live with one another; the majority are now simply villains.

In August of 2017, two law professors, University of Pennsylvania's Amy Wax and University of San Diego's Larry Alexander, penned an op-ed arguing that the breakdown in bourgeois values has led to much of the social discord and dysfunction of contemporary society. The bourgeois culture of the 1940s to 1960s laid out "the script we all were supposed to follow":

> Get married before you have children and strive to stay married for their sake. Get the education you need for gainful employment, work hard, and avoid idleness. Go the extra mile for your employer or client. Be a patriot, ready to serve the country. Be neighborly, civic-minded, and charitable. Avoid coarse language in public. Be respectful of authority. Eschew substance abuse and crime.

Wax and Alexander acknowledged the downsides of that era, but they also noted that bourgeois norms help the disadvantaged more than they help the wealthy, because the wealthy can afford their deviations. But, they note correctly, "all cultures are not equal" and bourgeois culture has benefits others do not.[52] A coalition of students and alumni responded to the essay in predictable fashion. Wax and Alexander were peddling the "malignant logic of hetero-patriarchal, class-based, white supremacy that plagues our country today. These cultural values and logics are steeped in anti-blackness and white hetero-patriarchal respectability . . ."[53] It goes on in that vein for a while.

It's all such nonsense. One has to wonder: If the Judeo-Christian and bourgeois norms of the 1940s and 1960s were so malignantly racist and sexist, how is it that the civil rights movement and feminism ever succeeded in the first place? America was far whiter, the government and leading institutions far more dominated by white men, and the society as a whole was far more religious in the 1960s than it is today. And yet the Civil Rights Acts passed (almost exclusively thanks to the votes of white males in Congress—a majority of them Republicans), universities became coed, and society became more tolerant and welcoming. Martin Luther King Jr. didn't demonize whites or the Founding; he appealed to the very ideals that are now declared illegitimate. He didn't vilify bourgeois values; he modeled them in public. He didn't denounce the Judeo-Christian tradition; the *Reverend* extolled them from his heart. And, by the way, why did the struggle for gay marriage succeed? Because it appealed not to radicalism but to bourgeois values about family formation.

It must be pointed out that this is not simply about rhetoric. The rhetoric yields reality. Anywhere these religious or bourgeois values come into conflict with the agenda of the new class, they must give way. The architects of Obamacare insisted that nuns—nuns!—must pay for birth control and abortion coverage. In Massachusetts, Boston's Catholic Charities closed down its adoption services because the state told it that if it wanted to find homes for orphans, it needed to place them with same-sex couples.[54] I'll spare the reader all of the controversies over transgender bathrooms, bakers being forced to make cakes for same-sex weddings, forcing the Marines to accept women, and the like.

Whatever one thinks about the merits of these individual policies, the larger point still stands. Under the progressive view of the state, tolerance only has one meaning: bending to a single vision of the culture. When activists say, "If you're not part of the solution, you're part of the problem," they are saying there are no safe harbors in the culture, no rights of exit from the agenda of "social justice." The Nazis borrowed the term *Gleichschaltung* from engineering to describe a doctrine whereby every institution, every Burkean "little platoon," must coordinate with the state or be crushed. My point here is not to single out the role of the state but to emphasize the larger climate of power politics.

As Alexis de Tocqueville most famously argued, our liberal order depends upon mediating institutions, or what he called "associations," that create and enrich the space between the individual and the state. These institutions—families, churches, businesses, schools, sports teams, charities, the Boy Scouts and Girl Scouts, etc.—are the microcosms that provide meaning for individuals in the larger macrocosm of the nation. By their nature, they must be culturally distinct in some meaningful way if they are to be "sticky." It is the cultural distinctiveness—the quirks of theology, custom, and mission—that appeal to some people and leave other people cold that provide members a sense of community, belonging, and meaning.

African-Americans understand this implicitly and often express it with great eloquence when it comes to their own historic institutions, both physical and cultural. Historically-black colleges have a rich and laudatory history in America. The black church has been a heroic spiritual, cultural, and political bulwark and safe haven. Jews, likewise, have an incredibly rich collective consciousness of not just the role their religion plays but the myriad customs that give their lives meaning and that have kept them culturally and religiously intact over millennia. The same goes for virtually every ethnic minority and identity group, from gays to the Amish to the deaf. Within broad parameters, there is nothing wrong with any of this, and very much that is right. The key to a thriving civil society is a multiplicity of institutions where diverse groups of people can find a home.

The one hitch is that you must have the "right to exit." Individuals must have the ability to leave communities and other institutions that do not serve their interests. The miserable, abused wife must be allowed to leave the marriage. The non-believer must be able to walk out of his church, mosque, or temple. The worker must be allowed to leave her job. The right to exit is not absolute. The soldier cannot desert his unit without paying a price. Divorce laws can be written in a way that allows for "cooling-off periods." Children cannot wander off in a huff. Employees can be held to account for contracts they voluntarily signed. But individuals must have the ultimate authority to say "this is not for me," and institutions must be allowed to have some cultural "stickiness" if they are going to be able to do their job. And that stickiness can only come from a certain degree of cultural distinctiveness that runs somewhat counter to the mainstream culture. What is true of the hippie commune and gay chorus is also true of the Catholic nunnery and the Boy Scout troop.

There was a time when the right to exit wasn't the problem, but the right to enter was. Jim Crow laws and sex and religious discrimination policies were immorally exclusive. The country had a series of big, democratic arguments about these barriers, and those arguments were consistent with the Western tradition, not in defiance of it.

Unfortunately, progressives could not take yes for an answer. The failure of ubiquitous and total equality to materialize overnight was seen as proof that classically liberal, color-blind policies were not enough, particularly among a whole class of activists who made a career of exaggerating the nature of the problems so as to justify their own status and power. Psychologically, the romantic desire to fight oppression, to be a person of radical commitment, was unfazed by success after success. Social justice has become an industry unto itself. Progressivism now lacks a limiting principle for governmental and social action. There's always more work to be done, more injustice to be identified—or imagined—and then rectified. As Democratic senator Chris Murphy said in a moment of jubilation when the effort to repeal the Affordable Care Act failed: "There is no anxiety or sadness or fear you feel right now that cannot be cured by political action."[55] This is a description not of politics but of religion.

Social justice warriors do not seek to simply destroy existing traditional Western culture (or what's left of it); they seek to create a new culture, or what Hillary Clinton called a "new politics of meaning."

On its best terms, this can be a defensible vision of social democracy, multiculturalism, and secularism. But that vision is almost entirely theoretical. Quite literally, it has simply never been tried on anything like the scope its proponents are attempting, save in places like the Soviet Union. And as that catastrophic experiment demonstrated, whenever you try to replace well-established cultural norms and traditions with an abstract new system, you do not open the door to a new utopia; you open the door to human nature's darker impulses.

Among the greatest benefits of old institutions is that they are old. Old trees can weather a storm that uproots saplings. Any institution that has been around for a long time has, through a kind of evolutionary adaptation, learned how to cope with crises. The Catholic Church has endured for more than 2,000 years, and in that time it has learned a few things. Judaism has been around for roughly twice as long, which at minimum speaks to the resources Jews have developed to survive.

The Japanese monarchy, the oldest continuous monarchy, dates back to 660 B.C. There is a reason the current Japanese constitution describes the emperor as "the symbol of the State and of the unity of the people."[56] In the literal ashes of World War II, the Japanese could still look to the emperor as a reassuring symbol of communal meaning.

What is true of nations is also true of institutions. Anyone who has relied on church or family during a personal storm understands how rooted institutions provide us not only physical shelter but, even more important, emotional, psychological, or spiritual shelter. We lash ourselves to these oaks of the culture. Chopping them down with the aim of building a perfect society is the perfect recipe for destroying a good society. Because when you destroy existing cultural habitats, you do not instantly convert the people who live in them to your worldview. You radicalize them. This is a point many on the left understand very well when it comes to American foreign policy. They are among the first to argue that nation building or "imperialism," invites a backlash. The war in Iraq did not deliver democracy, they argue; it delivered ISIS.

But when it comes to domestic cultural imperialism, many of the same people have a blind spot. They see nothing wrong with forcing Catholic institutions to embrace gay marriage or abortion. They think the state should force small business owners to celebrate views they do not hold. They brand any parent or institution that resists allowing men to use women's bathrooms as bigots. They constantly change the rules of our language to root out disbelievers so they can hold them up for mockery. In June of 2017, Senator Bernie Sanders voted against the confirmation of Russell Vought, President Trump's nominee for deputy director of the Office of Management and Budget. Vought had written that Muslims were not "saved" because they do not accept Jesus Christ.[57] This is not a radical interpretation of Christianity. It *is* Christianity. "I would simply say, Mr. Chairman, that this nominee is really not someone who is what this country is supposed to be about," Sanders said. "I will vote no." In other words, a faithful Christian cannot serve in government, according to Sanders. He has no such policy for Muslims who hold a very similar view toward Christians.[58]

Sanders's office issued a statement clarifying his position: "In a democratic society, founded on the principle of religious freedom, we can all disagree over issues, but racism and bigotry—condemning an entire group of people because of their faith—cannot be part of any public policy." This is correct on its face. No *public policy* can discriminate against someone on the basis of faith. But there was no evidence whatsoever that Vought would discriminate against Muslims at the OMB. Meanwhile, Sanders's own policy is that no one who actually believes in Christian doctrine has a right to make policy.

Later that same summer, Senators Dianne Feinstein and Dick Durbin interrogated a judicial nominee, Amy Coney Barrett, about her Catholic faith, insinuating time and again that one cannot be a devout Catholic and a judge. "Dogma and law are two different things," Feinstein said. "And I think whatever a religion is, it has its own dogma. The law is totally different. And I think in your case, professor, when you read your speeches, the conclusion one draws is that the dogma lives loudly within you, and that's of concern . . ."[59]

You can agree with Sanders, Feinstein, and Durbin if you like, but ask yourself, How do you expect believing Christians to respond to this? Will they instantly embrace this radical reinterpretation of our Constitution—which would have barred every president we've ever had from the office (to the extent that they were all truthful when they said they were Christians)—or would they feel like Sanders is trying to take their country away from them? No doubt there is a diversity of responses among even the most orthodox Christians to Sanders's views, but can anyone doubt that many would take offense?

IT IS A CLICHÉ of the left to say that "perception is reality." Well, the perceived reality for millions of white, Christian Americans is that their institutional shelters, personal and national, are being razed one by one. They do not like the alternatives they are being offered. Some fraction may indeed be racists, homophobes, or Islamaphobes, but most simply don't like what they are being offered because they do not know it or because they do know it but prefer what they perceive to be theirs. And yet people like Sanders insist that resistance to their program is not just wrong but evil.

The grave danger, already materializing, is that whites and Christians respond to this bigotry and create their own tribal identity politics. I don't think the average white American is nearly as obsessed with race, never mind invested in "white supremacy," as the left claims. But the more you demonize them, the more you say that "whiteness" defines white people, the more likely it is white people will start to defensively think of themselves in those terms. Some liberals will— and do—embrace a self-hating creed. Recall that Robert Frost said a liberal is a man so broad-minded he won't take his own side in an argument. But most white people will respond differently. They will take the identity peddlers' word for it and accept that whiteness is an immutable category. White working-class voters who said that they felt like "strangers in their own land" were 3.5 times more likely to vote for Trump.[60] In 2016, the more aggressively a person embraced the white identity, the more likely that person was to vote for Trump.[61]

Now, one last essential point needs to be made. Neither the left nor the state is entirely, or even in some cases primarily, to blame. Capitalism itself is a big part of the problem. The creative destruction of capitalism is constantly sweeping away traditional arrangements and institutions. The thriving communities that grew up around the steel and coal industries, only to be denuded by market forces, are just two obvious examples of how capitalistic innovation unsettles the status quo.

Whenever misfortune befalls us, we are instinctually inclined to assume there was agency behind it. Someone must be responsible! The ruling classes! The industrialists! The Globalists! The New Class! Immigrants! (And for generations of bigots: the Jews!) And while some of these actors may deserve some blame, in some sense the real demon lurking in the shadows is change itself. Populist demagogues promise not only that they have the answer to ease the pains of change ("Free silver! Tariffs! Share the wealth! Build a wall!"), but that they will punish the culprits responsible. Such promises are a thick miasma of snake oil containing healthy portions of nostalgia, demonization, and scapegoating.

Such siren songs—whether from technocrats or demagogues— are inevitable by-products of capitalism. That's because innovation and efficiency maximization are at eternal war with "the way we've always done it." Capitalism arouses in us feelings of nostalgia for an imagined—and, in some cases, actual—better past when people knew their place in the universe, and their work and their identity were inextricably intertwined.

Here lies the eternal tension inherent in Enlightenment-based societies. The extra-rational institutions of family, faith, and community in all their forms are in constant battle with the force of change and the sovereignty of the individual. Our inner Rousseauians crave community and group meaning. Our inner Lockeans demand that we be given the tiller in finding our own fate. Because capitalism is unnatural and government (broadly understood) is natural, we constantly look to the state to fix the very real problems and anxieties that inevitably emerge from capitalistic destruction.

No one wants to be replaced by a machine or told that her work is no longer valued. It is here where the left often has the better part of the argument, for they at least recognize the havoc that the market can wreak on those left behind. Donald Trump was not the first to appeal to the "Forgotten Man." He appropriated the phrase—without credit, of course—from Franklin Roosevelt, who argued that "better the occasional faults of a government that lives in a spirit of charity than the consistent omissions of a government frozen in the ice of its own indifference."[62]

The Luddites had a point. The Industrial Revolution destroyed whole ways of life for English communities. And while we should be grateful for the Industrial Revolution, one can understand why the immediate victims of it were not inclined to say "Thank you." Their rage as they saw this new system like a tornado razing their villages was wholly understandable.

But while we can concede the obvious merits of Roosevelt's views, there remains an inherent defect in this thinking. And it is at once a practical and a philosophical objection. When can you know? When can the neo-Luddites or the technocratic liberals know that the forces of creative destruction are not to the ultimate benefit of mankind or the nation? So far, the evidence is overwhelmingly on the side of innovation. When do you think we should have frozen technological progress? Would we have been better off if Rousseau went back in time and stopped the first man who put a fence around a piece of land and called it his own? Perhaps not. What about in Byron's age? When life expectancy in England was forty years,[63] and when as late as 1851, more than a third of all boys aged ten to fourteen worked, as did about a fifth of all girls?[64] Should we have frozen the economy during the 1950s? The wages were good, but life expectancy was sixty-five[65] and countless diseases were a death sentence.

The larger problem is that any attempt by the state, or an outraged populist movement, to suppress innovation and more humanely or rationally plan the economy inevitably leads to restrictions on our liberties. No doubt some are easy to tolerate and even welcome. (For instance, it bothers me not a whit that the state makes it difficult for consumers to find child pornography.) But economic liberty is ultimately inseparable from liberty. Socialist society, as Robert Nozick famously put it, must "forbid capitalist acts between consenting adults."[66]

The rising tide of protectionism in this country and across the West is merely the most obvious symptom of the larger malady. We live in a moment of ingratitude. Thankfulness is wanting, not just in regard to capitalism, but in regard to democracy itself. In our romantic rage against the machine, we do not differentiate between causes. The state gets blamed for the faults of capitalism. Capitalism gets blamed for the faults of the state. And everywhere we are told that it doesn't have to be like this and that some other tribe is responsible for our ills. And so we build coalitions of tribes determined to dethrone the authors of our misfortune.

This is the prologue to the story of Donald Trump's victory and the rise of the "alt-right." It is also the context for the ascent of Marine Le Pen, the victory of Brexit, and the new global crusade against "globalism." In the face of the staggering rebuke to the progressive project, we see progressives on their hands and knees searching amidst the wreckage they created, searching for the ideals they were all too happy to smash when they were in power.

11

Pop Culture Politics
Godzilla, Rock & Roll, and the Romantic Spirit

And their children wept, & built
Tombs in the desolate places,
And form'd laws of prudence, and call'd them
The eternal laws of God.

—WILLIAM BLAKE, *THE FIRST BOOK OF URIZEN* (1794)[1]

The fate of our times is characterized by intellectualization
and rationalization and, above all, by the disenchantment of
the world.

—MAX WEBER, *SCIENCE AS A VOCATION* (1917)[2]

"DON'T WRITE ABOUT ROMANTICISM."
    In the course of working on this book, I heard that advice—if not always in those words—from my wife, a brilliant writer and editor; my actual editor (who cleaved the original manuscript in half); and any number of trusted friends. Sometimes they just said it with their eyes. There's something about the word "romanticism" that elicits both an eye roll of the soul and a reflexive crouch of the mind. *What is romanticism again? I had to learn about that in college, but I never really got it.*

The academics haven't helped. It's a term that has been stretched and twisted like taffy. No word, not even "fascism," has proved more difficult to define, particularly among the scholars who study it.[3] For starters, every country has its own kind of romanticism, because romanticism expresses itself in the language and culture in which it appears. Thus, romanticism is often found everywhere and nowhere depending on whom you listen to. Adding to the problem, romanticism often manifests itself most acutely as a rebellion against definitions, distinctions, and classifications. The romantic is usually quick to say, "Don't label me, man."

Even Isaiah Berlin began his seminal 1965 A. W. Mellon lectures on the "Roots of Romanticism" by declaring he wasn't going to make that blunder. "I might be expected to begin, or to attempt to begin, with some kind of definition of Romanticism, or at least some generalisation, in order to make clear what it is that I mean by it. I do not propose to walk into that particular trap."[4] In 1923, the philosopher Arthur O. Lovejoy gave a lecture to the annual meeting of the Modern Language Association of America titled "On the Discrimination of Romanticisms." After getting some laughs by recounting all of the different people who'd been declared "the father of Romanticism"— Plato, Saint Paul, Francis Bacon, Immanuel Kant, etc.—he then listed all of the different kinds of romanticism and declared: "Any attempt at a general appraisal even of a single chronologically determinate Romanticism—still more, of 'Romanticism' as a whole—is a fatuity."[5]

In his acclaimed book *Bobos in Paradise: The New Upper Class and How They Got There*, David Brooks argues that modern American culture is suffused with romanticism. But perhaps because he was better at taking editorial advice, he rejected the term in favor of "bohemianism." "Strictly speaking, bohemianism is only the social manifestation of the Romantic spirit," Brooks writes. "But for clarity's sake, and because the word Romanticism has been stretched in so many directions, in this book I mostly use the word bohemian to refer to both the spirit and the manners and mores it produces."[6]

Given the success that book had, maybe I should have listened to those warning me off from romanticism. But I'm sticking with it because, as a historical and social phenomenon, it's the better term. No one talks about "Bohemian nationalism." So herewith I will offer some notes toward a definition.

As we saw in the early discussions of Rousseau, romanticism is often described as a rebellion against reason, and it often is. Others describe it as the primacy of emotions and *feelings*. That gets closer to it, I think. The emphasis on feelings certainly explains why romanticism's first and most powerful expression was artistic.

The Age of Reason was a revolution not just of the mind but of the whole of society. And for many, it felt like an invasion. In Germany and large swaths of Europe, that feeling was literally true. Romanticism, Joseph Schumpeter noted, "arose almost immediately as a part of the general reaction against the rationalism of the eighteenth century that set in after the revolutionary and Napoleonic Wars."[7] The poets—and painters, and novelists—were the frontline soldiers in the human soul's great counteroffensive against the Enlightenment. William Blake, the great romantic poet, loathed everything that John Locke and Isaac Newton bequeathed to the world. When Blake proclaimed, "A Robin Red breast in a Cage / Puts all Heaven in a Rage,"[8] the cage he had in mind was the Enlightenment. It wasn't quite the humans versus the machines; it was more like the champions of the soul against the promoters of machine thinking.

I happen to think the romantics were on to something. Even sticking to my promise to keep God out of this book, I believe that there is more to life than what can be charted, graphed, or otherwise mathematized. And these things are important. What we imbue with significance is in fact significant; there is meaning to the meaning we impose on things.

IT IS MY ARGUMENT in this chapter that the romantic era in our culture—including that slice we call popular culture—never ended. It has ebbed and flowed, I suppose, but it has always dominated much of what we call popular culture. And today it essentially defines our shared culture. In fact, "shared culture" might be a better term for popular culture because popular culture is seen as for the masses, when the truth is that almost everyone, rich and poor, goes to the movies, watches at least some popular TV shows, and is at least somewhat familiar with pop music. Class differences explain far less than age differences when talking about different tastes in popular entertainment.

The main reason I think the romantic era never ended is that it wasn't an era; it was a reaction. Until the scientific revolution and the Enlightenment, humans did not, as a rule, divide the world into secular and religious, the personal and political, reason and superstition. Science was magic and magic was science for most of our time on this earth. The ancient Roman priests who studied the entrails of birds to predict the future weren't asking anyone to make a leap of faith. This was sound science. And it was magic. And it was religion. Scholars have debated the strange and often beautiful relationship between magic and science for a very long time. Was medieval magic rational? Anti-rational? Non-rational? Were the alchemists just the first chemists?[9]

The Protestant Reformation, the Enlightenment, and the scientific revolution are widely credited with giving birth to a more secular and less superstitious world. All of that is true enough. But the process was more complicated than it may seem. The image at the heart of the Enlightenment is *light*—the idea being that science and reason banished the shadows of ignorance. But that metaphor is misleading when it comes to the human mind. The Enlightenment was really more like the Unbundling. In the medieval and primitive mind, science, magic, religion, superstition, and reason were all more or less fused together. The pieces started to separate with the Protestant Reformation, when magic and religion started to be considered unrelated things. Then science and religion drifted apart from each other. Then, after the Enlightenment, traditional religion and politics split off.

The pre-modern mind was like an enormous iceberg entering new waters, and as it got closer to the modern period, huge chunks calved off. But here is the important point: The chunks don't melt away, at least not completely. They just become smaller icebergs. The scientific revolution did not get rid of religion. The Age of Reason did not banish superstition. One need only look around to see that religion and superstition (not the same thing) endure. The triumph of reason didn't mean turning us all into Vulcans from *Star Trek*, slaves to cold logic. (Indeed, even Vulcans have emotions; they just work very hard to keep them in check.) Rather, after the Enlightenment, priority was increasingly given to reason in law, public arguments, and most institutions, at least most of the time.

That's what is so funny about the at times visceral hatred for Isaac

Newton among the early romantics (second only to their hatred for John Locke). To Blake and Coleridge and other romantics, Newton's physics had demystified the cosmos and our place in it, thus paving the way for a mechanistic and soulless universe. But for all of Newton's monumental contributions to science, he was, at heart, a mystic. He was more interested in alchemy than in gravity. He saw himself as an explorer of the occult, determined to rediscover the lost magical secrets of the ancients. As John Maynard Keynes once put it, Newton wasn't the first scientist; he was the last of the magicians. Thomas Edison and Alexander Graham Bell regularly attended séances. Edison tried to invent a phone to talk to ghosts. Guglielmo Marconi, the inventor of the radio, wanted to do the same thing using radio waves.

Today, neuroscientists and psychologists fill their days documenting the ways the human mind acts irrationally.[10] Our animal brains have programs and subroutines designed to keep us alive, not to determine the truth. The ability to reason is an important tool for survival. But is it more important than fear? Anger? Loyalty? Remember, for primitive man, survival was a collective enterprise, and the cognitive tools we developed were far more varied and complicated than simply rational. For instance, a superstition or taboo about the importance of cleanliness may be passed from one generation to another for a thousand years without a single shaman, priest, or parent making any reference to microbes or germs. But the group that follows prohibitions against eating unclean food has an evolutionary advantage all the same. Similarly, groups that adhere to notions of retributive justice—both internally for traitors and externally for strangers—will be more likely to pass on their genes. More broadly, groups that have a coherent vision of group meaning—religious, political, social, etc.— will likely be more successful at cooperating, and cooperation is the core evolutionary adaptation of humanity.

The Enlightenment didn't erase these apps from our brains. They're running all the time, generating emotional, instinctual responses to events and ideas that we sometimes recognize as part of our baser natures, and that we sometimes mistake for some higher ideal. Romanticism's emphasis on emotion and the irrational, the significance of that which cannot be seen or explained through science but can be felt intuitively, is the tribal mind's way of fighting its way back into the centrality of our lives. My argument here is that popular culture gives us the clearest window into the romantic dimension that we all live in. To demonstrate this, I will focus on some of the classic hallmarks of romanticism. But it needs to be emphasized that popular culture isn't romantic because of the lasting influence of some romantic writers and poets (though some influence is surely there). Popular culture is romantic because Enlightenment-based society naturally invites a romantic reaction; we crave the unity of meaning that we have lost, and we yearn for the enchantment purged from everyday life.

IT'S ONLY ROCK AND ROLL (BUT I LIKE IT)

I believe I could make this case almost entirely by looking at rock and roll—and rock and roll alone. My claim is not so much that there are elements of romanticism in rock and roll, but that *rock and roll is romanticism.* In fact, I suspect one could say something similar of popular music generally, so as to include hip hop and country music as well. What are the key themes of rock and roll and these other genres? Any list would include: defy authority and throw off the chains of "the Man," true love, damn the consequences, nostalgia for an imagined better past, the superiority of youth, contempt for selling out, alienation, the superiority of authenticity, paganism and pantheism, and, like an umbrella over it all, the supremacy of personal feelings above all else.

Rock and roll, from its most commercial forms to its most authentic, fancies itself as outside "the system." It claims a higher or truer authority based in feelings that, like the poets of earlier generations, defy the tyranny of the slide rule and the calculator. Its more grandiose champions put rock on a par with all of the higher forces, like a Titan or a god in eternal battle with the tyrannical deities of the system. "Christianity will go," John Lennon assured us. "It will vanish and shrink . . . We're more popular than Jesus now—I don't know which will go first, rock and roll or Christianity."[11] "You see," U2 guitarist The Edge tells us, "Rock and roll isn't a career or hobby—it's a life force. It's something very essential."[12]

Robert Pattison, in his *The Triumph of Vulgarity: Rock Music in the Mirror of Romanticism*, argues that rock and roll is vulgar both in the classic sense—"vulgar" is derived from the Latin *vulgus* meaning crowd or the common people—and in the snobbish sense of being crude. Because rock is democratic, it appeals to us all and makes no pretension to higher culture or higher ideals. It speaks to the gut, the pantheistic primitive in all of us. By now the reader should have a good sense of what the primitive is, but pantheism requires a bit of explication. Pantheism, from the Greek *pan* (all) and *theos* (god), is the belief that all of reality is divine, and that God (or gods) suffuses us and everything around us. Earth is heaven and heaven is earth.

Is there any art form that is more successful at re-enchanting the world, to borrow Max Weber's phrase, than music? Who hasn't had that feeling of being elevated or transported from the mundane world by music? "Music expresses that which cannot be put into words and that which cannot remain silent," observed Victor Hugo.[13]

Put on your headphones and walk down a busy city street; the world seems set to music. Or watch people listening to music on their iPods as they walk past you, giving new literalism to the line widely—and falsely—attributed to Nietzsche: "And those who were seen dancing were thought to be insane by those who could not hear the music."[14] This feeling is the conceit behind countless movies that use music to transport us to that feeling of isolated oneness with the world around us. (The recent film *Baby Driver* is a good example of the genre.)

Think about how humans first enjoyed music. A primitive band sits around the fire pounding drums and singing its treasured folk songs and chants. No doubt this practice was entertaining, but it was also a way to commune with the gods or with fellow members of the troop, or a means to honor revered ancestors or mourn fallen warriors, or a method of warding off evil spirits—or some combination of the above. It was democratic and personal, divine and worldly, all at once.

Rock and roll is the primitive's drumbeat hooked up to killer amps. It ties together meanings we are taught to keep separate; it ratifies the instincts we are instructed to keep at bay. It tells us, in the words of Jethro Tull, "Let's bungle in the jungle," because "that's all right with me."

Nowhere is the romantic mixture of pantheism, primitivism, and the primacy of feelings more evident than in rock's appeal to inner authority and authenticity. Despite the fact that we may be surrounded by thousands of fellow fans dancing or head banging in syncopated unison, rock still tells us that we must move to the beat of our own drummer. For Hegel, romanticism could be summarized as "absolute inwardness." This idea that the artist is a slave solely to his own irrational muse is no doubt ancient, but its obvious modern echoes can be found in the romantic philosophy of Friedrich Nietzsche's early writings. "Nietzsche," writes music historian Martha Bayles, "echoed the robust Romantic view that the only worthwhile use of reason in art is to confront, wrestle with, and finally incorporate the irrational."[15]

It is no accident that drugs and rock and roll are so linked in the popular imagination. Both promise to take us out of the realm of daily concerns and rational priorities. They are both forms of escapism from the workaday, from the shackles of the here and now. The ancients celebrated wine, women, and song. Today the mantra is "sex, drugs, and rock and roll"—and so long as we remain human, it will be ever thus.

Nor is it a coincidence that rock appeals most directly to adolescents. Your teenage years are the time when the civilized order and your inner primitive are most at war. It is when glandular desires are most powerful and our faculties of reason are the most susceptible to all manner of seductions. Everyone who has experienced teenage angst—which is to say everyone who has lived long enough to legally buy booze and cigarettes—knows full well that the romantic revolution and the Enlightenment wage war in every teenage heart.

It is also no coincidence that the post–World War II era of peace, prosperity, and conformity largely created the idea of the teenager. The buttoned-down 1950s gave adolescents something to rebel against. Similarly, the peace and prosperity of the post–Cold War world created the adolescent forty-year-old. The comfort of prosperity leads, in Schumpeterian fashion, to a cultural backlash against the established order and bourgeois values.

Now let us move on from rock and look instead to popular culture more generally. For it is my contention that the same romantic impulses that define rock and roll also define much of the rest of our culture as well.

HERE THERE BE MONSTERS

The simplest place to start: monsters. Primitive man believed in all manner of monsters, broadly defined. The Dungeons & Dragons geek in me wants to distinguish between monsters qua monsters and, say, dragons, spirits, orcs, and the like. But we'll stick with the broadest understanding of monster: unnatural creatures that terrify us. The primitive mind creates monsters to personify fears, and fear is one of the greatest defense mechanisms in the state of nature. The growl we hear from the back of a cave causes the mind to race to the worst possible scenario because the credo "Better safe than sorry" is written into nearly every animal's DNA. Young children have to be taught that there are no monsters lurking under their beds because humans are born with an innate sense of their vulnerability. In adults, fear of monsters endures, usually to manifest our anxiety about the unknown. The frontiers of medieval mapmakers' knowledge were marked off with the words "Here there be dragons."

From the late Medieval Period to the present day, we still worry that if we press the boundaries of the known or if we trespass on God's authority, we will find—or create—monsters. Part of the romantic indictment of science and reason is *hubris,* which not only means arrogance but in the original Greek means prideful defiance of the gods and their plan. How dare we try to tame nature or disenchant the world? In this way, monsters serve as instruments of a revenge fantasy against "the system." The monster that tears it all down is the ultimate radical.

At the end of Drew Goddard and Joss Whedon's screenplay of *The Cabin in the Woods,* two world-weary millennials, fed up with the hypocrisy of the world, willingly allow ancient evil Titans called "the Old Ones" to destroy the world rather than sacrifice their own lives. When told that five billion people will die, if they don't kill themselves before the sun comes up in eight minutes, one of the youths replies, "Maybe that's the way it should be. If you gotta kill all my friends to survive, maybe it's time for a change." In other words, for the millennial who plays by his own rules, planetary genocide is a just rebuke for not getting one's way.

The most influential monster story of all time is, of course, *Frankenstein*. Mary Shelley based Frankenstein's monster on the ancient Jewish legend of the Golem, a creature brought to life from inanimate material by magic. Dr. Frankenstein wasn't a magician but a man of science, but the morals of the story are largely the same: hubris, playing God, mucking about with nature, finding the divine spark in worldly things. It is not difficult to understand why Shelley's story of the mad scientist dabbling with mighty forces beyond his ken captivated the imaginations of millions of readers in the early 1800s.

Rousseau's romantic indictment of progress mirrors the biblical story of man's fall. Defying the natural law—i.e., God's commandment—Adam and Eve partake of the forbidden fruit of knowledge and, ever since, man has been living in sin, cast out from Eden. In Rousseau's version, when man embraced property and the division of labor, he left the happy life of the noble savage who lives in harmony with nature. The story of Frankenstein's monster follows the same pattern.

The original title of Shelley's story is largely forgotten: *Frankenstein; or, The Modern Prometheus*. In Greek mythology, the Titan Prometheus creates man out of clay and water—just like the Golem. Prometheus also gives man fire, against the will of Zeus, who famously punishes him for it by chaining him to a rock where an eagle would eat his liver every day, only to have it regenerate overnight.

The similarities between Dr. Frankenstein and Prometheus are too obvious to explore further—which is why Shelley invokes the Titan in her title. But it is interesting to note that electricity, then still a magical and miraculous phenomenon, played much the same role that fire did for the ancient mind. Indeed, it was Søren Kierkegaard who coined the phrase "Modern Prometheus" to describe Benjamin Franklin and his experiments with electricity.[16] For had not Franklin plucked the symbol of godly power—lightning—and yoked it to the reins of science?

Was this not a great act of hubris?

When news of Franklin's experiments in the New World reached the Old World, the shock was akin to the news of the first detonation of an atomic bomb.[17]

Since we're on the topic, the atom bomb also unleashed its own wave of monster stories. The etymology of "monster" is relevant: *warning, portent, demonstrate, show.* Consider Godzilla, King of Monsters (and one of the most enduring pop culture icons in the world, not just in Japan). The first Godzilla movie was released in 1954, less than a decade after the bombing of Nagasaki and Hiroshima, and just two years after the formal end of the American occupation of Japan— amidst an enormous controversy over a Japanese fishing boat damaged during some American nuclear testing in the Bikini Atoll.

But most important, Godzilla was also a kind of Frankenstein's monster, created by the invisible, seemingly magical force of atomic radiation. Deformities and mutations—precisely the kinds of conditions that gave birth to the original meaning of the word "monster"— were a very real consequence and omnipresent concern after the bombings. The fear that the atomic age would unleash unimaginable horrors was common around the world, but understandably acute in Japan.

"Godzilla has long mirrored public thinking in Japan," writes Chieko Tsuneoka in the *Wall Street Journal*. "The monster's origin as the mutant product of nuclear tests reflected Japan's trauma from the atomic bombings of World War II and its anxieties over postwar American H-bomb testing in the Pacific. In the 1970s, as Japan choked with industrial pollution, Godzilla fought the Smog Monster. In the early 1990s, when U.S.-Japanese trade frictions intensified, Godzilla fought King Ghidorah, a three-headed monster sent by a foreign-looking group called the Futurians to prevent Japan from developing into an economic superpower."[18]

The most recent Godzilla movie, 2016's *Shin Godzilla*, captures growing nationalist sentiments in Japan as the country is agonizing over whether to remilitarize in the face of Chinese and Russian aggression and perceived American unreliability. The idea is wrenching because Japan turned its back on nationalist militarism after World War II in favor of a market democracy and pacifism. (Indeed, the first Godzilla movie sixty-two years earlier was a pacifist allegory.) The twin fears facing Japan are, on the one hand, that bringing back nationalism and militarism will awaken old demons, and, on the other hand, that it may be necessary to do so for Japan to survive. In *Shin Godzilla*, the beast returns to his original role as villain, and the heroes of a Godzilla movie are the actual politicians and military, who are traditionally seen as well-intentioned but hapless fodder for monster feet. Once again, they play to type, but eventually rise to the challenge, finding the will to defeat the beast (for now—there will always be sequels).

William Tsutsui, author of *Godzilla on My Mind: Fifty Years of the King of Monsters* (2004), writes that "*Shin Godzilla* leaves no doubt that the greatest threat to Japan comes not from without but from within, from a geriatric, fossilized government bureaucracy unable to act decisively or to stand up resolutely to foreign pressure. Indeed, this movie could easily have been titled 'Godzilla vs. the Establishment,' as Tokyo's smothering quicksand of cabinet meetings, political infighting, and interagency logjams make Mothra, Rodan, and King Ghidorah seem like remarkably tame adversaries."[19]

Shin in Japanese can mean new, divine, or true, but the filmmakers refused to disclose which meaning they had in mind—which surely suggests they intended all three.[20]

Of course, Godzilla and Frankenstein barely scratch the list of monsters that populate the popular culture and the warnings they foretell. Indeed, there's a whole subliterature on what the villain-monsters in sci-fi movies really represent.

For example, one of my favorite horror films—and I don't like many—is *The Exorcist*, in part because it is not really a horror movie at all. *The Exorcist* tells the story of an innocent young girl who is possessed and befouled by a demon. It is a brilliant piece of theological and psychological commentary.

In the early scenes, when the scientists and doctors are trying to figure out what is wrong with the little girl, Regan, we are made to feel the limits of modern, sterile technology. Later, when the priests try to expel the demon from the child, we are asked to grapple with the very existence of evil. The younger priest, Father Damien Karras—a psychologist who prior to these events had largely lost his faith to secularism—asks: Why this girl? Father Merrin responds, "I think the point is to make us despair. To see ourselves as animal and ugly. To reject the possibility that God could love us."[21] Though I prefer Father Merrin's fuller response in the original novel:

> Yet I think the demon's target is not the possessed; it is us . . . the observers . . . every person in this house. And I think—I think the

point is to make us despair; to reject our own humanity, Damien: to see ourselves as ultimately bestial; as ultimately vile and putrescent; without dignity; ugly; unworthy. And there lies the heart of it, perhaps: in unworthiness. For I think belief in God is not a matter of reason at all; I think it is finally a matter of love; of accepting the possibility that God could love *us* . . .[22]

There are many themes to *The Exorcist*: the limits of reason and technology, the power of faith, the reality of evil, and the very deliberate glorification of religion in both the book and the screenplay, both written by William Peter Blatty. The monster that takes over Regan is a warning against the dangers of nihilism, secularism, and even capitalism, wrongly pursued.

While obviously a supernatural thriller, the film can better be understood as part of, and a response to, a dark turn in American movies in the early 1970s. Whatever idealism there had been in the 1960s had largely turned to dross, as the costs of free love and sticking it to the Man mounted up. The loss of faith in politics and international and domestic turmoil all contributed to a very bleak—if well-executed—time in American cinema. *The Exorcist* came out the same year as *American Graffiti, Mean Streets, Serpico, The Last Detail, Soylent Green, Walking Tall,* and *Magnum Force,* the sequel to the first *Dirty Harry* film.[23] The following year's top movies included: *Death Wish, Chinatown, The Godfather: Part II, The Parallax View,* and *Lenny.* The year after that included *One Flew Over the Cuckoo's Nest* and *The Stepford Wives.* What was the one thing these movies, including *The Exorcist,* all had in common? The idea that contemporary life was out of balance and off-kilter, inauthentic, or oppressive, and that elites and the system itself were broken, corrupt, or inadequate to the task of making life right.

"IT'S NOT SUPPOSED TO BE LIKE THIS"

The idea that the world—this world—is . . . *wrong,* off balance, fake, fraudulent, unnatural, has been one of the dominant themes of art since the Enlightenment. It is what motivated the romantic poets to fight back against what they saw as the mechanization of natural life. It is the central conceit of the *Matrix* films, in which a technologically oppressive system parasitically feeds off humanity. It can also be found in a host of baby boomer midlife crisis and middle-age anxiety movies and TV shows, such as Lawrence Kasdan's 1991 *Grand Canyon*. In what was supposed to be "*The Big Chill* of the 1990s" (that was how it was marketed), the film focuses on how a diverse set of characters are lost in the chaos of modern American life, lacking any shared experiences or mutual empathy and desperately looking for a sense of control or meaning. As Danny Glover says in one famous scene, "Man, the world ain't supposed to work like this."

In fairness, the same trope can be found in every generation. So-called Gen-X films were also full of generational angst. Winona Ryder and Ethan Hawke spent much of the 1990s making films dedicated to the proposition that the system is a succubus draining out the authenticity of life and the souls of youth. Here's Hawke in *Reality Bites*:

> There's no point to any of this. It's all just a . . . a random lottery of meaningless tragedy and a series of near escapes. So I take pleasure in the details. You know . . . a Quarter-Pounder with cheese, those are good, the sky about ten minutes before it starts to rain, the moment where your laughter become a cackle . . . and I, I sit back and I smoke my Camel Straights and I ride my own melt.

In another scene, Hawke literally answers the phone: "Hello, you've reached the winter of our discontent."[24]

Interestingly, the 1990s may have marked something of a high-water mark of this genre. One can speculate as to why. The 1980s had been a time when conformity and prosperity were on the rise. The end of the Cold War and the subsequent triumphalism of Western democratic capitalism appalled many of the artistic souls who had to endure it.

The execrable film *Pleasantville* was an extended metaphor on the horror of conformity. And so was the even more execrable 1999 film *American Beauty*. "I feel like I've been in a coma for the past twenty years. And I'm just now waking up," declares Kevin Spacey playing Lester Burnham, an updated version of the man in the gray flannel suit desperate to break the chains of conventional morality and selling out to the consumer culture. He commences a "self-improvement" regimen that includes all of the staples: sexual obsessions, pot smoking, flipping off the Man.

"Janie, today I quit my job. And then I told my boss to go fuck himself, and then I blackmailed him for almost $60,000. Pass the asparagus," Lester tells his daughter at the dinner table.[25]

In *Point Break* (1991) a small band—a tribe, if you will—of surfers living off the grid dedicate themselves to ripping off the system by donning masks of dead presidents and robbing banks. But Bodhi (Patrick Swayze) explains: "This was never about money for us. It was about us against the system. That system that kills the human spirit. We stand for something. To those dead souls inching along the freeways in their metal coffins . . . we show them that the human spirit is still alive."[26] The terrible remake of the film was even more ham-fisted in its treatment of these themes.

The romantic spirit is often at its least subtle when expressing its hatred for capitalism and the market. As John Steinbeck writes in *The Grapes of Wrath*, "The bank is something else than men. It happens that every man in a bank hates what the bank does, and yet the bank does it. The bank is something more than men, I tell you. It's the monster. Men made it, but they can't control it."[27]

The brilliant TV series *Mr. Robot* offers the most recent exposition of these themes. Set in contemporary New York, the show follows the mentally unstable computer programmer savant Elliot, hauntingly portrayed by Rami Malek. Elliot seems to live half in dream, consumed with an ongoing dialogue with the ghost (for want of a better word) of his dead father, a Rousseauian rebel determined to take down the system. As Elliot explains to a therapist:

> Oh, I don't know. Is it that we collectively thought Steve Jobs was a great man, even when we knew he made billions off the backs of children? Or maybe it's that it feels like all our heroes are counterfeit? The world itself's just one big hoax. Spamming each other with our running commentary of bullshit, masquerading as insight, our social media faking as intimacy. Or is it that we voted for this? Not with our rigged elections, but with our things, our

property, our money. I'm not saying anything new. We all know why we do this, not because *Hunger Games* books make us happy, but because we wanna be sedated. Because it's painful not to pretend, because we're cowards. Fuck society.[28]

(We later learn that he didn't, in fact, say anything at all to his therapist. It was just another inner monologue narrated by his authentic self.)

Elliot and his tribe of hackers, "F-Society," set out to tear down E Corp, which quickly becomes "Evil Corp." That might sound didactic, even propagandistic, but the show's creator, Sam Esmail, deftly avoids such pitfalls. The series is almost an allegorical tale of Rousseauians, who want to "save the world" by restoring it to something more human and natural, and the capitalistic Nietzscheans, who run the system through force of will and nihilistic disregard for morality. What both factions have in common is the romantic conviction that the only legitimate source of truth is found within oneself. In the first season, Tyrell Wellick, a brilliant corporate climber, explains what he felt after killing someone:

Two days ago I strangled a woman to death just with my hands. That's a strange sensation. Something so tremendous done by something so simple. The first ten seconds were uncomfortable, a feeling of limbo, but then your muscles tense, and she struggles and fights, but it almost disappears in the background along with everything else in the world. At that moment it's just you and absolute power, nothing else. That moment stayed with me. I thought I'd feel guilty for being a murderer, but I don't. I feel wonder.[29]

One of the most remarkable aspects of the series is how it exemplifies the romantic spirit in the technological age. Romanticism always speaks in the language of its time. That's partly why we think the romantic era ended: The language changed with the times.

But the two most egregious films of this neo-romantic genre must be *Fight Club* and *Dead Poets Society*. In *Fight Club*, which opened the same month as *American Beauty*, Edward Norton plays a young professional driven to madness by the cage of modern capitalism. The film is a riot of Rousseauian and Nietzschean vignettes masquerading as primal yawps. The premise of *Fight Club* is that young men are orphans of the system, forgotten, exploited, and downtrodden. They were born free but live in chains. "Like so many others," Norton explains, "I had become a slave to the Ikea nesting instinct."

The only way to rediscover the freedom and meaning bleached out of them by the system is to rekindle their primal, tribal inner flames and band together, first to fight each other and then to fight the system itself.

Norton's alter ego, Tyler Durden, explains:

Man, I see in fight club the strongest and smartest men who've ever lived. I see all this potential, and I see squandering. God damn it, an entire generation pumping gas, waiting tables; slaves with white collars. Advertising has us chasing cars and clothes, working jobs we hate so we can buy shit we don't need. We're the middle children of history, man. No purpose or place. We have no Great War. No Great Depression. Our Great War's a spiritual war . . . our Great Depression is our lives. We've all been raised on television to believe that one day we'd all be millionaires, and movie gods, and rock stars. But we won't. And we're slowly learning that fact. And we're very, very pissed off.

Another member of Fight Club advises, "Reject the basic assumptions of civilization, especially the importance of material possessions."[30]

And then there's *Dead Poets Society*, in which a group of young men at a straightlaced boarding school seek to break the chains of convention and defy the authority of the oppressive system they are destined to inherit. How do they do this? By embracing the work of the romantic poets (and a hodgepodge of later transcendentalists) who had declared war on the Enlightenment two centuries earlier!

The film begins with the students learning poetry by formula, plotting its "perfection along the horizontal of a graph" and its "importance" on the vertical in order to find the "measure of its greatness." It is almost as if the system has found its soulless answer to poet August Wilhelm Schlegel's question "What can a poem prove?" John

Keating, the student's new charismatic teacher played by Robin Williams, tells the boys to rip the introduction from their poetry text books.

He exhorts his charges to stop and to look inward for meaning and authority: "Boys, you must strive to find your own voice. Because the longer you wait to begin, the less likely you are to find it at all. Thoreau said, 'Most men lead lives of quiet desperation.' Don't be resigned to that. Break out!"

When one of the students discovers in an old yearbook that Mr. Keating was a member of something called the Dead Poets Society, Mr. Keating tells him, "No, Mr. Overstreet, it wasn't just 'guys,' we weren't a Greek organization, we were Romantics. We didn't just read poetry, we let it drip from our tongues like honey. Spirits soared, women swooned, and gods were created, gentlemen, not a bad way to spend an evening, eh?"

So inspired, the boys get into all manner of trouble. Neil, the leader of the band, takes to heart Thoreau's dictum, "To put to rout all that was not life; and not, when I had come to die, discover that I had not lived." He decides he's going to be an actor, against the wishes of his father, who wants him to dedicate himself to becoming a doctor. "For the first time in my whole life I know what I wanna do. And for the first time I'm gonna do it! Whether my father wants me to or not! Carpe diem!"

It all goes badly and Neil ultimately commits suicide out of despair at the prospect of having to sell out to the system. Mr. Keating is fired, but the surviving boys pay tribute to him by standing on their desks, shouting, "O Captain! My Captain!"

Throughout the film, we are always supposed to take Mr. Keating's side in every dispute. When the stodgy headmaster chastises him for his unorthodox techniques, Mr. Keating shoots back: "I always thought the idea of education was to learn to think for yourself." The headmaster responds, "At these boys' age? Not on your life. Tradition, John. Discipline. Prepare them for college and the rest will take care of itself."[31]

We are supposed to roll our eyes at this. But the headmaster is right, or at least less wrong than Mr. Keating. To be sure, Mr. Keating has something to teach the fogeys about how to make education interesting and entertaining. But what he is not doing is teaching the boys to think for themselves. He is teaching them to embrace the romantic imperative of finding truth—or at least the only truth that matters—within themselves. In other words, he is not teaching them to think for themselves; he is teaching them not to think at all. *Dead Poets Society* is a rock-and-roll song minus the rock and roll.

All of this matters, because films like this do not merely reflect our culture but also shape it, giving it voice and validation. Voted the greatest "school film" of all time, *Dead Poets Society*'s influence has been profound, not just on how normal people view education, but on how educators view themselves.[32]

I should note that this trope of a vampiric political or economic order sucking the life force out of humanity is usually described as left-wing, and in the hands of Hollywood it often is. But in other cultures and at other times, this romantic spirit has taken different—or allegedly different—forms. In the American South, the Southern Agrarian poets and writers were a decidedly conservative bunch, but their critiques of capitalism, democracy, and mass culture could easily be described as romantic. In the Soviet Union, the writers and intellectuals who yearned to restore the romantic and religious spirit of Mother Russia were not necessarily lovers of the free market. What they wanted was to restore the glory of soil, nature, church, and tradition to the sanitized world of Marxism. The Nazis were drenched in romanticism and romantic notions going back to gauzy myths of their pre-Christian Teutonic forefathers. In India, Hindu nationalists do not fit easily into our left-right schema (as far as I can tell), but in both their historic and contemporary desire to elevate ancient notions of folk, custom, and nation over "foreign" concepts like capitalism and socialism, they seem to fit perfectly well inside the romantic tradition. And, as will be discussed in another chapter, today romantic nationalism is in full, if noxious, flower amidst the fever swamps of the American right.

ISN'T IT BYRONIC?

The classic character of the romantic novel is the Byronic hero. In many of Byron's works, most famously *Childe Harold's Pilgrimage*, the protagonist is a rebellious soul plagued with the memory of wrongs he's committed in the past and determined to set things right, or at least atone for them. One can think of countless stock characters in film and television who fit this description. The brooding vampire with a soul archetype (*Angel, Vampire Diaries, Twilight*) is one. Martin Blank in *Grosse Pointe Blank* is a classically Byronic figure trying to do right after a career of doing wrong. Brad Pitt, Clint Eastwood, and Mel Gibson routinely play Byronic characters in such films as *Legends of the Fall, Fury, Unforgiven*, and *Lethal Weapon*.

One of the central traits of the Byronic hero is the man who "plays by his own rules." This theme has come to nearly define what we mean by a hero. A fascinating example of this can be found in the changing view of the Muslim prophet Muhammad during the romantic era. In Christian Europe, martyrdom was always held in high esteem. But giving your life was laudable when you were sacrificing it for a capital-*T* Truth, most specifically for the Christian faith. (Giving your life for your country was also highly valued, but this was often seen as just another form of religious self-sacrifice. See "Arc, Joan of.") But, Isaiah Berlin notes that by the 1820s "you find an outlook in which the state of mind, the motive, is more important than the consequence, the intention is more important than the effect."[33]

In Voltaire's play *Muhammad*, the prophet emerges, in Berlin's words, "as a superstitious, cruel and fanatical monster."[34] Voltaire probably didn't care much about the Islamic faith one way or another; he was trying to get around the censors, to attack organized religion, specifically Catholicism as practiced in France. By the 1840s, the height of the romantic period, Muhammad becomes a heroic man of will. In Thomas Carlyle's *On Heroes, Hero-Worship, and the Heroic in History*, Muhammad is "a fiery mass of Life cast up from the great bosom of Nature herself." Carlyle couldn't give a fig about the tenets of faith found in the Koran either. What he admired was Muhammad's radical commitment. The Muslim prophet's example served as an indictment of what Carlyle considered to be a "withered . . . second-hand century."[35]

Today, this fetishization of strength and will is everything in culture. It explains so much, from Donald Trump's cult of personality to fandom for countless athletes and hip-hop icons, not to mention the hints of grudging admiration one often hears for Muhammad's extremist followers.[36]

From *Rebel Without a Cause* to cooking shows, the man—or occasionally woman—who plays by his own code, even if that code is evil, has become the stock character of American popular culture. Batman, a.k.a. the Dark Knight, is not evil, but he is a vigilante who plays by his own rules. The pioneering comic book character Wolverine's slogan? "I'm the best there is at what I do, but what I do best isn't very nice." In the cult classic comic *Watchmen*, the character Rorschach's motto is "Never compromise. Not even in the face of Armageddon."[37] In the novel and Showtime TV series *Dexter*, we meet a brutal serial killer who has found a way to live with himself by following "the Code of Harry," named after his dead father (who appears as a ghost throughout the series). According to his code, it's okay for him to murder so long as he's murdering other serial killers (and, on rare occasions, people who might bring him to justice). Omar in the HBO series *The Wire* insists that he will only rob and kill other drug dealers and gangsters, because "a man's got to have a code." "The Mountain" in *Game of Thrones* explains that, while he's fine with slaughtering innocent people, he won't steal "because a man's got to have a code." He later steals, but the audience doesn't care.

In *Breaking Bad*, arguably the best television series ever made,[38] Vince Gilligan, the show's creator, set out to chronicle one man's descent from decency to decadence. The idea was to show how Mr. Chips could turn into Scarface.[39] Gilligan succeeded, but not before he seduced and corrupted the viewing audience too: By the time the story ended, fans no longer minded that Walter White had become a homicidal drug dealer. They rooted for him anyway.

Many of these Knights of the Self, warriors for their own code, end up dying in these stories. They are martyrs to the idea of "I did it my way." It would all look very familiar to the original romantics and their view on heroism from an inner-directed light.

WHAT WAS ONCE CONSIDERED the only noble motivation for a hero, a conception of good outside himself, has been replaced by what Irish philosopher David Thunder calls "purely formal accounts of integrity." According to Thunder, "purely formal accounts essentially demand internal consistency within the form or structure of an agent's desires, actions, beliefs, and evaluations." He adds that, under purely formal integrity, a person "may be committed to evil causes or principles, and they may adopt principles of expediency or even exempt themselves from moral rules when the rules stand in the way of their desires."[40]

In other words, if you stick to your code, no matter what you do, you can be seen as a hero. It's this sort of thinking that has led Hannibal Lecter, a character who barbarously murders and eats(!) innocent people, to be seen as something of a folk hero. In the film *The Silence of the Lambs*, he's a charming monster who has no problem with eating people but says that "discourtesy is unspeakably ugly to me." In the TV series *Hannibal*, the audience marvels at the cannibalistic gourmand, who cares not a whit for bourgeois morality, preferring instead a Gothic-gastronomic overlay to the laws of the jungle and a simultaneously barbaric and noble savage who does his own thing.

THE ALLURE OF TRIBAL JUSTICE

Why do movies and other modern myths find purchase in our imaginations? Anyone who has experience in even high school theater probably knows the phrase "willing suspension of disbelief." The term was coined by the poet Samuel Taylor Coleridge in his collaboration with fellow poet William Wordsworth on their groundbreaking work, *Lyrical Ballads*, widely seen as marking the birth of the English romantic movement. The idea of the willing suspension of disbelief, Coleridge explained, was twofold. Coleridge's contributions were to give voice to the "inward nature" of our irrational imagination, to make the supernatural characters seem real enough to the reader. Wordsworth came at the project from the opposite direction. His task was "to give the

charm of novelty to things of every day, and to excite a feeling analogous to the supernatural."[41]

In other words, Coleridge was tasked with making the supernatural seem real, while Wordsworth was assigned the job of making the
real seem supernatural. Combine these two approaches and you get
not only pantheism but the whole gamut of romantic art. The workaday is magical, and the magical is all around us.

But what interests me about the willing suspension of disbelief is
the *unwillingness* of it. No one walks into a theater or opens a book
or plays a song only after rationally committing to suspending their
disbelief. The "poetic faith" is already there as a feature of our inward
nature. The poetic faith, in this sense, is no different from any other
form of faith. When the faithful enter a church, mosque, or synagogue, they do not rationally argue themselves into believing; the program for belief is already up and running. Our faith is like our senses
of sight or touch or hearing: We don't turn it on and off; the engine is
always running. It is primal, hardwired.

WHAT FASCINATES ME is how our moral expectations in the world
of art differ from our expectations in the real world around us. The
people we are at work, at the grocery store, play by one set of largely
artificial rules: the rules of civilization. But beneath—or perhaps
beside—the person of manners, custom, and law resides a different
being. We've all heard the expression that some movie, novel, or piece
of music "transported" us. Perhaps "transported" is the wrong word.
Perhaps "liberated" gets closer to the mark. Comedians and pop psychologists often talk about our "inner caveman." The reason this stuff
appeals to us is because we sense there's a healthy dose of truth to the
idea. Beneath the layers of outward civilization lurks our more primal
self, who finds the world around us complicated and artificial. Our
primal self isn't a noble savage, but he does feel like a more authentic
person than the one who works hard and plays by the rules of modern
society.

The moral universe of cinema sometimes mirrors the real world,
but just as often the actors on the screen play roles more consistent
with the moral universe of our inner savage. It's like a scene in some

science fiction movie where the protagonist develops a roll of film and finds that the people he photographed are different from those he saw with his naked eye.[42] Art captures a reality that we tend to deny in the "real world" around us. In novels, movies, TV, rap music, video games, and almost every other realm of our shared culture, the moral language of the narrative is in an almost entirely different dialect from the moral language of the larger society.

For instance, we are rightly taught not to hit, steal, or torture. These rules, and ones like them, form the bedrock of virtually every halfway decent civilization. And yet, almost every time we go see an action movie, we cheer people who violate these rules. I am a sucker for a heist movie, but I don't think robbing banks is laudable. As a general rule, I stand foursquare against using violence to settle disagreements or respond to insults. But a John Wayne who didn't deck someone who insulted him wouldn't be John Wayne.

CONSIDER AN EXTREME EXAMPLE: torture. For the last two decades, America has been roiled by an intense and passionate debate over the use of what critics call torture and defenders call "enhanced interrogation." Many opponents of torture implicitly argue that it is worse than homicide. After all, almost no one disputes that there are times when the state has the power and authority to kill. But torture? Never. Not even in a ticking-time-bomb situation. In order to hold to this extreme position, torture opponents find they must argue that torture "never works."

This is dubious in what we call real life, but it is flat-out lunacy according to famously liberal Hollywood. Steven Bochco's *NYPD Blue* broke a lot of television taboos, but the least appreciated is its open endorsement of beating the truth out of suspects. In *Patriot Games*, Harrison Ford shoots a man in the knee to get the information he needs. In *Guarding Tess*, Secret Service agent Nicholas Cage blows off a kidnapper's toe with his service weapon. In *Rules of Engagement*, Samuel L. Jackson executes a prisoner to force another to talk. In *Pulp Fiction*, we delight at contemplating the "short-ass-life-in-agonizing-pain" of Ving Rhames's rapist ("I'ma get medieval on your ass."). In the TV series *24*, Kiefer Sutherland would routinely resort to torture if it meant thwarting some impending threat. And each time the audience cheers.

When we suspend disbelief, we also suspend adherence to the conventions and legalisms of the outside world. Instead, we use the more primitive parts of our brains, which understand right and wrong as questions of "us" and "them." Our myths are still with us on the silver screen, and they appeal to our sense of tribal justice. We enter the movie theater a citizen of this world, but when we sit down, we become denizens of the spiritual jungle, where our morality becomes tribal the moment the lights go out.

12

THE FAMILY'S LOSING WAR
AGAINST BARBARISM

IN THE FIRST PART OF THIS BOOK, I DISCUSSED THE VITAL role institutions play in a pluralistic society. Institutions are rules and customs for how groups of people self-organize and work together outside the state. Hence the term "mediating institutions"—the formal and informal organizations, customs, and rules that "mediate" the space between the individual and the state, often called "civil society." This is the world of work, church, and community. Most of the work of civilization and of our individual lives is conducted in this space.

By any measure, the most important mediating institution in any society is the family. Healthy, well-functioning families are the primary wellspring of societal success. Unhealthy, dysfunctional families are the primary cause of societal decline. The family is the institution that converts us from natural-born barbarians into, hopefully, decent citizens. It is the family that literally civilizes us. Before we are born into a community, a faith, a class, or a nation, we are born into a family, and how that family shapes us largely determines who we are.

The healthy family is also the keystone of civil society. Many of the most important mediating institutions relate not simply to individuals but to the families behind them. If you ever explore the question of how any thriving school, small town, sports league, church, mosque, synagogue, or almost any other non-government-run civic event or tradition does so well, the answer almost always involves the involvement of certain families, usually led by a few determined women and reinforced by cadres of obedient husbands and fathers.

"Capitalism," Joseph Schumpeter said, "does not merely mean that the housewife may influence production by her choice between peas and beans; nor that the youngster may choose whether he wants to work on a factory or in a farm; nor that plant managers have some voice in deciding what and how to produce. It means a scheme of values, an attitude toward life, a civilization . . ."[1] This scheme of values, this attitude toward life and civilization, begins in the family, which is traditionally defined as a marriage between one man and one woman and their children.

And this system is breaking down. The family as an engine of civilization is in deep trouble. In a way, the breakdown of the family is an illustration of my larger argument in miniature. Many critics of bourgeois morality are indeed right when they say that the nuclear family—one man, one woman, married to another—is not natural. It's not altogether unnatural either. But it's true that the historical and anthropological record is full of different types of families. Combatants on both sides of the intellectual wars of the family often commit the naturalistic fallacy: assuming that if something is "natural" it is right or good. Many traditionalists insist that the nuclear family is the natural way, "as God intended." Advocates for new ways of organizing and thinking about family point out all of the different ways families have been organized and say many forms are just as natural.

But whether it is natural or not misses the more salient point: The nuclear family *works*.

But before we explore that point, we should review—very quickly and summarily—the world we came from when it comes to families.

Non-human primates have a variety of sexual dynamics. In gorilla communities, the alpha male has sex with all the females. Among chimpanzees, it's more like a free-for-all, with males competing with each other for sex with as many partners as possible. In both species, the difference in size between males and females is a symptom of these sexual politics. Males must defeat other males to become the alpha or even to get a first shot at the most desirable females. Around 1.7 million years ago, our human ancestors started to deviate from this norm, and the size differential between the sexes shrank (though it still exists). "This shift in size is almost certainly a sign that competition between males had diminished because of the transition to the pair bond system," writes Nicholas Wade in *Before the Dawn: Recover-*

ing the Lost History of Our Ancestors.[2] The pair-bond is what you could call natural or primitive monogamy.

However, even chimps have a kind of stealth monogamy. The females may be obligated to have sex with all the males, but, once having fulfilled that duty, they tend to pick a favorite male "consort" they spend more time with. They even have trysts off in the forest with them for weeks at a time and delay their ovulation so they can increase the chances that their preferred partner succeeds.

Our human ancestors improved on this system with the pair-bond. Among the benefits of this adaptation, all the males—or at least a lot more of them—had a chance to reproduce, which introduced a good deal more social peace and stability to primitive societies. In this way, primitive monogamy may be the driver of mankind's success as a species. By taking the need to fight with other males out of the equation and giving each male an incentive to protect the group (specifically his own offspring), males became much more cooperative and willing to make sacrifices for their tribe (or, more accurately, their band or troop). In evolutionary terms, the pair-bond was a mixed blessing for the females. "The females," Wade writes, "must give up mating with all the most desirable males in the community and limit their reproductive potential to the genes of just one male. On the other hand they gain an implied guarantee of physical protection for themselves and their children, as well as some provisioning."[3]

But here's the problem: The pair-bond is not fully baked into our instinctual programming the way, say, the fight-or-flight instinct is. Monogamy is natural—except when it isn't. It's a tendency, not an imperative. Culture, law, material circumstances—and sometimes mere opportunity—can easily override this real but often weak evolutionary drive. Also, in a world where few humans lived past the age of thirty, the notion of being bound to one person for fifty, sixty, or seventy years seemed unimaginable.

Marriage, whatever form it takes, is a social construction, an artificial institution and cultural adaptation. For instance, in certain areas where resources are scarce, societies developed polyandry—the practice of one wife and many husbands. This was a common practice in the mountain communities of China and Tibet. Far more common is polygyny, the form of polygamous marriage where one man has many wives. Some 85 percent of human societies through history, according to one commonly cited estimate, have been formally polygynous, which is to say harems of wives were allowed.[4] This practice is still widespread throughout much of the Muslim world and Africa.

So polygyny is natural—*except for when it isn't*. As for what the God of the Bible intended, tell Abraham, Jacob, David, and Solomon that they were defying God's will. (Meanwhile, Jesus was remarkably silent on the topic, though the few hints that exist suggest he opposed it.)

Now, back to the more important point. Monogamous marriage of the sort that defines the nuclear family works better for society (although I can't speak to whether it works better for every individual). Societies where monogamy is the norm tend to be much more economically productive, politically democratic, socially stable, and friendlier to women's rights.

Men in monogamous societies are more economically productive than men in polygynous societies because each married man is a stakeholder in his own family, and there are more families. Large-scale polygyny tends to destabilize the male population as young, poor men find themselves increasingly desperate for sexual relationships. Eric D. Gould, Omer Moav, and Avi Simhon, in their paper "The Mystery of Monogamy," demonstrate that polygyny emerges in societies with high levels of inequality, where wealth is largely derived from natural resources, particularly land. In societies where wealth comes from human capital—ingenuity, innovation, etc.—the marriage market is defined by a search for *quality* (by males and females alike), while in societies where wealth comes from landholdings, the market is defined by the strictly male emphasis on *quantity*. "In particular," they write, "skilled men in modern economies increasingly value skilled women for their ability to raise skilled children, which drives up the value of skilled women in the marriage market to the point where skilled men prefer one skilled wife to multiple unskilled wives."[5]

This is surely too reductionist. Other historical, religious, and cultural factors must be involved in an institution that spans much of the globe and that existed in nearly every ancient society in one form or another. But Gould and his colleagues are also surely right when they write that it is no accident that monogamy is the norm in *every* economically advanced democratic society. It is impossible to know how much the traditional nuclear family is responsible for the social and democratic stability and economic growth of the last three hundred years, but there is little doubt that it played an important role. The institution of marriage as we know it on a society-wide level and a personal level requires work. Just as capitalism is sustained by how we talk about it, so is marriage.

As a practical matter, I don't object to claims that monogamy is natural or in sync with God's plan, because that is an important way civilizations talk about settled questions. Making the ideal of monogamy a matter of unquestioned dogma simply strikes me as a good idea, even if honesty requires us to acknowledge that is what we are doing. We talk about murder and rape as unnatural as a way to heap deserving opprobrium on the practice even though, as we've seen, neither is actually unnatural. Adultery is wholly natural, but we condemn it as a violation of important norms to keep the habit to a minimum. "Very often those things we have condemned as 'unnatural' are things that we know will flourish if we leave them alone," writes Robin Fox in *The Tribal Imagination: Civilization and the Savage Mind.*[6] We ban and condemn polygyny because we know that, if we don't, many men will imitate our gorilla cousins and our ancient human ancestors and form a harem.

In other words, when we say that traditional marriage is "natural," what we really mean—or should mean—is that it is "normal." We made traditional marriage normal through centuries of civilizational trial and error because countless generations of wise people figured out that it was a best practice for society. And over those centuries we heaped layer upon layer of law, tradition, and custom on top of the institution. It has become dogma so old that we have forgotten all of the reasons for it. But rather than respect its time-tested value, we instead subject it to the razor of reason. We think that, because we cannot see—or remember—its myriad functions, they must not exist.

The family—in form, function, and ideal—has changed a great deal in a remarkably short period of time. Divorce has lost most of its social stigma, as has out-of-wedlock birth. Even adultery and "open marriage" are accepted or even celebrated by certain segments of society, particularly among some bohemian elites. A recent *New York Times Magazine* essay asked the question "Is an Open Marriage a Happier Marriage?"[7] The popular medical website WebMD article on open marriage reports that "those who practice open relationships or polyamory often say they are 'hardwired' this way and that laying the ground rules for multiple relationships spares everyone hurt and disappointment."[8]

Open marriage is not an epidemic. But, again, that misses an important point. The way we talk about marriage has changed profoundly since the 1960s, and that by itself has profound consequences. Marriage as an institution depends upon how the society around it talks about it. The rhetoric around marriage affects its desirability, for both men and women. When the sophisticated opinion is "Who needs it?" there are real consequences, both in law but also in the far more important climate of expectations people have about how to live a fulfilling life. When the mainline Protestant churches caved in to the bourgeois cultural populism of the "me decade" by removing or loosening many of the stigmas, rules, and customs that attached to divorce, they were downgrading the status of marriage.

"Prior to the late 1960s," writes the University of Virginia's Brad Wilcox, one of America's leading marriage researchers (and an AEI colleague of mine), "Americans were more likely to look at marriage and family through the prisms of duty, obligation, and sacrifice. A successful, happy home was one in which intimacy was an important good, but by no means the only one in view. A decent job, a well-maintained home, mutual spousal aid, child-rearing, and shared religious faith were seen almost universally as the goods that marriage and family life were intended to advance."

This is what Wilcox calls the "institutional model" of marriage.[9] Sex was reserved—according to the ideal, at least—for marriage. Certainly marriage was the only legitimate, or at least desirable, model for having children. In short, the old attitude was that one must work for the marriage. The new attitude was that the marriage had better work *for me*. In 1962, roughly half of American women agreed with the statement "When there are children in the family parents should stay together even if they don't get along." By 1977, only one in five American women agreed.[10]

Where the culture goes, so goes the state. Ronald Reagan signed the first no-fault divorce law as governor of California in 1969. As so often happens, where California "leads," much of the nation follows.

In the decade and a half that followed, virtually every state in the Union followed California's lead and enacted a no-fault divorce law of its own. This legal transformation was only one of the more visible signs of the divorce revolution then sweeping the United States: From 1960 to 1980, the divorce rate more than doubled—from 9.2 divorces per 1,000 married women to 22.6 divorces per 1,000 married women. This meant that while less than 20 percent of couples who married in 1950 ended up divorced, about 50 percent of couples who married in 1970 did. And approximately half of the children born to married parents in the 1970s saw their parents part, compared to only about 11 percent of those born in the 1950s.[11]

No-fault divorce was just one way in which the state accelerated the cultural trend. Under the Great Society, with an overabundance of good intentions, the federal government started subsidizing women who had children out of wedlock. For instance, a program—Aid to Families with Dependent Children—originally intended to provide modest pensions for the widows of coal miners became a broad entitlement for single mothers, paid out on a per-baby basis. The problem is that the way the program was structured, the funds were cut off if the recipient got married, thus penalizing mothers for seeking a more stable family. Welfare reform in 1996 fixed some of these problems, but it didn't eliminate them. According to a study by C. Eugene Steuerle of the Urban Institute, a single mother working full-time at a minimum-wage job who marries a man also working full-time at the same wage would lose $8,060 in cash and noncash welfare benefits.[12]

Trying to pinpoint single causes for the profound transformation in attitudes and practices around marriage is pointless. This is a big, diverse society, and big, diverse phenomena have big, diverse causes. Still, the statistics speak for themselves. Roughly seven out of ten black children are born out of wedlock. The out-of-wedlock birth rate for whites (29 percent) is now higher than what it was for blacks (24 percent) when Daniel Patrick Moynihan issued his (in)famous 1965 report: *The Negro Family: The Case for National Action.*[13]

Since 1974, roughly one million children per year have experienced the dissolution of their family, and these children "are two to three times more likely than their peers in intact marriages to suffer from serious social or psychological pathologies."[14]

Now, it must be acknowledged that the transformation of ideas about marriage had some benefits. This is not all a tale of woe. Whatever complaints you might have about various forms of doctrinaire or radical feminism, the core gains from the women's rights movement are not ones even most social conservatives would be comfortable rolling back, starting, of course, with women's suffrage, but also the broader acceptance that women have an equal right to pursue happiness to men. I certainly wouldn't want to go back to a world where women's occupational choices were limited to a few "women's jobs" like teaching, retail sales, nursing, and working at telephone switchboards. As the son and husband of successful "career women" (already a kind of antiquated term) and the father of a teenage girl whom I expect to follow in their footsteps, I welcome many of these changes. Nor would I like to see anyone trapped in an unworkable marriage.

In other words, we can acknowledge that important progress has been made, but we should also recognize that the implosion of the institutional model of marriage has had profound consequences for society, especially children.

No matter how impressive a single mother—or a single father—may be, the simple fact remains that, as a generalization, two parents are better than one. Such statements are upsetting to many Americans, who believe that to say such a thing unfairly stigmatizes single parents and the children of single parents. One can sympathize with the desire not to make an already formidable burden even heavier, but facts do not care about feelings (which is why we are in the midst of a war on facts on all sides these days).[15]

A recent study by Princeton University and the left-of-center Brookings Institution reported that "most scholars now agree that children raised by two biological parents in a stable marriage do better than children in other family forms across a wide range of outcomes."[16]

Sociologists Sara McLanahan and Gary Sandefur determined that adolescent children of divorced parents were almost three times more likely to drop out of high school (31 percent to 13 percent for children of intact families). They also found that a third of adolescent girls with divorced parents became teen mothers (whereas 11 percent of girls from married parents became teen mothers). More than one in ten male children of divorce (11 percent) spent some time in prison before the age of thirty-two. "Only" 5 percent of boys from intact homes were ever incarcerated.[17]

It is a cruel fact of human nature that evolution makes us biased toward our own kin in ways the rational mind cannot always accept or explain. Andrew J. Cherlin reports that even remarriage isn't the solution many of us hope it will be. In *The Marriage-Go-Round: The State of Marriage and the Family in America Today*, Cherlin recounts that "children whose parents have remarried do not have higher levels of well-being than children in lone-parent families."[18]

Cherlin attributes this to the stresses associated with moving and bonding (or not bonding) with stepparents and siblings. No doubt that's part of it, but there are surely deeply rooted biological factors at play as well. "A parent's patience will tend to run out with stepchildren more quickly than with biological children," notes Steven Pinker, "and in extreme cases this can lead to abuse."[19] A dismaying study by Nicholas Zill of the Institute for Family Studies found that adopted children have a harder time at school than kids raised by their biological parents. What makes this so dismaying is that adoptive parents tend to be better off financially and are just as willing as traditional parents, if not more so, to put in the time and effort of raising kids.[20]

Zill's finding highlights the problem with traditional family triumphalism. Adoption is a wonderful thing, and just because there are challenges that come with adoption, no one would ever argue that the problems adopted kids face make the alternatives to adoption better. Kids left in orphanages or trapped in abusive homes do even worse. Similarly, the well-established finding that parents of non-biological children often struggle with non-biological offspring doesn't mean that people with children should not remarry. What is required in such marriages is extra effort to compensate for the inevitable pull of human nature.[21]

Obviously, I believe this is much more than an argument about economics, but looking at the family through an economic lens helps us see the real-world consequences in ways table-pounding rhetoric and nostalgic nostrums about "the way things used to be" cannot. Consider the stress so many families go through when elderly parents can no longer care for themselves. The pressures involved can hardly be captured solely by economic considerations. The feelings of obligation adult children have toward their parents and to their own children cannot be easily or fully translated into financial terms. But they can be illuminated by them. A RAND Corporation study found that elderly people with no children end up paying far more over their remaining lifetime for nursing home care. Why? Because they spend more time in nursing homes. People with children, particularly daughters, spend less because the kids make a nursing home less necessary.[22] The data are silent on the emotional significance, but it's not hard to fill in the blanks.

How we take care of the elderly is an important issue, but how we raise children matters more for the future of the country. The Brookings Institution's Isabel Sawhill—no Bible-thumping right-winger—has found that 20 percent of the increase in child poverty since 1970 can be attributed to family breakdown.[23] A study by Brad Wilcox found that states with more married parents do better on a broad range of economic indicators, including upward mobility for poor children and lower rates of child poverty.[24] On most economic indicators, the *Washington Post* summarized, "the share of parents who are married in a state is a better predictor of that state's economic health than the racial composition and educational attainment of the state's residents."[25]

Also left out of the conversation is the incredible economic benefit marriage has for men. Married men, controlling for all factors, make 44 percent more than single men.[26] Pascal-Emmanuel Gobry notes that the wage benefit for marriage is roughly equal to, if not greater than, that of going to college.[27] But, he adds, economists are quick to extol the vital importance of going to college but are loath to emphasize—or even talk about—the benefits of marriage.[28]

Ron Haskins, also of the Brookings Institution, has identified what he calls the "success sequence": "at least finish high school, get a full-time job and wait until age 21 to get married and have children." If young people do just these three things, in that order, they are almost guaranteed to climb out of poverty. "Our research shows that of American adults who followed these three simple rules, only about 2 percent are in poverty and nearly 75 percent have joined the middle class (defined as earning around $55,000 or more per year)."[29] Undoubtedly, some teenagers could be persuaded to follow these steps with appeals to cool reason. But is it really so ridiculous to claim that society as a whole would have an easier time persuading more kids to follow this sequence if they were in families that modeled this practice themselves? Or if celebrities and other elites openly promoted these lifestyles? Or if they put just a smidgen of stigma on out-of-wedlock births and "baby daddy" culture?

Indeed, this highlights the profound failure and hypocrisy of elites in our culture. Amidst all the talk of marriage's decline, an important trend often gets overlooked: Marriage among elites is doing okay. The divorce rate among affluent Americans stabilized in the late 1980s and has largely recovered, at least among whites. The share of young white women with college degrees who were married in 2010 was just over 70 percent. That's pretty much where it was in 1950.[30] Less than 9 percent of college-educated white women had an unwed birth in 2011, very close to the number for women in 1950.[31] A Pew Research Center analysis of the most recent U.S. Census Bureau data found that marriage is more correlated with socioeconomic status than at any time in our history.[32] College-educated Americans tend to get a degree, get married, and have children—in that order. Meanwhile, marriage, particularly among the working class, has gone out of style. (Charles Murray's *Coming Apart: The State of White America, 1960–2010* exhaustively documents these trends.) Not surprisingly, college-educated professionals tend to marry other college-educated professionals, widening the rift between elites and everyone else. "It is the privileged Americans who are marrying, and marrying helps them stay privileged," Andrew J. Cherlin, a sociologist at Johns Hopkins University, told the *New York Times.* Up to 40 percent of the growth in economic inequality may be attributable to changes in the pattern of marriage in the United States. "The people with more education tend to have stable family structures with committed, involved fathers," Princeton sociologist Sara McLanahan added. "The people with less education are more likely to have complex, unstable situations involving men who come and go."[33] Wilcox attributes these trends to the degradation of the institutional model of marriage and to the subsequent ascendancy of the "soul-mate" model. The romantic ideal of finding a soul mate has deep historical roots, but for most of human history, marriage was a political, religious, and economic institution largely removed from notions of "true love" and soul mates. That started to change not long after the economic miracle of the Lockean Revolution. Soul-mate marriage is not a uniquely American ideal, but it has been most intensely idealized and democratized in America, and this ideal is arguably America's greatest cultural export, though marriage for love is still not the norm in many parts of the non-Western world.[34]

The big change in recent years is the one Brad Wilcox identified. Finding a true life partner was always an important consideration, but it was not the *sole* criterion. It was always nice in an arranged marriage when the youngsters found each other agreeable, but it was hardly the only item on the checklist. Even after arranged marriages ceased to be an acceptable norm, the checklist approach endured. Women—and their parents—still defined a "good match" beyond the narrow calculus of finding "the one." Would the man be a good provider? Would the woman be a good mother? Did he or she come from a good family? Practice the right faith? And so on. A few generations ago, marrying purely for love was a luxury largely reserved for the affluent. We are in some respects returning to that model, the difference being that in the past the poor still got married. Not so much anymore.

Today, the soul-mate model works on the self-centered though not necessarily *selfish* view that there is a single person out there who will allow me to be the person I want to be. This pursuit of happiness, newly defined, has much to recommend it, particularly for women. I certainly wouldn't want to go back to a time when the choice of whom to marry didn't reside entirely with the couple involved (except in the case of my daughter, where I would like veto power!). The problem isn't that men and women have the right to choose their own life partners; it is that, culturally, the range of factors taken into account for that choice has narrowed. And that has drawbacks.

For starters, it is more likely to lead to divorce. If marriage is all about romantic notions of personal fulfillment, there is precious little left to fall back on when marriage isn't all you hoped it would be. By telling poor people, especially, that they must "hold out for 'the one,'" society is, if not closing, then at least narrowing access to the best institution for raising children, getting and staying out of poverty, and finding meaning beyond purely individualistic terms. It is remarkable that, in all of the hand-wringing about the rise in economic inequality, the issue of marriage's dissolution almost never makes an appearance in the debate.

Family lays all the crucial groundwork for the kind of person you will become. When I say that the family is the gateway to civilization, I mean that literally. The family *civilizes barbarians*. It imprints them with language, customs, mores, values, and expectations for how society should work. If culture is a conversation, then the family is where all conversation begins. To be sure, other institutions pick up and round out the work of the family. Some researchers claim that peers have more influence on kids than parents do. Maybe. But parents have a huge role in who their peers will be—from where they live to where they send their kids to school to what hobbies they pursue and associations they form. Still, as nearly every teacher in the world will tell you, the first and most important work starts in the home.

In 2012, *Washington Post* columnist Courtland Milloy asked a good question: Why is African-American participation in professional baseball at an all-time low?[35] Economics doesn't offer much insight. Baseball offers the highest return for professional athletes of any professional sport. But culture plays a big role, albeit one that is hard to quantify. Basketball and football are more popular and glamorous. Baseball is a slower sport, less amenable to television coverage. Public policy plays some role as well. Local governments find baseball diamonds an expensive line item.

But one partial answer jumped out: fathers. "If you did a survey, I believe you'd find that the one thing average and above average players have in common is a father," Gerald Hall Jr., the baseball director for a local youth league, told Milloy. "Baseball is, at heart, a father-and-son sport. And if you're a kid that has nobody to throw to, nobody to talk to, nobody to discipline you in the way that baseball demands, you're not likely to play the game."

Tony Davenport, a local coach, agreed. "You have to catch the kids early, start with the basics—how to hold a bat, the proper throwing motion, catch with the glove, not your hand," he said. "A lot of kids really enjoy it if they continue to be provided with guidance."

Basketball is a sport that's largely picked up from peers. So is football. But baseball is arcane. It requires explanation and patience. You don't have to subscribe to all the sentimental arguments about the importance of fathers to appreciate how an absent father creates difficulties. A simple division of labor suggests that it's hard for a single parent to both prepare or provide dinner (or work two jobs) and play catch with a kid or sit on a couch for a few hours watching and explaining a game at the same time. But here's the important part: This observation is true not just for baseball but for an entire suite of life lessons, skills, and tasks, from playing a musical instrument, to learning a trade, to understanding good habits.

Single parents—either never married or divorced—simply have less time to dedicate to parenting than they otherwise might. This has numerous knock-on effects. Struggling single parents are more likely to let the TV, iPad, or Xbox serve as a babysitter. They take less time vetting peers who might seduce their kids into bad habits. They model behaviors—like serial dating or understandably short tempers—that may not always be ideal.

Of course, the world is full of counterexamples of successful people raised by single parents. In many of these cases, grandparents or other members of the extended family stepped in. In others, the mother did it all. Some mothers *can* do it all. But that is a lot to ask of them, and not the best way to organize a society.

It all boils down to conversation, gratitude, and remembering. People tend to value what societies celebrate. The broader conversation about marriage, family, and parenthood has decayed. It's in better shape than it was in the days when Betty Friedan could liken housewives to concentration camp victims and fringe radicals were shouting "Smash monogamy!" Serious people don't say "A woman needs a man like a fish needs a bicycle" anymore. But the rhetoric about marriage and parenting is shot through with culture-war politics on the right and identity-politics victimology on the left. In the mushy middle, it's usually adorned with self-help nostrums and silly verbiage about DIY "life hacks."

Gay marriage notwithstanding, among the cosmopolitans at the commanding heights of our culture, it is simply déclassé to extol the benefits of the bourgeois married lifestyle, at least in a public forum. Meanwhile, intellectuals and activists hector and demonize anyone who bestows undue honor on marriage or, more often, scorn or stigma on promiscuity, divorce, or out-of-wedlock birth. Dan Quayle, who, as vice president, criticized the TV show *Murphy Brown* for celebrating out-of-wedlock birth, was vilified by cultural elites for his prudishness and Comstockery. But, as a matter of public policy, he was right.[36]

Those who would prefer to, at best, ignore the role of culture in the degradation of the family emphasize purely material explanations for the decomposition. The family, they say, has come apart because of the disappearance of the "family wage," which was held aloft by large levels of unionization. And while it would be foolish to argue that the structure of the economy plays no role in encouraging or discouraging people to form families, such claims are overblown.

The materialists aren't wrong that economic conditions are important. Their error is in assuming that economic explanations tell the whole story.

The sacrifices inherent to parenthood require an enormous amount of social support to remain attractive, particularly in an age when there are so many enjoyable distractions made possible by the mass affluence of capitalism. Joseph Schumpeter recognized that the family was the one indispensable institution to liberal democratic capitalism. The sacrifices it demands of parents, he said, "do not consist only of the items that come within the reach of the measuring rod of money."[37] They demand more intangible things, like time, emotional commitment, and the subordination of our wants and desires to the needs of our children. These sacrifices need to be honored, publicly and passionately.

At the beginning of this chapter, I suggested that the plight of the family traces the larger argument of this book in miniature. In case I did a poor job showing that, let me magnify the point. It is my argument that capitalism and liberal democracy are unnatural. We stumbled into them in a process of trial and error but also blind luck, contingency, and happenstance a blink of an eye ago. The market system depends on bourgeois values, i.e., principles, ideas, habits, and sentiments that it did not create and cannot restore once lost. These values can only be transmitted two ways: showing and telling. That is to say by modeling right behaviors and instructing people through words and images what right behavior looks like. Institutions, not the government, are the chief mechanisms for communicating and rewarding these values. Moreover, modernity itself requires that citizens have divided and diverse loyalties. One of these is loyalty to self: We all have a right to pursue happiness as we see it. But others include loyalty to family, friends, faith, community, work, etc. Our problems today can be traced to the fact that we no longer have gratitude for the Miracle and for the institutions and customs that made it possible. Where there is no gratitude—and the effort that gratitude demands—all manner of resentments and hostilities flood back in. Few actually *hate* the traditional nuclear family or the role it plays. But many are indifferent to it. And indifference alone is enough to invite the rust of human nature back in.

Hannah Arendt once observed that, in every generation, Western civilization is invaded by barbarians: We call them "children." The family is the first line of defense against this barbarian invasion. The metaphor is inapt, because parents aren't at war with babies themselves. But parents are at war with the darker side of human nature, which we all work to trim away from for our children by inscribing in their hearts notions of decency, fair play, and self-restraint. When parents fail to do that, other institutions, including the government, try to step in and remedy what they can. But no teacher, counselor, social service worker, priest, rabbi, imam, or police officer will deny that, when the family fails to do its part, the work of every institution downstream of the family becomes that much more difficult. This doesn't mean that every failed family produces criminals, never mind marauding barbarians. But when the family fails, it becomes harder to produce good citizens dedicated to the principles and habits that created the Miracle in the first place.

13

THE TRUMPIAN ERA
The Perils of Populism

L ET'S PICK UP WHERE WE LEFT OFF IN THE LAST CHAPTER. Civilization is an ongoing conversation: Change the conversation, you change the world. If a baby born today is no different from a baby born 50,000 years ago, then the only thing keeping that baby from growing up into a barbarian is the conversation he or she is born into. This is the moral of everything we have discussed so far.

Deirdre McCloskey says that the Miracle happened because of words and talk. "The economy is nothing without the words supporting it," she insists. "Capitalism, like democracy, is talk, talk, talk all the way down."[1] *

This is true about more than just the economy. It is true about politics, family, religion, and every human endeavor. We are a cooperative

---

* "A big change in the common opinion about markets and innovation, I claim, caused the Industrial Revolution, and then the modern world. The change occurred during the seventeenth and eighteenth centuries in northwestern Europe. More or less suddenly the Dutch and British and then the Americans and the French began talking about the middle class, high or low—the 'bourgeoisie'—as though it were dignified and free. The result was modern economic growth.

"That is, ideas, or 'rhetoric,' enriched us. The cause, in other words, was language, that most human of our accomplishments. The cause was not in the first instance an economic/material change—not the rise of this or that class, or the flourishing of this or that trade, or the exploitation of this or that group. To put the claim another way, our enrichment was not a matter of Prudence Only, which after all is a virtue possessed by rats and grass, too. A change in rhetoric *about* prudence, and about the other and peculiarly human virtues, exercised in a commercial society, started the material and spiritual progress. Since then the bourgeois rhetoric has been alleviating poverty worldwide, and enlarging the spiritual scope of human life. . . ." Deirdre N. McCloskey, *Bourgeois Dignity: Why Economics Can't Explain the Modern World* (Chicago: University of Chicago Press, 2010), xi.

species, and it was our ability to communicate concepts that sent us skyrocketing up the food chain.

One need not be too literal here. It's not, strictly speaking, the words themselves but how we use them, the concepts they form and convey. But it is axiomatically true that what can be created by conversation can be destroyed by conversation. A holiday dinner can be a lovely affair or a dark and dismal disaster, all depending on the course of the conversation. So it is with our civilization. The Glorious Revolution and the American Revolution represented the ascendance of a new bourgeois worldview that elevated liberty, commerce, innovation, hard work, and the autonomy of family and individual alike. This worldview bubbled up from below far more than it trickled down from above. The bourgeoisie asserted their rights. And once they were won, those rights steadily became more and more universal because that was the only way the conversation could go. Once you say that all men are created equal and that we are endowed by our Creator with inalienable rights to life, liberty, and the pursuit of happiness, it becomes ever more difficult to say, "Well, except for those people." Once you insist that the only legitimate form of government is government by consent of the people, it's very difficult to walk that back.

Indeed, until fairly recently, dictators and totalitarians had to claim the mantle of democracy, talking as if it were something even they had to believe in, if they wanted to be seen as legitimate rulers. The Soviet Union, Nazi Germany, Mussolini's Italy—they all insisted that they spoke for the people's will, even if they rejected the "mechanical" fictions of Western politics and held Potemkin elections. East Germany called itself the "German Democratic Republic." North Korea still goes by the name "Democratic People's Republic of Korea." Syria's Bashar al-Assad and the mullahs in Iran feel the need to hold elections and referenda for the sake of appearances, just like Saddam Hussein, Hosni Mubarak, and Napoleon before them. Even the deceit of dictators was a tribute paid to democracy's virtue.

In the West, the left and right argued about how and where to draw the line between social welfare and economic liberty, but the rest of the conversation usually boiled down to which party was more committed to democracy, free speech, and personal liberty. Progressives from FDR to Barack Obama believed that granting "economic rights" would liberate people. Recall that FDR proclaimed that "necessitous men are not free men."[2] Conservatives in the classical liberal tradition argued that this approach was a violation of liberalism properly understood and was destined to constrict freedom in the end. These disagreements were—and remain—intense, but if you took each side at its word, both believed they were on the side of liberty and each used rhetoric to that effect.

That started to change in the early part of the twenty-first century.

For the last two decades, the rhetoric of Western elites has grown increasingly hostile to democracy, free speech, and capitalism. One reason is the widespread belief that authoritarian societies develop faster and better than democratic and free-market ones. This is a very old notion that emerges in new wrappings every generation. Mussolini made the trains run on time. Lincoln Steffens returned from the Soviet Union to declare, "I have been over into the future, and it works."[3] They said it about Napoleon's command economy and they probably said it about Hammurabi's too. There's just something deeply seductive about the idea of society being run by a strong father figure or some wise council of experts.

This is particularly true among the class of people who believe they should be on just such a council. They cast their gaze abroad and look for examples of societies doing things the "right" way and then insist we should be following that example. That's what countless intellectuals in America said in the 1920s and early 1930s about fascist and communist regimes in Europe, and, like a dog returning to its vomit, they do so today.[4]

William Easterly, one of the most brilliant scholars of development economics alive today, documents how this cult of authoritarianism thrives among the global caste of development experts and the journalists who rely on them.[5] Part of the problem of looking to "successful" autocracies as models is that it is something of a statistical mirage. It's true that in the last fifty years nine out of ten of the countries with truly extraordinary economic growth have been autocracies. This suggests that autocracy offers the best path to prosperity. The problem is that, over that period, there were *eighty-nine autocracies.* In other words, being an autocracy, under the best of circumstances, offers perhaps a one-in-nine chance of leading to prosperity. But even this is misleading, because the policies implemented by the successful autoc-racies tend to move countries away from despotism.[6]

Lee Kuan Yew, the founding dictator of Singapore, is the global elite's favorite benign despot, and for good reason. His policies did lead to amazing economic growth. But how did he do that? By wrenching out the corruption—both in the conventional sense and in the way I've been using it—from Singaporean society. He was an at times brutal modernizer. In the 1990s, Singapore had one of the highest per capita execution rates in the world.[7] Under the "Singapore model," graft and other forms of bribery are ruthlessly proscribed, and the rule of law, including property rights and contract enforcement (under British common law), is just as ruthlessly protected. Lee Kuan Yew believed in low regulation, low taxation, and free trade.

In other words, the crucial ingredient of Singapore's growth wasn't despotism but the imposition of market mechanisms and, to some extent, the legacy of British colonialism. Lee Kuan Yew's success no doubt depended in part on his ability to not be corrupted by power and keep the country on a path to modernization—and, I would wager, eventual democratization—but it also stemmed from the unique nature of Singapore itself, a small island nation. But for every Lee Kuan Yew there are many more Hugo Chávezes, Fidel Castros, and Robert Mugabes. Betting on authoritarian states on the assump-tion you will get a Lee Kuan Yew is playing a lottery with millions of lives.

The more important point, however, is that fawning on dictator-ships is morally grotesque. It is ultimately just a form of power wor-ship. For instance, *New York Times* columnist and best-selling author Thomas Friedman has spent much of the last two decades gushing over China's enlightened authoritarian capitalism. Look to China, he insisted in column after column, speech after speech, and book after book. They only care about "optimal policies"!

Well, okay, let's look to China. Authoritarianism under the emper-ors and then under Mao immiserated, oppressed, or murdered hun-dreds of millions of people in China. Then, in the late 1970s, China introduced rudimentary markets and property rights. And, suddenly, the Chinese economy took off. For the first time, hundreds of millions of Chinese people could eat meat, enjoy electricity, and acquire other things long considered staples here and unattainable luxuries there. Yet, here in America, and around much of the developed world, the reaction to China's success was "Wow. It must have been the authoritarianism."

Friedman was in many respects the head cheerleader:

> Watching both the health care and climate/energy debates in Congress, it is hard not to draw the following conclusion: There is only one thing worse than one-party autocracy, and that is one-party democracy, which is what we have in America today. One-party autocracy certainly has its drawbacks. But when it is led by a reasonably enlightened group of people, as China is today, it can also have great advantages. That one party can just impose the politically difficult but critically important policies needed to move a society forward in the 21st century.[8]

It's worth explaining what Friedman means by "one-party democracy." At the time he wrote this, the Democratic Party controlled the House, the Senate, and the White House. But the party in the "one-party democracy" Friedman lamented was not the ruling party but the minority party, because it refused to capitulate to the majority. The benefit of autocracy is that it is autocratic and can dispense with persuasion and impose the best policies.

In his book *Hot, Flat, and Crowded: Why We Need a Green Revolution—and How It Can Renew America*, Friedman has a chapter titled "China for a Day (but Not for Two)." In it, he openly pines for America to be like China—but just for a day. On this day there would be no rule of law, no constitutional safeguards, and no democratic debate. Instead "enlightened" experts would simply be able to impose the best policies—i.e., the policies Friedman agrees with.

This is a perfect example of how words can camouflage things. His columns are full of the sorts of buzzphrases and jargon that fill the air at Davos meetings and TED talks. But what does "China for a day" mean that is substantively different from "king for a day" or "tyranny for a day" or, for that matter, "Nazis for a day"? Saying "China for a day" gives the "argument" a certain cachet, but that cachet is just a different label on the same ancient bottle. (Also, if there is any lesson worth taking to heart from the last thousand—or 10,000—years, it is that if you give people absolute power "just for a day," expect them to find reasons to give themselves an extension. Absolute power is like being granted a wish by a genie: The first thing you do is wish for more wishes.)

Ultimately, wanting to be "China for a day" is no different from talking about how our politics should be like the "moral equivalent of war" (another argument Friedman employs constantly, saying that we must fight climate change the way we fought World War II; "green" he explains, "is the new red, white and blue.")[9] We are hardwired to dispense with pleasantries and protocol when under attack. The technocrats understand this, which is why the Obama administration loved the phrase "A crisis is a terrible thing to waste." And it is why the Trump campaign was—and the Trump White House is—so eager to describe America as a violence-plagued hellscape when it serves their political agenda. "This American carnage stops right here and stops right now," the president declared in his inaugural address,[10] which he concluded with an upraised fist.

How we talk is merely a reflection of what we think. No wonder, then, that the state of public opinion in the West is depressing. A majority of young people no longer believe democracy is "essential."[11] Support for liberty is literally dying out. Among those born in the 1930s, 75 percent of Americans and 53 percent of Europeans say living under democratic government is "essential." Among people born in the 1980s, the number drops to the low 40s in Europe and the low 30s in America. Only 32 percent of millennials consider it "absolutely essential" that "civil rights protect people's liberty."[12]

"Citizens in a number of supposedly consolidated democracies in North America and Western Europe have not only grown more critical of their political leaders," write political scientists Roberto Stefan Foa and Yascha Mounk in the *Journal of Democracy*. "Rather, they have also become more cynical about the value of democracy as a political system, less hopeful that anything they do might influence public policy, and more willing to express support for authoritarian alternatives."[13]

There is ample evidence that support for the core rights that define a liberal order is eroding, most precipitously among young people (though it is possible that, as a reaction to the Trump presidency, some young people might develop a heightened appreciation for civil liberties). The younger you are, the less likely you are to support free-speech rights. Forty percent of eighteen- to thirty-four-year-olds told Pew they thought that speech offensive to minorities should be banned.[14] A survey of college students in 2015 found that a majority of students favor speech codes for both students and faculty. More than six in ten want professors to provide students with "trigger warnings" before discussing or presenting material some might find offensive. A third of the students couldn't name the First Amendment as the part of the Constitution that protects free speech. Thirty-five percent said the First Amendment doesn't apply to "hate speech" (it does), and 30 percent of self-identified *liberal students* said they believe the First Amendment is outdated.[15]

Presumably, most young liberals do not think support for free markets, democracy, and free speech is itself "hate speech." But it is remarkable how quickly activists can conclude that support for such things are "code words" for hateful ideals. (The *Harvard Crimson* has a long history of running articles insisting that the eminent scholar Harvey Mansfield, one of the last conservatives at Harvard, is a practitioner of "hate speech.") Duke historian Nancy MacLean published a book, *Democracy in Chains: The Deep History of the Radical Right's Stealth Plan for America*, in which she argues that the libertarian economics movement, specifically the public choice school, is a thinly concealed racist scheme designed to undermine democracy. Despite the fact the book was torn to shreds for dishonest and shabby scholarship—a work of "speculative historical fiction," according to MacLean's Duke colleague, Michael C. Munger—it was, as of this writing, a finalist for a National Book Award. Apparently the thesis is too seductive to care about the facts.[16] Just try to talk about individualism, inequality, merit, etc., on a college campus and see how long it takes before someone is offended. In many places where the new class controls the commanding heights of the culture, free speech has come to be defined as assault, and assault as free speech.[17]

Before the Obama administration's deception about a video causing the attacks on the American diplomatic outpost in Benghazi was debunked, liberal op-ed pages and radio and television shows lit up with calls to "fix" the First Amendment and curtail free speech in America, as if rioting barbarians halfway around the world have a heckler's veto on what Americans can say.

It is inevitable that, when the way people think and talk changes, the shape of our politics will change too. Across Europe, illiberal movements have been gaining steam for more than a decade. Marine Le Pen's National Front has the wind at its back, forcing artificial coalitions between traditional conservatives and socialists to keep it out of power. Emmanuel Macron succeeded in defeating Le Pen, but he needed to form a new party to do it: La République en Marche or simply En Marche, which in English is translated, variously, as "Forward!" or "Onward!" or "Working!" or "On the Move!" As of this writing, it is too soon to form a lasting judgment on Macron, but it appears that he has something of a Napoleonic streak to him. He pledges to go around the French Parliament and impose most of his reforms by decree. He has already extended the state of emergency declared in the wake of some horrific terrorist attacks in 2015.[18]

In Austria, a coalition similar to Macron's narrowly prevented Norbert Hofer from becoming the first right-wing nationalist leader of a Western European country since the end of World War II. In neighboring Hungary, president Viktor Orbán routinely talks of "building an illiberal new national state" modeled after the regimes in Russia, Turkey, and China.[19] "Liberal democratic states can't remain globally competitive," he insists.[20] Orbán's biggest political competition is Jobbik, an ultra-nationalist party that is economically left-wing and anti-capitalist and feeds off a deep reserve of anti-Semitism in the country. An estimated one in five Hungarians have extreme animosity toward Jews.[21] In Bulgaria, the nationalist-socialist party, Ataka (Attack), has made huge strides blending a populist anti-immigrant agenda with conventional economic and racial socialism (which, again, are more often than not synonymous historically).

In Greece, a hard-left nationalist party, Syriza, dominates, while the authoritarian right-wing party Golden Dawn is in a close third. Golden Dawn marches under a banner conveniently reminiscent of the official Nazi flag, displaying a black meander against a backdrop of red.[22] The party's lodestar is the Greek pro-fascist dictator Ioannis Metaxas, who ruled from 1936 to 1941.[23]

In Britain, the triumph of the Brexit movement, while salutary on the whole, arguably owed its relatively narrow margin of victory to an undercurrent of nativist and nationalist sentiment (fomented to some extent by Vladimir Putin's social media troll army). More troubling is the illiberalism of Jeremy Corbyn, the unreconstructed leftist who leads the Labour Party and rejects Tony Blair's project to reconcile the party with liberal democratic capitalism. A left-wing populist and fervent opponent of all things "Zionist," Corbyn struggles to avoid the charge of anti-Semitism while pandering to members of his coalition who cannot avoid the charge.

Turkey's Recep Tayyip Erdoğan, in just a few short years, has gone a long way to meld the illiberal policies of Atatürk with the illiberal theology of the Ottomans, persecuting journalists and imprisoning political opponents by the thousands. As of this writing, Venezuela under Nicolás Maduro continues to prove that things can always get worse under a populist-socialist dictatorship. The oil-rich basket case is now in the throes of Weimar-level hyper-inflation. Parents are forced to give away their children because they cannot feed them as Maduro blames the country's economic woes on the "bourgeois parasites."[24]

In July of 2017, President Trump visited Warsaw, Poland, and gave a stirring defense of Western civilization, much of which I agreed with. But the speech had an overlay of nationalism to it that did not go unnoticed by the increasingly authoritarian Polish government. The ruling party, Law and Justice, is committed to a campaign of delegitimizing the press, the independent judiciary, and even the apolitical nature of the military under a program called "repolanization."[25]

Tragically, the dream of liberalism is dying away in illiberal countries as well. The "Green" movement in Iran has been crushed from above but has also withered from below. "The educated young who were the backbone of the Green movement are now demoralized and apathetic thirty- and forty-somethings—a transformation not unlike what happened to China's pro-democracy movement after the 1989 Tiananmen Square massacre," writes Sohrab Ahmari.

". . . The situation is equally grim in the Arab lands," he adds. "Save for Tunisia, the Arab Spring uprisings of 2010 and 2011 have everywhere yielded civil war, state failure, or a return to the repressive status quo ante." Public opinion surveys "suggest that the region's young aspire to stability, not political freedom."[26] The demoralization of young Arabs is understandable given the failure of the Arab Spring to deliver on its promises, but one has to wonder whether some of that despair derives from the growing global consensus that democracy is losing its appeal.

THE TRUMP ERA

And then, of course, there's Donald Trump. Though you wouldn't know it from the writings of many liberal intellectuals and journalists, President Trump is very different from far-right and neo-fascist demagogues in some important respects—but, of course, he's dismayingly similar in others. The differences are worth discussing first.

Unlike Marine Le Pen, Norbert Hofer, Viktor Orbán, and other illiberal politicians, Trump is not deeply immersed in nationalist ideology—or any ideology. In no way whatsoever is Trump an intellectual. To say someone isn't an intellectual does not mean he is not intelligent. The question of Trump's intellect is an open one to all but his most committed followers and detractors—and to Trump himself, who constantly insists that he is man of unimpeachable genius. He certainly possesses a formidable cunning that often catches his opponents off guard. But it is also clear that he knows very little about American political history, and that makes him a fascinating political creature.

For instance, many of his favorite slogans—"the silent majority," "the forgotten man," "America first," and even "Make America Great Again"—have deep historical roots that he appears to have no appreciation for. He learned the phrase "America first" from a *New York Times* reporter who was trying to understand his political philosophy.[27] "America first" has a complicated and storied pedigree in American politics, as it was the rallying cry of a broad coalition of non-interventionists who wanted to keep America out of World War II in Europe. Over time, it took on a particularly sinister connotation, as the most vocal faction in it was objectively pro-German in the European conflict. In an interview with the *Washington Post*, Trump was informed that the phrase "the Silent Majority" was used by Richard Nixon in his 1972 campaign.[28] It remains unclear whether anyone has explained to him that "the Forgotten Man" was FDR's slogan in his effort to appeal to the disaffected masses of the Great Depression. Even "Make America Great Again" is not original to him; it was used repeatedly by Ronald Reagan in his 1980 campaign (though he meant something very different).

Trump's ideological commitments are similarly inchoate. Over the last thirty years, he has been consistent about only a handful of ideas—protectionism, the wisdom of "taking the oil" from Middle Eastern countries we invaded, and some fairly vague platitudes about cutting back regulations—but, beyond that, he's been all over the map on guns, immigration, abortion, taxes, health care, etc. Unlike traditional American conservatives, his lodestars have never been limited government, the Constitution, individual liberty, or, needless to say, "traditional values." There is little reason to believe that he has anything more than a thumbless grasp of such concepts. Rather, his watchwords have always been "winning" and "strength." His key promise to voters was that America will "win again" and that, if elected, our leaders will no longer be "weak." "Winning solves a lot of problems," Trump said in an interview with the *Washington Post*.[29]

It should go without saying—but doesn't today—that winning and strength are entirely amoral values. Successful cheaters and murderers "win." Good parents do not teach their children that the only thing that matters is winning, nor do they insist that being strong is more important than being decent. A morally and philosophically serious person does not place personal victory as the highest value.

For Donald Trump, "winning"—at business, in television ratings, and in politics—is all that matters. Suggesting that one of his opponents was akin to a pedophile and that another was the son of an accomplice to Kennedy's assassination are justified by the fact that he won. He even explains away the fact that he constantly whines on the grounds that it is a useful tool for winning. "I keep whining and whining until I win."[30] Hence his commitment to render all news reporting that doesn't show him as a winner as not just unfair or biased but "fake."

Trump's ignorance of the politics that came before him, it turned out, was a great advantage politically. The elite political class—on the left and the right, but most importantly in the fiercely arrogant middle—invested too much in the power of political shibboleths and taboos. Trump simply steamrolled over them, speaking in his own authentic manner. For those of us who place a great deal of importance in words, Trump sounded not only ignorant but vulgar. But for millions of voters he sounded real, and his vulgarity proved he wasn't part of the "establishment" that so many blamed for the sorry status quo. This was his greatest advantage over Senator Ted Cruz, a deeply establishmentarian politician who knew all of the lyrics of populism but could not convincingly carry the tune.

Similarly, Trump's anti-political political rhetoric is a clear echo of the language of the 1930s, on both sides of the Atlantic. "The time for empty talk is over," Trump declared in his inaugural address (and again at his speech at the Conservative Political Action Conference [CPAC] in February of 2017). "Now arrives the hour of action!"[31] He loves to talk of the "blood of patriots."

The 1930s marked a high-water mark in the international cult of "Action!" FDR, Mussolini, Hitler, and countless other leaders all tried to tap into the widespread belief that decadent Western capitalism and "Manchester liberalism" were inadequate to the challenges of the day. In America, FDR tapped into this intellectual fad in an attempt to preserve democracy (if not necessarily capitalism) when he promised "bold, persistent experimentation." To this day—I have learned to excess—progressives fail to appreciate what is implied in a policy of "experimentation." The very idea of experimentation presumes that there are no a priori dogmatic, principled constraints on the investigation. "Take a method and try it," FDR said.[32] It sounds so reasonable, but the implication is that democracy, property rights, civil rights, etc., are not prior constraints on political behavior. The whole point of our Constitution was to put certain questions out of the reach of rulers and voters alike. "Experimentation" says all options are on the table—the very definition of the authoritarian method. "I'm a conservative, but at this point, who cares?" an exasperated Donald Trump remarked at the California Republican Party convention. "We've got to straighten out the country."[33]

"Fascism appealed, first of all, to the pragmatic ethos of experimentation," observed the late John Patrick Diggins.[34] Ideology was a deadweight, holding back nations from reaching their true potential. Hitler despised theorists who spoke of principle and doctrine, calling them "ink knights." What Germany needed, according to Hitler, was a "revolt against reason" itself, for "intellect has poisoned our people!"[35]

The point is not that Trump is a Hitler. He's not: Hitler could have repealed Obamacare quite easily! Nor is he an FDR or a Mussolini. It is that he represents a reversion to a natural type of leader who speaks and thinks in tribal terms. His thinking and rhetoric are less interesting than the fact that his thinking and rhetoric found purchase with so many Americans, particularly supposed champions of constitutionalism and limited government.

Trump is a thoroughly romantic figure in so many ways. He puts his faith not in God or the Constitution or any abstract rules but in his own instincts: "I'm a very instinctual person, but my instinct turns out to be right."[36] "Experience has taught me a few things," Trump explains. "One is to listen to your gut, no matter how good something sounds on paper."[37] In numerous interviews, Trump has explained that his instincts are more reliable than facts. If it feels right to him, it's right. That's why he once explained in a sworn deposition that his net worth depends heavily on how he feels about himself any given morning.[38] That is also why, as a businessman, he was happy to lie to business partners, abuse eminent domain, and do anything he could get away with under the law.

As the Trump presidency has unfolded, it's become clear that Trump's feelings—particularly his insecurities, his megalomania, etc.—determine the vast majority of his decisions. His refusal to stop attacking the parents of a slain Muslim-American soldier during the campaign was indicative of his entire approach to life. If you disagree with or criticize him, you deserve whatever insults and attacks he can muster. And his attacks on a judge of Mexican descent highlighted how democratic norms and decorum have no weight when balanced on the scale of his feelings.

And while his capacity to personalize every conflict and relationship is the central theme of his psyche, his reliance on feelings does have broader policy and political consequences as well. As a candidate, he encouraged crowds to "knock the crap" out of protestors.[39] As president, Trump has condoned and celebrated excessive force for police officers.[40] He famously admires Vladimir Putin, and whenever he's pressed on the fact that he admires a murderous autocrat, he throws America under the bus, arguing that Americans have no right to judge because we do terrible things too.[41] There is no venue where he will forgo advancing his own political interests or settling some score, be it an address to a Boy Scout jamboree or to uniformed military.

Were Trump able to check his id and think beyond the horizon of his instincts in the moment, he would be a far more formidable demagogue. Fortunately, he cannot, and so the constitutional architecture of our government, combined with the patriotic commitments of most of the people who work for him, is more than adequate to constrain his will to power as president. Still, it is precisely these qualities in him that make him so fascinating. Beneath his suits and his abnormally long ties, he is a throwback, a kind of generic prototype of premodern man, obsessed with being the alpha of the group. Because he is bereft of any coherent ideology and largely immune to any of the norms of good character, Donald Trump is, in many respects, a perfect example of how capitalism, absent the extra-rational dogmas of morality, creates creatures of pure appetite, guided only by the most rudimentary software of human nature. He cares about sex and power, dominating others, and having his status affirmed. He puts family above all other considerations, but defines the family's interests in terms of wealth and dynastic glory. He views others as instruments of his will whose value is measured in their loyalty to him, a loyalty that is rarely reciprocated. When asked what sacrifices he made comparable to those of parents who lost a child in war, he couldn't even name any sacrifice at all.[42] He is a knight, in the Nietzschean sense, and he makes his own morality.

Alas, rather than see these facts as flaws, many voters saw them as admirable features. Donald Trump's improvisational, almost glandular style of politics, combined with his unapologetic ignorance of democratic norms and undiluted resentment toward elites, made him an ideal vessel for the frustrations and anger of not just the Republican base but millions of disaffected non-traditional and Obama voters who felt they had no voice in politics as usual. Indeed, doctrinaire conservatives were among the last to rally to Trump's banner, a fact easily forgotten now that so many conservative ideologues and intellectuals have retrofitted their worldview to rationalize and accommodate Trumpism.

In short, Donald Trump is the most successful populist politician in American history, with the possible exception of President Andrew Jackson. Many conservative commentators have convinced themselves that Trump's victory was the product of his own incredible political genius. There is scant evidence to support this claim. This is not necessarily a slight against Trump. Politics is about moments more than anything else. The right politician at the wrong time will almost always lose against the wrong politician at the right time. Trump flirted with running for president in 2000 on the Reform Party ticket and again in 2012. Both times he opted not to, at least in part because he had no chance of winning. The point is simply that Trump won the presidency because the time was ripe for him to do so, and even then he barely pulled it off.[43]

Just as it's always advisable to be a well-stocked water seller during a drought, it's good to be a populist at a moment of widespread thirst for populism. It's worth remembering that there were two authentic populists in the 2016 presidential race, the other being Vermont senator Bernie Sanders. There is reason to believe that, if the Democratic establishment had not circled the wagons around Hillary Clinton, the quintessential technocratic progressive new-class candidate, Sanders could have won the Democratic primaries. Even if that were not the case, the fact remains that populism is high in the saddle on both the left and the right, here and abroad.

THE PERILS OF POPULISM

Populism, which essentially means nothing more than "peoplism," is not a doctrine. It is an orientation and a passion. In theory and in its rhetoric, it elevates "the people," but in reality it only speaks for a subset of them. It shares with nationalism a romantic glorification or sanctification of the group. Those in the group are part of the tribe, the cause, "the movement," or any other abstraction that triggers "the coalition instinct" discussed earlier. They are us, we, the ones we have been waiting for. "The people" simultaneously claim to be victims and superior to the victimizers, with a more rightful claim on power. They may claim to be "the 99 percent"—they aren't—but they mean that they are 100 percent of those who matter. "For populists," writes Jan-Werner Müller, "this equation always works out: any remainder can be dismissed as immoral and not properly a part of the people at all. That's another way of saying that populism is always *a form of identity politics* (though not all versions of identity politics are populist)."44

As an outspoken conservative critic of the president, I've been subjected to near-constant anger and scorn from Trump supporters, including many who were once admirers of mine. (Indeed, one of the most painful revelations of the last two years has been to discover so many people disappointed in me for not living down to their expectations.) I bring this up because it's been fascinating to hear from so many Trump supporters who fly under the banner of "We the People." It is a constant refrain. But it's also untrue. The Trump supporters' use of "We the People" is a perfect illustration of Müller's point. Donald Trump lost the popular vote and, as of this writing, has approval ratings in the mid-30s. Donald Trump, by any objective metric, is not the paladin of "We the People." He is the representative of the people his supporters believe to be the only people who matter.

Populism and nationalism often go together, but not all populist movements are nationalist, nor are all nationalist movements populist. Before he took his populism to the national stage, William Jennings Bryan was, properly speaking, a Nebraska-firster. Likewise, George Wallace was populist for "the people of Alabama," by which he meant the white people of Alabama who supported Jim Crow. Al Sharpton rose to fame as a populist demagogue representing himself first and a subset of blacks in Harlem second. Donald Trump talks often about "the American people," but his definition of who qualifies as the American people often begins and ends with those Americans who support Donald Trump. The "only important thing," Trump announced at a rally in the spring of 2016, "is the unification of the people—because the other people don't mean anything."[45]

Populist movements in America have tended to be cast on the left side of the political spectrum—except when they've been avowedly racist or anti-Semitic, in which case liberal historians and political analysts go to great lengths to disassociate and exonerate progressivism from any such associations. In Europe, where the upper classes have replaced the old notions of inherited nobility and aristocracy with elite technocracy, populism tends to be associated with demagoguery, pandering, and backward thinking. The bankers and bureaucrats scoff at the little people who resist the tides of globalization as bitter losers.

And there's some truth there. Populist movements do tend to be coalitions of losers. I do not mean that in a pejorative sense but in an analytical one. Populist movements almost by definition don't spring up among people who think everything is going great and they're getting a fair shake. Populism is fueled by resentment, the sense that the "real people" are being kept down or exploited by the elites or the establishment or, in the numerous extreme cases of populism, shadowy conspirators. "Conspiracy theories," Müller writes, are "not a curious addition to populist rhetoric; they are rooted in and emerge from the very logic of populism itself."[46]

FDR came up with the phrase "the Forgotten Man" not because he himself was much of a populist but because he needed to siphon off support from his many populist challengers. But the phrase was a brilliant encapsulation of the source of populist discontent. To be forgotten is to feel disrespected, left out, left behind. It breeds a soul-poisoning sense of ingratitude for the status quo and a burning sense that things were better in the past. It was this sentiment that the romantic nationalists of Europe tapped into. All of us are familiar with the way paranoia can fester when we have been excluded; we invent theories about how our enemies—or friends—are working against us.[47] Populism often works under the same dynamic, but on a mass scale.

The first populist movements in the United States were mostly agrarian and rural. Farmers, for obvious reasons, were not at the cutting edge of social change. The rapid industrialization and urbanization of American life understandably led rural communities to feel that their country was getting away from them. The tendency of young men to leave their communities in search of a new life in the big city aroused feelings of resentment among those who stayed behind (and amplified feelings of alienation and rootlessness among those who left). The ever-increasing sophistication of financial capitalism made many feel like tools or pawns of forces outside of their control.

This is one reason why populist movements, here and in Europe, are attracted to various forms of "producerism," an economic doctrine that distinguishes between "good" economic activity—building with your hands, toiling in the soil, etc.—and the mere manipulation of capital. William Jennings Bryan distinguished between those who worked with their hands making things and "the idle holders of idle capital."[48] Producerism is often associated with "right-wing" populist movements, but one can see its relationship to Marxist notions of the labor theory of value and exploitative capital. When Benito Mussolini was transitioning from socialism to fascism, he stopped calling his newspaper *Il Popolo d'Italia* (*The People of Italy*), a "socialist daily," in favor of a "producers' daily."[49] To listen to Donald Trump, the only jobs that matter are manufacturing and construction. He talks about the trade deficit obsessively, never mentioning that America has a significant trade surplus in services or that trade deficits are the product of large foreign investment in America.

Historically, the demonization of "idle capital" provided a fertile medium for the oldest of conspiracy theories: anti-Semitism. Thomas E. Watson, a prominent Georgia populist, started out as a defender of poor blacks and whites alike, arguing that the poor needed to unite against the monied interests. But because populism has no limiting principle save the need to feed off and stoke resentment, he eventually embraced white supremacy, anti-Catholicism, and anti-Semitism. The 1892 Populist Party platform proclaimed, "A vast conspiracy against mankind has been organized on two continents, and it is rapidly taking possession of the world."[50]

In Europe in the 1930s and in much of the Arab world today, the widespread belief that the Jews or Zionists are the author of every problem of the world has made anti-Semitism the easiest route to pander to the masses.

"Populists . . . look at the supposedly secret deals that run the world 'behind the scenes,'" observed Christopher Hitchens, This is "child's play," he added. "Except that childishness is sinister in adults."[51] Hitchens was making a more profound point than he might have realized. The corruption of democracy comes from human nature, and children are always closer to our natural state than adults. Adults—hopefully—have been civilized. Children are born barbarians, and their instincts are the same in every era. Populism is a barbaric, childish yawp coming out of democratic man.[52]

Donald Trump's constant insistence that "the system is rigged"—even as he runs the system—fits neatly into the mainstream of the populist tradition—as does most of the rhetoric from Bernie Sanders and, to a slightly lesser extent, Elizabeth Warren. At times, Trump's persecution complex is quite amusing. His relentless tweets asking why the government hasn't done this or that make it sound like he can't actually ask his employees directly. But Trump's indictment of the "globalist" conspiracy against "the people" has some more ominous echoes as well.

In the final weeks of the 2016 presidential race, Trump's campaign went into overdrive. In an October 13 speech, he railed against "the global special interests" that "don't have your good in mind."[53] In an ad touted as his "closing argument," Donald Trump railed against a global "political establishment" that has vampirically "bled our country dry." Over images of various supposedly villainous globalists—most of them Jewish—Trump inveighed against this sinister cabal. While the screen showed Goldman Sachs CEO Lloyd Blankfein, Trump declared, "It's a global power structure that is responsible for the economic decisions that have robbed our working class, stripped our country of its wealth and put that money into the pockets of a handful of large corporations and political entities."[54] (The fact that large swaths of his administration are run by the Goldman Sachs/Wall Street/Davos crowd is a stirring tribute to his lack of ideological—or just plain logical—coherence.)

The ad invited vociferous charges of anti-Semitism, with some likening it to the nineteenth-century anti-Semitic conspiracy forgery *The Protocols of the Elders of Zion*. Such complaints might be heavy-handed, though it doesn't seem inconceivable that Steve Bannon, Trump's avowed nationalist campaign manager, was feeding the troll army of alt-right bigots he helped bring out of the floorboards. I don't think Bannon or Trump are anti-Semites, but it's much harder to defend them against the charge of gross cynicism in their willingness to play fast and loose with populist rhetoric and their willingness to feed an army of racist and anti-Semitic trolls.[*]

But, again, the important point is not that people in Trump's orbit—or their kindred spirits in Europe—traffic in populist and nativist appeals. It is that we have blundered into a time when such appeals *work*. There have always been populist opportunists in every country and in every age. But healthy societies with healthy institutions can usually fend them off like a weak virus. The rhetoric of the demagogues is drowned out by the much larger conversation. The dismaying thing about the moment we are in is that demagoguery on the left and the right is in such high demand.

Demagoguery—appealing to the gut instincts of the mob or the crowd—is an ancient form of rhetoric. The term comes from ancient Greeks who first defined a demagogue as a leader of the common people. Only later did it come to mean playing on the passions of the public to foment immediate and unthinking action or hatred toward

---

[*]   I have some personal experience on this front. As a conservative critic of Donald Trump, I was subjected to an onslaught of anti-Semitic attacks by members of the alt-right. These were no dog whistles. On Twitter, my face was Photoshopped into gas chambers with that of a smiling Donald Trump poised to press the button. A common meme was the image of a corpse hung from the struts of a helicopter, the implication being this was what I had to look forward to under a Trump presidency. When I mentioned on Twitter that my brother died from his addictions, I was queried by ebullient alt-righters whether he had been turned into a lampshade or a bar of soap. The Anti-Defamation League found that I ranked sixth on their ranking of Jewish journalists subjected to anti-Semitic attacks during the 2016 presidential campaign, with my friend Ben Shapiro as number one, and my similarly named fellow journalist Jeffrey Goldberg as number three. (See "ADL Report: Anti-Semitic Targeting of Journalists During the 2016 Presidential Campaign: A Report from ADL's Task Force on Harassment and Journalism," p. 6. https://www.adl.org/sites/default/files/documents/assets/pdf/press-center/CR_4862_Journalism-Task-Force_v2.pdf.) What dismayed me more than the bigoted attacks was the relative silence of many traditional conservatives who thought that it was not worth taking a more vocal stand against bigotry in the name of their candidate.

the system. Demagoguery is quite obviously linked to romanticism, because both elevate the importance of emotion and feelings above reason and fact. But the practice of demagoguery is far more ancient, because it is grounded in human instinct. In primitive societies, where strangers are presumed to be enemies and where survival requires inflaming a zealous defensiveness of the group and demonizing hatred for the other, the ability to see the world in black-and-white is a competitive advantage. A talent for stirring up passion—and the ability to have one's passion stirred up—is a source of strength. For unity is the fruit of passion. In other words, demagoguery is a natural human trait. Containing, channeling, and dispelling dangerous popular passions is what civilizations *do.* The Constitution does many things, but one of its chief functions is to blunt and divert the power of demagogues and the masses that listen to them. This was once understood and celebrated by conservatives. Not so much today.

Again, if Trump had been able to keep his instincts in check, he would have been a much more formidable president and a more effective demagogue. If he had a better read on the moment, he would have given a very different inaugural address, reaching out to Democrats for some massive share-the-wealth program of big-infrastructure spending and the like. He would have siphoned some of the populist passion that drove the Sanders campaign. Instead, as so many new presidents do, he misread the election results, antagonizing Democrats and appeasing his most zealous supporters. As a conservative and as an American, this makes me happy, at least in the short term, because by galvanizing opposition against him, he has unwittingly strengthened the system of checks and balances. But in the long term I worry more, because he has demonstrated that conservatism, at least as expressed by the Republican Party and its more loyally allied media outlets, is not immune to the tribal desire for strongmen.

Donald Trump did not cause this corruption on the right; he exploited it. And, having succeeded, he is accelerating it. If civilization is just a conversation, then Donald Trump is already a very consequential president, because he has profoundly changed the conversation of our democracy.

14

THINGS FALL APART
The American Experiment at Risk

FOR MANY AMERICANS, INCLUDING MOST LIBERALS BUT also a good number of conservatives, libertarians, and others, Donald Trump's sudden emergence as a political force raised the question: *Where did this monster come from?*

Of course, that's not entirely fair to Trump and many of his supporters. For many voters, Donald Trump was not the monster but the savior, the heroic—albeit flawed—champion called forth by the times. He was the Shin Godzilla of our moment, rising up to destroy the establishment and awaken the true spirit of the American nation. For others, he was simply the preferable option between two bad choices. Ample polling during the campaign showed that more Trump voters thought of their vote as against Clinton than for Trump.[1] And if, for example, as a conservative, your overriding concern is the future of the Supreme Court, Trump was the right choice at the time.

Whichever perspective you subscribe to, the real point is that Trump was not a creature out of the blue. Both his election and his presidency were symptoms of trends long in the making. Any exhaustive attempt to explain how Donald Trump succeeded in his hostile takeover of the Republican Party would require a whole book—at least. So I will simply focus on what I believe are the most important factors and the ones that most directly touch on the themes of this book.

As I have labored to illustrate, human nature holds constant. The world changed over the last three hundred years, not because we evolved into more enlightened beings, but because we stumbled into a new way of talking and thinking about how society should be organized. That changed way of thinking was the revolutionary event, but the revolution was sustained and secured by a host of institutions, both in terms of rules but also in the more concrete sense of actual associations and organizations. Those associations and organizations are commonly lumped into the term "civil society." It comprises everything from churches and schools to bowling leagues and 4-H clubs. The old form of civil society is not dead, but it is everywhere retreating, like a once great reef bleached by acidic waters.

That simile is intentional. I've always thought of civil society to be like a great reef in the ocean. The coral provides a rich ecosystem in which a vast variety of life resides, which is why they are sometimes called "the rain forests of the sea." They constitute less than 0.1 percent of the worldwide ocean surface but account for a staggering 25 percent of all marine species.[2]

For most of human prehistory, there was really only one institution: the tribe or band. It may have been subdivided into some smaller units: the family, the hunters versus the gatherers, etc. But they were all subsumed into the tribe itself.

After the agricultural revolution, the division of labor created space for more institutions, some of which could even be in conflict with one another. There was "space" outside the state. And in that space, institutions grew over time, at coral pace. This ecosystem changed little, and when it did, it did so very slowly, allowing humans to adapt. The reef was made up of only a few distinct colonies of coral: the family, the local community, the church, a relative handful of occupations, usually supervised by guilds of one sort or another, and, of course, the state, including the military. Then, for reasons discussed at length earlier, there was the miraculous explosion of institutions. And with that explosion came a staggering burst of human prosperity and creative genius, which only expanded and extended the whole process.

Creating a nurturing environment for mediating institutions is a form of social engineering, arguably the greatest feat of social engineering in human history, but not in the way we normally define the term. It is social engineering of the sort I described when discussing the differences between English gardens and French ones. English gardens create a zone of liberty where people and institutions are free to prosper. Humans serve as pollinators, moving from one institution to another, gaining sustenance and providing it at the same time. It is social engineering without any intended goal other than the flourishing of the garden itself.

If you can forgive the whiplash of going back and forth between metaphors, civil society in the modern era is akin to creating artificial reefs. Drop a pile of concrete or sink an oil rig to the bottom of the Gulf of Mexico and wait. Soon coral, algae, barnacles, oysters, and other creatures attach themselves to it. As they accumulate, fish take up residence in the new shelter. (Oil rigs in Southern California host up to twenty-seven times more fish than natural rocky reefs in the same area.)[3] I hate the expression "If you build it, they will come," but in this case it's apt. And when they do come, they flourish.

The hitch to this metaphor is that the state cannot build the reefs; it can only protect them. If you've ever been scuba diving or snorkeling, you probably know that swimmers aren't supposed to touch the coral with their bare hands. We have oils in our skin that disrupt the membranes of coral and can even kill a whole colony. The state is a greasy-handed tourist in civil society. Except when it is extremely careful—which it usually is not—when it intervenes in institutions, it harms them and often kills them.

Civil society has a different currency from the market economy and the state. Voluntary associations operate on the economy of love and community, charity and reciprocity. The Salvation Army, the Catholic Church, the Boy Scouts, garden clubs, and Civil War reenactment societies operate based on shared values and different principles from a welfare agency or jobs program. When the state stomps its way in and tells these groups how they must operate, it is usually harmful. When the state takes over the functions being performed by civil society, it is toxic.

That is not the intent, of course. The government is usually "here to help." The government does many good and important things. But what it cannot do is love you.

Politicians delight in likening the country to a family. This is a dangerous analogy. Welfare programs—including numerous middle-class entitlements—are justified on the grounds that we all belong to the same American family, families take care of their own, and in the family there is no shame in asking for help. The problem here is twofold. Anyone who has asked a family member—particularly the wrong family member—for money knows that shame often plays a big role in the experience, particularly if you ask more than once. Family generosity has its limits, and it comes with strings attached. This is because generosity is different from entitlement, and familial assistance brings with it complex forms of reciprocity, guilt, expectations, etc.

My brother, Josh, was plagued by addiction. My parents aided him many times before he died. All of their help—financial, emotional, and every other kind imaginable—came with conditions, lectures, hugs, tears, guilt, encouragement, and ultimatums. The government cannot play that role. None of these psychological factors is at work with a government check. Can a bureaucrat call you at ten o'clock at night, like your uncle Irving, and hock you about the money you owe him?

Former Texas senator Phil Gramm tells a story about talking to a group of voters. He was asked what his policy on children was. He said something like "My policy derives from the fact that no one can love my children as much my wife and I do."

A woman in the audience interrupted him and said, "No, that's not true: I love your children as much as you do."

Graham shot back his answer: "Oh, really? What are their names?"

The second problem is that welfare is not received as charity; it is seen as an entitlement. When you tell people—particularly *strangers*—they are entitled to something they did not earn or work for, you are teaching a profound—and often profoundly pernicious—lesson about how life itself works. For instance, when societies assume that the government is there to provide all of the wants and needs for the poor, not only do the poor become less motivated to help themselves, but the affluent also become less motivated to help them. European countries, the imagined better models for social organization, have seen their civil societies atrophy. The churches are subsidized, but the pews are empty. The prevailing attitude is that the state is there to help those in need, so why should people give any more? "That's what I pay taxes for." Meanwhile, in America, the most charitable developed country in the world, religion is privatized and the source of immeasurable social generosity.

"Studies of charitable giving in the United States show that people in the least religious fifth of the population give just 1.5 percent of their money to charity," writes Jonathan Haidt. "People in the most religious fifth (based on church attendance, not belief) give a whopping 7 percent of their income to charity, and the majority of that giving is to religious organizations." Haidt adds that "it's the same story for volunteer work: religious people do far more than secular folk, and the bulk of that work is done for, or at least through, their religious organizations."[4] Civil society encourages people to be other-directed, to help not for a check but for the psychic or spiritual reward of being needed. That kind of participation is a source of values and virtues that sustain democracy and capitalism.

Mediating institutions also provide a sense of meaning, community, and even identity that gives people a sense of belonging and fulfillment.

Arthur C. Brooks, the president of the American Enterprise Institute (where I am a Fellow), has written extensively on the importance of "earned success." Earning success is not synonymous with making money or becoming famous. The essence of earned success, which Brooks says is the very essence of American exceptionalism, is the sense of personal satisfaction that comes from hard work and achievement. It can take the form of money, but money isn't what purchases a sense of earned success. People who are simply given money—from the lottery or an inheritance—get a brief psychological sugar high from the windfall, but that wears off rapidly. What generates lasting happiness is the conviction that your labors are valued, that you have made a meaningful contribution, that you are needed. A stay-at-home mother who raises happy, healthy children can have high levels of earned success, while a wealthy stockbroker can have low earned success. Priests, schoolteachers, artists, writers—no matter their financial status—can have high levels of earned success if they feel like they made a difference in the world.

The reason the American experiment is so bound up in earned success is that our system was designed to let people choose their own path to earned success. This is what the "individual pursuit of happiness" means. And the more mediating institutions we have, the more paths to earned success there are.

Brooks contrasts earned success with "learned helplessness," a term coined by the eminent University of Pennsylvania psychologist Martin E. P. Seligman. Learned helplessness has clinical definitions related to the study of depression, but in this context it is what you get when the incentives for work and rewards for merit get out of whack. When people feel their fate is out of their hands, when they are not captains of themselves, they respond accordingly.[5] Marx thought alienation was endemic to capitalism, but anyone who has lived in or even visited a communist society knows that alienation is even more prevalent in state-run economies. One can feel like a cog in the machine in a free-market society, but the free-market society by definition allows for the right to exit systems, jobs, careers, etc., that do not serve the interests of the individual. Statist systems do not recognize the right to exit.

But the right to exit is a right in name only *if you have no place to exit to.* Mediating institutions provide such safe havens. A man may be miserable in his work but feel rich in his life outside of work—if he is needed or valued or esteemed by his friends, family, church, or the volunteer fire department.

Every ideological flavor of statist, from the Marxist left to the monarchist right, has argued for the last three hundred years that the state must be given the power to cure the alienation of the market, bind the wounds of division, and act like a loving parent caring for its children. It does not work. But the more people believe it does, the more they turn their backs on the only thing that does: *us.* We build the reefs where people find an emotional or psychological home. And when the state touches them, it wounds them.

THERE'S A REASON WHY American liberals express such admiration for the European model: They tend to think like Europeans. American liberals are three times more likely than conservatives to tell pollsters they want the government to "do more" to reduce income inequality. At the same time, conservatives who believed that the government should not tackle income inequality gave four times as much money to charity as liberals. In 2002, people who said the government is "spending too much money on welfare" were more likely to help a homeless person with a gift of food or money.[6] When we outsource compassion for others to the government, we free ourselves up to think only about ourselves.

To be fair, the belief that the state, and only the state, can satisfy the allegedly ever greater complexities of modern life is sincerely held and does derive from real compassion. The point isn't that those who want the state to handle everything are evil or selfish—after all, they want to pay higher taxes to help others. The point is that they are blind to the costs of their compassion. In Barack Obama's second inaugural, he proclaimed:

> For the American people can no more meet the demands of today's world by acting alone than American soldiers could have met the forces of fascism or communism with muskets and militias. No single person can train all the math and science teachers we'll need to equip our children for the future, or build the roads and networks and research labs that will bring new jobs and businesses to our shores. Now, more than ever, we must do these things together, as one nation and one people.[7]

Look closely at what he is saying here. In his vision of America, there are only two actors on the national stage: the federal government and the individual. Forget mediating institutions; even state and local governments—which, being closer to the ground, are better equipped to understand the challenges people face—don't enter the picture. As Yuval Levin writes in his seminal *Fractured Republic: Renewing America's Social Contract in the Age of Individualism*, "This emaciated understanding of the life of our nation is precisely why the Left is for now poorly equipped to help America adjust to twenty-first-century realities." By reducing American life to the individual or the state, with nothing important in the middle, we sweep aside all of the nooks and crannies of life where people live and interact. The cliché that "government is just the word for the things we do together" renders invisible the vast ecosystem of civil society where people voluntarily cooperate and find meaning in their lives. This vision, Levin writes, "flattens the complex, evolved topography of social life and leaves us no way out of the corrosive feedback loop of individualism and centralization."[8]

This is the vision not of the English garden but of a field yielding a single crop. Every stalk of wheat is equal in its sameness to the other and its need for nurturing by the government. Atomism, another form of alienation, is the feeling of being alone in the world, with no one to help you. Such feelings of isolation are inevitable when the state crowds out all the little nooks and crannies of civil society where people *actually live.* Levin notes that "collectivism and atomism are not opposite ends of the political spectrum, but rather two sides of one coin."[9]

As a video played on the first day of the 2012 Democratic Convention put it, "Government's the only thing that we all belong to."[10] That same year, Barack Obama's campaign released a slideshow ad called "The Life of Julia." It was about a fictional woman named Julia and all that the government will do for her over her entire lifetime. Each slide begins with the words "Under President Obama . . ." and then proceeds to explain some specific benefit she receives from the state, from government-provided education under Head Start as a kindergartner to support in high school as part of Obama's Race to the Top program. In college, "under President Obama," she gets a tax credit and government-supported health care. And so it goes. After graduation, she gets help from Equal Pay laws, and government subsidies defray her student loans and pay for her birth control. Later, "under President Obama: Julia decides to have a child." When she's old, "under President Obama," she signs up for Medicare. And ultimately, "under President Obama," she gets to retire and live off social security and even volunteer in a "community garden."[11]

Leaving aside the weird implication that Barack Obama is sort of president for life in this formulation, the most interesting implication of the ad is what's *not* there. Julia has no family, save for her one child, who vanishes from her life after he turns eighteen. But there are no parents, no husband, no loved ones whatsoever. There is no church, no voluntary association of any kind, until, of course, Julia's golden years, when she has the time to volunteer for a community garden. The state, in other words, takes the place of family, friends, community, and religion.

The desire to be part of a family of some kind is one of the most deeply felt emotional instincts humans have. It's why nearly every TV show is really about families, either traditional ones or virtual ones.

The desire for family is of a piece with what Robert Nisbet called "the quest for community." Indeed, one reason the "Life of Julia" ad resonated with anyone it is that it offered a vision of belonging to something, an opportunity to have the state step in and fill the holes in your soul. This story—that the state can be your family or provide you with a sense of community—is incredibly powerful and popular. It also leaves conservatives and especially libertarians at a distinct disadvantage. As a matter of core ideology, we do not see the state as a good, reliable, or even possible substitute for the sense of social solidarity and belonging that can only come from civil society, starting with family. (Or at least most of us didn't before the rise of Trump.)

This vision of the state being our mother or father is popular because it appeals to something deep within us, which is why you can find such appeals in every era of human history. Indeed, this vision is in its own way tribal. We are all equal, we are all dependent on one another, we all need a Big Man—be it Barack Obama or Donald Trump—to lead us and punish our enemies, however defined. But why is it so compelling right now?

One obvious but partial reason is that the economy has been failing large swaths of Americans. Because capitalism is unnatural, it must deliver the goods or people will say, "Why bother?" And, since the year 2000, America's market economy has not been holding up its end of the bargain. "It turns out," writes prominent demographer Nicholas Eberstadt, "that the year 2000 marks a grim historical milestone of sorts for our nation. For whatever reasons, the Great American Escalator, which had lifted successive generations of Americans to ever higher standards of living and levels of social well-being, broke down around then—and broke down very badly."[12]

Between early 2000 and late 2016, America got vastly richer. The net worth of American households and nonprofit institutions more than doubled, from an estimated $44 trillion to $90 trillion. But per capita growth has only averaged about 1 percent. In other words, the distribution of economic prosperity across the whole society has been painfully unequal. Nicholas Eberstadt estimates that if we merely had the postwar economic growth that was normal before 2000, per capita GDP would have been 20 percent higher in 2016.[13]

The scope of the problem becomes more apparent when one looks at the state of work in America. "Work rates have fallen off a cliff since the year 2000 and are at their lowest levels in decades," Eberstadt writes. The official statistics are merely mediocre, but they are also deceptive, because they only track people looking for work. For every unemployed American male between twenty-five and fifty-five looking for work, "there are another three who are neither working nor looking for work." Meanwhile the work rate for women outside the home— "one of our society's most distinctive postwar trends," Eberstadt points out—has been thrown into reverse. Work rates for prime age women "are back to where they were a generation ago, in the late 1980s."[14]

At the end of Barack Obama's presidency, after roughly ninety straight months of admittedly lackluster economic growth, the share of American males of prime work age who were employed was lower than it was at the tail end of the Great Depression in 1940—when the official unemployment rate was above 14 percent. Since 1948, the share of men over the age of twenty who do not work for pay has more than doubled.[15]

Again, the overall story is not bleak, but the narrative for one large segment of the American people has been. The rest of America has prospered. In 1979, the upper middle class was 12.9 percent of the population; as of 2014, it was 29.4 percent.[16] According to the Census Bureau, after adjusting for inflation, the share of households with annual income of $100,000 or more rose from 8 percent in 1967 to 26.4 percent in 2015.[17] In 2015, according to the Pew Research Center, there were 11 percent fewer Americans in the middle class than in 1971, but that's because 7 percent moved into higher groups while 4 percent fell behind. The share of Americans in the upper middle and highest tiers grew by 50 percent from 1971 to 2015.[18]

But while it is important to note that income inequality has heightened in large part because the rich got richer and the middle class got much bigger, that doesn't change the fact that a big chunk of Americans are stuck. And they just happen to be a disproportionate share of Donald Trump's base.*

---

* I should note that, as this book went to press, many economic indicators were quite positive, particularly the stock market, which the president now cites as a key measure of economic health. It remains to be seen how deeply those trends are felt at the bottom of the economy.

Many want to blame capitalism for this stalling of the economy. And it's certainly fair to note that the market's creative destruction often leaves some people holding the bag. Despite Donald Trump's claims, the coal industry was hurt more by innovation and the market than by the Obama administration. The invention of fracking and other techniques made natural gas a more economically viable commodity than coal. The Obama administration didn't help the industry, but creative destruction hurt more.[19] Similarly, automation has done more to destroy manufacturing jobs than outsourcing or bad trade deals. American manufacturing is actually doing great.[20] Manufacturing output is near an all-time high and remains the largest sector of the economy.[21] The hitch is that, because of innovation, manufacturing simply requires fewer people to do the same job. We manufacture twice as much as we did in 1984 but with a third fewer workers.[22]

Also, it should not surprise anyone that when billions of people enter the global labor force thanks to the spread of capitalism and massive improvements in global transportation and communications, winners abroad will create some losers domestically. Still, while it is right and proper for Americans to care more about Americans than about non-Americans, we should not lose sight of the fact that the spread of markets around the world has led to the largest and quickest decline in poverty in all of human history. That it takes time for the American economy to adjust to the sudden expansion of the global market system is not an indictment of the market system. But the way our elites have managed that adjustment is an indictment of them.

There is a reason why the Obama campaign thought "The Life of Julia" would be persuasive. There's a reason why very smart political consultants opened the Democratic Convention with the words "Government is the one thing we belong to." And there is a reason why Donald Trump blamed "deindustrialization" on the "failed leadership" in Washington. When civil society is healthy, most people do not look to Washington for the answers to their problems. We look closer to home. It is only when the forests have been cleared that we can see distant peaks. But when the family and civil society are depleted or dysfunctional, we do not lose our desire to "belong" to something, nor do we lose our need for help when misfortune befalls us. And there is the state offering to fill in where other institutions have failed or fled. Statists have argued since the Founding that the government in Washington is the answer to our problems. That argument is more persuasive when the forests have been cleared away and all eyes look naturally to Washington.

This trend benefited Barack Obama because his political philosophy is consistent with it and his campaign always encouraged the idea that he was the representation of a national awakening of some kind. His slogan "We are the ones we've been waiting for" was a brilliant if creepy new age form of populism. But the erosion of civil society and the traditional economy also helped Donald Trump. Where Obama pressed a technocratic progressive vision of the government as every citizen's partner and helpmate, Donald Trump offered nostalgia and nationalism.

I'll get to the specifics of Donald Trump's message in a moment. But I need to take a moment to deal with nationalism as an ideology generally. There is a raging debate in conservative circles about nationalism that divides many traditional allies and friends. At *National Review,* where I am a senior editor, some of my colleagues have led the charge for conservatism to embrace what my friends Richard Lowry and Ramesh Ponnuru call "benign nationalism":

> It includes loyalty to one's country: a sense of belonging, allegiance, and gratitude to it. And this sense attaches to the country's people and culture, not just to its political institutions and laws. Such nationalism includes solidarity with one's countrymen, whose welfare comes before, albeit not to the complete exclusion of, that of foreigners. When this nationalism finds political expression, it supports a federal government that is jealous of its sovereignty, forthright and unapologetic about advancing its people's interests, and mindful of the need for national cohesion.[23]

On the surface, my only objections to this are terminological. But terminology matters, given that rhetoric shapes how we think about the world we live in. What Lowry and Ponnuru are referring to here, by my lights, is not really nationalism but patriotism. Nationalism is a universal phenomenon. Generically, it has no ideological content save glorification of whatever nation it manifests itself in. In this, it is somewhat similar to generic conservatism and radicalism. A conservative in Russia wants to conserve very different things from a conservative in the United Kingdom. A radical in Spain wants to tear down very different things from what a radical wants to tear down in Saudi Arabia. Likewise, a nationalist celebrates different things in every nation.

One could make the same argument about patriotism, of course. A patriot here is different from a patriot over there. But in the American context, patriotism is defined by adherence to a set of principles and ideals that is higher than mere nationalism. It is also a cultural orientation that is inherent to the idea of American exceptionalism. Despite a common misunderstanding on both the right and the left, American exceptionalism never meant "We're better than everyone else." It wasn't jingoism; it was an observation. Until the last decade or so, the long-running argument over American exceptionalism wasn't whether we are or are not exceptional but whether our obvious exceptionalism was a good thing. For the left, which wanted America to be more like Europe, it was bad. For the right—both the isolationist and internationalist factions—American exceptionalism was something to be proud of. But it never meant "nationalism."

Nationalism by definition is concerned with the collective will or spirit. Like arguments about the moral equivalent of war, the fundamental assumptions and emotional heart of nationalism are the cult of unity. We're all in it together! Let's unite around a cause larger than ourselves! The word "fascism" is based on *fasces*—a bundle of sticks around an axe—which was the symbol of Roman authority and meant "strength in numbers." In America, patriotism can include these things in moments of crisis, but it never loses sight of the fact that the fundamental unit of our constitutional order is not the group but the individual. To the nationalist, the heroic entity is the righteous crowd; to the patriot, the hero is the man who, with law on his side, stands up to the crowd. G. K. Chesterton captured the difference well: "'My country, right or wrong,' is a thing that no patriot would think of saying. It is like saying, 'My mother, drunk or sober.'"[24]

I have always argued that a little nationalism is essential to the American project. Nationalism is a pre-rational, emotional, ultimately *tribal* commitment to one's home country. This place is mine and I love it not least because it is mine. We are products of the nations we hail from, and a minimal amount of gratitude and appreciation for where we come from is good and healthy. But if a little nationalism is healthy, too much of it is poisonous. Indeed, all poisons are determined by the dose. In other words, nationalism is not, properly speaking, an ideology at all; it is a passion, like lust. Sexual attraction is important for every marriage, but no healthy marriage is based on *lust*. Strong unions depend on shared values, commitment to certain principles and projects that are more important than the self. So it is with nations. The Founders recognized that political passion is dangerous, which is why they set up a system designed to keep it in check.

Historically, nationalism has always been at war with such artificial restraints on the will of the people, which is why historians usually use the term "romantic nationalism." Romantic nationalism emerges in the waning days of the French Revolution when French and German intellectuals—and the masses—rebelled against the cold rationality and legalisms of the Enlightenment. The Jacobins of the Great Terror were committed nationalists, convinced that the French were God's chosen people. They inscribed the words "The citizen is born, lives and dies for the fatherland" above every altar and plastered it on every thoroughfare.[25] Robespierre did not shrink from embracing nationalism: "I am French, I am one of thy representatives. . . . O sublime people! Accept the sacrifices of my whole being; happy is the man who is born in your midst; happier is he who can die for your happiness."[26]

In Germany, intellectuals like Johann Gottfried Herder and Johann Fichte rose up against first the Enlightenment-based autocracy of Frederick the Great and then the cold militaristic pragmatism of Napoleon's empire. Reason and science served to disenchant the world, to borrow Max Weber's phrase, and nationalism was a "re-enchantment creed" (to borrow Ernest Gellner's words). Nationalism, with its myths and fables, would restore some of the meaning lost to the Age of Reason. Marxism would soon provide another such creed. Herder and Fichte borrowed heavily from Rousseau and his idea of creating a society based upon the general will, which Herder redefined as the *Volksgeist* or spirit of the people.[27]

He and Fichte used the German language as the defining feature of

the mythical German nation. French was the language of Enlightenment thinking, which suppressed the authentic German soul. "Spew
out the ugly slime of the Seine," Herder exhorted. "Speak German, O
you German!"[28] "Men are formed by language far more than language
is by men," Fichte believed. The German tongue was pure, he insisted,
because it had defied the corruption of not just the slime of the Seine
but the foreign ideas of the Roman Empire and its alien Latin tongue.
"The Germans still speak a living language and have done so ever since
it first streamed forth from nature, whereas the other Teutonic tribes
speak a language that stirs only on the surface yet is dead at the root."
Fichte was not a biological racist—though he was no fan of the Jews—
but his ideas about language would later lend themselves to the more
virulent ethnic nationalism of the Nazis: "Of all modern peoples it is
you in whom the seed of human perfection most decidedly lies and
to whom the lead in its development is assigned. If you perish in your
essentiality, then all the hopes of the entire human race for salvation
from the depths of its misery perish with you."[29]

Racial essentialism, tribal superiority, the elevation of passion and
myth—nationalism is not only powerless against these things, it is the
medium by which these passions grow like bacteria in a petri dish.
Nationalism works on the assumption that the search for meaning
and spiritual redemption is a collective enterprise. Lowry and Ponnuru's "benign nationalism" is certainly at odds with such things,
because the best part of American culture stands athwart mindless
passions. But all the valuable work in the concept of benign nationalism is done by the word "benign," not "nationalism."

That's because nationalism shorn of negating qualifiers has no
internal checks, no limiting principles that mitigate against giving in
to collective passion. And that is why nationalism taken to its logical extreme must become statism or some form of socialism. It is a
vestigial nostrum of Marxism and Leninism that nationalism and
socialism are opposites. But everywhere nationalism has free rein,
it becomes some kind of socialism. And every time socialism is set
loose in an actual nation, it becomes nationalism. Take a speech by
Hugo Chávez or Fidel Castro and replace words like "nationalist" and
"nationalize" with "socialist" and "socialize"; the meaning of the sen-

tence will not change. When you nationalize an industry, you socialize it, and vice versa. When you leave the page and leap into the real
world, the terms are not opposites; they are synonyms.

Nationalism uncaged has to become statism, because the state
is the only institution that is supposed to represent all of us. Which
brings us back to Donald Trump.

In his inaugural address, President Trump laid out his vision of
the new order:

> At the bedrock of our politics will be a total allegiance to the
> United States of America, and through our loyalty to our country
> we will rediscover our loyalty to each other.[30]

This is the same song sung by Barack Obama, just set to a different
tune, aimed at different ears. Both men bought into the idea that all
of America's problems could be fixed from Washington. Their programs and rhetoric were different in all sorts of important ways, but
the underlying assumption of both men was that, if we have the right
person sitting in the Oval Office, we can transform the country, or
"Make America Great Again."

In this, Trump differed from traditional conservatives, who argue
that Washington is too powerful and too involved in our lives and
the economy. Trump argued—or shouted—that Washington elites
were too weak, too stupid, to fix our problems. He insisted it would
be "easy" to provide better health care to everyone while spending less
money at the same time. He could, singlehandedly, counter the tide
of globalization through his superior deal making. There would be so
much winning, he warned his followers that they would one day suffer
from chronic winning fatigue.[31]

Just as the decay of civil society made the hearts of liberals—but
not just liberals—receptive to Barack Obama's re-enchantment creed of
"fundamentally transforming" America, it made many conservatives—
but not just conservatives (Trump won millions of votes from Obama
voters)[32]—receptive to Trump's "America first" nationalism.

Ultimately, the question of whether polarization in American politics breeds tribal thinking or tribal thinking breeds polarization can
only be answered with "Both." But what is clear is that a large amount

of Trump's support, in the election and to this day, stems from a desire to fight fire with fire. In hundreds of arguments, conversations, and debates with Trump's most enthusiastic supporters—and many of his reluctant ones—the loudest refrain is that we live with Trump or we die with Hillary. For the true believers, this was an exciting choice. For the more skeptical ones, it was a lamentable but necessary one. The traditional American conservative vision of limited government and free markets had passed its sell-buy date. The choice now is progressivism or nationalism.

Progressivism, in other words, conjured a nationalist backlash that is less an alternative to the statism of the left and more a right-wing version of it. We should take a moment to look at how it happened.

There's a deep confusion within progressivism. On the one hand, progressives take deep pride in their role as agents of "social change." Often they have every reason to be proud. If you believe in the causes of, say, civil rights and feminism, why wouldn't you celebrate your accomplishments? But at the same time, progressives want to claim that any effort to resist the forces of "progress" is an act of aggression in the culture war. From abortion and gay marriage to the hot fad for transgender rights, progressives want every institution and community to bend the knee to their movement. And when anyone refuses, the resisters are cast as the aggressors.

The slogan "Make America Great Again" worked on many levels because it is so diversely interpretable. But a key part of Trump's "MAGA" appeal was the notion that we could return to a simpler— often mythological—time where middle-class jobs dangled from the trees like ripe fruit, the police had a free hand to deal with troublemakers, and "political correctness" didn't ruin everyone's fun. "MAGA," particularly when adorned with all of the other nationalist and populist rhetoric, fell in the great Herdian tradition of conjuring myths of an imagined past where "we the [right] people" weren't humiliated by foreigners at home or abroad.

Even among the ranks of Trump-supporting conservatives who understood he was in all likelihood selling snake oil, this mind-set won the argument. Michael Anton, a multimillionaire hedge fund partner and part-time intellectual who now works for the Trump administration, wrote a famous pseudonymous essay for the *Clare-*

mont Review of Books titled "The Flight 93 Election." In it, he argued that America was essentially doomed if Hillary Clinton was elected. So, like the passengers who overpowered the terrorists on 9/11, there was no choice but to back Trump. Selfless courage was required (but not so much courage as to risk losing his job by publishing under his own name).[33] This argument was widely subscribed to by many leading conservatives, even many who had once been passionate opponents of Trump. The imperial arrogance of progressive social engineers and social justice warriors had earned an apocalyptic backlash so powerful that even clear-eyed conservatives who recognized Trump's dishonesty and demagoguery couldn't resist it. Indeed, as much as I hold Trump in contempt, I am still compelled to admit that, if my vote would have decided the election, I probably would have voted for him.

"Make America Great Again" captured the spirit of the backlash. It invoked nostalgic claims about trade, foreign policy, crime, culture, and economics. But the most salient and illustrative platform of the Trump agenda was immigration.

The Swiss writer Max Frisch famously said of the guest workers his country imported that "we wanted workers, but we got people instead."[34] That insight applies most poignantly to Europe. The massive influx of immigrants from the Middle East, North Africa, and South Asia had the predictable consequence, testing national and local institutions and giving rise to huge spikes in populism and calls for more authoritarianism.

Many on the left concede that immigration is fueling a populist backlash, but they then take the position that the backlash is racist and bigoted and therefore politically illegitimate. No doubt mass immigration elicits racist and other bigoted attitudes in some segments of the population. But relying on these sorts of explanations encourages a kind of smug virtue signaling: *People who don't like immigration are backward bigots—unlike me.*

Such responses not only miss the complexity of the issue but also encourage further resentment among the segments of society being demonized. In a sense, it is a kind of victim blaming. For instance, at the bottom of the socioeconomic ladder, work is far more often a matter of physical labor. If you have little or no education, working with your hands is usually your only option. Importing large numbers of competitors who keep wages down—*or are perceived to be doing so*—is not going to be celebrated by day laborers with nearly the gusto that one hears from journalists and the well-heeled. If we started importing very large numbers of pundits who could do the same job as the editors of the *New York Times* for half the price, one might find a bit more nuance in their pages.

I tend to believe that high levels of immigration, particularly skills-based immigration, are economically desirable policies. Also, the evidence that low-skilled immigration is a net detriment to the country is not as cut-and-dried as some claim. (The field of economics that studies immigration is shot through with methodological and ideological problems.)[35] But the simple fact is that, as with trade and automation, all economic policies create winners and losers. Proponents of very large levels of immigration almost invariably tend to be in the winners column, and a dismayingly high proportion of them also tend to be condescendingly dismissive of the complaints of the losers. When I talk to wealthy audiences, I will often point out that the people in the room only know two kinds of immigrants: extremely hardworking manual laborers who tend to do their landscaping or clean their homes and offices, and extremely hardworking and highly educated wealthy "citizens of the world" like themselves. In neither instance do the members of the audience have any reason to feel threatened by immigrants, economically or culturally. (Their children will not be going to the overwhelmed public schools of the day laborers, and if the children of affluent immigrants attend their children's private schools, all the better: "Diversity" is a wonderful thing.) Being rich can mean being able to afford generosity at someone else's expense.

Regardless, it's a mistake to put all the emphasis on economic arguments about immigration. Economists are very good at describing the world through models, but they tend to downgrade, dismiss, or demonize the cultural and psychological costs of immigration. So when it comes to immigration, economists talk about workers, labor costs, productivity, and all manner of costs and benefits. But those models are silent on all the other costs and benefits—social cohesion, civic and institutional health, community trust—that are difficult to quantify.

But it's not impossible. A recent paper by Ronald Inglehart of the University of Michigan and Pippa Norris of Harvard's Kennedy School of Government found that the bulk of the evidence points to the rise of populism in America and Europe having more to do with "cultural backlash" than economic dislocation.[36] Their cultural backlash theory includes issues other than immigration. Feminism, gay rights, and other forms of progressive change are part of the psychological mix. But there's reason to believe that immigration is probably the biggest driver of cultural backlash in populist strongholds.

A recent study by researchers at the London School of Economics found that, while levels of unemployment didn't correlate very tightly with populist support for Brexit, levels of immigration did. An earlier 2012 study found that opposition to immigration had less to do with economic concerns than worries about what newcomers would do to "the composition of the local population" and how it would affect "their neighborhoods, schools and workplaces."[37]

A lot of the political science literature on this topic is replete with ad hominem labels (or technically neutral labels used in ad hominem ways): "racism," "xenophobia," "nativism," "bigotry," "isolationism," etc. And while it is tragically true that it is easy to find examples to back up such descriptors, the tragedy is compounded when we use these terms as a blanket condemnation of anyone who has objections to mass-scale immigration. In other words, all racist xenophobes and white supremacists are opposed to immigration, but not all immigration opponents are racists and xenophobes. *National Review* magazine has been at the forefront of those arguing that if responsible politicians don't deal with the legitimate concerns of voters with regard to immigration, the issue will be taken up by irresponsible politicians—because, in the minds of voters, they are the only ones talking about the problem. The 2016 election proved us right.

Donald Trump's rhetoric on immigration during the campaign was like a mirror of the most cartoonish platitudes of the left. While pro-immigration absolutists scoff at any suggestion that immigrants are anything other than the noblest of Americans, Trump often painted immigrants—particularly illegal immigrants—as the dregs of humanity. For instance, Hillary Clinton said that Islam has "nothing whatsoever to do with terrorism."[38] And Donald Trump, by vowing to ban *all* Muslims (at least initially), made it clear that he thinks Islam has *everything* to do with terrorism. The same dynamic played itself out with his constant invocation of the statistically unrepresentative number of crimes committed by illegal immigrants. This rhetorical tactic helped Trump in two ways. First, he demagogically played on the natural tribal instinct of fear of others. But second, he signaled that he was willing to defy the "politically correct" rules of the "weak" and "stupid" establishment.

In other words, the left painted with a broad brush in a single color and so did Trump. And when that happens, there is no room for the shading and contrasts necessary to describe the world as it actually is. One scholar who has tried is Harvard sociologist Robert D. Putnam, a decent left-wing liberal who is arguably America's leading social scientist on civil society and community. In a massive survey of over 30,000 Americans, he found that there was an undeniable correlation between increased diversity and breakdowns in community. He is adamant that racism isn't the primary explanation. (In fact, supporters of the idea that racism is the primary driver of anti-immigrant sentiment have never paid much attention to the immigration controversies of the nineteenth and early twentieth centuries, or the anti-immigrant sentiments in Africa and the Middle East in which race plays no role.)

According to Putnam, people who live in more diverse communities tend to "distrust their neighbors, regardless of the color of their skin, to withdraw even from close friends, to expect the worst from their community and its leaders, to volunteer less, give less to charity and work on community projects less often, to register to vote less, to agitate for social reform more but have less faith that they can actually make a difference, and to huddle unhappily in front of the television."[39]

In short, he writes, "People living in ethnically diverse settings appear to 'hunker down'—that is, to pull in like a turtle."[40] Putnam hated his findings and recognized that they would not be well received by his peers. So he spent a year retesting the numbers for some other explanations. He couldn't find any.

In ethnically or culturally homogenous communities, there is more social trust and more social capital. People who share languages, customs, faiths, institutions, and plain old history are simply more likely to work out their differences and problems without looking to the government to do it for them. In short, a shared culture builds trust, which is essential to democracy and economic growth. "Trust," writes Francis Fukuyama, "is the expectation that arises within a community of regular, honest, and cooperative behavior, based on commonly shared norms, on the part of members of that community."[41]

Think of the typical postcard hamlet in Europe, where kids dress in communal garb, parents organize festivals, and everyone goes to the same church. Is it any wonder that there would be a larger reservoir of social trust and cooperativeness in such a community than in a diverse city full of strangers and newcomers? Sweden and other Scandinavian countries have been the beau ideal of American progressives for generations. What has been hard for those same progressives to grapple with is that ethnic homogeneity and a strong cultural consensus make social democracy much easier to pull off. One can say, without fear of contradiction, that the influx of immigrants and refugees into these countries—and others, like Germany, the U.K., the Netherlands, France, etc.—has not contributed to greater social peace.

There is no value judgment here. Traditional small-town life can be wonderful. It can also be stultifying for those who want something more—or merely something *else*. The Medieval German expression *Stadtluft macht frei* ("City air makes you free") captured this distinction. Moving to the city has always meant escaping from the more ordered and tradition-bound ways of rural life.

The customs—festivals, May Day dances, whatever—of traditional communities aren't merely quaint cultural activities; they are circuits of social trust, solidarity, and cooperation. It is right and good to value inclusiveness. But inclusiveness can go only so far and do so much. Christians can visit a mosque, but they probably can't pray there regularly. People who speak Korean are simply going to have a hard time forging relationships with people who don't.

The share of the foreign-born U.S. population is at its all-time high. In 1960 the foreign-born population was obviously smaller in absolute terms and as a share of the country, but it also overwhelmingly consisted of immigrants from Europe and Canada (84 percent), people who have an easier time assimilating into the majority culture.[42] Mexicans made up 6 percent of the foreign-born population, and other

Latin Americans another 3.5 percent, for a total of 9.5 percent of the foreign-born population. In 2014, 27.7 percent came from Mexico and another 23.9 percent from other Latin American countries.[43] Of the 48 million students enrolled in K-12 public schools in 2012, nearly one in four spoke a language other than English at home.[44]

People often note that we've had similar proportions of foreign-born students in public schools before (though we are in uncharted territory when it comes to the absolute numbers). They cite the success immigrants who came through Ellis Island had at finding and achieving the American dream. That is a great story and one that I love. What they leave out is that in those days America at the state, local, and federal levels was absolutely determined to turn immigrants into Americans. Sometimes that effort was too draconian—as in World War I—when German speakers were essentially persecuted for even speaking their native language in public.* But the schools, churches, and popular culture had both the tools and the will to encourage assimilation.

Today, all of the will is on the other side of the equation. There is a large and aggressive educational and political lobby that works against assimilation and strives to create ever more incentives for immigrants—as well as native-born ethnic groups—to maintain their minority identity at all costs.

Assimilation is still popular among many immigrants and many native-born Americans. But it is on the outs precisely where it is most needed. In the University of California system, an administration memo cautions faculty and staff not to use certain language that can lead to "micro-aggressions"—which the UC system defines as "the everyday verbal, nonverbal, and environmental slights, snubs, or insults, whether intentional or unintentional, that communicate hostile, derogatory, or negative messages to target persons based solely upon their marginalized group membership." One example of an

---

* They also leave out the fact that the U.S. economy was geared in such a way that it could absorb waves of immigrants. George Borjas notes that, in 1914, 75 percent of the workforce at the Ford Motor Company were immigrants (George J. Borjas, *We Wanted Workers: Unraveling the Immigration Narrative* [New York: W. W. Norton, 2016], p. 52). Industrial America is not doing nearly as poorly as some claim, thanks largely to huge advances in automation and innovation. But does anyone believe it can absorb waves of unskilled foreign-born workers the way it once did?

offensive, hostile, or derogatory statement: saying "America is a melting pot." This sends the signal that the speaker expects minorities to "assimilate to the dominant culture."[45]

Well, yeah.

Whatever your preferred policy on immigration might be—my own is to simply have one *and enforce it*—it should be remembered that fear and distrust of strangers is entirely natural. I do not like the demagoguery and demonization of immigrants that is thriving on the right these days, but the fact is that such responses are a feature of human nature. That doesn't excuse overt acts of bigotry or cruelty, but it should at least instill a little humility and empathy in people who think "nativism" is nothing more than know-nothingism. Many of the people concerned with immigration know something far better than their critics do: Their communities are changing in ways they do not like.

Donald Trump tapped into the frustrations of millions of people fed up with the failed promises of politicians who said they would do something about the problem. I don't like how he did it, and I think he will ultimately fail in fulfilling most of his promises—probably resulting in even more populist anger. But that doesn't mean the concerns he tapped into were wholly illegitimate.

Again, polarization fuels these trends and these trends fuel polarization.

To understand how, it's important to understand the degree to which the erosion of civil society has caused millions of Americans to flock to partisan politics as a source of tribal meaning. Political parties in America were not always particularly ideological. If someone told you she was a Republican or a Democrat in, say, 1950, you would need more information before you could guess whether she was a conservative or a liberal. There were very progressive Republicans and there were very conservative Democrats. But in the last few decades, starting in the 1960s and intensifying with almost every passing year, the parties have become not only more ideological but tribal. "Today, political parties are no longer just the people who are supposed to govern the way you want. They are a team to support, and a tribe to feel a part of. And the public's view of politics is becoming more and more zero-sum: It's about helping their team win, and making sure the other team loses," writes Amanda Taub, who covers social science for the *New York Times*.[46]

"Partisanship, for a long period of time, wasn't viewed as part of who we are," explain political scientists Shanto Iyengar and Sean J. Westwood. "It wasn't core to our identity. It was just an ancillary trait. But in the modern era we view party identity as something akin to gender, ethnicity or race—the core traits that we use to describe our-selves to others." But now partisanship is becoming a bigger predictor of behavior and attitudes than race.[47]

As other sources of meaning wither, and as we think of ourselves as residents of the national community rather than local ones, the stakes of politics inevitably increase, not just in terms of policy but psychologically. The logic of sports and war takes over. If they win, we lose, and vice versa. Citizens in California and New York become invested in partisan fights in North Carolina or Indiana as if they were skirmishes in a larger war.

This tribal us-versus-them worldview is intensified on social media, where it is easier to find like-minded but virtual "friends" a thousand miles away than it is to have a conversation with your actual neighbor. On both sides of the political aisle, the point of politics ceases to be persuasion and becomes instead victory, humiliation, and rubbing it in. Studies have shown that when people see someone being shocked with electrodes, the parts of the *observer's brain* that feel pain light up as well. In one study, this empathetic response was more likely when the observer was told the victim was a fan of their favorite soccer team. But when the observer was told the subject was a fan of a rival team, the observer's pleasure centers brain lit up instead.[48] This is pure tribalism, and it is wired into us. When one of my people suffers, I feel pain. When "the other" suffers, I take delight.

I am unaware of whether similar experiments were conducted using ideological or political tribes, but I have no doubt that the same thing would happen. The suffering of liberal avatars is something for conservatives to revel in, and vice versa. In the aftermath of terror attacks and mass shootings, the left openly hopes that the perpetrator was an angry white male belonging to some "right-wing hate group."

When the murderer is confirmed as a radical Muslim, many right-wingers struggle to contain their glee that their worldview has been confirmed.

Facebook and Twitter have become platforms where you boast of your purity and commitment to the good things and how your ideological opposites are not only corrupt but metaphysically committed to the bad things. (There is a curious paradox of tribal polarization on the left and the right. People tend to argue both that the enemy is totally committed to its evil ideology and that he is willing to sell out for personal profit.) "You want to show that you're a good member of your tribe," Westwood told the *New York Times*. "You want to show others that Republicans are bad or Democrats are bad, and your tribe is good. Social media provides a unique opportunity to publicly declare to the world what your beliefs are and how willing you are to denigrate the opposition and reinforce your own political candidates."[49]

The desire for news that satisfies the popular lust for what might be called ecstatic schadenfreude—obscene pleasure at the sadness of others—has created a market, and when there is a market entrepreneurs rush in. Hence the rise of "fake news" aimed at the trollish hordes on the left and right who think saying "Your tears are delicious" or "Butthurt" is an argument. Bias is endemic to all journalism. Fraud, however, while not new to journalism, is experiencing a kind of new golden age. Outright fabrications fly around the Internet, fueled by pay-for-click ad rates and a burning desire among millions of people to see reality bend in their direction. Meanwhile, half-truths, which are often the most effective whole lies, saturate even respectable news organizations. Headlines have always erred on the side of the sensational. But in an era when millions of people only read the headlines, and when much of the political conversation takes place in the 140-character realm of Twitter, the national conversation has become a noxious smog of feelings and desired yet fake facts. If a fanatic is someone who can't change his opinion and won't change the subject, then fanaticism runs amok on the left and the right these days. Of course, when a president believes that lies are true if they *feel* true to him, falsehood has a powerful megaphone.

Tyler Cowen, a brilliant economist at George Mason University, takes the somewhat too cynical view that much of ideological discourse can be boiled down to a desire to see the relative status of one group lowered or raised.[50] He was talking about the rarefied world of academics and intellectuals. But it seems obviously even truer in the trenches of the political culture. Whatever you make of the underlying merits of the issues related to the Black Lives Matter movement, symbolically it is very much an argument about the relative status of groups. The effort to force Christian bakers to make wedding cakes for same-sex marriages against their will has very little to do with tolerance and a great deal to do with a vengeful spirit that shouts out: "You will be made to care!" When Hillary Clinton wrote off roughly half of Donald Trump's supporters as a "basket of deplorables,"[51] those supporters turned it into a badge of honor and a foil for rhetorical vengeance.

Again, I must point out that all of these trends are interrelated to and mutually reinforcing of each other, but one can only think critically about phenomena by isolating them. Mass immigration erodes mediating institutions, and the decline of these authentic communities fuels the migration to "virtual communities" online where resentments are reinforced as like congregates with like, lending support to statements and attitudes we would normally never express in real life. This reinforcement encourages people to say them in real life. The resulting backlash is then celebrated as "winning" on the Internet, which can be increasingly monetized. Immigration and economic churn make people feel insecure, so they go on Facebook, where people curate their lives to make it seem like everything is going swimmingly, and this breeds feelings of envy and status/class anxiety. As Montesquieu said, "If one only wished to be happy, this could be easily accomplished; but we wish to be happier than other people, and this is always difficult, for we believe others to be happier than they are."[52]

And all of these trends cause people to search for new sources of identity—in race, gender, sex, faith, and political affiliation—and as these shallow categories of self-understanding harden, tribal polarization intensifies. What we often call tribalism in modern democracies is actually more properly speaking what you might call "coalitionalism." But coalitionalism isn't a word, and sounds too much like normal politics, which has always been about building coalitions, even for tyrants, since the word was invented. Tribalism gets closer to the reality of our polarization.

CONSERVATISM WAS MOVING IN the direction of identity politics for white people long before Trump, and it may have ended up where it is today sooner or later had he never run for president. But I believe the precipitating cause for the right's surrender to populism and tribalism was the failure of the Tea Parties. The populist movement that rose up to oppose President Obama was the only American populist cause I have ever sympathized with, never mind supported. (I spoke to many Tea Party rallies.) Why? Because as much as I dislike and distrust crowds, the Tea Parties married populism to the principles of the Founding, demanding the government live within its means and abide by the Constitution. I met countless people from the little platoons of civil society who had become animated with passion for the primary documents of our civilization. They held book clubs and seminars in living rooms and rec centers. They studied how the debt and the deficit work. When they held rallies, a few cranks would show, as happens whenever political enthusiasm is high and people gather. But the cranks were held at bay. The crowds cleaned up after themselves and took their citizenship seriously. There was passion, but it was married to principle.

They succeeded in getting many politicians elected. But ultimately they failed by the standards they set for themselves at the outset. The banks got bailed out. Obamacare stayed in place. The debt grew bigger. Taxes went up. But those failures are not what turned so many Tea Partiers into tribalists. It was the fact that, despite espousing the principles of the Constitution and arguing for wholly defensible and patriotic goals (whether you agree with them as a policy matter or not), they were still demonized by the media and Hollywood as racist yokels and boobs. This highlights the cancerous dynamic at work. If you tell people that, in effect, fighting for the Constitution and universal principles is just a "white thing," then many of those whites will eventually agree with you. They will see the Constitution as the document of "real Americans." But because the Constitution limits their power, they will eventually conclude that loyalty to the Constitution is a waste of time. What starts as a claim that only white people care about the Constitution ends with no one caring about the Constitution. We're not quite there yet, but in many quarters we're close. As bizarre as it sounds, there is a growing faction on the right who worship the by-any-means-necessary left-wing agitator Saul Alinsky. They believe the left brilliantly used his tactics to take over the country, and because we are in an existential battle, we must emulate their tactics. Chiefly, if the other side won't be constrained by the rules, then "we" shouldn't be either.

When Trump's critics decry his violation of "democratic norms," the immediate response is "What about Obama?"

And that is a very good question. But my response is: "I criticized Obama for his violations of democratic norms. So I am consistent when I criticize Trump for the same thing." The most reliable retort for Trump's biggest backers is: "Well, why should we abide by the rules when they don't?"

Donald Trump waded into this maelstrom of dysfunction and intensified it even further.

For years conservatives have complained that Republicans surrender too easily. And as a senior editor of *National Review*, I would lose my executive washroom privileges if I dared claim this wasn't true. I don't need to recount the history of the New Deal or the Great Society to demonstrate that the GOP often finds itself dragged along in the tide of ever-growing government. Moreover, while I think that conservatives have the right side of the argument on many cultural issues, this record of failure helps explain why Republicans often focus on symbolic social issues that rev up the base. The only problem is that Republicans often throw in the towel on those fights too. Part of this is simply the nature of conservatism. We tend, as Hayek said, to get pulled in directions not of our own choosing. In principle, that doesn't bother me, because giving society time to digest inevitable changes is an important function. Still, it would be nice to win more.

Donald Trump tapped into this frustration as well, as all of his Charlie Sheen–like outbursts about "winning" illustrate. The problem is that winning and fighting are not stand-alone principles. In my numerous debates with many of Trump's biggest conservative supporters, I was constantly astounded by how many supposedly—or formerly—principled conservatives had embraced "winning" and "fighting" as ends unto themselves. Trump could hurl the crudest epithets to defend an objectively immoral or politically indefensible position, and the response from his cheerleaders was "At least he fights!" Trump has become an avatar of "we the people," and winning has become decoupled from the substance of any victory. When he cannot declare victory, it is because others failed him or unfairly thwarted him. When he declares victory, the substance doesn't matter. When he does the incomprehensible, it is part of a genius we cannot appreciate. In short, for many people, it is simply a cult of personality.

In the primaries, pollsters asked Republicans whether they favored single-payer health care, and the vast majority said no. When they were told Donald Trump supports it (accurate at the time), nearly a plurality suddenly supported it.[53] In August of 2017, a poll found that half of Republicans would support postponing the 2020 elections if Donald Trump favored it.[54]

At the Conservative Action Political Committee—CPAC—meeting in February 2017, Trump advisor Kellyanne Conway suggested that the *C* in "CPAC" will be replaced with a *T* for a "Trump."[55] That was a glib exaggeration, but listening to the audience cheer as he threw aside free trade in favor of his preferred "economic nationalism," one could see how the ember of truth in her comment could grow into a flame.

Barack Obama had a similar cult of personality. Celebrities pledged allegiance to the president.[56] One columnist speculated whether he was a "Lightworker," which he defined as "that rare kind of attuned being who has the ability to lead us not merely to new foreign policies or health care plans or whatnot, but who can actually help usher in *a new way of being on the planet*, of relating and connecting and engaging with this bizarre earthly experiment."[57] Deepak Chopra proclaimed he represented "a quantum leap in American consciousness."[58] "Barack Obama is our collective representation of our purest hopes, our highest visions and our deepest knowings . . . ," proclaimed life coach Eve Konstantine. "He's our product out of the all-knowing quantum field of intelligence."[59] The mainstream media ignored all of this—and so much more—because they were besotted with him too. "We thought he was going to be . . . the next messiah," Barbara Walters confessed.[60] And this, too, fueled deep feelings of resentment among millions of dissenting Americans who were not motivated by racism but by simple disagreement, healthy skepticism, or plain old partisanship. But they were called racists nonetheless.

The liberal pundits, reporters, and politicians who look at Donald Trump and ask "Where did this monster come from?" didn't create Donald Trump—and they certainly didn't vote for him—but they helped pile the kindling high for the flames of backlash to come.

Scholars studying such diverse phenomena as Islamic terrorism, white supremacy, street gangs, and cults have found that the key recruitment tool is always the same: the promise of meaning and belonging. Human beings are hardwired to want to belong, to be part of a cause larger than themselves, and to be valued for their contribution to that cause. Young people with scant social capital—i.e., dysfunctional families, unresponsive schools and communities, etc.—are the most susceptible to such appeals precisely because they have few alternative sources of meaning and belonging. This is the core insight of every Big Brother program and Boys & Girls Club. But the poor, the poorly educated, and those "left behind" by capitalism are not the only people susceptible to such appeals. *We all are.* Many of the 9/11 terrorists were well educated. Osama Bin Laden was rich. Modernity itself leaves many cold if they don't have the resources or opportunity to find healthy sources of meaning and belonging.

In April 1993, Hillary Clinton delivered a commencement address to the University of Texas at Austin in which she declared that "we need a new politics of meaning. We need a new ethos of individual responsibility and caring. We need a new definition of civil society which answers the unanswerable questions posed by both the market forces and the governmental ones, as to how we can have a society that fills us up again and makes us feel that we are part of something bigger than ourselves."[61]

In my first book, I subjected Clinton to withering criticism for her politics-of-meaning speech. I now think I was somewhat unfair. Her *diagnosis* had merit. It was consistent with the long tradition of critics of the Enlightenment and the Industrial Revolution to address the "social question." People crave the sense of tribal solidarity that allowed us to evolve and to climb to the top of the food chain. Where I still stand in stark disagreement with Clinton is her *remedy* for the problem: more centralization. Like Obama, Clinton's answer is to give the state more power in an effort to satisfy our longing for meaning. That approach only fuels the problem, because it makes the state the only source of meaning in our lives, which in turn fuels resentment among the millions who find the state's definition of meaning wanting. Prior to the Glorious Revolution, a Catholic in England felt that a Protestant on the throne was a threat to his or her whole place in the universe. And vice versa.

That is the direction we are heading, and that direction is *backward*. When the president or a party in power is invested with that kind of meaning and significance, the "outs" feel like they are strangers in their own land. And the party in power does everything it can to exacerbate that feeling. Then, when the other party gets in, it gets its payback. The only solution is to break the cycle by making the state less important and letting the dying reefs of civil society grow back to health.

That doesn't mean there aren't important things for the state to do. But what the state cannot do is fill the holes in our souls. That is what monarchs who ruled by divine right claimed, and it is what theocrats preach.

CONCLUSION

Decline Is a Choice

"The question of whether America is in decline cannot be answered yes or no. There is no yes or no. Both answers are wrong, because the assumption that somehow there exists some predetermined inevitable trajectory, the result of uncontrollable external forces, is wrong. Nothing is inevitable. Nothing is written. For America today, decline is not a condition. Decline is a choice."

—CHARLES KRAUTHAMMER, 2009[1]

I HAVE TRIED TO KEEP GOD OUT OF THIS BOOK, BUT, AS A sociological entity, God can't be removed from it. I start the story of the Miracle in the 1700s, because that is where prosperity started to take off like a rocket. But a rocket doesn't materialize from thin air on a launchpad. The liftoff is actually the climax of a very long story.

Simply put, we got where we are because of God. I don't mean this as an argument for providence or divine intervention. I believe in God, but if you don't, you cannot discount the importance of God as a human innovation. I don't mean gods—plural—but God as a single omniscient being looking at us in all of our private moments. Prior to the god of the Jews, gods were more like prickly servants than masters. Humans picked their deities to support their passions, to grant their wishes, to justify their conquests. The Romans, Greeks, Hindus, Vikings, ancient Chinese, Japanese, and others created gods to match their feelings, from hate and anger to lust and compassion. The Hebrew god reversed the division of labor, demanding that the people work for him, not the other way around. The Hebrew god recognized the moral sanctity of the individual Jew, both male and female. The Christian god universalized that moral sanctity. From its earliest days, Christianity recognized that every person was due a certain measure of justice, and every person was obliged to respect others as children of God. The golden rule "Do unto others as you would have them do unto you" is the seed from which grew the concept of the individual.[2] Christianity, in other words, introduced the idea that we are born into a state of natural equality. For the Romans and Greeks, aristocracy was natural, and some men were simply by nature slaves. Of course, even after Christianity conquered Europe, the natural tendency of elites to lock in their advantages endured. Christianity's emphasis on human dignity and equality did not destroy monarchy, aristocracy, serfdom, or slavery for more than sixteen centuries. But the fuse, one could argue, was lit.

Christianity performed another vital service. It created the idea of the secular. As we've seen, Christianity divided the world between the City of Man and the City of God, in Saint Augustine's famous account. These cities are entirely metaphorical, describing states of mind, not actual city-states. Those who live in the City of God devote themselves to love of God. Those who live in the City of Man devote themselves to their self-interests. Augustine clearly preferred the City of God. But he acknowledged that human societies would always be marked by this "fundamental cleavage" between those of faith and those without. The secular and the faithful had to live among each other and work to create political systems that protected their common interests in "earthly peace" and other "necessaries of this life."[3] Now, Saint Augustine was surely more of a theocrat than this makes it sound. But his realism about the nature of this world created a new space between the religious and the secular. For Augustine, society was divided, not between nobles and peasants (or slaves) or between rich and poor, but between believer and non-believer. And most important: The ultimate task of identifying who was who was left to God, not man.[4]

Protestantism made its contributions, too, as we've seen. Martin Luther's emphasis on "faith alone" as the measure of righteousness liberated the individual conscience from the monopoly of the Catholic Church. It also led to an explosion of sects, which not only created new institutions and new habits of the heart—including a revolutionary respect for innovation—but also forced the state, ultimately, to expand the borders of liberty and tolerance.

The West's advance was the product of a series of creative tensions: between balancing the rights of the individual and the powers of the state; between the dominant faith and religious minorities; between faith and reason; between religion and government; etc. But there were also creative tensions inside the human heart, some of which are as old as the human heart: between desire and responsibility; between self-expression and self-discipline; between the yearning to shine as an individual and participate in, and contribute to, the community; and, again, between faith and reason. These tectonic plates of human nature shifted and bumped up against each other, within society and within our own souls.

But there was one thing that informed all of these passions and ideas: *the idea that God was watching.* The greatest check on the natural human desire to give in to your feelings and do what feels good or even what feels "right" can be captured in a single phrase: "God-fearing." The notion that God is watching you even when others are not is probably the most powerful civilizing force in all of human history. Good character is often defined as what you do when no one is watching. It is surely true that many atheists are people of good character. It is also true that peace has increased as society has become more secular (which is not to say that correlation is causation). But the very notion of what constitutes good character comes from countless generations of people trying to figure out how they should behave when only God knew what they were doing. And that is the most important tension: between our base instinctual desires and what God expects of us. This tension created space for reason to become a crucial moral tool in our lives. The medieval Doctors of the Church used reason to deduce and to discover God's will and to breach the divides between all people by appealing to conscience. The rabbinical Jewish tradition has its own deep history of using reason and debate to discover the otherwise hidden will of God.

This is obviously not true of every society everywhere. Some societies substituted the honor of their ancestors for God—and that is a very different thing. The ghosts of ancestors do not necessarily tell you to treat strangers as worthy of respect. Regardless, in the West, where the Miracle happened for the first and only time in human history, it was God, as defined by organized Christianity and informed by Judaism, who shaped our understanding of what right and proper behavior was. Religion provides a framework for how people approach the world, for how they prioritize wants and desires, for how they structure their days and their lives. It is—or was—the primary source of ideas about why you should get out of bed and how to behave once you did. God had a magnetic pull on the otherwise inner-directed compass of human nature, pointing us toward something better.

Regardless of whether you believe in God or not, it is simply the case that the idea of God has shrunk in society and in our own hearts. If you believe that man has a strong religious instinct, if I've convinced you that nature—including human nature—abhors a vacuum, then you have to believe that God's absence creates an opening for all manner of ideas to flood in. As the famous line (attributed to Chesterton) goes: "When men choose not to believe in God, they do not thereafter believe in nothing, they then become capable of believing in anything."[5] This, as we've seen, explains all manner of totalitarian efforts to create a heaven on earth, to replace a religion that places utopia in the hereafter with a "scientific" religion that will usher in a new heaven on earth in the here and now.

But that is not the only possibility. Totalitarian movements have a very poor track record of making people happier, and so even people alienated by capitalism and democracy recognize that such movements may not deliver what they desire. And so they look elsewhere. Some retreat into themselves, in search of their own inner-defined meaning, obsessing over, say, physical fitness.[6] Some might retreat into the virtual world of video games. Others might look for new, exotic religions that promise to provide answers they think traditional religion cannot. Some just fanatically pursue wealth or celebrity as an end in itself rather than a means to one.

But most of these things require work and effort, and for many that's too high a price of admission. In *Liberal Fascism*, I argued that fears of America ever becoming an authoritarian or totalitarian police state were wildly misplaced. The greater threat, I argued, lay not in Orwell's *1984* vision of a boot stomping on a human face forever but in Aldous Huxley's *Brave New World*. In Huxley's famous 1932 novel of a futuristic society (set in A.D. 2540), children are hatched in artificial wombs, and citizens are kept happy and docile by taking a drug called soma. As I noted in *Liberal Fascism*, *Brave New World* raises questions that are more relevant and vexing than Orwell's *1984*. Everyone understands why *1984*'s society of perpetual war and propaganda is undesirable. But in *Brave New World* everyone is more or less *happy*. The Miracle was built on the bourgeois idea that everyone had the right to *pursue* happiness, implying it would take effort and work. But what if we can just have happiness delivered? As technology—computers, robots, artificial intelligence, genetic engineering, and pharmacology—improves, and as entertainment becomes ever more immersive, why go to all the trouble of pursuing happiness when it can come to you on your couch? There's an app for that, as they say.

My rebuttal remains the same: The promise of such a society is fool's gold.

Earned success is the secret to meaningful happiness. The government can improve your net worth with a check, but it cannot improve your *self-worth*. Likewise, entertainment is not a substitute for effort, and it is certainly a poor replacement for God. But the pursuit of fool's gold has led many people to tragic ends. One of the great morals of life, for individuals and civilizations alike, is "You are what you worship."[7] The theory that capitalism came out of Protestantism may not explain it all, but it explains a lot. Believing that God is not only watching you but has high expectations creates one kind of society. Believing that getting "likes" on Facebook, Twitter, Instagram, or Snapchat (or whatever comes next) undoubtedly creates another kind. The average iPhone user unlocks his or her phone at least eighty times per day, and that number is rising every year.[8] And yet, despite the fact each of us has access to more information in our pockets than any scholar in the world had twenty years ago, we don't use it. We drown in information but we starve for knowledge. As I was finishing this chapter in 2017, a poll from the Annenberg Public Policy Center of the University of Pennsylvania reported more than one out of three people couldn't name a single right listed in the First Amendment. Only one in four Americans, 26 percent, can name all three branches of government. That's down from 38 percent in 2011! A third of Americans can't name a *single* branch of government.[9]

Ignorance of government, in itself, is not necessarily horrifying. But it is troubling, not least because of the national obsession with encouraging people to vote. If you don't know what the executive branch *is*, why is it vital that you vote for president? Democracy is supposed to rely on an informed electorate, after all. The answer to this question—why vote?—is invariably romantic, not reasoned. People must express their will! They must participate! Yes, yes, fine. But voting should be the culmination of one's civic engagement, not the gateway to it. Yet the tide pushes the other way. Legislators in California and elsewhere increasingly want children to vote. Others want people to vote online so as to not have to suffer the inconvenience of *pursuing* democracy.[10] Better to have it delivered like open phone lines during *American Idol*.

In 1961, John Courtney Murray delivered a brilliant lecture titled "Return to Tribalism." He had a prophetic warning: "I suggest that the real enemy within the gates of the city is not the Communist, but the idiot." He did not mean idiot in the "vernacular usage of one who is mentally deficient" but rather in the "primitive Greek usage." To the Greeks, the idiot was the private individual who "does not possess the public philosophy, the man who is not master of the knowledge and the skills that underlie the life of the civilized city. The idiot, to the Greek, was just one stage removed from the barbarian. He is the man who is ignorant of the meaning of the word 'civility.'"[11] (The word "idiot" didn't take on the connotation of stupid, low-IQ, etc., until the fourteenth century.)[12]

No doubt this sounds outrageously elitist. So be it. I am an elitist in the sense that I believe in objective standards of right and wrong, excellence and sloth. But let us also be clear: Our elites are a problem as well. Patrick J. Deneen, a brilliant and intellectually anachronistic (in a good way) professor at the University of Notre Dame, writes:

> My students are know-nothings. They are exceedingly nice, pleasant, trustworthy, mostly honest, well-intentioned, and utterly decent. But their brains are largely empty, devoid of any substantial knowledge that might be the fruits of an education in an inheritance and a gift of a previous generation. They are the culmina-

tion of western civilization, a civilization that has forgotten nearly everything about itself, and as a result, has achieved near-perfect indifference to its own culture.

He goes on to explain that his students—not just at Notre Dame but at other elite schools where he has taught, such as Princeton and Georgetown—are all smart: "They are superb test-takers, they know exactly what is needed to get an A in every class (meaning that they rarely allow themselves to become passionate and invested in any one subject)." He adds, "They build superb resumes" and "are the cream of their generation, the masters of the universe, a generation-in-waiting to run America and the world."

But . . .

ask them some basic questions about the civilization they will be inheriting, and be prepared for averted eyes and somewhat panicked looks. Who fought in the Peloponnesian War? Who taught Plato, and whom did Plato teach? How did Socrates die? Raise your hand if you have read both the *Iliad* and the *Odyssey*. The *Canterbury Tales*? *Paradise Lost*? The *Inferno*?

Who was Saul of Tarsus? What were the 95 theses, who wrote them, and what was their effect? Why does the Magna Carta matter? How and where did Thomas Becket die? Who was Guy Fawkes, and why is there a day named after him? What did Lincoln say in his Second Inaugural? His first Inaugural? How about his third Inaugural? What *are* the *Federalist Papers*?

A few hands may go up at this or that question, but that is usually a fluke, accidental knowledge from a quirky class. In short, they are idiots in the original Greek sense. Very clever idiots. Maybe even brilliant idiots. But, in the true meaning of the term, that is no contradiction. "They have learned exactly what we have asked of them—to be like mayflies, alive by happenstance in a fleeting present," Deneen laments.[13] The liberal arts as originally conceived were intended to be an antidote to this form of idiocy by equipping students with the arguments and knowledge necessary to protect and defend *liberty*.

Instead, these are the leaders of tomorrow that the leaders of today have created. They are the children of the new class, so ignorant of their own civilization that they have no response to those who insist with righteous passion that our civilization is not worth defending. They are a reserve army of ingratitude uninterested in defending the very soapboxes they stand on and, often, all too eager to take a sledgehammer to them in the name of fighting "hate speech." In college, the privileged children of our elite live the most bespoke lifestyles of any humans in history, getting their wants and desires fulfilled on demand. Among the affluent, most do not work to pay their tuitions. They think it is normal that others prepare their food, clean their dorms, fraternities, and sororities, and protect them from not just physical violence but allegedly "violent" ideas—and yet they are convinced they are "independent." Is it any wonder that they want to make society as whole as sheltered and nurturing as the only world they've known? Is it any wonder that they let their feelings and desires guide their sense of right and wrong?

"WHAT ORWELL FEARED WERE those who would ban books," Neil Postman wrote in *Amusing Ourselves to Death: Public Discourse in the Age of Show Business:*

> What Huxley feared was that there would be no reason to ban a book, for there would be no one who wanted to read one. Orwell feared those who would deprive us of information. Huxley feared those who would give us so much that we would be reduced to passivity and egoism. Orwell feared that the truth would be concealed from us. Huxley feared the truth would be drowned in a sea of irrelevance. Orwell feared we would become a captive culture. Huxley feared we would become a trivial culture, preoccupied with some equivalent of the feelies, the orgy porgy, and the centrifugal bumblepuppy.... In *1984*, Orwell added, people are controlled by inflicting pain. In *Brave New World*, they are controlled by inflicting pleasure. In short, Orwell feared that what we fear will ruin us. Huxley feared that what we love will ruin us.[14]

The primacy of feeling—that quintessential hallmark of romanticism—has now become a live idea about how we should organize our lives. "It is ideas which rule the world, because it is ideas that define the way reality is perceived . . ." This line from Irving Kristol is one of his more famous quotes.

But it's only half the sentence. Here it is in full:

> "[Adam Smith] could not have been more wrong. *It is ideas which rule the world, because it is ideas that define the way reality is perceived; and, in the absence of religion, it is out of culture—pictures, poems, songs, philosophy—that these ideas are born.*"[15]

Kristol's point was that conservatives—and defenders of liberty generally—were losing the battle of ideas because they had not come to grips with the fact that the popular culture had left religion behind. Popular culture, with its emphasis on hedonism, animism, or just simple feeling, is the primary public conveyor of meaning in our lives, and it is, with a few exceptions, unattached from (and often hostile to) higher understandings of meaning, morality, or religion. Much of classical music, painting, and architecture was dedicated to the greater glory of God.

We are becoming what we worship, and what we worship is ourselves. Outside of the occasional country-western song, when was the last time you engaged with mainstream popular culture that was dedicated to anything like the greater glory of God? Refreshment of the soul is another matter. But that's the point. In popular culture, nearly all efforts to refresh the soul fall under the tiresome cliché "spiritual but not religious" or, more likely, "discovering yourself"—not God.

All drama, all comedy, and virtually all entertainment is about human feelings. Characters on the page or the screen may use reason, but reason is always subservient to their emotional motivations. This is nothing new. It has been true from the first play or poem.

The difference now is that our feelings have become an end in themselves. How we feel—not what we conclude—is the higher truth. The gut has defeated the mind.

This—not immigration, inequality, or identity politics—explains why populism is so close to the surface in our life. We want our feelings ratified. Populism is not an ideology. It is a feeling. Populists have programs, but the program is merely a manifestation of popular feeling. "The people of Nebraska are for free silver and I am for free silver," proclaimed William Jennings Bryan (who was no fool). "I will look up the arguments later."[16] For populists, abstract principles are a handicap. Huey Long, the legendary populist governor of Louisiana, once asked a reporter from *The Nation*, "What's the use of being right only to be defeated?" For Long, "the time has come for all good men to rise above principle" so we could make "every man a king." In other words, what was required was will and strength to smash "the establishment."[17]

It was inevitable when we stopped looking up to God for meaning and started looking down into ourselves that we would look to find fulfillment, belonging, and meaning in tribes and crowds. "Classically, there are three ways in which humans try to find transcendence—religious meaning—apart from God . . . ," the theologian and pastor Eugene Peterson writes, "through the ecstasy of alcohol and drugs, through the ecstasy of recreational sex, through the ecstasy of crowds. Church leaders frequently warn against the drugs and the sex, but at least, in America, almost never against the crowds."[18] The crowd is reassuring, fulfilling and uplifting. It satisfies our evolutionary sweet tooth for being part of the tribe. Elias Canetti writes in *Crowds and Power* that inside the crowd "distinctions are thrown off and all feel *equal. . . .* It is for the sake of this blessed moment, when no-one is greater or better than another, that people become a crowd."[19]

The animating spirit—i.e., the *feeling*—of populism is the spirit of the crowd. Partisans of the left love their crowds, seeing in them moral uplift and "people power." Partisans of the right love their crowds, seeing in them proof that the "silent majority" is no longer silent. But each side sees the crowds of the other side as something very different and threatening: a demonic "other." But what they all seem to miss is that finding succor and strength in numbers is tribal passion. It may sometimes be necessary and even noble—in, say, Tiananmen Square, or the streets of Tehran, or the 1963 March on Washington—but the nobility is derived solely from the object of their strength, not from the strength itself. Unity is amoral because unity is force, and force can be used for evil just as much as it can for good. Giving in to the passion of the crowd is inherently corrupting, because it seeks no higher authority than itself and says you have righteous entitlement to act on your gut.

It takes moral leadership to keep a crowd from becoming a mob and losing its way, and moral leadership can come only from conversation, from reminding the crowd that their unity is a means, not an end.

But the culture of feeling is about more than just throngs in the street. It creates a mind-set, an orientation, a sense of entitlement about how the world around us is supposed to unfold. The idea that we could keep our politics walled off and separate from the rest of the culture is fanciful nonsense. In the chapter about popular culture, I noted that, when we watch movies, we watch with our tribal mind more or less intact.

But what happens when news—by which I mean real facts and events affecting our lives—is processed as just another form of entertainment? Political reporting tends to be framed as a drama, with a hero pitted against protagonists. Pundits and reporters covering former president Barack Obama had the tendency to cover every political drama on the calculus of whether he would emerge victorious. Whether his desired policy was sound or constitutional was, at best, a secondary consideration. Today, so much of the pro-Trump media plays the same game. "Will Trump win?" "Will this give Trump a win?" These are the new ideological litmus tests for many on the right. The crowds, virtual and literal, increasingly invest in our politicians—and celebrities generally—our feelings of self-worth. Love me, love my politician.

This desire for the hero to win, regardless of whether the victory is objectively desirable, is not merely romantic. It is also tribal. It says that my team must triumph, our will must be satisfied, and all impediments are equally illegitimate. Barack Obama himself said dozens of times that he didn't have the constitutional authority to unilaterally grant amnesty to so-called Dreamers. But the moment he decided to do it anyway, there was nary a peep of protest from members of his own team. What mattered was his victory. In an instant, the Republicans who *agreed* with President Obama for years when he said he couldn't do it became fools and villains for not changing their minds in lockstep with the president.

When I set out to write *Liberal Fascism* some fifteen years ago, Charles Murray gave me some vital advice. He told me that if, in the course of my research, I didn't change my mind on at least a half dozen important questions, I was doing it wrong. His point was that writing a book is an interactive, self-educational process. If you have all the answers before you start—as so many political writers do these days—you aren't writing a serious book. You're propagandizing.

I hope readers see this as a serious book. I've certainly learned a great deal in writing it. (The original manuscript was twice the length of the copy you're holding.) There were any number of intellectual and historical surprises along the way that changed my thinking.

The most relevant realization is that I now believe I was wrong about the threat of authoritarianism, as I described it in *Liberal Fascism*. It's not that the Huxleyan dystopia is not the more likely path America might take, but rather that there's no reason to believe the descent would stop there. A society that wallows in feelings and entertainment is not necessarily sustainable, either. When technology and all the myriad forms of simulation that come with it—pharmacological, auditory, visual, pornographic, etc.—advance at a geometric pace, so does our capacity to become numb to it. Like a patient in pain, we need ever more of the morphine drip just to get a fraction of the satisfaction.

"We make men without chests and expect from them virtue and enterprise," C. S. Lewis warned in *The Abolition of Man*. "We laugh at honor and are shocked to find traitors in our midst."[20] The "Chest," in Lewis's poetic telling, is one of the "indispensable liaison officers between cerebral man and visceral man. It may even be said that it is by this middle element that man is man: for by his intellect he is mere spirit and by his appetite mere animal."[21] In other words, the Chest is where reason and passion merge to form decency, civility, probity, and honor, rightly understood.

Self-indulgence and self-worship strip men of their chests, leaving them ill-equipped to defend what requires defending and hungry for some kind of meaning.

The young Muslim men who left Europe and America to go fight for ISIS had every form of entertainment and distraction available to them, but they found it unsatisfying. The same goes for the alienated and numb cadres who swell the ranks of neo-Nazis, antifa, and countless other groups. They crave meaning that our leading institutions no longer feel compelled to provide, or are even capable of providing, at least for those who need it most.

Francis Fukuyama, the modern popularizer of the idea of the end of history (with his essay and later book of the same name), anticipated this problem on a grand scale. "Perhaps this very prospect of centuries of boredom at the end of history will serve to get history started once again," he wrote.[22]

But Fukuyama was optimistic. He thought it would take centuries of ennui, while the evidence suggests that this challenge faces every generation and every heart. Just as capitalism has within it the seeds of its own destruction (as Schumpeter saw), the soft despotism of the Huxleyan life invites its own collapse. The siren call of glory, greatness, national solidarity, or tribal redemption—or vengeance—becomes ever more seductive, at first with alienated individuals but ultimately with groups and even nations. We've seen this pattern before. In the aftermath of Napoleon, the West enjoyed the greatest run-up of prosperity in human history. For a century, there were no large-scale wars in Europe. But when the prospect of war approached in 1914, the cream of Western civilization, on both sides of the Atlantic, leapt at the opportunity to prove their glory and their nations' greatness. In the aftermath of the war, Julien Benda was alone in recognizing that, for all the bloodshed, the urges had not been purged. Thinkers across the West were still dedicating themselves to the "intellectual organization of political hatreds."[23] Benda saw that the tribalisms of nationality, ethnicity, race, and class would lead to a second war even more terrible than the first. We are still far from that, but it's not hard to imagine how today's streams could become rivers. Rhetoric yields its own reality, because it transmits ideas, and ideas still rule the world.

This realization dawned on me during the course of this project, not on the page but in real life.

When I started, no serious person—probably including the current president himself—believed that Donald Trump was a plausible candidate for president. His rise in the primaries and his ultimate victory posed a professional challenge—and distraction—I had never planned on.

The fact that Trump's rise occurred against the backdrop of my thinking about human nature, tribalism, romanticism, and corruption made the whole experience more poignant and acute. In many ways, the existential challenge Trump and *Trumpism* posed to the conservative movement seemed a microcosm of the challenges Western civilization itself faces.

Consider the emergence of the so-called alt-right. The reason to fret about the growth and (relative) popularity of the alt-right is not that its adherents will somehow gain the power to implement their fantasies. No, the reason to be dismayed by them is that these intellectual weeds could find any purchase at all. They should have been buried beneath layers and layers of bedrock-like dogma with no hope of finding air or sunlight. But such is the plight we face. The bedrock is cracked. The soil of our civil society is exhausted, and the roots of our institutions strain to hold what remains in place.

Just as any civilization that was created by ideas can be destroyed by ideas, so can the conservative movement. That is why the cure for what ails us is dogma. The only solution to our woes is for the West to re-embrace the core ideas that made the Miracle possible, not just as a set of policies, but as a tribal attachment, a dogmatic commitment.

But we live in a culture that never wants its favorite shows to end. The desire to be entertained has rewired much of our civilization, because it has rewired our minds. When everything needs to be entertaining, we judge everything by its entertainment value. Entertainment is fundamentally romantic and tribal. It cuts corners, jumps over arguments, elevates passion, and lionizes heroes. Try to make an exciting movie about how laws are made and policy is implemented—without creating heroes of willpower and villains of greed, without skipping the reasonable arguments on both sides. It is almost impossible.

Donald Trump broke the fourth wall between reality-show entertainment and politics. He feeds off interpersonal conflict and drama. He's organized his life and presidency not around policy or ideology or even politics properly understood but around *ratings*. He bulldozed his way through the primaries, first and foremost, because he was so damn entertaining. Saying someone is entertaining is not necessarily a compliment. Horror movie villains are entertaining. But in an entertainment-driven age, being entertaining can be an advantage even if it is not inherently a virtue.

The rise of Trump showed me that the American right was far more susceptible to the corrupting tug of human nature than I had ever imagined. And that breaks my heart. More importantly, I no longer have the confidence I once did that this country is largely immune to authoritarianism. It can survive Trump, of that I have no doubt. But the rise of Trump proved to me that conservatism is far more fragile than I thought, more susceptible to the mob mentality than I ever appreciated. I would very much like to believe that this is a fever that will break. And at times I think it probably will, particularly as the Trump administration fails to deliver on his more grandiose promises to Make America Great Again. But Barack Obama failed to "fundamentally transform America" and the response from the left wasn't to become more moderate and reasonable. It was to redouble its passions for another try. There is no reason to be confident the same won't happen on the right. And that will leave traditional conservatives as ideologically homeless as our libertarian cousins have been.

Modern American conservatism is a bundle of ideological commitments: limited government, natural rights, the importance of traditional values, patriotism, gratitude, etc. But underneath all of that are two bedrock assumptions upon which all of these commitments stand: the beliefs that ideas matter and that character matters. We can have debates about what ideas are important and what good character means. Indeed, the reason we can have debates is that we believe that ideas matter. This is our debt to the Enlightenment: that through reason and argument we can identify good ideas and bad. Modern American conservatism arose in the 1940s and 1950s on the back of arguments made necessary by the threat of communism: arguments for Western civilization, the free market, the Constitution, property rights, and all of the underlying concepts that led to the Miracle.

DONALD TRUMP STANDS ATHWART both of these pillars of conservatism. His relationship to ideas is entirely ad hoc and instrumental, by his own admission. He boasts that he is not committed to any doctrine save the need for eternal flexibility. As for his character, suffice it to say, any standard of good character that conservatives championed over the last fifty years—honest business dealings, sexual probity, humility, restraint, piety, rhetorical decency—is a bar he would need a ladder to touch. I'll put it more simply: He is not a good person. If you described him in the abstract to any conservative (or liberal) a decade ago, this would be incontrovertible. He's boorish and crude. He freely admits his greed, his whining, and his deceptions. He is only civil when civility redounds to his benefit. He respects the law only when he can use it as a weapon, and he sees other people as instruments of his will.

And his biggest supporters don't care, and too many rank-and-file conservatives don't care very much. Forget conservatives: That Americans can see him as a representative of America's best self is a profound corruption of American idealism. Trump appeals to the desire for a tribal Big Man—or, if Trump had his way, a king.

Of course, thanks to the Founding, we don't have titles of nobility. But that hasn't stopped us from trying to create new ones. In America, where wealth and celebrity serve as substitutes for ancient notions of aristocracy, Trump took quite seriously the (possibly apocryphal) concept of droit du seigneur, the alleged right of nobles to extract sex from their vassals and serfs. He infamously boasted that his fame allowed him to accost women. "When you're a star, they let you do it. You can do anything . . . grab them by the pussy."

While such behavior is indefensible, there is nothing inherently wrong with wanting to playact as an aristocrat, since we do not, in fact, live in a world of inherited titles. But here lies the problem. Trump leapt from his world of playacting aristocracy and attained real power. And he brought many of the assumptions of his illusionary world with him. As we've seen, Western civilization has struggled to beat back the universal human preference for nepotism for millennia. In one fell swoop, Trump has brought it back to the center of political life. His children are ministers with open-ended portfolios in his government, even as they maintain their business interests. As his son, Eric, correctly explained, nepotism is a "factor of life." But he also added that it is "a beautiful thing."[24] And it can be a beautiful thing in civil society, where building a dynasty for your family is part of the American dream, at least for some. But Eric leapt from that private realm of a family business and imposed it on the people's business.

All this is a small example of the larger pattern and problem of conservative surrender to Trumpism. It is not an alternative to the worst facets of progressivism. It is a new right-wing *version* of them, grounded not so much in ideas as in populist grievance and a cult of personality.

This is but one panel in the great tapestry of conservative corruption. During the 2016 Republican primaries, a slew of right-wing radio and TV show hosts followed the famous dictum, "There go the people. I must follow them, for I am their leader."[25] To be sure, some were early adopters who were always more interested in marketing than ideas. They used their talent at guessing where their customers were going and met them there. Others fell one by one to the seduction of popularity and populism. The fact that a celebrity managed to do this from the right is particularly significant—and damning.

The same conservatives who insisted that Bill Clinton's "affair" with an intern was cause for impeachment saw little to object to in a man whose commitment to marital fidelity is arguably even weaker than Bill Clinton's. Conservatives who had claimed Rudy Giuliani was unfit for the presidency because of his three marriages and his stance on gay rights leapt to defend or dismiss Trump's three marriages and his even greater support for gay rights. Self-described libertarians who spent decades championing free trade, unrestrained immigration, and the cult of Ronald Reagan reversed course and hopped on board the Trump train, eagerly embracing positions they had once denounced as backward and racist.

This unqualified support of a leader regardless of the arguments he makes and the actions he takes is precisely the sort of thing that terrified the crafters of our Constitution, which is probably why Trump sees the Constitution as so archaic. As of this writing, a plurality (45 percent) of Republicans say that the courts should have the power to shut down news outlets that publish stories that are "biased or inaccurate."[26]

The evidence for the corrupting power of tribal politics and Trump's cult of personality is all around us. In 2011, only 30 percent of white Evangelicals said that "an elected official who commits an immoral act in their personal life can still behave ethically and fulfill their duties in their public and professional life." In 2016, that number more than doubled, to 72 percent. White Evangelicals used to be the religious group that was least tolerant of immoral acts by public officials. In the wake of Trump, they are now the *most* tolerant demographic. In fact, they are now far more tolerant of immoral acts than the average American.[27]

When the Democrats are back in power, what yardsticks of principle will be available for Republicans to hold them accountable? Under Obama, conservatives lamented the abuse of executive orders. Will that really be an argument they'll be able to make after Trump? What standard of sexual impropriety now bars someone from the presidency? How will conservatives decry "crony capitalism" in Trump's wake? Who will have the nerve to say the government shouldn't be "picking winners and losers" in the market after Trump has jawboned one company after another into giving him political victories? What standards of presidential decorum, honesty, and rhetoric can survive four years of Trump's Twitter tirades and petty insults?

Donald Trump is no dictator, thanks largely to the Constitution and the American people, but you can see how the distance between dictatorship and democracy has shrunk. Before I wrote *Liberal Fascism*, I subscribed to the view best described by the phrase "It can't happen here." Then, after studying the domestic moral horror of the Wilson administration, I modified my view to "It can't happen here—for long."* But this view was too generous. Since the New Deal, the

---

*   Under Wilson, America embraced totalitarianism, imprisoning, persecuting, and censoring dissidents. The government deployed extra-legal violence against domestic enemies. It demonized ethnic groups. The Committee for Public Information was the first modern propaganda ministry, releasing thousands of government agents to foment war lust and ideological conformity. But then the war ended and Wilson's stroke effectively ended his presidency even before he left office. In 1920 the Republicans ran on a "return to normalcy" and, once in power, released the political prisoners, dismantled Wilson's propaganda ministry and war socialism, and embraced free-market principles once again, unleashing unprecedented prosperity. (See Jonah Goldberg, *Liberal Fascism: The Secret History of the American Left, from Mussolini to the Politics of Change* [New York: Broadway Books, 2009 (2007)], pp. 106–20.) America's first truly modern war brought out the tribal instinct and, for a time, we abandoned our commitment to the principles of our civilization. But our commitment

conservative movement has been the primary champion of the principles of limited government, free markets, and constitutionalism. But the experience of watching Donald Trump seduce the right has caused me to wonder whether that commitment endures.

Which brings me back to corruption. Like the old joke about the turtle on a fence post—"It must have gotten there somehow"—we know the Miracle happened. The evidence is around us, everywhere. We have good theories about how and why it happened, but they are ultimately just theories. All we know for sure is *what* happened, because that can be measured. But the second law of thermodynamics tells us that nothing in this world can resist nature without effort.

Imagine a brand-new car in a field. Left untouched for a decade or two, it will still be the same car. But when you return to it, the paint will be faded. Rust will have taken hold in parts. The tires will be flat. Perhaps the windshield will be cracked from so many winters and summers. No doubt bugs and birds will have established nests among the weeds that have taken root in the nooks and crannies. In a century, a passerby will find a shell and some relics. In a thousand years—or maybe ten thousand; nature doesn't care—it may be like there was never a car there at all. Nature takes back everything, unless you fight it off with every pitchfork at your disposal, and even then, every victory is temporary, requiring the next steward to take the pitchfork like a baton.

On the 150th anniversary of the Declaration of Independence, in the greatest statement about that document ever uttered save for the Gettysburg Address, Calvin Coolidge observed:

> About the Declaration there is a finality that is exceedingly restful. It is often asserted that the world has made a great deal of progress since 1776, that we have had new thoughts and new experiences which have given us a great advance over the people of that day,

---

to those principles reasserted themselves, weakened but for the most part intact. It's worth noting that FDR lamented the reassertion of the old dogma of individual liberty. In his execrable 1944 State of the Union address, FDR said that if we returned to the "normalcy" of the 1920s, we would be in effect surrendering at home to the forces of fascism we were fighting abroad. (See Franklin D. Roosevelt, "4—State of the Union Message to Congress, January 11, 1944," American Presidency Project, John Woolley and Gerhard Peters, eds. http://www.presidency.ucsb.edu/ws/?pid=16518.)

and that we may therefore very well discard their conclusions for something more modern. But that reasoning can not be applied to this great charter. *If all men are created equal, that is final. If they are endowed with inalienable rights, that is final. If governments derive their just powers from the consent of the governed, that is final. No advance, no progress can be made beyond these propositions. If anyone wishes to deny their truth or their soundness, the only direction in which he can proceed historically is not forward, but backward toward the time when there was no equality, no rights of the individual, no rule of the people. Those who wish to proceed in that direction can not lay claim to progress. They are reactionary. Their ideas are not more modern, but more ancient, than those of the Revolutionary fathers.* [Emphasis mine.][28]

I believe this with all my heart. I believe that, conceptually, we have reached the end of history. We are at the summit, and at this altitude left and right lose most of their meaning. Because when you are at the top of a mountain, any direction you turn—be it left toward socialism or right toward nationalism or in some other clever direction—the result is the same: You must go down, back whence you came.

But as much as I believe all of this to be true, as a practical matter in the real world, it is only true so long as a sufficient number of Americans believe it, too, and work to keep that belief alive. Coolidge was right about the finality of the Declaration as an idea. But that idea, absent the hard work of caretakers, will rust away, reclaimed by human nature.

And more than faith and belief, more than reason and data, the indispensable ingredient for that work to be successful is *gratitude*. *Webster's Dictionary* defines "ingratitude" as: "forgetfulness of, or poor return for, kindness received."[29] The key word is "forgetfulness." Gratitude is impossible without memory. How can we repay a kindness we do not remember? But "forgetfulness" has a special meaning here. It is not merely a lapse of memory. "Remember" is an active verb. In the Bible, it is an action, not a passive function of the brain: "Remember the Sabbath day, to keep it holy" is an instruction to *do something*, attentively and mindfully. When we fail to remember to keep these principles alive in our hearts, and to remind ourselves why we should give thanks for them, we grow ungrateful for them.

There are no permanent victories. The only victory worth fighting for—because it is the only victory that is achievable—is to hand off this civilization to the next generation and to equip that generation to carry on the fight and so on, and forever. We cannot get rid of human nature and humanity's natural tribal tendencies. But we know that, under the right circumstances, our tribal nature can be grafted to a commitment to liberty, individualism, property rights, innovation, etc. It *happened* in England, accidentally but organically.

It happened in America by *choice*. America talked itself into existence. The Founders argued the Constitution out of the ether and they believed it could work so long as people of good character fended off the inevitable entropy of human nature. They wrote it down and made it hard to change to help us in that effort. The only thing that gives the Constitution real lasting power is our commitment to it, and there's nothing preventing us from walking away from it other than our refusal to do so.

And we cannot be forced to stay committed to our principles. We can only be persuaded to. Reason alone won't carry the load, but the task is impossible without it. Parents must cultivate their barbarian children into citizens, and the rest of us must endeavor to keep the principles of our civilization alive by showing our gratitude for it. The Miracle of human prosperity from 1700 to now looks like a rocket taking off. Some think we've achieved a permanent and stable orbit from which we can look down on the tiny speck that is our tribal past. But there's no such thing as a stable orbit. We must accelerate and maintain the equipment or fall back to the place whence we came. When the gravitational hand of nature reclaims objects from the heavens, the term for that in physics is "orbital *decay*." So it is with our civilization. Give up fighting for it, give up holding human nature at bay, abandon our principles for any reason—selfishness, sloth, forgetfulness, ambition, ingratitude, whatever—and you choose to give in to decay.

Decline is a choice. Principles, like gods, die when no one believes in them anymore.

APPENDIX

Human Progress

This book rests on a few core arguments. They are:

- We are living in an unnaturally prosperous time. Our prosperity is not merely material but political and philosophical. We live in a miraculous time, by historical standards, where every human born is recognized by law and culture as a sovereign individual with inalienable rights. This is not normal in humanity's natural environment. It is, to use the label I have used throughout this book, a Miracle.
- We stumbled into this Miracle without intending to, and we can stumble out of it.
- Human nature not only exists but is fundamentally unchanging.
- If we do not account for and channel human nature, it will overpower and corrupt the institutions that make prosperity possible.

The easiest of these propositions to demonstrate is that we are living in a uniquely prosperous time. It may seem obvious to some, but this "Great Fact," as Deirdre McCloskey calls it, is denied, denigrated, or dismissed by many. Ironically, the Great Fact is demeaned most vehemently by those who believe that material conditions—i.e., economics—represent the heart of political morality. The very essence of socialism—in all of its myriad flavors—is the dogmatic conviction that the virtue of society is determined almost entirely by how fairly wealth and resources are distributed.

This is an entirely legitimate and defensible worldview. But it has practical problems when turned into public policy. As Margaret Thatcher liked to say, "The problem with socialism is you eventually run out of other people's money."[1] We'll deal with those issues later. There's another more fundamental problem that needs to be dealt with here. All forms of socialism—in the broadest sense—subscribe to an entirely subjective understanding of poverty. The poorest among us are measured against the richest among us. In other words, when poverty is defined subjectively, a millionaire is poor in a community of billionaires. If one considers poverty to be an objective condition instead of a relative one, the poorest among us live better than the richest in our natural environment. One could quibble with this by pointing to the plight of some homeless people, but the average member of the working poor in the United States in 2018 lives better by any imaginable material measure than the wealthiest human a thousand years ago. And by many measures, a typical poor person today lives better than a rich person even a hundred years ago.

This is not an argument for saying we shouldn't do more to help poor people today. It is merely an observation that our standards are so contingent and time-bound that we often lose sight of the mind-boggling progress we've made in a remarkably short period of time. This appendix is intended to demonstrate that progress.

If the time line of human history were a landscape, humans lived in a wasteland for most of it, living off the land, eating tubers, acorns, bugs, and small mammals. "The most important thing to know about prehistoric humans," writes Yuval Noah Harari, "is that they were insignificant animals with no more impact on their environment than gorillas, fireflies or jellyfish."[2] It was only recently that humans became the apex predator on this planet. Our species only started hunting at all about 400,000 years ago, and long after that our prehistoric ancestors were as likely to be hunted as to hunt. Many of our first tools were used to crack open bones to get the marrow. According to some experts, that may have been our niche. "Just as woodpeckers specialize in extracting insects from the trunks of trees," Harari suggests, "the first humans specialized in extracting marrow from bones. This is because the first members of genus *Homo* were scavengers, picking over the abandoned kills of superior predators.[3]

It probably isn't necessary to dwell on the poverty of our pre-*Homo sapiens* forebears. So let us fast-forward a few hundred thousand years to consider the Yanomamö, a tribe living on the banks of the Orinoco River along the border of Brazil and Venezuela. They are one of the few stone-tool–making hunter-gatherer societies left in the world. They live mostly off subsistence hunting, small-garden agriculture, and a little trade; some Yanomamö make baskets, hammocks, and other items to sell to nearby villages.

In a very rough estimate by Eric Beinhocker, the Yanomamö make on average about $90 a year. (It has to be a rough estimate, Beinhocker notes, because the Yanomamö don't use money, never mind compile statistics.) According to Beinhocker, "It took about 2,485,000 years, or 99.4 percent, of our economic history to go from the first tools to the hunter-gather level of economic and social sophistication typified by the Yanomamö."[4] In other words, for nearly all of human history, the Yanomamö would be considered *incredibly rich*. As economist Todd Buchholz puts it, "For most of man's life on earth, he has lived no better on two legs than he had on four."[5]

But by modern, official metrics, the Yanomamö are worse than poor. The World Bank defines poverty as living on $1.90 per day.[6] Again, putting this in terms of money is a bit misleading, but it captures the material poverty of subsistence or near-subsistence living that defined human habitats for almost all of human history. It should also go without saying that the Yanomamö live without access to health care. A trivial injury for you or me can be a death sentence for them. Yanomamö poverty also encompasses the fact that the typical tribesman faces a paucity of choices about how to spend his or her life. If you subscribe to some "noble savage" nostrums or believe that ignorance is bliss, you might think they have a good deal. Who needs to study art or literature or practice medicine when you can live an "authentic" life of hunting, gathering, and basketmaking? But that option is more or less available to everyone reading this book, and yet you are not heading out for the wilderness.

While the readers of this book live in the oasis of the now, the Yanomamö still live on the outskirts of it.

After the onset of the agricultural revolution, it took about 12,000 years for humans to go from the $90-a-year Yanomamö standard of living to that of the ancient Greeks in 1000 B.C. ($150-a-year), according to economist J. Bradford DeLong. And it wasn't until A.D. 1750 that income reached $180 per year—a doubling of income from Yanomamö standards, yes . . . but over nearly 14,000 years.[7] Economic historian David S. Landes was not exaggerating when he said that "the Englishman of 1750 was closer in material things to Caesar's legionnaires than to his own great-grandchildren."[8] Douglass C. North and his colleagues write in *Violence and Social Orders: A Conceptual Framework for Interpreting Recorded Human History* that "over the long stretch of human history before 1800, the evidence suggests that the long-run rate of growth of per capita income was very close to zero."[9]

In other words, if the 200,000-year life span of *Homo sapiens* were a single year, the vast majority of human economic progress would have transpired in roughly the last fourteen hours.[10]

THE SPOILER, OF COURSE, is that no one truly knows why the Miracle happened. There are many theories but no consensus. The best explanation is that ideas changed. Starting in the 1700s, in a remote corner of Europe, people started to believe that the individual was sovereign, that innovation was good, that the fruits of our labors belong to us. We invented the notion of God-given rights and a way to organize the larger society—the extended order outside of family and tribe—that allowed humans to trade and make contracts rather than club each other. We stumbled into a non–zero-sum system that made people freer and wealthier. I have called this the Lockean Revolution, but John Locke no more created it than Adam Smith created capitalism when he described it.

I should pause here to explain that my aim in this appendix—or to some extent even in this book—is not to offer an explanation for why the Miracle happened but merely to demonstrate that it happened at all. From the vantage point of human history, this explosion of prosperity is as miraculous as the goose that lays the golden egg waddling into a peasant's home and producing unimagined wealth. I have already laid out the different theories about the *why*. But the *what* is what matters here.

The Chinese have a useful concept: "the rectification of the names." Confucius argued that when words no longer describe the world as it is, justice becomes impossible. "If names be not correct, language is not in accordance with the truth of things," Confucius wrote. "If language be not in accordance with the truth of things, affairs cannot be carried on to success."[11]

The age we live in is disconnected from the past. That is a good thing. That, in fact, is the Miracle. But there is a downside. When you amputate historical memory, you end up taking the present for granted. If you were born and raised in an oasis, you would be forgiven for not appreciating the misery of living in the desert. Westerners act as if the prosperity of today is simply natural, and, as a result, they have a cavalier attitude toward the ideas and institutions that make our prosperity possible. Recognizing our good fortune is the first step in securing it for posterity. The average American and West European lives the most bespoke lifestyle in human history, and yet we are angry that it is not even more tailored to our desires. In short, we are ungrateful. And in our ingratitude we indulge the devil on our shoulder that is human nature.

Unless you are reading this naked in the woods, nothing around you right now is natural. It is artificial. It is manufactured. And it is wonderful. But we refuse to see it that way. As Irving Kristol said, "When we lack the will to see things as they really are, there is nothing so mystifying as the obvious."[12] So let me return to demystifying the obvious.

According to economic historian Angus Maddison, the Western world's economy from A.D. 1 to A.D. 1820 grew at 0.06 percent per year, or 6 percent per century—that is, essentially no growth at all.[13] World per capita GDP rose from $467 in A.D. 1 to a mere $666 in 1820.[14] Deirdre McCloskey estimates that, prior to the Industrial Revolution, pretty much everybody lived on about $3 a day.[15] In material terms, even the marginally more fortunate lords and barons lived closer to what we would today call a subsistence lifestyle. Virtually everyone throughout most of human history has lived in what we today have the luxury of calling poverty.

Economic growth took off in the 1700s, starting in England, and has been accelerating ever since.[16] Maddison estimates that the goods and services produced between 2001 and 2010 constitute 25 percent of all goods and services produced since A.D. 1.[17] McCloskey's figures put the difference between what our ancestors lived on and what we live on today as that between $3 and $100 a day (for bourgeois nations).[18] J. Bradford DeLong finds a thirty-seven-fold increase in world per capita income from 1750 to the late 2000s, from $180 per person to $6,600 per person.[19] And even the modern world's poorest places experience growth rates unlike anything before the Industrial Revolution.[20] Global GDP has soared, from an estimated $150 billion in A.D. 1 to more than $50 trillion as of 2008.[21] Observed macroscopically, we are closer to Eden than Eden ever was.

The Bernie Sanders chorus would not dispute this: They recognize that enormous wealth has been accumulated. They merely argue that the poor have been left behind. That's false. In the great migration out of the desert of time, the poor may have been at the back of the caravan, but they have lived in the oasis too. And as the West has marched deeper into the oasis, more of the world has followed us into it.

Around the world, the number of people considered poor has decreased both relatively *and* absolutely—an incredible feat, given massive increases in population.[22] For all of human history before the modern era, what we call poverty was simply the Way Things Are. It remained so in most of the world as recently as 1820. By one dire account, in 1820, 94.4 percent of the world's population lived on the equivalent of less than $2 a day, and 83.9 percent lived on less than $1 a day that year. As of 2015, only 9.6 percent of the world's population lived on less than $1.90 a day.[23]

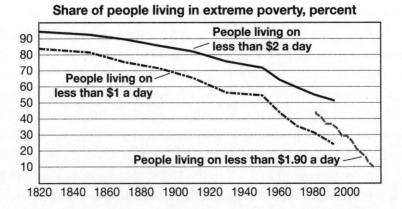

Share of people living in extreme poverty, percent

The figures are even more impressive in raw numerical terms. As recently as 1970, almost 27 percent of people worldwide lived in absolute poverty (less than one 1987 dollar a day). A little more than 5 percent did as of 2006.[24]

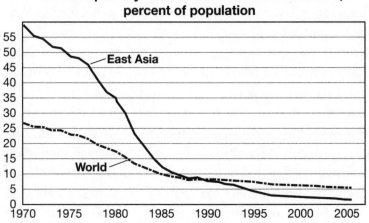

Absolute poverty rates in East Asia and the world, percent of population

Decry "globalization" all you like. It certainly has come at a price for some citizens of the developed world. But the spread of market forces to the far corners of the globe has been the chief driver of the largest eradication of poverty in human history. Between 1990 and 2010, the percentage of the population in developing countries living in poverty fell from 43 to 21 percent, a reduction of almost one billion people.[25] In 2015, for the first time in human history, less than 10 percent of the world's population was considered extremely poor.[26] The United Nations estimates more poverty was reduced in the last fifty years than in the previous five hundred.[27]

One of the great cleavages between left and right is a disagreement over the definition of freedom. The left tends to define freedom in material terms, the right in political ones. FDR argued that "necessitous men are not free men."[28] Thus the state must provide or guarantee health care, income (or employment), etc. This is so-called positive liberty. The right prefers "negative liberty"—freedom from government interference. What often gets left out of the debate is the fact that economic growth and technological innovation do more to provide positive liberty than any government possibly could.

THE ULTIMATE FINITE RESOURCE is time. Technology cannot create more hours in the day, but it allows us to do more with the hours we have by reducing the amount of labor required to accomplish desired tasks. One of the dominant aspects of a precapitalist, preindustrial world was the sheer amount of work required to perform even the most menial tasks, and the staggering number of workers required to perform them. Today's world is increasingly leaving the burdensome toil of the past behind.

To take just one example, consider the percentage of the total population employed in agriculture. Often romanticized, farming is, in fact, backbreaking labor. Fortunately, fewer and fewer people are actually doing it. When China first began to open itself up to markets in 1978 (a little more than a generation ago), 70.5 percent of the population worked in agriculture. After four decades of market-driven transformation, that figure in 2015 was 28 percent.[29] Unlike in China, no one in the United States has memories of a majority-agricultural workforce. But as recently (in the grand historical scheme of things) as 1870, 46 percent of the population worked on farms. In 1940, well within American cultural memory, 17.3 percent of the population still worked in agriculture. As of 2009, 1.1 percent did.[30] Available data worldwide show a similar pattern.[31]

Technology has lightened the burden of labor more generally as well. In 1950, the average annual number of hours worked per worker was 2,226.47 hours (about a forty-three-hour workweek in a fifty-two-week year). In 2016, it was 1,855.04 (about a thirty-six-hour workweek in a fifty-two-week year).[32]

Because of the vast time scope and the many countries involved in discerning such a figure, many of which either stopped existing or only began to exist or report data at some point during the measured period, it is worth taking these figures with at least a grain of salt. But the trend they describe is undeniable. And it is made possible by incredible increases in productivity. Again, available figures have their limitations. But those we do have paint an amazing picture: global labor productivity at $9.30 per hour worked in 1950, and at $36.64 per hour worked in 2015 (measured in 2014 U.S. dollars).[33]

Simply put: Getting more done in less time means less work. Indeed, the lightening of human toil that capitalism has enabled is

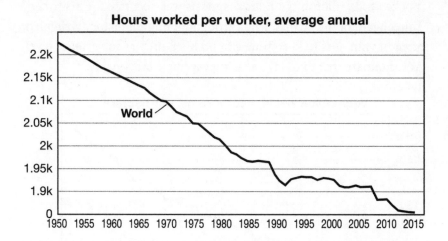

Hours worked per worker, average annual

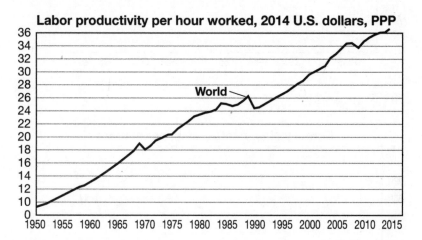

Labor productivity per hour worked, 2014 U.S. dollars, PPP

so thorough that major public policy debates in developed countries center around getting *more* people to work—a debate that would have made no sense to any of our ancestors. This is a vital challenge, to be sure. It is increasingly obvious that work—meaningful, valued work—is essential to human happiness. Creating new sources of such work may be one of the most important political and cultural tasks of the next century. But let's be clear: This is a good problem to have compared to the historical alternatives.

Another way in which capitalism is liberating is that it has allowed humanity to escape the Malthusian trap. Thomas Malthus, writing in the late eighteenth century, believed that the increase in population would always outpace the means of food production. For this, he is mocked today, but in truth his diagnosis was accurate for his time.[34] Think again of the farmer, who throughout human history struggled, often in vain, just to keep himself and his family at subsistence level. And compare that to today's soaring vegetable crop yields:[35]

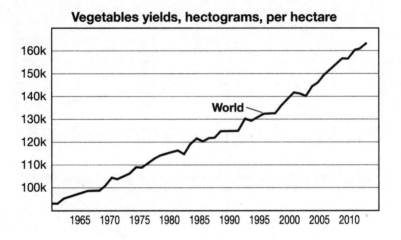

Vegetables yields, hectograms, per hectare

and cereal yields:[36.]

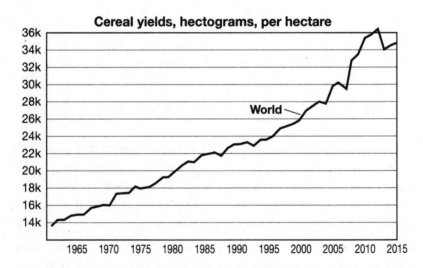

Cereal yields, hectograms, per hectare

Malthus may have accurately described his time, but capitalism lifted what seemed like an eternal curse of mankind.

Consider the New Testament miracle of the loaves and fishes, in which Jesus fed 5,000 people with a few baskets of bread and fish. The apostle Philip called this crowd so vast that not even more than half a year's wages could have fed them all.[37] Half of the median wage today in America would amount to something like $28,000,[38] with which one could purchase multiple satisfying food items for the vast crowd. And this is only one example of the transformative power of capitalism. To keep things biblical, consult a study by Brian Wansink and C. S. Wansink that found that depictions of the Last Supper have grown both tastier and more generous over time, reflecting the increase in food options and portions over the centuries.[39] To be more numerate, consider, for example:

- The world produced only 53.6 percent as much food in 1961 as it did on average in 2004–2006, whereas in 2013 it produced 119 percent as much.[40]
- Meat consumption per person in developing countries has nearly doubled since 1964.[41]
- The global average food supply per person per day has risen by more than 600 calories since 1961:[42]

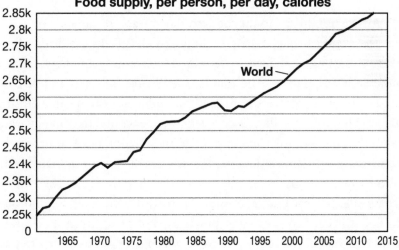

- The overall food consumption shortfall among food-deprived persons has declined precipitously since as recently as 1992.[43]
- And, most stunning, the worldwide total of undernourished persons has plummeted since 1992, when it approached 1 billion, to now less than 700 million.[44]

We also have more and cheaper energy than ever before. World-wide access to electricity—a utility that, let us not forget, simply did not exist for human use for thousands of years before the modern age—has steadily increased, from 75.65 percent in 1990 to 84.58 percent in 2012:[45]

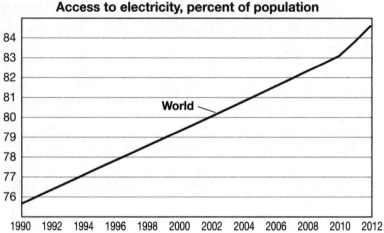

Access to electricity, percent of population

All are testaments to the modern-day miracle of capitalism.

The skeptical reader may be annoyed that I am crediting all of these things to capitalism. After all, science and technology are not inherently "capitalist." And that is true. People invented and discovered things long before anything like a capitalist system came online. But, as I have already discussed at length, science and technology were routinely made subservient to politics and religion prior to the Lockean Revolution. Innovation was literally a crime or sin in many parts of the world, because innovation was a threat to the established order. The freedom of the market economy is really the freedom to innovate, to find efficiencies in existing practices, and/or to invent new practices that render the old ways obsolete. People may have been free to build a better mousetrap that may have existed for millennia, but the freedom to bring a better mousetrap to market is a remarkably recent development.

Capitalism is actually the most liberating force in human history. Matt Ridley estimates that, with the average human consuming 2,500 watts per second, it would require 150 humans pedaling on exercise bikes to power the lifestyle to which each person in the world is becoming increasingly accustomed. For Americans, the number is 660 people.[46] Economist Mark J. Perry estimated the number of domestic servants the average American would need to replace the technology we all rely on. To maintain the same level of convenience would require the physical output of about 600 people (keep these figures in mind next time you watch *Downton Abbey*, with its apparent multitude of servants).[47] Either way, the proliferation of energy has immensely benefited mankind.

But even if the world were running out of resources (which it is not), we are continuing to do more with less, thanks to the market's peerless ability to maximize efficiency in ways impossible to central planners. According to a 2013 study by the Alliance to Save Energy, "U.S. economic output expanded more than three times since 1970 while demand for energy grew only 50%," resulting in millions fewer barrels of oil used than otherwise would have been. University of Manitoba natural scientist Vaclav Smil—Bill Gates's favorite expert on these issues—identified some areas that drove this efficiency: modern steel production requires only 20 percent of the energy it did in 1900; aluminum production requires 70 percent less energy now than it did then; manufacturing nitrogen fertilizer requires 80 percent less energy now than it did then. Similarly, technologist Ramez Naam calculates that the energy required to heat a house has decreased 50 percent since 1978, and the amount of energy required for water desalination is down 90 percent since 1970.[48] The United States now uses half as much energy per unit of GDP as in 1950, and the world uses 1.6 percent less energy for each dollar of GDP growth every year.[49] The U.S. also uses no more water today than it did in 1980, despite a population increase of some 80 million.[50]

This efficiency has appeared in material production as well. Vaclav Smil points out that producing a dollar of value in the United States in 1920 required 10 ounces of material, whereas now it requires only 2.5. And the 11 million cell phones that existed in 1990 weighed 7,000 tons, whereas the 6 billion or so that exist today collectively weigh only one hundred times more.[51]

To go back to farming for a moment, we are not simply achieving the massive increase in yields by plowing in more inputs. In fact, we're doing it with fewer greenhouse emissions.[52]

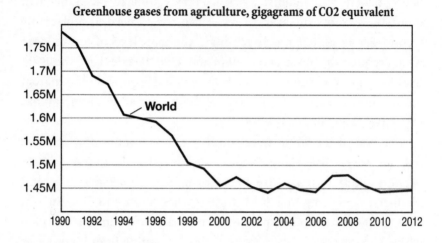

Greenhouse gases from agriculture, gigagrams of CO2 equivalent

Contrary to what you may be hearing, resources are bountiful, and our innovation-driven efficiency in using them wisely is on the rise.

Capitalism has also completely transformed transportation, a depressingly primitive affair from the invention of the wheel to the first passenger train, limited, as it was, by "hoof and sail."[53] Here is historian William Manchester's account of travel in the Middle Ages:

> Travel was slow, expensive, uncomfortable—and perilous. It was slowest for those who rode in coaches, faster for walkers, and fastest for horsemen, who were few because of the need to change and stable steeds. The expense chiefly arose from the countless tolls, the discomfort from a score of irritants. Bridges spanning rivers were shaky (priests recommended that before crossing them travelers commend themselves to God); other streams had to be forded; the roads were deplorable—mostly trails and muddy ruts, impassable, except in summer, by two-wheeled carts—and nights en route had to be spent in Europe's wretched inns. These were unsanitary places, the beds wedged against one another, blankets crawling with roaches, rats, and fleas; whores plied their trade and then slipped away with a man's money, and innkeepers seized guests' baggage on the pretext that they had not paid.[54]

Manchester also relates some contemporary travel times, in days, from Venice—a commercial center of the medieval world—to various other places: Damascus (80 days), Alexandria (65), Lisbon (46), Constantinople (37), Valladolid (29), London (27), Palermo (22), Nuremberg (20), Brussels (16), Lyons (12), Augsburg (10).[55] Columbus's first voyage took more than two months.[56] In 1830, a trip from New York to Chicago took three weeks.[57] All of these journeys are now achievable in less than a day. And, thanks to the market, the ability to travel is available to more people every year.[58] Just as capitalism has gone a long way toward liberating us from darkness and toil, it has also toppled the tyranny of distance.

While it's certainly true that capitalism and economic growth have come at a cost to the environment, free-market societies are far better stewards of the environment than command economies. Moreover, capitalism provides the means to remedy the damage.

Forests in wealthy countries have been expanding for decades.[59] Despite widespread forecasts to the contrary, Europe's forests grew during the 1980s and 1990s.[60] From 1960 to 2000, India's forests grew by 15 million hectares (larger than the state of Iowa). Leaving out the heavily developing nations of Brazil and Indonesia, global forests have grown by roughly 2 percent since 1990.[61] And forest area has grown in the United States and China, the world's two wealthiest countries.[62]

Innovation allows us to replace diminishing or depleted resources with better ones. Ronald Bailey notes that "railroads, the 19th cen-

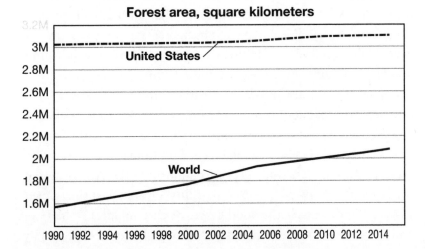

Forest area, square kilometers

3.2M
3M
2.8M
2.6M
2.4M
2.2M
2M
1.8M
1.6M

United States

World

1990 1992 1994 1996 1998 2000 2002 2004 2006 2008 2010 2012 2014

tury's 'modern' form of transportation, consumed nearly 25 percent of all the wood used in America, for both track ties and fuel."[63] Today, however, we no longer use wood for fuel, and we use it much less as a construction material (and paper usage is plummeting thanks to the digital revolution).

Similarly, when we decide that the by-products of industry are becoming a problem, the market allows us to innovate techniques that fix the problem. Hence, recently, energy-related carbon dioxide emissions in the U.S. have been on a downward trend, not upward:[64]

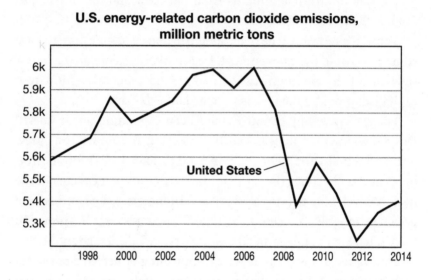

U.S. energy-related carbon dioxide emissions, million metric tons

Because we are doing more with less, and because capitalism's wealth allows us to spare what once we might have heedlessly plundered from the earth, capitalism is ultimately good for the environment. "Pollution levels are falling in rich countries and will begin to drop in poor countries as they become wealthier," writes Bailey.[65]

Capitalism has also made us healthier. It has, for example, led to longer lives for more people. For premodern societies as a whole, life expectancy was under forty years.[66] The shades (souls) of ancient Greeks often met Hades by age eighteen; most Roman shades met Pluto by twenty-two. A 2002 study of pre-Columbian Native American skeletons found that few people lived past fifty, or even past thirty-five.[67] Not many Europeans in the Middle Ages reached middle age; half were dead before their thirtieth birthday. A young girl could expect to live to twenty-four. Men fortunate enough to survive past their thirties or early forties could reasonably expect to live a bit longer but would outwardly resemble senior citizens by what we still consider middle age.[68]

We're a lot better off than that today. Even the global average life expectancy at birth in 1960, at 52.48 years, would have compared favorably to anything from the past. But in 2015 that same figure was 71.6 years.[69]

Life expectancy at birth, years

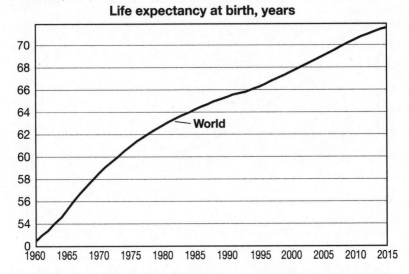

Today, the average person born worldwide can expect to live decades longer than anyone in the past could have reasonably hoped for. Capitalism literally gives the average person "new life" in the sense that old age was, for the average person, an unrealistic ambition. Technology cannot create more time, but it can give us the opportunity to have more of it.

But capitalism gives new life in another way: We are simply more likely to *live* in the first place.[70] In premodern societies, almost one-third of children died before age five. Infant mortality in hunter-gatherer societies was almost thirty times greater than in America today, and child mortality was more than one hundred times greater. The average worldwide population-weighted child mortality rate was 43 percent in 1800. The worst-off countries in 1800 suffered the death of half of all children, but even the best-off countries endured the passing of about a third of all children. In America, as recently as 1890, infant mortality was 22 percent of new births.[71]

Today, the worldwide, population-weighted child mortality rate is 3.4 percent. Child mortality is 1.3 percent in China, which, along with Brazil, has experienced a fourfold decrease of child mortality over the past four decades.[72] Since 1960 the worldwide infant mortality rate has declined from 121.9 per 1,000 live births to 31.7:[73]

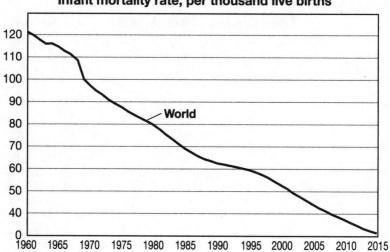

Infant mortality rate, per thousand live births

Similarly, the mortality rate worldwide for all ages has decreased from 16.03 per 1,000 people in 1960 to 8.09 per 1,000 people in 2013.[74]

Think of all the value created because people simply *lived*.

This has been happening in part simply due to the correlation between health and wealth.[75] More specifically, it's from better medical care. Consider just a few aspects of medical care in the past. Would you like to be treated by the medieval doctors described by William Manchester?

> The stars were known to be guided by angels, and physicians were constantly consulting astrologers and theologians. Doctors diagnosing illnesses were influenced by the constellation under which the patient had been born or taken sick; thus the eminent surgeon Guy de Chauliac wrote: "If anyone is wounded in the neck when the moon is at Taurus, the affliction will be dangerous." Thousands of pitiful people disfigured by swollen lymph nodes in their necks mobbed the kings of England and France, believing that their

Death rate, per 1,000 people

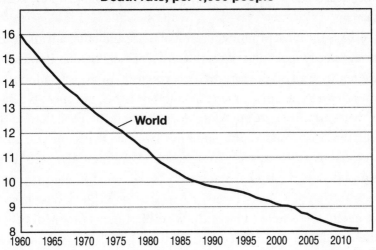

scrofula could be cured by the touch of a royal hand. One document from the period is a calendar, published at Mainz, which designates the best astrological times for bloodletting. Epidemics were attributed to unfortunate configurations of the stars . . .[76]

Would you entrust your teeth to "dentists" in medieval England, who relied on "herbal remedies, charms, and amulets" for both cleaning and removal?[77] Would you like to have a limb amputated before the first painless surgery with anesthetic in 1846?[78] Would you trust medical examinations before 1896, when blood pressure instruments and X-ray machines—the latter costing only 20 percent in 2012 of what they cost in 1910[79]—were invented? Or before 1901, before electrocardiograms, which weren't even used widely until the 1920s?[80] Or would you even like to be alive in America in the 1920s, when, according to Lewis Thomas, former dean of the Yale and New York University Schools of Medicine, going to a doctor probably *lowered* your chances for survival and most mothers by necessity became domestic nurses?[81] Or around the same time, when sepsis infection killed nearly half of major-surgery patients?[82] Even as recently as 1990, the number of women dying in or from childbirth worldwide was far higher than today.[83] And as recently as a decade ago, sequencing a genome cost millions of dollars versus $10,000 today.[84] The steady advance of medical care has gone a long way toward improving overall health outcomes.

Perhaps the most prominent result of these and other advances has been the steady reduction of death from disease. Pharaoh Rameses V could not with all his power prevent his own death from smallpox. (In fairness, there's no cure for smallpox today, either, but there is a vaccine that works as a cure up to four days after infection.) Nathan Rothschild, the richest man in the world in 1836, died that same year from what today is an easily treatable infection.[85] While Calvin Coolidge was president of the United States in 1924, his son died within a week from infection of a blister he got playing on the White House lawn.[86] And, again, these were some of the wealthiest, most powerful people in the world. Life was much worse for most;[87] malaria, typhoid fever, and dysentery killed thousands annually.[88]

Today, however, a wide variety of diseases—mumps, rubella, malaria, measles, sleeping sickness, elephantiasis, and river blindness—are drastically retreating worldwide, suggesting that "the total eradication of many diseases is now a realistic prospect."[89] In America, the death rate from infectious disease was only 2 percent in 2009.[90] Other disease indicators have also significantly improved. Malaria, typhoid fever, and dysentery are non-factors in the developed world,[91] with the last in particular probably being better known as a video game meme ("You have died of dysentery") than a deadly disease.[92] Seventy-five percent fewer people died from strokes in 2013 than did in the 1960s.[93] AIDs peaked in the late 1990s; by 2010 incidence had decreased 20 percent from 1997.[94] Cancer is still a terrible scourge, but we're dealing with it better than ever. Apart from lung cancer, cancer incidence and death rate fell 16 percent from 1950 to 1997 and accelerated thereafter; once smoking decreased, lung cancer began to fall as well.[95] As the number of artificial chemicals has dramatically increased over the past four decades, overall cancer death rates and age-adjusted cancer incidence have both declined. Half of all cancer patients died within five years of their diagnosis in the 1970s; 68 percent now live past that. Overall cancer incidence has declined 0.6 percent annually since 1994, saving 100,000 people today who otherwise would have died from the disease. The death rate from leukemia is 7.1 per 100,000, half of what environmental alarmist Rachel Carson fretted over in *Silent Spring.*

An estimated 10,450 children were diagnosed with cancer in 2014, less than 1 percent of overall cancer deaths, and 80 percent of those diagnosed survive five years or more, up from 50 percent in the 1970s.[96]

Cancer causes 186 of every 100,000 deaths annually, but that's in large part because far more Americans live past the age of sixty-five, the median age of cancer diagnosis. Americans in the early twentieth century did not live long enough to develop 75 percent of today's cancers.[97] Non-disease-based indicators have improved as well: Disability rates in Americans over sixty-five decreased from 26.2 percent to 19.7 percent between 1982 and 1999 (twice as fast as the mortality rate decreased).[98] Historically, if you managed to make it to old age, it was unlikely you could be productive, never mind prosperous. Today, senior citizens in developed countries are a mass class of people.

We're also more literate and more educated than ever before. For most of human history, most people—and more women than men—were illiterate. The great stories, such as the *Iliad*, *Odyssey*, and *Beowulf*, were told orally long before they were ever written down. Education of any kind was a privilege of the elite. As recently as 1820, only 12 percent of the world's population was literate. The wealth created by capitalism has changed all of this. By 2014, only 15 percent of the world's population remained illiterate—almost a complete inversion in less than two hundred years.[99]

Education has also increased. The average amount of years of education worldwide has increased from 2.97 years in 1950 to 8.99 in 2015:[100]

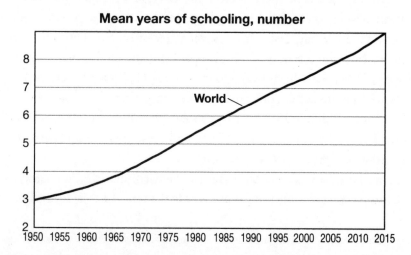

Mean years of schooling, number

World

Thanks to capitalism, education and literacy are no longer the privilege of the elite but increasingly common to all.[*]

Capitalism has also completely transformed communication. For the entirety of human history until about 170 years ago, the travel speed of news was limited to the travel speed of people: i.e., by "foot, horse, sail, or, more recently, rail," as economist Robert J. Gordon points out.[101] History records many darkly comic examples of this defect in communication. Thus did the Athenians in the Peloponnesian War, at first having decided to destroy the rebellious Mytileneans, send one boat to do just that. Changing their minds the next day, their only recourse was to send another boat after the first, with instructions to row as fast as it could to arrive in time to dissuade the first boat.[102] The Battle of New Orleans, technically the final skirmish of the War of 1812, occurred after the War of 1812 had actually ended.[103] The first telegram, sent in 1844, inaugurated a new era in human communication.[104] But as impressive as its early innovations must have been to those who experienced them, they seem laughably primitive to us today because of the pace of technological advance. And the technology continues to evolve: In 2010, each American household had nearly 2.6 cell phones; in 2013, 91 percent of American adults had a cell phone.[105] Mobile cell phone subscriptions have increased from 0.27 per 100 people in 1990 (think Gordon Gekko and his brick phone in 1987's *Wall Street*) to 105.74 per 100 people(!) in 2014.[106]

The calls made on these devices, moreover, are cheaper. We take for granted today that a fixed-price phone service covers most essentially instantaneous long-distance calls, yet as recently as seventy years ago such a call would require multiple operators and could cost an hour's wages.[107] We even have technology—Facebook, Twitter, Skype—that allows free, instantaneous communication without a phone. For the first time in human history, two people can call one another *without even knowing where the other is*.[108] That is a testament to the incredible transformative power of capitalism.

Markets have also utterly transformed computing. *Iron Sky*, an absurd science fiction film, illustrates this point. In this 2012 film, a

---

[*]   Increasingly, education might also be an enemy of capitalism, as I discussed earlier.

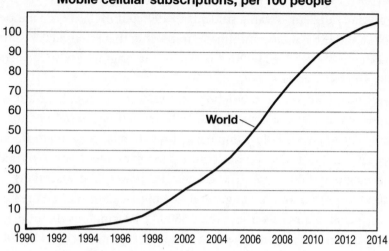

Mobile cellular subscriptions, per 100 people

Nazi cadre secretly escaped to the dark side of the moon at the end of World War II and spent the intervening years plotting an invasion of Earth. Their plans receive a considerable boost when they steal an American astronaut's smartphone, which alone has more computing power than the totality of their equipment up to that point.[109] Sound far-fetched? Well, yes. But the computing power differential is highly plausible. ENIAC, one of the first "modern" computers, debuted in 1946, right around the time the Nazis flee to the moon in *Iron Sky*. It weighed 27 tons, required 240 square feet (22.3 square meters) of floor space, and needed 174,000 watts (174 kilowatts) of power, enough to (allegedly) dim all the lights in Philadelphia when turned on.[110] In 1949, *Popular Mechanics* predicted that one day a computer might weigh less than 1.5 tons.[111] In the early 1970s, Seymour Cray, known as the "father of the supercomputer," revolutionized the computer industry. His Cray-1 system supercomputer shocked the industry with a world-record speed of 160 million floating-point operations per second, an 8-megabyte main memory, no wires longer than four feet, and its ability to fit into a small room. The Los Alamos National Laboratory purchased it in 1976 for $8.8 million, or $36.9 million in today's inflation-adjusted dollars. But as predicted by Moore's Law (the number of transistors that can fit on a microchip will double roughly every twenty-four months),[112] modern computing has improved and spread beyond even the wildest speculations of people living at the time of any of these computers (certain science fiction excepted). A team of University of Pennsylvania students in 1996 put ENIAC's capabilities onto a single 64-square-millimeter microchip that required 0.5 watts, making it about 1/350,000th the size of the original ENIAC.[113] And that was twenty years ago.

Popular Mechanics' prediction proved correct, though a bit of an (understandable) understatement. Still, try telling its 1949 editorial staff that today we hold computers in our hands, place them in our pockets, and rest them on our laps. Laptop computers with 750 times the memory, 1,000 times the calculating power, and essentially an infinitely greater amount of general capabilities as the Cray-1 are now available at Walmart for less than $500.[114] Bearing out the *Iron Sky* comparison, a smartphone with 16 gigabytes of memory has 250,000 times the capacity of the *Apollo 11* guidance computer that enabled the first moon landing.[115] A life's wages in 1975 could have bought you the computing power of a pocket calculator in 2000.[116] In 1997, $450 could have bought you 5 gigabytes of hard-drive storage that is free today.[117] A MacBook Pro with 8 gigabytes of RAM has 1.6 million times more RAM than MANIAC, a 1951 "supercomputer."[118] Forget angels on the head of a pin: Intel can fit more than six million transistors onto the period at the end of this sentence.[119]

What this all means for the consumer is an unprecedented spread of technology. Today's cell phones exceed the computing power of machines that required rooms mere decades ago. Nearly half the world uses the Internet, up from essentially zero in 1990.[120]

Today, then, computers are better, faster, smarter, more prevalent, and more connective than ever before. In the 1990s, progressive policy makers fretted over something called "the digital divide." They convinced themselves that, absent government intervention, the Internet would be a plaything for the wealthy. They raised new taxes, transferred wealth, paid off some constituents, and claimed victory. But the truth is that the Internet was always going to be for everyone, because that is what the market does. It introduces luxuries for the wealthy, and the wealthy subsidize innovations that turn luxuries— cell phones, cars, medicine, computers, nutritious food, comfortable homes, etc.—into necessities. It is the greatest triumph of alchemy in

Internet users, per 100 people

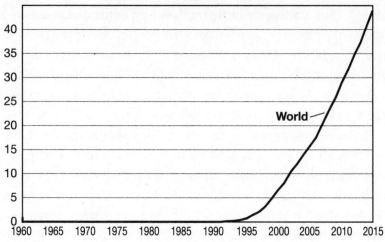

all of human experience, and the response from many in every generation is ingratitude and entitlement.

NOW, NONE OF THIS is to say that this miraculous explosion in material prosperity has not come with costs. Such is the nature of this life. Everything has trade-offs.

Nor is it to say that government hasn't played a role in evening out some of the excesses of human enrichment. But paternalistic government is as old as the first Big Man leading the first band of hairless apes running across the savannas of Africa. Paternalism is the logic behind the rule of every Caesar, king, pasha, sultan, commissar, and emperor. Paternalism did not create the Miracle. Human ingenuity unleashed by the miracle of liberty, chiefly economic liberty—which yields political liberty—made this possible.

And yet, in the modern era, every generation takes the Miracle for granted. We are told, by people who should know better, that capitalism is making us sicker, poorer, and more exploited. That we are falling farther behind and therefore must look even farther behind us to some mythological golden age when we had it better. One typical poll result revealed that 66 percent of Americans believe that extreme poverty has "almost doubled in the past 20 years, 29 percent think it has not changed, whereas only 5 percent correctly stated that it has halved." The numbers are no better elsewhere in the developed world: 58 percent of Britons assumed extreme poverty had increased and a third thought it had stayed the same.[121] These pessimists answer in vain Thomas Babington Macaulay's inquiry: "On what principle is it, that when we see nothing but improvement behind us, are we to expect nothing but deterioration before us?"[122]

The free-market system depends on values, ideas, and institutions outside of the realm of economics to function, a topic I covered in the second half of this book. But for now the important point is this: The free-market system is not merely the best anti-poverty program ever conceived; it is quite literally the *only* anti-poverty system ever invented. Poverty is the natural human condition, and it remained the steady state of human affairs for nearly all of human history. Socialism as a label is a relatively recent invention. But socialism as an idea is beyond ancient. Socialism is the economics of the tribe. We evolved as a cooperative, resource-sharing species. This is one reason why the idea of socialism keeps coming back. It's in our brains, alongside myriad other factory-preset ideas and desires: that capitalism is unnatural; individual liberty and free speech are unnatural; liberal democratic capitalism is at war with human nature in every generation.

It is a common theme in literature: Every wish comes with a catch. From Goethe's and Marlowe's *Faust*, to Kipling's "Sing-Song of Old Man Kangaroo," to Hans Christian Andersen's "Galoshes of Fortune," to a half dozen episodes of *The Twilight Zone*, we must be careful what we wish for. The Miracle of now is the answer to a thousand generations of wishes by people whose lives were poor, nasty, brutish, and short. Capitalism is the greatest peaceful cooperative endeavor for human enrichment ever created—by orders of magnitude. The catch? *It doesn't feel like it.* It doesn't feel cooperative. It doesn't even feel peaceful. It is full of uncertainty and tumult.

Capitalism cannot provide meaning, spirituality, or a sense of *belonging*. Those things are upstream of capitalism. And that's okay. Capitalism is an economic system that is fantastic at doing what we claim we want from economic systems: growth and prosperity. The problem is that what we say we want from an economic system and what we actually want are often different things. Economics is a sphere of the larger civilization, and we want more than what mere capitalism can provide. We want meaning. We want to feel like we're part of the tribe. But just as a hammer makes for a terrible knife, capitalism is a tool ill-suited for filling the holes in our souls.

Meaning comes from family, friends, faith, community, and countless little platoons of civil society. When those institutions fail, capitalism alone cannot restore them. As a result, human nature starts making demands of the political and economic systems that neither can possibly fulfill. Liberty, economic and political, is recast as the source of our problems. Having lost faith in other realms, we lose faith in the Miracle itself, and we cast about for what feels more natural: tribalism, nationalism, or socialism in one guise or another.

Most people recognize that "consumer confidence" is important for the economy. When people feel optimistic about their own financial situation and the prospects for the overall economy, they are more likely to spend money and businesses invest more in workers and equipment. Tragically, we spend vastly more time talking about consumer confidence than we do about civilizational confidence, and yet civilizational confidence is vastly more important. Western civilization created the Miracle, even if it did so by accident. When we lose our confidence—and pride—in what it has accomplished, we are committing a suicidal act on a civilizational scale.

Notes

INTRODUCTION

1. Richard Rorty, *Consequences of Pragmatism: Essays, 1972-1980* (Minneapolis: University of Minnesota Press, 1982), p. xlii.
2. I am indebted to Joshua Greene, author of *Moral Tribes: Emotion, Reason, and the Gap Between Us and Them* (New York: Penguin, 2013), for this thought experiment.
3. Robin Fox, *The Tribal Imagination: Civilization and the Savage Mind* (Cambridge, MA: Harvard University Press, 2011), p. 6.
4. "GDP, 1990 International Dollars," Human Progress. http://humanprogress.org/f1/2128. All figures from Human Progress, a project of the Cato Institute. Marian L. Tupy and Chelsea Follett were extremely helpful to us for this portion of the project.
5. Todd G. Buchholz, "Dark Clouds, Silver Linings," in *New Ideas from Dead Economists: An Introduction to Modern Economic Thought* (New York: Penguin Group, 2007 [1990]), p. 313.
6. I use the word "tribal" because it is the more serviceable adjective. Technically, humans evolved in smaller units called bands. But "bandal" isn't a word, and "tribe," the next unit of organization up from band, captures the point just as well.
7. With the exception of a few nocturnal lower primates and the higher primate, the orangutan, virtually all primates live in communities.
8. Sebastian Junger, *Tribe: On Homecoming and Belonging* (New York: Grand Central, 2016, Kindle edition), pp. 2–3.
9. "Thousands of Europeans are Indians, and we have no examples of even one of those Aborigines having from choice become European," a French émigré writer, Hector Saint John de Crèvecoeur, observed in 1782. "There must be in their social bond something singularly captivating and far superior to anything to be boasted of among us." "Crèvecoeur seemed to have understood that the intensely communal nature of an Indian tribe held an appeal that the material benefits of Western civilization couldn't necessarily compete with," Junger writes. "If he was right, that problem started almost as soon as Europeans touched American shores. As early as 1612, Spanish authorities noted in amazement that forty or fifty Virginians had married into Indian tribes, and that even English women were openly mingling with the natives." Ibid., p. 10.
10. The Austrian writer Ernst Fischer found that Marx's vision was an extension of "the romantic revolt against a world which turned everything into a commodity and degraded man to the status of an object." The socialist scholar Michael Löwy, in a deeply researched essay, "The Romantic and the Marxist Critique of Modern

Civilization," concludes that as "a matter of fact Romantic anti-capitalism is the forgotten source of Marx, a source that is as important for his work as German neo-Hegelianism or French materialism." But Paul Johnson sums it up best: "There was nothing scientific about him; indeed, in all that matters he was anti-scientific." Michael Löwy, "The Romantic and the Marxist Critique of Modern Civilization," *Theory and Society* 16, no. 6 (November 1987), p. 897; Paul Johnson, *Intellectuals* (New York: HarperCollins, 2009, Kindle edition), Kindle location 1233-37.

11. Thirty years after its publication, its Amazon sales rank was 5 in books on political science as of 1/17/18. It's an unrelenting indictment of America as a force of evil. It remains one of, if not the most, widely used textbooks in American high schools and colleges. "Given a choice between a book that portrayed America honestly—as an extraordinary success story—and a book that portrayed the history of America as a litany of depredations and failures, which do you suppose your average graduate of a teachers college, your average member of the National Education Association, would choose?" asks Roger Kimball. He adds, "To ask the question is to answer it." Roger Kimball, "Professor of Contempt," *National Review* online, February 3, 2010. http://www.nationalreview.com/article/229071/professor-contempt-roger-kimball

12. Howard Zinn, *A People's History of the United States* (New York: HarperCollins, 2005 [1980]), p. 10.

13. "163. The Hen and the Golden Eggs," *Aesop's Fables* (trans. G. F. Townsend, 1867. See Aesopica: Aesop's Fables in English, Latin, & Greek. http://mythfolklore.net/aesopica/townsend/163.htm

14. "Avyan 24. Of the goos and of her lord," *Aesop's Fables* (trans. William Caxton, 1484. See Aesopica: Aesop's Fables in English, Latin, & Greek. http://mythfolklore.net/aesopica/caxton/724.htm

15. I am indebted to Paul Rahe for calling the significance of this scene to my attention. For his full argument, see Paul Rahe, "Don Vito Corleone, Friendship, and the American Regime," in *Reinventing the American People: Unity and Diversity Today*, Robert Royal, ed. (Washington, D.C.: Ethics and Public Policy Center, 1995), pp. 115-35.

1: HUMAN NATURE

1. Paul Bloom, *Just Babies: The Origins of Good and Evil* (New York: Broadway Books, 2013, Kindle edition), pp. 23-29.

2. Ibid., pp. 110-111.

3. Ibid., p. 14.

4. Carl Schmitt, *Glossarium: Aufzeichnungen der Jahre 1947-1951*, Eberhard Freiherr von Medem, ed. (Berlin: Duncker & Humblot, 1991), pp. 4-5, 243. Quoted in Claudia Koonz, *The Nazi Conscience* (Cambridge, MA: Belknap Press/Harvard University Press, 2003), p. 293.

5. Bloom, *Just Babies*, p. 15.

6. Donald E. Brown, "Human Universals, Human Nature & Human Culture," *Daedalus* 133, no. 4 (special issue: "On Human Nature," Fall 2004), pp. 47-54.

7. Steven Pinker, *The Blank Slate: The Modern Denial of Human Nature* (New York: Penguin Publishing Group, 2003 [2002], Kindle edition), p. 6.

8. Ibid.

9. Jean-Jacques Rousseau, "The Second Part," sec. 207, "A Dissertation on the Origin and Foundation of the Inequality of Mankind," *The Social Contract and Discourses*, Online Library of Liberty, 1761. http://oll.libertyfund.org/titles/rousseau-the-social-contract-and-discourses#lf0132_head_066

10. Arthur Herman, *The Idea of Decline in Western History* (New York: Free Press, 1997), p. 29.

11. Charles Baudelaire, "The Salon of 1846," *Romanticism: The Documentary History of Western Civilization*, John B. Halsted, ed. (London: Palgrave Macmillan, 1969), p. 119.

12. Francis Fukuyama, *The Origins of Political Order: From Prehuman Times to the French Revolution* (New York: Farrar, Straus and Giroux, 2011), p. 73.

13. Deirdre N. McCloskey, *Bourgeois Dignity: Why Economics Can't Explain the Modern World* (Chicago: University of Chicago Press, 2010), pp. 154-55.

14. Steven Pinker, "A History of Violence," *New Republic*, March 18, 2007. https://newrepublic.com/article/77728/history-violence

15. Matt Ridley, "Farewell to the Myth of the Noble Savage," *Wall Street Journal*, January 25, 2013. http://www.wsj.com/articles/SB10001424127887323940004578257720972109636

16. Nicholas Wade, *Before the Dawn: Recovering the Lost History of Our Ancestors* (New York: Penguin Publishing Group, 2006), p. 151.

17. Chagnon was besieged by anthropologists, indigenous activists, and Catholic missionaries for his relentlessly bleak portrait native of the primitive societies he suffered. The typical charges of colonial bias, Western chauvinism, and racism were hurled at him. But he was ultimately vindicated by subsequent research, most notably the work of Alice Dreger of Northwestern University. See Alice Dreger, "Darkness's Descent on the American Psychological Association: A Cautionary Tale," *Human Nature* 22, no. 3 (September 2011), pp. 225-46. http://link.springer.com/article/10.1007%2Fs12110-011-9103-y. See also Matt Ridley, "Farewell to the Myth of the Noble Savage," *Wall Street Journal*, January 25, 2013.

18. Napoleon Chagnon, "Life Histories, Blood Revenge, and Warfare in a Tribal Population," *Science* n.s., 239, no. 4843 (February 26, 1988), pp. 985-92. http://www.class.uh.edu/faculty/tsommers/moral%20diversity/bood%20revenge%20yanomamo.pdf

19. Marvin Harris was the reigning authority in the early 1960s when Chagnon first set out for the Amazon to do his research. The Columbia professor was a cultural materialist, which is a fancy way of saying he was a Marxist. He rejected that notions of honor or contests over women could lead to perpetual bloodshed. Instead, he bought the theory put out by his former student Daniel Gross, who in 1975 published a paper postulating that the scarcity of animal protein in the Amazon was the only reason tribes there resorted to war. He told Chagnon: "If you can show me that the Yanomami get the protein equivalent of one Big Mac per day, I'll eat my hat." The protein studies are still hotly debated, with partisans of Chagnon finding whole Happy Meals' worth of protein and opponents finding slightly less. But as far as Chagnon's larger argument goes, he has been vindicated. Still, even if it were the case that the typical Yanomamö warrior ate less animal fat than Gwyneth Paltrow on a cleanse fast, it doesn't matter much for my larger argument. First of all, rates of violence are remarkably constant across time and geography for primitive societies. Surely some of them had enough protein? Second, if a relative shortage of tree sloths and bush pigs can lead to staggering levels of violence and infanticide, the fact remains that the Yanomamö live in constant violence. And given that resource scarcity defined virtually every human society before the agricultural revolution—and well beyond it—it would be racist, not to mention woefully ignorant, to assume that other human populations didn't respond to scarcity in the same way. See Emily Eakin, "How Napoleon Chagnon Became Our Most

Controversial Anthropologist," *New York Times*, February 13, 2013. http://www.ny
times.com/2013/02/17/magazine/napoleon-chagnon-americas-most-controversial
-anthropologist.html?mcubz=1

20. Michael Graulich, "Aztec Human Sacrifice as Expiation," *History of Religions* 39,
no. 4 (2000), p. 353.

21. Robert J. Sharer and Loa P. Traxler, *The Ancient Maya*, 5th edition (Stanford, CA:
Stanford University Press, 1994 [1946]), pp. 543–44.

22. Bradley J. Parker, "The Construction and Performance of Kingship in the Neo-
Assyrian Empire," *Journal of Anthropological Research* 67, no. 3 (Fall 2011), p. 372.

23. Matthias Schulz, "The Worst Ways to Die: Torture Practices of the Ancient World,"
Spiegel Online International, May 15, 2009. http://www.spiegel.de/international/zeit
geist/the-worst-ways-to-die-torture-practices-of-the-ancient-world-a-625172.html

24. Marvin Zalman, "Miranda v. Arizona," in Rolando V. del Carmen et al, *Criminal
Procedure and the Supreme Court: A Guide to the Major Decisions on Search and
Seizure, Privacy, and Individual Rights* (Lanham, MD: Rowman & Littlefield, 2010),
p. 240.

25. Steven Pinker recounts his visit to the Museum of Medieval Torture (Museo della
Tortura e di Criminologia Medievale) in San Gimignano, Italy: "I think even the
most atrocity-jaded readers of recent history would find something to shock them in
this display of medieval cruelty. There is Judas's Cradle, used in the Spanish Inquisi-
tion: the naked victim was bound hand and foot, suspended by an iron belt around
the waist, and lowered onto a sharp wedge that penetrated the anus or vagina; when
victims relaxed their muscles, the point would stretch and tear their tissues. The
Virgin of Nuremberg was a version of the iron maiden, with spikes that were carefully positioned so as not to transfix the victim's vital organs and prematurely end
his suffering. A series of engravings show victims hung by the ankles and sawn in
half from the crotch down; the display explains that this method of execution was
used all over Europe for crimes that included rebellion, witchcraft, and military
disobedience. The Pear is a split, spike-tipped wooden knob that was inserted into
a mouth, anus, or vagina and spread apart by a screw mechanism to tear the victim open from the inside; it was used to punish sodomy, adultery, incest, heresy,
blasphemy, and "sexual union with Satan." The Cat's Paw or Spanish Tickler was a
cluster of hooks used to rip and shred a victim's flesh. Masks of Infamy were shaped
like the head of a pig or an ass; they subjected a victim both to public humiliation
and to the pain of a blade or knob forced into their nose or mouth to prevent them
from wailing. The Heretic's Fork had a pair of sharp spikes at each end: one end was
propped under the victim's jaw and the other at the base of his neck, so that as his
muscles became exhausted he would impale himself in both places." Steven Pinker,
The Better Angels of Our Nature: Why Violence Has Declined (New York: Penguin
Publishing Group, 2012 [2011], Kindle edition), Kindle location 3063–67.

26. Steven A. LeBlanc, *Constant Battles* (New York: St. Martin's, 2003), p. 8.

27. See item 15 in "The Code of Hammurabi," L. W. King, trans., Avalon Project, Yale
Law School. http://avalon.law.yale.edu/ancient/hamframe.asp

28. Richard Hellie, "Slavery," *Encyclopaedia Britannica*. https://www.britannica.com/
topic/slavery-sociology

29. Thomas Sowell, "The Real History of Slavery," in *Black Rednecks and White Liberals*
(New York: Encounter, 2005), p. 113.

30. "Where then there is such a difference as that between soul and body, or between
men and animals (as in the case of those whose business is to use their body, and
who can do nothing better), the lower sort are by nature slaves, and it is better for

them as for all inferiors that they should be under the rule of a master." Aristotle, "Book One, Part V," in *Politics*, Benjamin Jowett, trans., Internet Classics Archive. http://classics.mit.edu/Aristotle/politics.1.one.html

31. One might object and say that the Founders, for all their wisdom, did not consider Africans fully human. That's surely true of some of them. But not only is that a poor excuse, it's a flimsy explanation. The original English settlers of the Virginia Company tried to turn local Indians into slaves, but it didn't work for various reasons, the most obvious being it was easy for them to escape. The English also tried using white Europeans as quasi-slaves—i.e., indentured servants—but that didn't work either. (In fact, the first blacks brought to America were made indentured servants, not slaves.)

32. Reuters Staff, "Chronology—Who Banned Slavery When?," Reuters, March 22, 2007. https://www.reuters.com/article/uk-slavery-idUSL1561464920070322

33. Jerome Reich, "The Slave Trade at the Congress of Vienna: A Study in English Public Opinion," *Journal of Negro History* 53, no. 2 (April 1968), pp. 139–40.

34. See "Slavery Abolition Act." *Encyclopaedia Britannica*. https://www.britannica.com/topic/Slavery-Abolition-Act; "1863 Abolition of Slavery," Rijks Studio. https://www.rijksmuseum.nl/en/rijksstudio

35. Ibid.

36. Don Bourdeaux, "Capitalism and Slavery," Café Hayek, August 25, 2009. http://cafehayek.com/2009/08/capitalism-and-slavery.html

37. Adam Smith, "I.8.40: Of the Wages of Labour," in *An Inquiry into the Nature and Causes of the Wealth of Nations*, Library of Economics and Liberty. http://www.econlib.org/library/Smith/smWN3.html

38. Adam Smith, "III.2.9: Of the Discouragement of Agriculture in the Ancient State of Europe After the Fall of the Roman Empire," in *An Inquiry into the Nature and Causes of the Wealth of Nations*, Library of Economics and Liberty. http://www.econlib.org/library/Smith/smWN3.html

39. Abraham Lincoln, "House Divided Speech: Springfield, Illinois, June 16, 1858," Abraham Lincoln Online. http://www.abrahamlincolnonline.org/lincoln/speeches/house.htm

40. Daron Acemoglu and Alexander Wolitzky, "The Economics of Labor Coercion," *Econometrica* 79, no. 2 (March 2011), p. 555. http://economics.mit.edu/files/8975

41. Harry Wu, "The Chinese Laogai," Victims of Communism Memorial Foundation. http://victimsofcommunism.org/the-chinese-laogai/

42. John Stuart Mill, "Essay V: On the Definition of Political Economy; and on the Method of Investigation Proper to It," in *Essays on Some Unsettled Questions of Political Economy*, Online Library of Liberty. http://www.econlib.org/library/Mill/mlUQP5.html

43. Richard Leakey and Roger Lewin, *People of the Lake: Mankind and Its Beginning* (Garden City, NY: Anchor, 1978), p. 139.

44. Fukuyama, *The Origins of Political Order*, p. xii.

45. Adam Smith. "III.1.8: Of the Love of Praise, and of That of Praise-worthiness; and of the Dread of Blame, and That of Blame-worthiness," in *The Theory of Moral Sentiments*, Library of Economics and Liberty. http://www.econlib.org/library/Smith/smMS3.html#Part%20III.%20Of%20the%20Foundation%20of%20our%20Judgments%20concerning%20our%20own%20Sentiments%20and%20Conduct,%20and%20of%20the%20Sense%20of%20Duty

46. See Frans de Waal, *Chimpanzee Politics: Power and Sex Among the Apes* (Baltimore, MD: Johns Hopkins University Press, 2007 [1983]).

47. Russ Roberts, "Munger on Slavery and Racism," Library of Economics and Liberty, August 22, 2016. http://www.econtalk.org/archives/2016/08/munger_on_slave.html

48. See Jonah Goldberg, *The Tyranny of Clichés: How Liberals Cheat in the War of Ideas* (New York: Sentinel, 2012), pp. 175–79.

49. Davis Benioff and D. B. Weiss, "You Win or You Die," *Game of Thrones*, Season 1, Episode 7.

50. Jonathan Haidt, *The Righteous Mind: Why Good People Are Divided by Politics and Religion* (New York: Knopf Doubleday, 2012, Kindle edition), pp. 165–66.

51. Paul Bloom. *Just Babies: The Origins of Good and Evil* (New York: Broadway Books, 2013, Kindle edition), p. 95.

52. Charles Darwin, "Chapter V: On the Development of the Intellectual and Moral Faculties During Primeval and Civilised Times," *The Descent of Man and Selection in Relation to Sex*, Project Gutenberg. http://www.gutenberg.org/cache/epub/2300/pg2300.html

53. Paul H. and Sarah M. Robinson, *Pirates, Prisoners, and Lepers: Lessons from Life Outside the Law* (Lincoln, NE: Potomac Books, 2015, Kindle edition), Kindle location 672–75.

54. Ibid., Kindle location 670–71.

55. Blake Seitz, "Bernie Sanders Was Asked to Leave Hippie Commune for Shirking, Book Claims," *Washington Free Beacon*, April 19, 2016. http://freebeacon.com/politics/bernie-sanders-asked-leave-hippie-commune/

56. See Amy Shuman, "Food Gifts: Ritual Exchange and the Production of Excess Meaning," *Journal of American Folklore* 113, no. 450 (special issue: "Holidays, Ritual, Festival, Celebration, and Public Display," Autumn 2000), pp. 495–508.

57. Eugene Scott, "Trump Believes in God, but Hasn't Sought Forgiveness," CNN, July 18, 2015. http://www.cnn.com/2015/07/18/politics/trump-has-never-sought-forgiveness/

58. Sharing food through "ritual exchange" produces what Amy Shuman calls "excess meaning." In other words, the significance of the act is far greater than the material content of what is given. If someone important in your life ever invited you to eat dinner with their family, you understand the value of the gesture is far greater than the cost of the groceries or the time value of the effort put into the preparation. Rules about hygiene as they relate to food have a rather obvious grounding in evolution. Haidt discusses at great length how different societies have developed arcane and elaborate rules about how to deal with food. The Hua of New Guinea, for example, believe that "in order for their boys to become men, they have to avoid foods that in any way resemble vaginas, including anything that is red, wet, slimy, comes from a hole, or has hair. It sounds at first like arbitrary superstition mixed with the predictable sexism of a patriarchal society. [American psychologist Elliot] Turiel would call these rules social conventions, because the Hua don't believe that men in other tribes have to follow these rules. But the Hua certainly seemed to think of their food rules as moral rules. They talked about them constantly, judged each other by their food habits, and governed their lives, duties, and relationships by what the anthropologist Anna Meigs called 'a religion of the body.'" Jonathan Haidt, *The Righteous Mind: Why Good People Are Divided by Politics and Religion* (New York: Knopf Doubleday, 2012, Kindle edition), p. 14.

59. Ernest Gellner, *Plough, Sword, and Book: The Structure of Human History* (Chicago: University of Chicago Press, 1989), pp. 118–12.

2: CORRUPTING THE MIRACLE

1. Horace, *Epistles*, Book I, epistle x, line 24, Latin Library. http://www.thelatinlibrary
   .com/horace/epist1.shtml
2. Ronald Reagan, "First Inaugural Address—January 5, 1967," Governors' Gallery,
   California State Library. http://governors.library.ca.gov/addresses/33-Reagan01
   .html
3. Beelzebub is the name for the Babylonian deity Baal, who was turned into a demon
   by Jews, Christians, and Muslims. See Liaquat Ali Khan, "Beelzebub: An Unfairly
   Demonized Deity?," Huffington Post, April 23, 2017. http://www.huffingtonpost
   .com/liaquat-ali-khan/beelzebub-an-unfairly-dem_b_9759936.html
4. William Golding, *Lord of the Flies* (New York: Berkeley, 2003 [1954]), p. 143.
5. "corruption, n," *OED Online*, Oxford University Press, June 2017.
6. Robert Nisbet writes in *Prejudices*: "But the word corruption had more general and
   diverse use even during the Middle Ages. Not only human flesh but organic life in
   general, language, study of the classics, morality, conduct in diplomacy and commerce, art, and though infrequently, political rule could all serve as referents for the
   word. Very often during the Renaissance and after were references to Earth itself,
   widely believed to be undergoing gradual decay and disintegration, with its eventual cracking up and disappearance a matter of certain foreknowledge. From the
   time of the word's appearance in the English language in roughly the fourteenth
   century, down through the nineteenth century, all branches of literature and art
   were rich in diverse applications of it. Although from about the sixteenth century
   on uses of a political nature became commoner as a result of the increasing promi-
   nence of the political state in Western life, such uses in no way interfered with or
   cut down on applications of the word to the host of nonpolitical referents." Robert
   Nisbet, *Prejudices: A Philosophical Dictionary* (Cambridge, MA: Harvard University Press, 1983), p. 61
7. William Shakespeare, *The Tragedy of Hamlet, Prince of Denmark*, Act IV, Scene III,
   The Complete Works of William Shakespeare. http://shakespeare.mit.edu/hamlet/
   full.html
8. Nicholas Wade, *Before the Dawn: Recovering the Lost History of Our Ancestors* (New
   York: Penguin, 2006), p. 149.
9. Jonathan Gottschall, "Explaining Wartime Rape," *Journal of Sex Research* 41, no. 2
   (May 2004), p. 130. http://www.nlgmltf.org/pdfs/11-Gottschal-wartime-rape.pdf
10. Jonathan Gottschall, ibid., after reviewing the horrific prevalence of wartime rape
    around the world in the twentieth century, writes:

    *There is no reason to believe that mass wartime rape was less common prior to
    the 20th century. Perhaps most well documented historical wars include examples
    of widespread military rape. For instance, mass rape is well documented in the
    wars between Jews and their enemies described in the Bible (e.g., Deuteronomy,
    21; Isaiah, 13:16; Lamentations, 5:11; Zechariah, 14:2), in Anglo-Saxon and Chi-
    nese chronicles (Littlewood, 1997), in Medieval European warfare (Meron, 1993),
    during the crusades (Brownmiller, 1975, p. 35), in Alexander's conquest of Persia
    (Hansen, 1999, p. 188), in Viking marauding (Karras, 1990), in the conquest of
    Rome by Alaric (Ghiglieri, 2000, p. 90), in the petty wars of Ancient Greeks (Finley,
    1954), and so on. It is important to note that the level and extent of mass rape in
    many conflicts—for instance, the German "rape of Belgium" in World War I has
    been hotly contested by scholars (Gullace, 1997). Yet, a review of the historical evi-
    dence conveys the distinct impression that whenever and wherever men have gone*

> to war, many of them have reasoned like old Nestor in the Iliad, *who concludes his pep talk to war-weary Greek troops by reminding them of the spoils of victory:* "So don't anyone hurry to return homeward until after he has lain down alongside a wife of some Trojan." (Homer, 1999, Book 2, 354–55).

11. C. S. Lewis. *The Screwtape Letters* (New York: HarperCollins, 2001 [1942]), p. 161.

12. John Locke, *Some Thoughts Concerning Education*, sec. 115, Online Library of Liberty. http://oll.libertyfund.org/titles/locke-the-works-vol-8-some-thoughts-concerning-education-posthumous-works-familiar-letters

13. Arthur Herman, *The Idea of Decline in Western History* (New York: Free Press, 1997), pp. 15–16.

14. Jonah Goldberg, *The Tyranny of Clichés: How Liberals Cheat in the War of Ideas* (New York: Sentinel, 2012), p. 8.

15. Ibid., p. 9.

16. Ibid.

17. Deuteronomy 31:29. https://www.biblegateway.com/verse/en/Deuteronomy%2031:29

18. See James 4:4. https://www.biblegateway.com/verse/en/James%204%3A4

19. Francis Fukuyama, *The Origins of Political Order: From Prehuman Times to the French Revolution* (New York: Farrar, Straus and Giroux, 2011), p. 43.

20. Ibid., p. 17.

21. Mancur Olson, *The Rise and Decline of Nations: Economic Growth, Stagflation, and Social Rigidities* (New Haven, CT: Yale University Press, 1987), p. 1.

22. Ibid.

23. Adam Bellow, *In Praise of Nepotism* (New York: Knopf Doubleday, Kindle edition, 2003), Kindle location 3245–49.

24. In his first letter to the Corinthians, Paul says: "To the unmarried and the widows I say that it is well for them to remain single as I do. But if they cannot exercise self-control, they should marry. For it is better to marry than to be aflame with passion" (1 Cor. 7:8–9). https://www.biblegateway.com/passage/?search=1+Corinthians+7:8-9

25. Marshall Connolly, "A Very Brief History of Priestly Celibacy in the Catholic Church," Catholic Online, August 24, 2016. http://www.catholic.org/news/hf/faith/story.php?id=70507

26. "Pope Gregory's goal was to end corruption and rent seeking within the church by attacking patrimonialism, the ability of bishops and priests to have children. He was driven by the same logic that led the Chinese and Byzantines to rely on eunuchs, or the Ottomans to capture military slaves and tear them from their families: if given the choice between loyalty to the state and to one's family, most people are driven biologically to the latter. The most direct way to reduce corruption was therefore to forbid officials to have families in the first place." Fukuyama, *The Origins of Political Order*, p. 265.

27. See Santiago Cortés-Sjöberg, "Why Are Priests Celibate?," U.S. Catholic. http://www.uscatholic.org/glad-you-asked/2009/08/why-are-priests-celibate. Martin Luther, agreeing with Horace about the futility of fully keeping nature at bay, opposed priestly celibacy on the grounds that it led to masturbation. "Nature never lets up," Luther said, "we are all driven to the secret sin. To say it crudely but honestly, if it doesn't go into a woman, it goes into your shirt." See Helen L. Owen, "When Did the Catholic Church Decide Priests Should Be Celibate?," History News Network, October 2001. http://historynewsnetwork.org/article/696

28. "Pope Callistus III," Catholic Encyclopedia, New Advent. http://www.newadvent .org/cathen/03187a.htm

29. "Pope Innocent XII," Catholic Encyclopedia, New Advent. http://www.newadvent .org/cathen/08022a.htm

30. Bellow, *In Praise of Nepotism*, Kindle location 1595-96.

31. Ibid., Kindle location 1592-1607.

32. Ibid., Kindle location 1609-10.

33. Cemal Kafadar, *Between Two Worlds: The Construction of the Ottoman State* (Berkeley and Los Angeles, CA: University of California Press, 1995), pp. 111-13.

34. *The Republic of Plato*, 414c-415c, Allan Bloom, trans. (New York: Basic Books, 1968), pp. 93-94.

35. Fukuyama, *The Origins of Political Order*, pp. 190-91.

36. "Janissary," *Encyclopaedia Britannica*. https://www.britannica.com/topic/Janis sary-corps

37. The Praetorians of ancient Rome, like the Ottoman Janissaries and the Chinese eunuchs, eventually became their own interest group tribe as well. In A.D. 193 the Praetorian Guard not only assassinated the emperor Pertinax but then put the throne up for auction to the highest bidder. Ultimately, Titus Flavius Sulpicanus bought control of the Roman Empire for the price of 25,000 sesterces per Praeto-rian. See B. G. Niebuhr, "Lecture CXXXV," *Lectures on the History of Rome, from the Earliest Times to the Fall of the Western Empire* (London: Lockwood, 1870), pp. 738-39.

38. Maria Konnikova, "The Limits of Friendship," *New Yorker*, October 7, 2014. http:// www.newyorker.com/science/maria-konnikova/social-media-affect-math-dun bar-number-friendships.

39. Some critics of Dunbar's number think it is too high, since most primitive human bands were much smaller than that, roughly forty to fifty people.

40. Hayek believed that the tribal impulse was a permanent threat to the Open Society and the rule of law and nearly every collectivist enterprise was an attempt to satisfy our atavistic nostalgia for our tribal past: "It should be realized, however, that the ideals of socialism (or of 'social justice') which in such a position prove so attrac-tive, do not really offer a new moral but merely appeal to instincts inherited from an earlier type of society. They are an atavism, a vain attempt to impose upon the Open Society the morals of the tribal society which, if it prevails, must not only destroy the Great Society but would also greatly threaten the survival of the large numbers to which some three hundred years of a market order have enabled mankind to grow." He adds: "The persistent conflict between tribal morals and universal justice has manifested itself throughout history in a recurrent clash between the sense of loyalty and that of justice. It is still loyalty to such particular groups as those of occupation or class as well as those of clan, nation, race or religion which is the greatest obstacle to a universal application of rules of just conduct. Only slowly and gradually do those general rules of conduct towards all fellow men come to prevail over the special rules which allowed the individual to harm the stranger if it served the interest of his group." F. A. Hayek, *Law, Legislation and Liberty, Volume 2: The Mirage of Social Justice* (Chicago: University of Chicago Press, 1976), pp. 146–148.

41. See William Butler Yeats, "The Second Coming," Poetry Foundation. https://www .poetryfoundation.org/poems/43290/the-second-coming

3: THE STATE

1. Thomas Hobbes, "Chapter XIII: Of the Natural Condition of Mankind, As Concerning Their Felicity, and Misery," *Leviathan*, sec. 9, Edwin Curley, ed. (Indianapolis: Hackett, 1994), p. 76.

2. Olson: "Thus we should not be surprised that while there have been lots of writings about the desirability of 'social contracts' to obtain the benefits of law and order, no one has ever found a large society that obtained a peaceful order or other public goods through an agreement among the individuals in the society." Mancur Olson, "Dictatorship, Democracy, and Development," *American Political Science Review* 87, no. 3 (September 1993), p. 568.

3. Ibid.

4. Ibid., p. 567.

5. Ibid., p. 568.

6. Ibid., p. 567.

7. "The State's criminality is nothing new and nothing to be wondered at," Albert Jay Nock wrote. "It began when the first predatory group of men clustered together and formed the State, and it will continue as long as the State exists in the world, because the State is fundamentally an anti-social institution, fundamentally criminal. The idea that the State originated to serve any kind of social purpose is completely unhistorical. It originated in conquest and confiscation—that is to say, in crime." Albert Jay Nock, "The Criminality of the State," *American Mercury*, March 1939, accessed via Mises Daily, Mises Institute, December 29, 2006. https://mises.org/library/criminality-state

8. Diego Gambetta, in his seminal work *The Sicilian Mafia: The Business of Private Protection*, takes this argument much further. The Mafia, he argues, filled a market niche in Italian society when the government became an unreliable enforcer of property rights. For a percentage, the Mafia would do what the government could not or would not do. Prison gang leaders in California and Texas are another perfect example of stationary bandits in modern society. In *The Social Order of the Underworld: How Prison Gangs Govern the American Penal System*, David Skarbek describes how the Big Men of our penal system exact taxes from their members and other inmates in exchange for protection from roving bandits. After all, the first rule of prison is that everyone needs friends.

9. This is not to say that we aren't hardwired to believe in some conception of property. We have an innate sense of fairness, and taking what belongs to another tends to violate it. In bands of chimpanzees, if a strong ape takes food from a weaker one, the weaker one will complain. The alpha or a small group of allied chimpanzees may also intervene to make things right. In early hunter-gatherer societies, that role falls to the Big Man or some other tribal leader. But whether or not he opts to intervene is a social and political question. There is no written code or rule that says he must intervene.

10. "While there are many historical examples of competitive state formation, no one has ever observed the pristine version, so political philosophers, anthropologists, and archaeologists can only speculate as to how the first state or states arose," writes Francis Fukuyama in *The Origins of Political Order: From Prehuman Times to the French Revolution* (New York: Farrar, Straus and Giroux, 2011), pp. 81-82.

11. Charles Tilly, "Reflections on the History of European State-Making," p. 42. http://psi424.cankaya.edu.tr/uploads/files/Tilly,%20Reflections%20on%20State%20Making.pdf

    Tilly has a four-point job description that tracks fairly closely to Olson's stationary bandit. First, a leader, warlord, or feudal chieftain (the labels don't matter much) becomes the undisputed power in his territory, usually by destroying external rivals. Second, the lord turns on his domestic rivals, real and potential, and eliminates or neutralizes them. Third, the lord offers "protection"—just as the mob does—to "clients" in his territory. This basically means destroying the commercial enemies of his commercial supporters. And finally, he sets up a system of taxation to "acquire means to carry out first three." Tilly's focus was on state formation in Europe. His theories, as Francis Fukuyama argues, apply very easily to China as well. But Tilly's theory of predatory state formation becomes more controversial when you travel farther afield.

12. Douglass C. North and Robert Paul Thomas, *The Rise of the Western World: A New Economic History* (New York: Cambridge University Press, 1973), p. 2.

13. Ibid., p. 1.

14. Ernest Gellner, *Plough, Sword, and Book: The Structure of Human History* (Chicago: University of Chicago Press, 1989), p. 16.

15. See Chelsea German, "$1,500 Sandwich Illustrates How Exchange Raises Living Standards," Human Progress, September 25, 2015. http://humanprogress.org/blog/1500-dollar-sandwich-illustrates-exchange-raises-living-standards; https://www.youtube.com/watch?v=URvWSsAgtJE

16. Max Weber, "Politics as a Vocation," *From Max Weber: Essays in Sociology*, H. H. Gerth and C. Wright Mills, eds. and trans. (New York: Routledge, 2009), p. 78. Elsewhere, Weber deems a state worthy of the name "insofar as its administrative staff successfully upholds a claim on the 'monopoly of the legitimate use of physical force' in the enforcement of its order." Max Weber, *Economy and Society: An Outline of Interpretive Sociology*, Vol. I, Part One: "Conceptual Exposition: I. Basic Sociological Terms: 17. Political and Hierocratic Organizations," Guenter Roth and Claus Wittich, eds. (Berkeley and Los Angeles: University of California Press, 1978 [1968]), p. 54.

17. This is true even today, even in the most progressive societies. In San Francisco, Stockholm, or Amsterdam, if you break the law and the state knows about it, eventually people with guns will find you and tell you to stop. This is so not just for grave crimes but for innocuous ones too. If you refuse, say, to sort your trash properly, you may get a letter or an email telling you to comply with the law. If you ignore the letter, you might get a visit from a government official. You might get fined. If you refuse to pay the fine, you'll get another. And another. The process will play out until the state dispatches armed gendarmes to force compliance or to punish you. If you doubt that even the most innocuous institutions of the welfare state you live under is supported by the threat of force, ask yourself why the Social Security Administration recently purchased 174,000 rounds of hollow-point bullets. See Stephen Ohlemacher, "Why Does Social Security Need 174,000 Bullets?," Associated Press. http://katu.com/news/nation-world/why-does-social-security-need-174000-bullets-11-19-2015

18. Take your pick: "to put force or strength into"; "to add force to, intensify, strengthen (a feeling, desire, influence); to impart fresh vigour or energy to (an action, movement, attack, etc.). Obs.; to exert one's strength (obs.); to exert oneself, strive . . . ; to bring force to bear upon; to use force upon; to press hard upon; to overcome by violence; to take (a town) by storm; to force, ravish (a woman); to compel, constrain, oblige . . . ; to produce, impose, effect, by force; to force, obtrude (something) on a person; to compel by physical or moral force (the performance of an action, conformity to a rule, etc.); to impose (a course of conduct on a person); to compel

the observance of (a law); to support by force (a claim, demand, obligation). From "enforce, v," *OED Online*, Oxford University Press, June 2017.

19. Gellner, *Plough, Sword, and Book*, p. 17.

20. Jeremy Egner, "'Game of Thrones' Recap: The Faith and the Crown," *New York Times*, April 26, 2015. https://artsbeat.blogs.nytimes.com/2015/04/26/game-of-thrones-recap-the-faith-and-the-crown/

21. Yuval Noah Harari, *Sapiens: A Brief History of Humankind* (New York: HarperCollins, 2015, Kindle edition), p. 122.

22. "Sir Arthur's Quotations," The Arthur C. Clarke Foundation. https://www.clarke foundation.org/about-sir-arthur/sir-arthurs-quotations/

23. "The most significant thing about writing," Ernest Gellner observed, "is that it makes possible the detachment of affirmation from the speaker. Without writing, all speech is context-bound: in such conditions, the only way in which an affirmation can be endowed with special solemnity is by ritual emphasis, by an unusual and deliberately solemnized context, by a prescribed rigidity of manner." Gellner, *Plough, Sword, and Book*, p. 71.

24. "The Code of Hammurabi," L. W. King, trans., Avalon Project, Yale Law School. http://avalon.law.yale.edu/ancient/hamframe.asp

25. Ibid., no. 15.

26. Ibid., nos. 196–99.

27. Ibid., no. 195.

28. Ibid., no. 104.

29. Claude Hermann Walter Johns, "Babylonian Law—The Code of Hammurabi," *Encyclopedia Britannica*, 11th edition, cited on the Avalon Project, Yale Law School. http://avalon.law.yale.edu/ancient/hammpre.asp

30. We risk getting into a lengthy discussion of the differences between law and legislation, but I will skip all that. Today we think legislation is simply the process of writing laws. But this is not how legal theorists understood things for most of human history. Some laws exist whether or not there is *legislation* to support them. The state does not have a law that says the person in front of you in line at Starbucks gets to order his coffee before you do, yet nearly all of us recognize and obey this rule without aid of the police. Geese follow no written law when they fly in V formation; rather, they discovered a law that says the V formation is the best way to fly. If someone cuts the line, the other customers or the cashier will enforce the unwritten or hidden law. There is an ancient tradition in legal thinking that says that all written laws should be an effort to discover and clarify such unwritten laws. In *Minos*, Socrates debates a companion about the nature of the law. The unnamed man says that law is "things loyally accepted." Socrates protests. He asks, "So speech, you think, is the things that are spoken, or sight the things seen, or hearing the things heard? Or is speech something distinct from the things spoken, sight something distinct from the things seen, and hearing something distinct from the things heard; and so law is something distinct from things loyally accepted? Is this so, or what is your view?" The companion changes his definition: "State opinion, it seems, is what you call law." Ah, but can't the state make poor judgments? Socrates asks. Cannot the government make mistakes? Socrates himself offers a better different definition. "And again, in writings about what is just and unjust, and generally about the government of a state and the proper way of governing it, that which is right is the king's law, but not so that which is not right, though it seems to be law to those who do not know; for it is unlawful." Plato, *Minos*, 313a–317c, Gregory R. Crane, ed., Perseus Digital Library, Tufts University. http://www.perseus.tufts

.edu/hopper/text?doc=Perseus%3Atext%3A1999.01.0180%3Atext%3DMinos%3A
section%3D313a

31. Kevin D. Williamson, "Gay Marriage: Where Do We Put the Sidewalks?" *National Review* online, June 26, 2011. http://www.nationalreview.com/corner/270523/gay -marriage-where-do-we-put-sidewalks-kevin-d-williamson

32. Matt Ridley notes that this code itself was an emergent property. "No group of inmates met to decide it. Although transgressors were punished with ostracism, ridicule, assault or death, punishment was decentralised. Nobody was in charge. And the convict code 'facilitated social cooperation and diminished social conflict. It helped establish order and promote illicit trade.'" Matt Ridley, *The Evolution of Everything: How New Ideas Emerge* (New York: HarperCollins, 2015), p. 237.

33. David Skarbek, *The Social Order of the Underworld: How Prison Gangs Govern the American Penal System* (Oxford, U.K.: Oxford University Press, 2014). Quoted in Ridley, *The Evolution of Everything*, p. 238.

34. Later, it should be noted, Henry had second thoughts. "Canossa became a symbol of secular submission, but improperly so; the emperor's contrition was short-lived. Changing his mind, he renewed his attack, and, undeterred by a second excommunication, drove Gregory from Rome . . ." William Manchester, *A World Lit Only by Fire* (Boston: Little, Brown, 1993 [1992]), p. 11.

35. See, for example, Catriona Kelly, "Riding the Magic Carpet: Children and Leader Cult in the Stalin Era," *Slavic and East European Journal* 49, no. 2 (Special Forum Issue: "Russian Children's Literature—Changing Paradigms," Summer 2005), pp. 199-224.

36. "Chris Rock: Obama like 'Dad of the Country. And When Your Dad Says Something, You Listen,'" Breitbart TV, February 6, 2013. http://www.breitbart .com/video/2013/02/06/chris-rock-obama-is-americas-dad-you-have-to%20-listen -to-him/

4: THE BIRTH OF CAPITALISM

1. Joel Mokyr, *A Culture of Growth: The Origins of the Modern Economy*, Graz Schumpeter Lectures (Princeton, NJ: Princeton University Press, Kindle edition, 2016), p. 4.

2. In his *Riddle of the Modern World: Of Liberty, Wealth and Equality*, Cambridge University anthropologist Alan MacFarlane reports that "the emergence of our modern world and its very nature is a mystery. We are very confused as to how it came about." He adds, "There is still a large gap in the explanation of how the transition to the modern world has occurred." Alan McFarlane, *The Riddle of the Modern World* (New York: St. Martin's, 2000), p. 2. Ernest Gellner, who was not often inclined to admit he didn't have an answer to any question, marveled at "the circuitous and near-miraculous routes by which agrarian mankind has, *once only*, hit on this path" to modernity. Ernest Gellner, *Plough, Sword, and Book: The Structure of Human History* (Chicago: University of Chicago Press, 1989), p. 204.

3. Eric Jones, "Afterword to the Third Edition," *The European Miracle: Environments, Economies and Geopolitics in the History of Europe and Asia*, 3rd edition (Cambridge, U.K.: Cambridge University Press, 2003 [1981]), p. 257.

4. If you are looking for that argument, might I suggest Robert H. Nelson's *God? Very Probably: Five Rational Ways to Think About the Question of a God* (Eugene, OR: Cascade, 2015).

5. Daniel Hannan, *Inventing Freedom: How the English-Speaking Peoples Made the Modern World* (New York: HarperCollins, 2013, Kindle edition), Kindle location 205-9.

6. Ibid., Kindle location 4686-4701.

7. For those interested in this topic, Lisa Jardine's *Going Dutch: How England Plundered Holland's Glory* (New York: HarperCollins, 2008) is a sweeping history of Holland's influence on England.

8. Ralph Raico, "The 'European Miracle,'" in *The Collapse of Development Planning,* Peter Boettke, ed. (New York: New York University Press, 1994), p. 41. McCloskey also writes that "we do not yet know for sure why the making and using of new knowledge kept going in northwestern Europe, though many historians suspect that Europe's political fragmentation, 'the ancient clotted continent,' was the ticket to the modern world. It led to incessant war (excepting occasional successes in utopian schemes of peacemaking as the Treaty of Venice [1454]), but also comparative liberty for enterprise." Deirdre N. McCloskey, *Bourgeois Dignity: Why Economics Can't Explain the Modern World* (Chicago: University of Chicago Press, 2010), p. 109.

9. Hannan, *Inventing Freedom*, Kindle location 1293-95.

10. Ibid., Kindle location 1307-10.

11. Ibid., Kindle location 1302-4.

12. Francis Fukuyama, *The Origins of Political Order: From Prehuman Times to the French Revolution* (New York: Farrar, Straus and Giroux, 2011), p. 233.

13. Karl Marx and Friedrich Engels, *Manifesto of the Communist Party*, "Chapter I: Bourgeois and Proletarians," Marxist Internet Archive. https://www.marxists.org/archive/marx/works/1848/communist-manifesto/ch01.htm

14. Fukuyama, *The Origins of Political Order*, p. 233.

15. Ibid.

16. Hannan, *Inventing Freedom*, Kindle location 1179-82.

17. For a somewhat counter view see: Edward D. Re, "The Roman Contribution to the Common Law," *Fordham Law Review* 29, no. 3 (1961). http://ir.lawnet.fordham.edu/cgi/viewcontent.cgi?article=1673&context=flr

18. Hannan, *Inventing Freedom*, Kindle location 1198-1200.

19. Ibid., Kindle location 771-73.

20. Peggy Noonan, "A Cold Man's Warm Words: Jefferson's Tender Lament Didn't Make It into the Declaration," *Wall Street Journal*, July 2, 2012. https://www.wsj.com/articles/SB10001424052748703571704575341403234545296

21. Thomas Jefferson et al., "Declaration of Independence: A Transcription," America's Founding Documents, National Archives. https://www.archives.gov/founding-docs/declaration-transcript

22. Hannan, *Inventing Freedom*, Kindle location 724-26.

23. Patrick Henry, "Virginia Ratifying Convention," June 5, 1788. From *The Founders' Constitution*, Volume 1, Chapter 8, Document 38. http://press-pubs.uchicago.edu/founders/documents/v1ch8s38.html

24. Hannan, *Inventing Freedom*, Kindle location 127-31.

25. Barack Obama, "8—Farewell Address to the Nation from Chicago, Illinois—January 10, 2017," American Presidency Project, John Woolley and Gerhard Peters, eds. http://www.presidency.ucsb.edu/ws/?pid=119928http://www.realclearpolitics.com/video/2017/01/10/watch_live_president_obamas_farewell_address.html

26. James Madison, "*Federalist* No. 48: These Departments Should Not Be So Far Separated as to Have No Constitutional Control over Each Other," Constitution Society. http://www.constitution.org/fed/federa48.htm

27. Herbert Butterfield, *The Whig Interpretation of History* (London: G. Bell, 1931, Kindle edition), Kindle location 226-28.

28. "The Gunpowder Plot: Three Years in the Making," BBC. http://www.bbc.co.uk/timelines/z3hq7ty

29. As historian Jay Wieser writes, "Hannan argues that the Norman Conquest marked the fall of a medieval Germanic Eden and launched a millennium-long struggle between Whig forces of liberty and Tory forces of statism and aristocracy. This eternal bright line never existed," Wieser adds, "and it is odd that Hannan, himself a member of the British Conservative party, thinks it does. The Normans, rather than importing continental villainy, were themselves Germanic (from the Scandinavian branch), and the later, unimpeachably Germanic Habsburgs and Hohenzollerns were no lovers of freedom." Wieser also notes that many of the notions of religious freedom and limits on the monarch were imported from Holland after the Glorious Revolution. Jay Weiser "Anglospheremonger," *Weekly Standard*, October 6, 2014. http://www.weeklystandard.com/anglospheremonger/article/806152

30. James Peron, "The Evolution of Capitalism: Why Did Europe Develop a System of Market Capitalism?," Foundation for Economic Education, June 1, 2000. http://fee.org/freeman/detail/the-evolution-of-capitalism

31. McCloskey, *Bourgeois Dignity*, pp. 332-35.

32. "It is a fact that the Protestants (especially certain branches of the movement to be fully discussed later) both as ruling classes and as ruled, both as majority and as minority, have shown a special tendency to develop economic rationalism which cannot be observed to the same extent among Catholics either in the one situation or in the other. Thus the principal explanation of this difference must be sought in the permanent intrinsic character of their religious beliefs, and not only in their temporary external historico-political situations. It will be our task to investigate these religions with a view to finding out what peculiarities they have or have had which might have resulted in the behavior we have described. On superficial analysis, and on the basis of certain current impressions, one might be tempted to express the difference by saying that the greater other-worldliness of Catholicism, the ascetic character of its highest ideals, must have brought up its adherents to a greater indifference toward the good things of this world. Such an explanation fits the popular tendency in the judgment of both religions. On the Protestant side it is used as a basis of criticism of those (real or imagined) ascetic ideals of the Catholic way of life, while the Catholics answer with the accusation that materialism results from the secularization of all ideals through Protestantism. One recent writer has attempted to formulate the difference of their attitudes toward economic life in the following manner: 'The Catholic is quieter, having less of the acquisitive impulse; he prefers a life of the greatest possible security, even with a smaller income, to a life of risk and excitement, even though it may bring the chance of gaining honor and riches. The proverb says jokingly, "either eat well or sleep well." In the present case the Protestant prefers to eat well, the Catholic to sleep undisturbed.'" Max Weber, *The Protestant Ethic and the Spirit of Capitalism*, "Chapter I: Religious Affiliation and Social Stratification," 1905, Marxist Internet Archive. https://www.marxists.org/reference/archive/weber/protestant-ethic/ch01.htm

33. Ibid.

34. Joyce Appleby, *The Relentless Revolution: A History of Capitalism* (New York: Norton, 2010), p. 17. Quoted in McCloskey, *Bourgeois Dignity*, p. 145.

35. Ibid.

36. Jerry Z. Muller, *The Mind and the Market: Capitalism in Modern European Thought* (New York: Knopf, 2002), p. 167.

37. Karl Marx, "The Metaphysics of Political Economy: Fourth Observation," *The Poverty of Philosophy* (Mansfield Centre, CT: Martino, 2014), p. 121.

38. Don Boudreaux, "Slave to a Myth," Café Hayek, December 20, 2014. http://cafe hayek.com/2014/12/slave-to-a-myth.html

39. The word "thrift" was originally more capacious than its meaning today, combining the concepts of not just fiscal prudence, saving, temperance, and profit. Neither these broader meanings nor the narrower modern sense of fiscal prudence were invented by Protestants. McCloskey finds calls to thriftiness across eras and civilizations, from biblical times to the writings of Buddha. The "prehistory of thrift," she writes, "extends back to the Garden of Eden" and is in fact "laid down . . . in our genes." Meanwhile, McCloskey writes:

> *Saving rates in Catholic Italy or for that matter Confucian Buddhist Taoist China were not much lower, if lower at all, than in Calvinist Massachusetts or Lutheran Germany. According to recent calculations by economic historians, in fact, British investment in physical capital as a share of national income (not allowing for seed investment) was strikingly below the European norm—only 4 percent in 1700, as against a norm of 11 percent, 6 percent as against 12 percent in 1760, and 8 percent against over 12 percent in 1800. Britain's investment, though rising before and then during the Industrial Revolution, showed less, not more, abstemiousness than in the less advanced countries around it.*

Quoted from McCloskey, *Bourgeois Dignity*, pp. 131–32.

40. Charles C. W. Cooke, "Anglosphere Attitudes," *National Review* 66, no. 2, February 10, 2014. https://www.nationalreview.com/nrd/articles/369268/anglosphere -attitudes

41. White, according to Erick Erickson, is literally a "trinity denying heretic." See Erick Erickson, "An Actual Trinity-Denying Heretic Will Pray at Trump's Inauguration," Resurgent, December 28, 2016. http://theresurgent.com/an-actual-trinity-denying -heretic-will-pray-at-trumps-inauguration/

42. C. V. Wedgwood. *The Thirty Years War* (New York: New York Review Books, 2005), p. 506. I should note that the next sentence reads, "Instead, they rejected religion as an object to fight for and found others."

43. Quoted in James Q. Wilson, *American Politics, Then & Now: And Other Essays* (Washington, D.C.: AEI, 2010), p. 144.

44. McCloskey, *Bourgeois Dignity*, p. 8

45. Elizabeth Palermo, "Who Invented the Printing Press?," LiveScience, February 25, 2014. https://www.livescience.com/43639-who-invented-the-printing-press.html

46. Ronald Bailey, *The End of Doom* (New York: St. Martin's, 2015), p. 89.

47. Benoît Godin, "'Meddle Not with Them That Are Given to Change': Innovation as Evil," Project on the Intellectual History of Innovation Working Paper No. 6, 2010, pp. 16–27. http://www.csiic.ca/PDF/IntellectualNo6.pdf

48. Deirdre N. McCloskey, "Creative Destruction vs. the New Industrial State: Review of McCraw and Galbraith," *Reason*, October 2007. Accessed via http://www.deirdre mccloskey.com/articles/galbraith.php

49. McCloskey, *Bourgeois Dignity*, p. 421.

50. Bailey, *The End of Doom*, pp. 89–90.

51. Sheilah Ogilvie, "'Whatever Is, Is Right'? Economic Institutions in Pre-Industrial Europe" (Tawney Lecture 2006), CESIFO Working Paper No. 2066, pp. 13–14. https://papers.ssrn.com/sol3/papers.cfm?abstract_id=1004445#

52. Jerry Z. Mueller, *The Mind and the Market: Capitalism in Western Thought* (New York: Alfred A. Knopf, 2005), p. 5.

53. Marian L. Tupy, "Anti-Capitalism Through the Ages," Foundation for Economic Education, September 15, 2016. https://fee.org/articles/anti-capitalism-through -the-ages/

54. Ibid.

55. Mueller, *The Mind and the Market*, p. 6.

56. Ibid.

57. Mueller, *The Mind and the Market*, pp. 5–6.

58. Larry Siedentop, *Inventing the Individual: The Origins of Western Liberalism* (Cambridge, MA: Belknap Press/ Harvard University Press), pp. 338–39.

59. Mueller, *The Mind and the Market*, p. 167.

60. Thomas McCraw, *Prophet of Innovation: Joseph Schumpeter and Creative Destruction* (Cambridge, MA: Belknap Press/ Harvard University Press, 2009 [2007]), p. 79.

61. "The function of entrepreneurs," Schumpeter writes, "is to reform or revolutionize the pattern of production by exploiting an invention or, more generally, an untried technological possibility for producing a new commodity or producing an old one in a new way, by opening up a new source of supply of materials or a new outlet for products, by reorganizing an industry and so on." Joseph A. Schumpeter, *Capitalism, Socialism and Democracy*, 3rd edition (New York: Harper Perennial Modern Thought, 2008 [1942]), p. 132.

62. Ibid., p. 143.

63. Ibid., p. 162.

64. Ibid., p. 249.

65. When the French poet Gérard de Nerval famously walked his pet lobster through the Tuileries gardens—"It does not bark and it knows the secrets of the deep," he quipped—it was cheap and largely harmless performance art. When Flaubert completed his novel *Salammbô*, he hopefully anticipated that, "It will 1) annoy the bourgeois . . . ; 2) unnerve and shock sensitive people; 3) anger the archeologists; 4) be unintelligible to the ladies; 5) earn me a reputation as a pederast and a cannibal. Let us hope so." David Brooks, *Bobos in Paradise: The New Upper Class and How They Got There* (New York: Simon & Schuster, 2010, Kindle edition), p. 67.

66. Joel Mokyr, *The Gifts of Athena: Historical Origins of the Knowledge Economy* (Princeton, NJ: Princeton University Press, 2002), p. 278.

67. According to Nietzsche, the knight doesn't need to hate his enemies; it is sufficient for him to simply know they *are* his enemies. Because the ruler deals in the currency of power and will, he can identify his foe simply by virtue of the fact that his enemy's interests conflict with his own. Once he has defeated his enemy or come to some other satisfactory resolution to their conflict, he is no longer his enemy. There is no need to lose respect for one's adversary. One sees this dynamic among military men often. Men of (conventional) power respect other men of power. But the priest full of *ressentiment* needs to hate his enemy, to see in his every move proof that he is evil, representing all that the priest despises. Here is how Nietzsche contrasts the knight from the priest:

> *A man like this shakes from him, with one shrug, many worms which would have burrowed into another man; actual "love of your enemies" is also possible here and here alone—assuming it is possible at all on earth. How much respect a noble man has for his enemies!—and a respect of that sort is a bridge to love . . . For he insists*

on having his enemy to himself, as a mark of distinction, indeed he will tolerate as enemies none other than such as have nothing to be despised and a great deal to be honoured! Against this, imagine "the enemy" as conceived of by the man of ressentiment—and here we have his deed, his creation: he has conceived of the "evil enemy," "the evil one" as a basic idea to which he now thinks up a copy and counterpart, the "good one"—himself!

He also says:

While the noble man is confident and frank with himself (gennaˆ iov, "of noble birth," underlines the nuance "upright" and probably "naïve" as well), the man of ressentiment is neither upright nor naïve, nor honest and straight with himself. His soul squints; his mind loves dark corners, secret paths and back-doors, everything secretive appeals to him as being his world, his security, his comfort; he knows all about keeping quiet, not forgetting, waiting, temporarily humbling and abasing himself. A race of such men of ressentiment will inevitably end up cleverer than any noble race, and will respect cleverness to a quite different degree as well: namely, as a condition of existence of the first rank, whilst the cleverness of noble men can easily have a subtle aftertaste of luxury and refinement about it:—precisely because in this area, it is nowhere near as important as the complete certainty of function of the governing unconscious instincts, nor indeed as important as a certain lack of cleverness, such as a daring charge at danger or at the enemy, or those frenzied sudden fits of anger, love, reverence, gratitude and revenge by which noble souls down the ages have recognized one another. When ressentiment does occur in the noble man himself, it is consumed and exhausted in an immediate reaction, and therefore it does not poison, on the other hand, it does not occur at all in countless cases where it is unavoidable for all who are weak and powerless. To be unable to take his enemies, his misfortunes and even his misdeeds seriously for long—that is the sign of strong, rounded natures with a superabundance of a power which is flexible, formative, healing and can make one forget.

Friedrich Nietzsche, *On the Genealogy of Morality*, Keith Ansell-Pearson, ed.; Carol Diethe, trans. (Cambridge, U.K.: Cambridge University Press, 2007 [1994]), pp. 21-22.

68. McCloskey, "Creative Destruction vs. the New Industrial State."
69. Schumpeter, *Capitalism, Socialism and Democracy*, p. 145.
70. Quoted in Matthew Continetti, "The Seer," *National Review* 67, no. 5. March 23, 2015. https://www.nationalreview.com/nrd/articles/414923/seer
71. George Orwell, "Second Thoughts on James Burnham." http://orwell.ru/library/reviews/burnham/english/e_burnh.html
72. Francis Fukuyama, "The End of History?" *National Interest*, no. 16 (Summer 1989), p. 4.
73. Abraham Lincoln, "Address Before the Young Men's Lyceum of Springfield, Illinois," Constitution Society, January 27, 1838. http://www.constitution.org/lincoln/lyceum.htm

5: THE ETERNAL BATTLE

1. Locke writes in the *Second Treatise*:

Though I have said above, Chapter II, That all Men by Nature are equal, I cannot be supposed to understand all sorts of Equality. Age or Virtue may give men a just

Precedency. Excellency of Parts and Merit may place others above the Common Level. Birth may subject some, and Alliance or Benefits others, to pay an observance to those to whom Nature, Gratitude, or other Respects, may have made it due; and yet all this consists with the Equality which all Men are in respect of Jurisdiction or Dominion one over another, which was the Equality I there spoke of as proper to the Business in hand, being that equal Right that Every Man hath to his Natural Freedom, without being subjected to the Will or Authority of any other Man.

John Locke, "Chap. VI: Of Paternal Power," sec. 54, "The Second Treatise of Government: An Essay Concerning the True Original, Extent, and End of Civil Government," *Two Treatises of Government*, Peter Laslett, ed. (Cambridge, U.K.: Cambridge University Press, 1988 [1960]), p. 304. I will be using this version throughout for quotations from Locke, preserving his usage of English.

2. Jean-Jacques Rousseau, "A Discourse on Political Economy," *The Social Contract and the Discourses*, Online Library of Liberty. http://oll.libertyfund.org/titles/rousseau-the-social-contract-and-discourses#lf0132_head_069

3. Michael Locke McLendon, "The Overvaluation of Talent: An Interpretation and Application of Rousseau's Amour Propre," *Polity* 36, no. 1 (October 2003), p. 115.

4. Barack Obama, "Remarks at the Town Hall Education Arts Recreation Campus—December 4, 2013," American Presidency Project, John Woolley and Gerhard Peters, eds. http://www.presidency.ucsb.edu/ws/index.php?pid=104522

5. John Maynard Keynes, "Chapter 24: Concluding Notes on the Social Philosophy Toward Which the General Theory Might Lead," *The General Theory of Employment, Interest, and Money*, Project Gutenberg. http://gutenberg.net.au/ebooks03/0300071h/printall.html

6. I am drawing my account of Locke's life largely from Peter Laslett, "II. Locke the Man and Locke the Writer," in John *Locke, Two Treatises of Government*, pp. 16–44.

7. Those looking for a full account should consult Michael Barone's *Our First Revolution: The Remarkable British Upheaval That Inspired America's Founding Fathers* (New York: Crown, 2007, Kindle edition), from which my account derives.

8. Michael Barone writes: "Other rulers followed [Louis XIV's] example. In Bavaria and Brandenburg forceful rulers broke the power of the estates, as did the rulers of the Rhenish Palatinate and Baden. A similar process occurred in the domains of the Austrian Hapsburgs. Denmark and, a quarter-century later, Sweden developed absolutist government, while in Spain and Portugal the power of the legislative assemblies, the Cortes, was sharply curtailed . . . Many in the smaller German states feared the trend would prevail there . . . Republicanism was on the wane, alive in the bustling Netherlands and backward Switzerland, ailing in a declining Venice and extinct in most of the rest of Italy (with the conspicuous exception of the small city of Lucca), defunct after the Restoration in England. The forces resisting absolutism were those asserting ancient, arguably feudal, rights, and local particularity: the vestiges of the past. Absolutism, seemingly modern and efficient, seemed the way of the future." Michael Barone, *Our First Revolution*, Kindle location 145–49.

9. Ibid., Kindle location 2938–39.

10. William of Orange, "Declaration of the Prince of Orange, October 10, 1688," Jacobite Heritage. http://www.jacobite.ca/documents/16881010.htm

11. Edmund Burke, *Reflections on the Revolution in France*, Constitution Society. http://www.constitution.org/eb/rev_fran.htm

12. Locke, "Chap. V: Of Property," sec. 49, "The Second Treatise of Government," p. 301.

13. Locke, "Chap. II: Of the State of Nature," sec. 4, ibid., p. 269.

14. Ibid.

15. Locke, "Chap. III: Of the State of War," sec. 19, ibid., pp. 280–81.

16. Ibid., sec. 24, p. 284.

17. Mancur Olson, "Dictatorship, Democracy, and Development," *American Political Science Review*, 87, no. 3 (September 1993), p. 568.

18. Locke, "Chap. V: Of Property," sec. 27, ibid., "The Second Treatise of Government," pp. 287–88.

19. Ibid., sec. 41, p. 297.

20. John Locke. "Book II—Chapter I: Of Ideas in General, and Their Original," *An Essay Concerning Human Understanding*, Online Library of Liberty. http://oll.libertyfund.org/titles/locke-the-works-vol-1-an-essay-concerning-human-understanding-part-1#lf0128-01_label_314

21. Steven Pinker, *The Blank Slate: The Modern Denial of Human Nature* (New York: Penguin, 2003 [2002], Kindle edition), pp. 5–6.

22. Locke, "Chap. II: Of the State of Nature," sec. 6, "The Second Treatise of Government," p. 271.

23. James T. Kloppenberg, *Toward Democracy: The Struggle for Self-Rule in European and American Thought* (Oxford, U.K.: Oxford University Press, 2016), p. 158.

24. Locke, "Chap. XI: Of the Extent of the Legislative Power," sec. 142, "The Second Treatise of Government," p. 363.

25. Locke, "Chap. IX: Of the Ends of Political Activity," sec. 131, ibid., p. 353.

26. Locke, "Chap. IV: Of Slavery," sec. 22, ibid., p. 284.

27. Kloppenberg, *Toward Democracy*, p. 138.

28. Michael Locke McLendon, "Rousseau, Amour Propre, and Intellectual Celebrity," *Journal of Politics* 71, no. 2 (April 2009), pp. 507–8.

29. Jean-Jacques Rousseau, *The Confessions* (London: Wordsworth, 1996), p. 641.

30. Leo Damrosch, *Jean-Jacques Rousseau: Restless Genius* (New York: Houghton Mifflin, 2005), pp. 390–91.

31. Voltaire, "On the Advantages of Civilisation and Literature: To J.J. Rousseau," 30 August 1775, Letters from Voltaire: A Selection, Voltaire Society of America. https://www.whitman.edu/VSA/index.html

32. David Edmonds and John Eidinow, "Enlightened Enemies," *Guardian*, April 28, 2006. https://www.theguardian.com/books/2006/apr/29/philosophy

33. David Hume, "Letter 407: To Adam Smith," *The Letters of David Hume, Volume 2: 1766–1776*, J. Y. T. Craig, ed. (Oxford, U.K.: Oxford University Press. 2011), p. 165.

34. Elena Russo, "Slander and Glory in the Republic of Letters: Diderot and Seneca Confront Rousseau," *Republics of Letters* 1, issue 1. http://arcade.stanford.edu/rofl/slander-and-glory-republic-letters-diderot-and-seneca-confront-rousseau

35. Ibid.

36. Tim Blanning, *The Romantic Revolution: A History*, Modern Library Chronicles (New York: Random House, 2011, Kindle edition), Kindle location 281–90.

37. Jean-Jacques Rousseau, "Book I: Chapter I: Subject of the First Book," "The Social Contract, or Principles of Political Right," *The Social Contract and Discourses*, Online Library of Liberty. http://oll.libertyfund.org/titles/rousseau-the-social-contract-and-discourses#lf0132_label_057

38. Jean-Jacques Rousseau, "The First Part," sec. 130–31, "A Discourse on the Moral Effects of the Arts and Sciences," *The Social Contract and Discourses*, Online Library of Liberty. http://oll.libertyfund.org/titles/rousseau-the-social-contract-and-discourses#lf0132_head_058

39. Jean-Jacques Rousseau, *Emile, or On Education*, Allan Bloom, trans. (New York: Basic Books, 1979), p. 37.

40. Jean-Jacques Rousseau, *Dialogues, Oeuvres*, 1:935. Quoted in Eugene L. Stelzig, *The Romantic Subject in Autobiography: Rousseau and Goethe* (Charlottesville, VA, and London: University Press of Virginia, 2000), p. 46.

41. Jean-Jacques Rousseau, "The Second Part," sec. 207, "A Dissertation on the Origin and Foundation of the Inequality of Mankind," *The Social Contract and Discourses*, Online Library of Liberty. http://oll.libertyfund.org/titles/rousseau-the-social-contract-and-discourses#lf0132_head_066

42. Ibid., sec. 214.

43. Ibid., secs. 214-15.

44. Rousseau, "The Second Part," sec. 152, "A Discourse on the Moral Effects of the Arts and Sciences," *The Social Contract and Discourses*, Online Library of Liberty. http://oll.libertyfund.org/titles/rousseau-the-social-contract-and-discourses#lf0132_head_059

45. These quotes come from an early draft of Rousseau's *Discourse on the Origins and Foundations of Inequality*, quoted in Paul A. Rahe, "The Enlightenment Indicted: Rousseau's Response to Montesquieu," *Journal of the Historical Society* 8, no. 2 (June 2008), p. 293.

46. Quoted in James Schall, *Political Philosophy and Revelation: A Catholic Reading* (Washington, D.C.: Catholic University of America Press, 2013), p. 122.

47. Jean-Jacques Rousseau, "Book IV: Chapter VIII: Civil Religion," sec. 121, "The Social Contract, or Principles of Political Right," *The Social Contract and Discourses*, Online Library of Liberty. http://oll.libertyfund.org/titles/rousseau-the-social-contract-and-discourses#lf0132_label_146

48. Ibid., secs. 122-23.

49. Robert Nisbet, *The Present Age: Progress and Anarchy in Modern America* (New York: Harper & Row, 1988), p. 52.

50. Quoted in Conor Cruise O'Brien, "Rousseau, Robespierre, Burke, Jefferson, and the French Revolution," in Jean-Jacques Rousseau, *The Social Contract and The First and Second Discourses*, Rethinking the Western Tradition series, Susan Dunn, ed. (New Haven, CT, and London: Yale University Press, 2002, Kindle edition), Kindle location 4134. It should be noted in Rousseau's partial defense that he believed the Social Contract would not lend itself neatly to nationalism because he believed communities must be small, like his beloved Geneva, to work. But ideas merely influence events, they do not dictate them, and Rousseau's ideas deeply influenced nationalist movements across Europe.

51. Richard Pipes, *Property and Freedom* (New York: Knopf, 1999), p. 42.

52. Quoted in O'Brien, "Rousseau, Robespierre, Burke, Jefferson, and the French Revolution," Kindle location 4136-43.

53. Ibid., Kindle location 4147-50.

6: THE AMERICAN MIRACLE

1. Herbert Butterfield, *The Whig Interpretation of History* (London: G. Bell, 1931, Kindle edition), Kindle location 308-10.

2. "The Glorious Revolution set in motion a series of developments, some immediate, some taking several decades, that restored throughout the American colonies the extraordinary degree of political autonomy that Charles and James had sought to end." James T. Kloppenberg, *Toward Democracy: The Struggle for Self-Rule in European and American Thought* (Oxford, U.K.: Oxford University Press, 2016), p. 176.

3. Thomas Y. Davies, "Recovering the Original Fourth Amendment," *Michigan Law Review* 98, no. 3 (December 1999), pp. 547-750; "The meaning and origin of the expression: An Englishman's home is his castle," The Phrase Finder. http://www .phrases.org.uk/meanings/an-englishmans-home-is-his-castle.html

4. Thomas Jefferson, "Letter to Henry Lee—May 8, 1825," *Thomas Jefferson: Writings*, Merrill D. Peterson, ed. (New York: Library of America, 1984), pp. 1500-1. http:// teachingamericanhistory.org/library/document/letter-to-henry-lee/

5. Mostly the Virginia constitution, which he had written, and the Virginia Declaration of Rights drafted by George Mason. These, in turn, were deeply indebted to the English Bill of Rights from 1688-89. Rather than crafting a novel expression of principle, Jefferson's achievement, writes Pauline Maier, "lay instead in the creative adaptation of preexisting models to different circumstances." See Pauline Maier, *American Scripture: Making the Declaration of Independence* (New York: Vintage Books, 1988), p. 104.

6. Gordon S. Wood, "Dusting Off the Declaration," *New York Review of Books*, August 14, 1997. http://www.nybooks.com/articles/1997/08/14/dusting-off-the-declaration/

7. Abraham Lincoln, Full text of "Abraham Lincoln's lost speech, May 29, 1856." https://archive.org/stream/abrahamlincoln00linc/abrahamlincoln00linc_djvu.txt

8. Abraham Lincoln, "Speech on the Kansas Nebraska Act at Peoria, Illinois" (abridged), TeachingAmericanHistory.org. http://teachingamericanhistory.org/ library/document/speech-on-the-kansas-nebraska-act-at-peoria-illinois-abridged/

9. Abraham Lincoln, "Address at the Dedication of the National Cemetery in Gettysburg, Pennsylvania—November 19, 1863," American Presidency Project, John Woolley and Gerhard Peters, eds. http://www.presidency.ucsb.edu/ws/?pid=73959

10. Martin Luther King Jr., "I Have a Dream," Address Delivered at the March on Washington for Jobs and Freedom, August 28, 1963, Martin Luther King Jr., Research and Education Institute—Stanford University. https://kinginstitute.stanford.edu/ king-papers/documents/i-have-dream-address-delivered-march-washington -jobs-and-freedom

11. Carl Becker, in his *Declaration of Independence* (1922), declared, "The Declaration, in its form, in its phraseology, follows closely certain sentences in Locke's second treatise on government." Charles and Mary Beard insisted in 1930 that Locke provided the foremost of the "textbooks of revolution" for the Founders. Merle Curti wrote in 1937: "No one has seriously questioned the great influence of John Locke on American thought during the latter part of the eighteenth century." More recently J. W. Peltason writes in his book *Understanding the Constitution* that Locke's *Two Treatises of Government* "was thought to be an authoritative pronouncement of established principles. Locke's ideas provided ready arguments for the American cause, and they were especially embarrassing to an English government whose own source of authority was based on them." See Oscar and Lilian Handlin, "Who Read John Locke? Words and Acts in the American Revolution," *American Scholar* 58, no. 4 (Autumn 1989), pp. 546-47. The English philosopher Maurice Cranston says Locke's "influence on the Founding Fathers exceeded that of any other thinker." See Maurice Cranston. "Locke and Liberty," *Wilson Quarterly* (Winter 1986), p. 82. http://archive.wilsonquarterly.com/sites/default/files/ articles/WQ_VOL10_W_1986_Article_02.pdf

Here, again, we face the dilemma of the intellectual historian trying to connect dots from one mind to another across the generations. Because while it is certainly true that some of the Founders had read Locke, it is surprisingly difficult to find contemporary concrete testimonials to his overwhelming influence on the Founders' political thought. Oscar and Lilian Handlin make a powerful case that the Founders were not close students of Locke's political writing (see the entire essay cited above). Historians, they write, have "commonly ascribed many revolutionary ideas and sometimes even actions to the influence of John Locke, without troubling to investigate the channels of transmission" (Handlin and Handlin, "Who Read John Locke?," p. 546).

12. Ibid., p. 549.
13. James Wilson, "Remarks of James Wilson in the Pennsylvania Convention to Ratify the Constitution of the United States, 1787," Online Library of Liberty. http://oll .libertyfund.org/titles/wilson-collected-works-of-james-wilson-vol-1
14. Somewhat disturbingly, if Jefferson is to be believed, Hamilton paused for a long moment and then said, "The greatest man, that ever lived, was Julius Caesar." See Thomas Jefferson, "To Dr. Benjamin Rush, Monticello, January 16, 1811," American History: The Letters of Thomas Jefferson, 1743–1826. http://www.let.rug.nl/usa/ presidents/thomas-jefferson/letters-of-thomas-jefferson/jefl208.php
15. John Locke, "A Letter Concerning Toleration," *A Letter Concerning Toleration and Other Writings*, Online Library of Liberty. http://oll.libertyfund.org/titles/locke-a -letter-concerning-toleration-and-other-writings
16. "Act for Establishing Religious Freedom, January 16, 1786," Library of Virginia. http://edu.lva.virginia.gov/docs/ReligiousFree.pdf
17. Donald Lutz found that Montesquieu and Locke account for 60 percent of all references to Enlightenment thinkers in the political literature of 1760s America. In the 1770s that share went up to 75 percent. Montesquieu was cited more in work discussing constitutional design, while Locke was invoked more in arguments justifying a break with England. See Donald S. Lutz, "The Relative Influence of European Writers on Late Eighteenth-Century American Political Thought," *American Political Science Review* 78, no. 1 (March 1984), p. 192.
18. Clinton Rossiter, *The Political Thought of the American Revolution, Part 3* (New York: Harcourt, Brace & World, 1963), p. 8.
19. John Adams, "From John Adams to Jonathan Sewall, February 1760," Founders Online, National Archives. https://founders.archives.gov/?q=locke&s=1111311111 &sa=&r=20&sr
20. Thomas Paine, "Of the Present Ability of America, with Some Miscellaneous Reflections," *Common Sense*, Constitution Society. http://www.constitution.org/ tp/comsense.htm
21. David Azerrad, "The Declaration of Independence and the American Creed," Heritage Foundation, July 3, 2013. http://www.heritage.org/research/commen tary/2013/7/the-declaration-of-independence-and-the-american-creed
22. Thomas Jefferson, "Queries 14 and 19, 145–49, 164–65," in *The Founders' Constitution*, Volume 1, Chapter 18, Document 16, University of Chicago Press. http://press-pubs.uchicago.edu/founders/documents/v1ch18s16.html
23. Thomas Jefferson, "Preamble to a Bill for the More General Diffusion of Knowledge—Fall 1778," in *The Founders' Constitution*, Volume 1, Chapter 18, Document 11, University of Chicago Press. http://press-pubs.uchicago.edu/founders/ documents/v1ch18s11.html
24. Holly Brewer, "Entailing Aristocracy in Colonial Virginia: 'Ancient Feudal Restraints' and Revolutionary Reform," *William and Mary Quarterly* 54, no. 2 (April 1997), p. 307.
25. David Boaz, "The Man Who Would Not Be King," Cato Institute, February 20, 2006. https://www.cato.org/publications/commentary/man-who-would-not-be-king

26. James Madison, "*Federalist* No. 51: The Structure of the Government Must Furnish the Proper Checks and Balances Between the Different Departments," Constitution Society. http://www.constitution.org/fed/federa51.htm

27. "When any number of Men have so consented to make one Community or Government, they are thereby presently incorporated," Locke wrote, "and make one Body Politick, wherein the Majority have a Right to act and conclude the rest." John Locke, "Chap. VIII: Of the Beginning of Political Societies," sec. 95, "Second Treatise of Government," *Two Treatises of Government*, Peter Laslett, ed. (Cambridge, U.K.: Cambridge University Press, 1988 [1960]), pp. 330–31.

28. In 1802, Napoleon offered a referendum on a new constitution that would make him the permanent consul of France (much like the rulers of the Roman Empire), a.k.a. dictator for life. It received 99 percent of the vote. In 1804 he issued another plebiscite, this one on the question of whether he should be named emperor of France. The official results were even better (though just shy of 100 percent). See "From Life Consulship to the Hereditary Empire (1802–1804), Napoleon.org (Fondation Napoleon). https://www.napoleon.org/en/history-of-the-two-empires/timelines/from-life-consulship-to-the-hereditary-empire-1802-1804/

29. The identity of Brutus is still debated. Among the leading candidates are Melancton Smith or Robert Yates or perhaps John Williams.

30. Brutus, "No. 25—Objections to a Standing Army" (Part II), *The Federalist vs. Anti-Federalist Dispute: The Original Arguments for Each* (Seattle, WA: Amazon Digital Services, 2011, Kindle edition), p. 542.

31. See, for example, Charles Lyttle, "Deistic Piety in the Cults of the French Revolution," *Church History* 2, no. 1 (March 1933), pp. 22–40.

32. Quoted in James W. Caesar, "Foundational Concept and American Political Development," *Nature and History in American Political Development: A Debate* (Cambridge, MA: Harvard University Press, 2006), p. 20.

33. See Yuval Levin, *The Great Debate: Edmund Burke, Thomas Paine, and the Birth of Right and Left* (New York: Basic Books, 2013).

34. James Madison, "*Federalist* No. 10: The Utility of the Union as a Safeguard Against Domestic Faction and Insurrection (continued)," Constitution Society. http://www.constitution.org/fed/federa10.htm

35. "Adam Smith on the Need for 'Peace, Easy Taxes, and a Tolerable Administration of Justice,'" Online Library of Liberty. http://oll.libertyfund.org/quote/436

36. Daniel Hannan, *Inventing Freedom: How the English-Speaking Peoples Made the Modern World* (New York: HarperCollins, 2013, Kindle edition), Kindle location 2104–13.

37. Henry Fairlie, "The Shot Heard Round the World," *New Republic* 199, no. 3/4, July 18–25, 1988, p. 20.

38. Ibid., p. 25.

39. Robert Wright, "Why the American Revolution Was Really an Economic Revolution," Learn Liberty, July 7, 2016. http://www.learnliberty.org/blog/why-the-american-revolution-was-really-an-economic-revolution/

40. Fairlie, "The Shot Heard Round the World," p. 25.

41. Ibid., p. 23.

42. Ibid., pp. 22–23.

43. Daniel J. Boorstin, *The Americans: The Democratic Experience* (New York: Knopf Doubleday, 1974 [1973], Kindle Edition), Kindle locations 1823–25.

44. Ibid., Kindle location 1825–31.

45. The phrase "the New World" has acquired a vaguely negative connotation as it con-

jures longstanding grievances about the displacement of natives in the Americas. Columbus didn't "discover" America, reads the familiar indictment, he helped Europeans conquer it. From the vantage point of the indigenous peoples of the Americas, there's really no refuting this perspective (even if such conquest was the story of all humanity, including among the indigenous peoples of America, until the Lockean Revolution began to unfold, and even then for a good while after).

46. Boorstin, *The Americans*, Kindle location 1836-40.
47. Ibid., Kindle location 4054-56.
48. Ibid., Kindle location 4062-65.
49. Boorstin adds that "businessmen were urged to domicile their newly created legal entities in Delaware rather than in Massachusetts, in New Jersey rather than in Pennsylvania, in Nevada rather than in New York. The less populous states, such as Delaware, New Jersey, and Nevada, were especially eager and ingenious in the competition." Ibid., Kindle location 8056-62.
50. Henry Hazlitt, "Capitalism Without Horns," *National Review* 14, no. 10, March 12, 1963, p. 201.
51. Burton Folsom, *The Myth of the Robber Barons: A New Look at the Rise of Big Business in America* (Herndon, VA: Young America's Foundation, 1991).
52. Max Roser, "Economic Growth," Our World in Data. https://ourworldindata.org/economic-growth
53. Boorstin, *The Americans*, Kindle location 153-54.

7: THE ELITES

1. George Washington, "Circular to the States," June 8, 1783, in *The Founders' Constitution*, Volume 1, Chapter 7, Document 5, University of Chicago Press. http://press-pubs.uchicago.edu/founders/documents/v1ch7s5.html
2. John Adams, "Defence of the Constitutions of the Government of the United States," in *The Founders' Constitution*, Volume 1, Chapter 15, Document 34, University of Chicago Press. http://press-pubs.uchicago.edu/founders/documents/v1ch15s34.html
3. John Adams, "From John Adams to Benjamin Rush, 27 December 1810," Founders Online, National Archives. https://founders.archives.gov/documents/Adams/99-02-02-5584
4. Ibid., https://founders.archives.gov/documents/Adams/99-02-02-5585
5. C. W. Cassinelli, "The Law of Oligarchy," *American Political Science Review* 47, no. 3 (September 1953), pp. 773-84.
6. Daron Acemoglu and James Robinson, *Why Nations Fail: The Origins of Power, Prosperity, and Poverty* (New York: Crown Business, 2012, Kindle edition), p. 148.
7. Ibid.
8. Ibid., p. 150.
9. James Madison, "Federal Convention: Wednesday, June 6," Debates on the Adoption of the Federal Constitution, in the Convention Held at Philadelphia, in 1787; With a Diary of the Debates of the Congress of the Confederation; As Reported By James Madison, a Member and Deputy from Virginia, Elliot Jonathan, ed. (Washington, D.C.: Printed for the editor, 1845), p. 163.
10. "Table 4. Population: 1790 to 1990," Census.gov, U.S. Census Bureau. https://www.census.gov/population/censusdata/table-4.pdf
11. Max Roser, "Economic Growth," Our World in Data. https://ourworldindata.org/economic-growth
12. See Jonah Goldberg, "Your 'Robber Baron,' My American Hero," *National Review* 58, no. 10, June 5, 2006, pp. 30-31.

13. Andrew Carnegie, "Wealth," *North American Review*, No. CCCXCI, June 1889. https://www.swarthmore.edu/SocSci/rbannis1/AIH19th/Carnegie.html

14. William Leuchtenburg, *The FDR Years: On Roosevelt and His Legacy* (New York: Columbia University Press, 1995), p. 284.

15. "What, then, is the State as a sociological concept? The State, completely in its genesis, essentially and almost completely during the first stages of its existence, is a social institution, forced by a victorious group of men on a defeated group, with the sole purpose of regulating the dominion of the victorious group over the vanquished, and securing itself against revolt from within and attacks from abroad. Teleologically, this dominion had no other purpose than the economic exploitation of the vanquished by the victors. No primitive state known to history originated in any other manner." Franz Oppenheimer, "Theories of the State," *The State: Its History and Development Viewed Sociologically*, John M. Gittman, trans. (Indianapolis: Bobbs-Merrill, 1914), p. 15.

16. Albert Jay Nock, *Our Enemy, the State* (Caldwell, ID: Caxton Printers, 1950), pp. 49–50.

17. Katie Louchheim, *The Making of the New Deal: The Insiders Speak* (Cambridge, MA, and London: Harvard University Press, 1983), p. 275.

8: THE PROGRESSIVE ERA

1. Thomas C. Leonard, *Illiberal Reformers: Race, Eugenics, and American Economics in the Progressive Era* (Princeton, NJ: Princeton University Press, 2016), p. xi.

2. Jonah Goldberg, "Richard Ely's Golden Calf," *National Review* 61, no. 24, December 31, 2009, p. 34.

3. Ibid.

4. Leonard, *Illiberal Reformers*, p. 24.

5. Ibid.

6. Richard Theodore Ely, *The Social Law of Service* (New York: Eaton & Mains, 1896), pp. 162–63.

7. Samuel Zane Batten, *The Christian State: The State, Democracy, and Christianity* (Philadelphia: Griffith & Rowland Press, 1909), p. 14. Accessed via: https://ia600609.us.archive.org/12/items/christianstatest00batt/christianstatest00batt.pdf

8. Quoted in Michael McGerr, *A Fierce Discontent: The Rise and Fall of the Progressive Movement in America* (New York: Free Press, 2003), p. 66.

9. Walter Rauschenbusch, *Christianizing the Social Order* (Waco, TX: Baylor University Press, 2010), p. 330.

10. Leonard, *Illiberal Reformers*, p. 104.

11. Ibid.

12. Quoted in Robert Nisbet, *The Sociological Tradition* (New Brunswick, NJ: Transaction, 2004 [1966]), p. 273.

13. See Jonah Goldberg, *Liberal Fascism: The Secret History of the American Left from Mussolini to the Politics of Change* (New York: Broadway Books, 2009 [2007]), p. 97.

14. Woodrow Wilson, "The Study of Administration," *Political Science Quarterly* 2, no. 2 (June 1887), p. 204. Phillip Hamburger writes: "More generally, though, Americans adopted German ideas to overcome the constitutional obstacles to administrative power. Once these Germanic justifications were popularized, there was no need to cite Germans, and after 1914 Americans had particularly strong reasons to repackage the Continental ideas to suit domestic sensibilities. But it is no coincidence that when Americans defended the constitutionality of administrative law, they relied on ideas familiar from German academics. Indeed,

throughout the twentieth century, Germanic anti-constitutional ideas were among the leading constitutional justifications for administrative power." Philip Hamburger, *Is Administrative Law Unlawful?* (Chicago: University of Chicago Press, 2014), p. 462.

15. Wilson, "The Study of Administration," p. 215.
16. Ibid., p. 214.
17. Quoted in Charles Murray, *By the People: Rebuilding Liberty Without Permission* (New York: Crown Forum, 2015), p. 73.
18. Hamburger, *Is Administrative Law Unlawful?*, p. 371.
19. Woodrow Wilson, *Constitutional Government in the United States* (New York: Columbia University Press, 1908), p. 16.
20. Woodrow Wilson, "What Is Progress? From *The New Freedom*, Chapter 2," in *American Progressivism: A Reader*, Ronald J. Pestritto and William J. Atto, eds. (Lanham, MD: Lexington Books, 2008), p. 50.
21. Ibid., p. 51.
22. John Dewey, *Liberalism and Social Action* (Amherst, NY: Prometheus Books, 2000), p. 40.
23. Ibid., p. 27.
24. Ibid., p. 42.
25. Thomas G. West, "Progressivism and the Transformation of American Government," in *The Progressive Revolution in Politics and Political Science*, John Marini and Ken Masugi, eds. (Lanham, MD: Rowman & Littlefield, 2005), p. 16.
26. F. J. Goodnow, "The American Conception of Liberty," in *American Progressivism: A Reader*, p. 57.
27. Ibid., p. 62.
28. Ronald J. Pestritto, "The Birth of the Administrative State: Where It Came From and What It Means for Limited Government," Heritage Foundation, November 20, 2007. http://www.heritage.org/research/reports/2007/11/the-birth-of-the-adminis trative-state-where-it-came-from-and-what-it-means-for-limited-government
29. Thomas Jefferson, "From Thomas Jefferson to Edward Carrington, 27 May 1788," Founders Online, National Archives. https://founders.archives.gov/documents/Jefferson/01-13-02-0120
30. Woodrow Wilson, *Woodrow Wilson: The Essential Political Writings*, Ronald J. Pestritto, ed. (Lanham, MD: Lexington Books, 2005), p. 23.
31. Walter Lippmann, *The Essential Lippmann: A Political Philosophy for Liberal Democracy*, Clinton Rossiter and James Lare, eds. (Cambridge, MA: Harvard University Press, 1982), p. 88.
32. Ibid., p. 85.
33. James Madison, "*Federalist* No. 10: The Utility of the Union as a Safeguard Against Domestic Faction and Insurrection (continued)," Constitution Society. http://www.constitution.org/fed/federa10.htm
34. Pestritto, "The Birth of the Administrative State."
35. Richard Milner, "Tracing the Canals of Mars: An Astronomer's Obsession," Space .com, October 6, 2011. https://www.space.com/13197-mars-canals-water-history -lowell.html
36. This list comes from Thomas Leonard's indispensable book *Illiberal Reformers*, pp. x–xi.
37. Quoted in McGerr, *A Fierce Discontent*, p. 282.
38. William Leuchtenberg, *The FDR Years: On Roosevelt and His Legacy* (New York: Columbia University Press, 1995), p. 39.

39. G. J. Meyer, *The World Remade: America in World War I* (New York: Bantam Books, 2016), p. 550.

40. See Goldberg, *Liberal Fascism*, p. 109.

41. Ibid., p. 117.

42. Ibid., p. 115.

43. Robert Higgs, "How War Amplified Federal Power in the Twentieth Century," Independent Institute, July 1, 1999. http://www.independent.org/publications/article.asp?id=113

9: THE ADMINISTRATIVE STATE

1. Ryan Teague Beckwith, "Read Steve Bannon and Reince Priebus' Joint Interview at CPAC," *Time*, February 23, 2017. http://time.com/4681094/reince-priebus-steve-bannon-cpac-interview-transcript/

2. An influential group of conservative writers and scholars—mostly associated with the Claremont Institute in California and Hillsdale College in Michigan—embraced Donald Trump early on in large part because they believed the real estate developer and reality show impresario might be like a bull in the china shop that is the administrative state. Despite my deep respect for—and friendships with—many of these scholars, I thought this was a profound error. Many arguments, most collegial, some not, ensued. But one thing conservative opponents and supporters of Trump agree on is the danger posed by the administrative state.

3. Quoted in Matthew Continetti, "The Managers vs. the Managed," *Weekly Standard*, September 21, 2015. http://www.weeklystandard.com/the-managers-vs.-the-managed/article/1028522

4. Philip Klein, "The Empress of ObamaCare," *American Spectator*, June 4, 2010. https://spectator.org/39516_empress-obamacare/

5. Ibid.

6. Christopher C. DeMuth, "Unlimited Government," *American*, January 1, 2006. http://www.aei.org/publication/unlimited-government/print/

7. Rudy Takala, "FCC Commissioner: Expect a Broadband Internet Tax," *Washington Examiner*, March 2, 2016. http://www.washingtonexaminer.com/fcc-commissioner-expect-a-broadband-internet-tax/article/2584747

8. See, for example, Katie McAuliffe, "Fraud Still Plagues the FCC's Universal Service Fund," *The Hill*, February 14, 2017. http://thehill.com/blogs/pundits-blog/technology/319446-fraud-still-plagues-the-fccs-universal-service-fund

9. DeMuth, "Unlimited Government."

10. "Public Company Accounting Oversight Board 2017 Budget by Cost Category, 2015-2017," Public Company Accounting Oversight Board. https://pcaobus.org/About/Administration/Documents/Fiscal%20Year%20Budgets/2017.pdf

11. Charles Murray, *By the People: Rebuilding Liberty Without Permission* (New York: Crown Forum, 2015), pp. 68-69.

12. Philip Hamburger, *Is Administrative Law Unlawful?* (Chicago: University of Chicago Press, 2014), p. 7.

13. Ibid., p. 6.

14. Ibid.

15. James Madison, "*Federalist* No. 47: The Particular Structure of the New Government and the Distribution of Power Among Its Different Parts," Constitution Society. http://www.constitution.org/fed/federa47.htm

16. See p. 27 of Justice Thomas's concurring opinion in *Department of Transportation,*

et al., Petitioners vs. Association of American Railroads. https://www.supremecourt
.gov/opinions/14pdf/13-1080_f29g.pdf

17. Hamburger, *Is Administrative Law Unlawful?*, pp. 5–6.
18. Emily Zanotti, "EPA Causes a Major Environmental Disaster, the Question Is:
    Will It Fine Itself and Fire Those Involved?," Watts Up with That?, August 10,
    2015. https://wattsupwiththat.com/2015/08/10/epa-causes-a-major-environmental
    -disaster-the-question-is-will-it-fine-itself-and-fire-those-involved/
19. Hamburger, *Is Administrative Law Unlawful?*, p. 363.
20. Murray, *By the People: Rebuilding Liberty Without Permission*, p. 5
21. Ibid., p. 6.
22. Hamburger, *Is Administrative Law Unlawful?*, pp. 370–71.
23. It's worth recalling that, under Wilson, civil service reform in Washington meant,
    as much as anything, purging blacks from government. Wilson re-segregated
    Washington, D.C., and pioneered the practice of requiring photos with job applica-
    tions, the better to ensure that no "inferior" races made it through. See Nancy J.
    Weiss, "The Negro and the New Freedom: Fighting Wilsonian Segregation," *Politi-
    cal Science Quarterly* 84, no. 1 (March 1969), pp. 61–79.
24. Quil Lawrence, "U.S. Office of Special Counsel Calls Out VA Firing of Whistle-
    blowers," NPR, September 17, 2015. http://www.npr.org/2015/09/17/441222434/u-s
    -office-of-special-counsel-calls-out-va-firing-of-whistleblowers
25. John Locke, "Chap. VI: Of Paternal Power," sec. 138, "The Second Treatise of
    Government: An Essay Concerning the True Original, Extent, and End of Civil
    Government," *Two Treatises of Government*, Peter Laslett, ed. (Cambridge, U.K.:
    Cambridge University Press. 1988 [1960]), p. 301.
26. F. A. Hayek, *The Road to Serfdom* (New York: George Rutledge, 1944), p. 108.
27. Dennis Cauchon, "Some Federal Workers More Likely to Die Than Lose Jobs," *USA
    Today*, July 19, 2011. http://usatoday30.usatoday.com/news/washington/2011-07-18
    -fderal-job-security_n.htm
28. "National Treasury Employees Union: Party Split by Cycle," OpenSecrets.org
    (Center for Responsive Politics). https://www.opensecrets.org/pacs/lookup2
    .php?strID=C00107128
29. "American Federation of Government Employees: Total Contributions by Party of
    Recipient," OpenSecrets.org (Center for Responsive Politics). https://www.opense
    crets.org/orgs/totals.php?id=D000000304&cycle=2016
30. Quoted in Hamburger, *Is Administrative Law Unlawful?*, p. 368.
31. Mancur Olson demonstrated this in his 1965 work *The Logic of Collective Action.*
    Almost twenty years later Jonathan Rauch fleshed out the thesis in his *Demoscle-
    rosis: The Silent Killer of American Government* (New York: Three Rivers, 1995). In
    2015 the problems diagnosed by Olson and Rauch had gotten so bad that Charles
    Murray published his *By the People*, which called for dismantling the administra-
    tive state through massive civil disobedience and grinding courtroom lawfare.
32. Even in the last twenty years, the growth is somewhat staggering. The total amount
    of money spent on lobbying more than doubled between 1998 and 2016, from $1.45
    billion to $3.15 billion. See "Lobbying Database," OpenSecrets.org (Center for
    Responsive Politics). https://www.opensecrets.org/lobby/
33. Rauch continues: "If you see others rushing to lobby for favorable laws and regula-
    tions, you rush to do the same so as not to be left at a disadvantage. But the govern-
    ment can do only so much. Its resource base and management ability are limited,
    and its adaptability erodes with each additional benefit that interest groups lock

in. In fact, the more different things it tries to do at once, the less effective it tends to become. Thus if everybody descends on Washington hunting some favorable public policy, government becomes rigid, overburdened, and incoherent. Soon its problem-solving capacity is despoiled. Everybody loses." Jonathan Rauch, *Government's End: Why Washington Stopped Working* (New York: PublicAffairs, 1994), p. 270.

34. R. H. Coase, "The Federal Communications Commission," *Journal of Law and Economics* 2 (October 1959), p. 36.

35. James Q. Wilson, *Bureaucracy: What Government Agencies Do and Why They Do It* (New York: Basic Books, 1989), p. 76.

36. Milton Friedman, *Capitalism and Freedom* (Fortieth Anniversary Edition) (Chicago: University of Chicago Press, 2002 [1962]), p. 138.

37. James Davis, *Medieval Market Morality: Life, Law and Ethics in the English Marketplace, 1200–1500* (Cambridge, U.K.: Cambridge University Press, 2012), p. 298.

38. Deirdre N. McCloskey, *Bourgeois Equality: How Ideas, Not Capital or Institutions, Enriched the World* (Chicago: University of Chicago Press, 2016), p. 462. I tried to answer this rhetorical question. The answer is that there were 1,976 pharmacies in Holland in 2011, according to the World Health Organization. (See page 8 of: http://www.who.int/medicines/areas/coordination/netherlands_pharmaceutical_pro file.pdf.) In the United States there were 64,356 in 2011 (http://journals.plos.org/plosone/article?id=10.1371/journal.pone.0183172). Adjusting for population (circa 2011: http://databank.worldbank.org/data/reports.aspx?source=2&series=SP.POP .TOTL&country), there are roughly twice as many pharmacies per person in the U.S. as there are in Holland.

39. He continues: "These men and women, most of whom are only part-time officials, may have a direct economic interest in many of the decisions they make concerning admission requirements and the definition of standards to be observed by licensees. More importantly, they are as a rule directly representative of organized groups within the occupations. Ordinarily they are nominated by these groups as a step toward a gubernatorial or other appointment that is frequently a mere formality. Often the formality is dispensed with entirely, appointment being made directly by the occupational association—as happens, for example, with the embalmers in North Carolina, the dentists in Alabama, the psychologists in Virginia, the physicians in Maryland, and the attorneys in Washington." Walter Gellhorn, "The Right to Make a Living," *Individual Freedom and Governmental Restraints* (Baton Rouge: Louisiana State University Press, 1956), p. 106. Quoted in Milton Friedman, *Capitalism and Freedom*, p. 140.

40. Morris P. Kleiner and Alan B. Krueger, "The Prevalence and Effects of Occupational Licensing," NBER Working Paper No. 14308, September 2008, pp. 2–3. http://www.nber.org/papers/w14308

41. Jeffrey Zients and Betsey Stevenson, "Trends in Occupational Licensing and Best Practices for Smart Labor Market Regulation," The White House: President Barack Obama, July 28, 2015. https://obamawhitehouse.archives.gov/blog/2015/07/28/trends-occupational-licensing-and-best-practices-smart-labor-market-regulation

42. "Braiding: IJ Untangles Regulations for Natural Hair Braiders," Institute for Justice. http://ij.org/issues/economic-liberty/braiding/

43. For starters, see "Economic Liberty: The Institute for Justice Files Lawsuits Nationwide to Defend Honest Enterprise," Institute for Justice. http://ij.org/issues/economic-liberty/

44. See "Certification, Licensing, and Charters," Tennessee Department of Agriculture. https://www.tn.gov/agriculture/article/ag-businesses-certification

45. George Gilder, *Wealth and Poverty: A New Edition for the Twenty-First Century* (Washington, D.C.: Regnery, 2012), p. 326.

46. Nick Sabilla, "Are Taxi Medallions Too Big to Fail?," Fox News, August 16, 2016. http://www.foxnews.com/opinion/2016/08/16/are-taxi-medallions-too-big-to-fail -too.html

47. Peter Jamison, "Outrage After Big Labor Crafts Law Paying Their Members Less Than Non-Union Workers," *Los Angeles Times*, April 9, 2016. http://www.latimes .com/local/cityhall/la-me-union-minimum-wage-20160410-story.html

48. Benjamin T. Smith, "Teachers, Education Reform, and Mexico's Left," *Dissent*, October 7, 2013. https://www.dissentmagazine.org/online_articles/teachers -education-reform-and-mexicos-left

49. Marion Lloyd, "Striking Mexico Teachers See Jobs as Things to Sell," *Houston Chronicle*, October 13, 2008. http://www.chron.com/life/mom-houston/article/ Striking-Mexico-teachers-see-jobs-as-things-to-1642091.php

50. Information available at "Historical Data Sets and Trends Data," Doing Business: Measuring Business Regulations, World Bank, http://www.doingbusiness.org/ Custom-Query. The World Bank has a vast set of data on the ease of doing business; the easiest way to find the figures I used is to create your own data set, though, unfortunately, this process does not generate a unique URL. At any rate, I created my data set using the link above by restricting my topics to "Enforcing Contracts," "Dealing with Construction Permits," and "Registering Property," restricting my years to "Doing Business" editions 2007, 2009, 2016, and 2017, and restricting the countries I wanted data for to Greece and the United States.

51. J. D. Harris, "The Decline of American Entrepreneurship—in Five Charts," *Washington Post*, February 12, 2015. https://www.washingtonpost.com/news/on -small-business/wp/2015/02/12/the-decline-of-american-entrepreneurship-in-five -charts/?utm_term=.1392d11fe67c

52. Daniel Bell, *The Coming of Post-Industrial Society: A Venture in Social Forecasting* (New York: Basic Books, 1976), p. 361.

53. Quoted in Matt Continetti, "The Managers vs. the Managed," *Weekly Standard*, September 21, 2015. http://www.weeklystandard.com/the-managers-vs.-the -managed/article/1028522

54. See Natalie Goodnow, "'The Bell Curve' 20 years later: A Q&A with Charles Murray," AEIdeas (American Enterprise Institute), October 16, 2014. http://www.aei .org/publication/bell-curve-20-years-later-qa-charles-murray/

55. Adam Liptak, "An Exit Interview with Richard Posner, Judicial Provocateur," *New York Times*, September 11, 2017. https://www.nytimes.com/2017/09/11/us/politics/ judge-richard-posner-retirement.html?_r=0

56. David Brooks, "How We Are Ruining America," *New York Times*, July 11, 2017. https://www.nytimes.com/2017/07/11/opinion/how-we-are-ruining-america.html

10: TRIBALISM TODAY

1. Barack Obama, "Remarks Following the New Hampshire Primary—January 8, 2008," American Presidency Project, John Woolley and Gerhard Peters, eds. http:// www.presidency.ucsb.edu/ws/index.php?pid=62272

2. Peter Schramm, "American by Choice," *Weekly Standard*, June 27, 2007. http:// www.weeklystandard.com/article/14917

3.   *Chae Chan Ping v. United States*, Legal Information Institute, Cornell Law School. https://www.law.cornell.edu/supremecourt/text/130/581

4.   Mark Lilla, "The End of Identity Liberalism," *New York Times*, November 18, 2016. https://www.nytimes.com/2016/11/20/opinion/sunday/the-end-of-identity-liberalism .html?mcubz=1

5.   University of Wisconsin-Madison offers a "Problem of Whiteness" course: http:// www.cnn.com/2016/12/23/health/college-course-white-controversy-irpt-trnd/ index.html. Carl Sandburg College outlaws "disparaging comments": http://www .campusreform.org/?ID=9455. Salon declares that white men must be stopped: http://www.salon.com/2015/12/22/white_men_must_be_stopped_the_very _future_of_the_planet_depends_on_it_partner/. Feminist geographers warn against citing too many white men: http://www.nationalreview.com/article/ 449507/feminist-geographers-warn-against-citing-too-many-white-men-scholarly -articles. King's College in the U.K. replaces portraits of bearded white scholars with a "wall of diversity": http://www.telegraph.co.uk/education/2017/07/14/top-uk -university-replaces-busts-portraits-bearded-white-scholars/. Culture and gender- studies researcher argues that Newtonian physics hurts minorities: http://www .nationalreview.com/article/448102/quantum-physics-oppressive-marginalized -people. Oxford University declares that avoiding eye contact is racist: http://www .telegraph.co.uk/education/2017/04/22/students-avoid-making-eye-contact-could -guiltyof-racism-oxford/. Elite Manhattan grade school teaches students that they are born racist: http://nypost.com/2016/07/01/elite-k-8-school-teaches-white -students-theyre-born-racist/

6.   Ibram Rogers, "'Merit Plea' Inherently Racist as Argument Against Affirmative Action," Diverse Education, November 19, 2012. http://diverseeducation.com/ article/49589/

7.   Ian Schwartz, "Van Jones: Republicans Who Want a Colorblind Meritocracy Have a Racial 'Blind Spot,'" RealClearPolitics, December 5, 2016. https://www .realclearpolitics.com/video/2016/12/05/van_jones_republicans_who_want_a _colorblind_meritocracy_have_a_racial_blind_spot.html

8.   *Anderson Cooper 360 Degrees*, CNN Transcripts, August 2, 2017. http://transcripts .cnn.com/TRANSCRIPTS/1708/02/acd.01.html

9.   Lauren Rankin, "Colorblindness Is the New Racism," PolicyMic, July 22, 2013. https://mic.com/articles/55867/colorblindness-is-the-new-racism#.rqbARSvWO

10.   Adia Harvey Wingfield, "Color-Blindness Is Counterproductive," *Atlantic*, Septem- ber 13, 2015. http://www.theatlantic.com/politics/archive/2015/09/color-blindness -is-counterproductive/405037/

11.   Zach Stafford, "When You Say You 'Don't See Race,' You're Ignoring Racism, Not Helping Solve It," *Guardian*, January 26, 2015. https://www.theguardian.com/com mentisfree/2015/jan/26/do-not-see-race-ignoring-racism-not-helping

12.   Ta-Nehisi Coates, *Between the World and Me* (New York: Spiegel & Grau, 2015), p. 50.

13.   Ibid., p. 10.

14.   Ibid., p. 6.

15.   Ibid., throughout; see, for example, p. 66.

16.   Ibid., p. 42.

17.   Dana Bash and Emily Sherman, "Sotomayor's 'Wise Latina' Comment a Staple of Her Speeches," CNN, June 8, 2009. http://www.cnn.com/2009/POLITICS/06/05/ sotomayor.speeches/

18. Wendy Doniger, "All Beliefs Welcome, Unless They Are Forced on Others," On Faith. https://www.onfaith.co/onfaith/2008/09/09/all-beliefs-welcome-unless-the/578

19. There are many variables at play. Men tend to gravitate toward more dangerous work—construction, mining, logging, etc.—which is why men accounted for 92.3 percent of workplace fatalities in 2014. Men also work longer hours than women, no doubt in part because of the unequal division of labor when it comes to raising children. For more on this, see Mark J. Perry, "Some Thoughts on Equal Pay Day and the 23 Percent Gender Pay Gap Myth," AEIdeas (American Enterprise Institute), April 11, 2016. http://www.aei.org/publication/some-thoughts-on-equal-pay-day-and-the-23-gender-pay-gap-myth/

20. "Cracking the Gender Code: Get 3x MORE Women in Computing," Accenture and Girls Who Code, p. 3. https://www.accenture.com/t20161018T094638__w__/us-en/_acnmedia/Accenture/next-gen-3/girls-who-code/Accenture-Cracking-The-Gender-Code-Report.pdf

21. Scott Alexander, "Contra Grant on Exaggerated Differences," Slate Star Codex, August 7, 2017. http://slatestarcodex.com/2017/08/07/contra-grant-on-exaggerated-differences/

22. Christine Rosen, "You Will Not Think Outside the Box," *Commentary*, September 2017. https://www.commentarymagazine.com/articles/you-will-not-think-outside-box/

23. Nancy P. McKee and Linda Stone, *Gender and Culture in America*, 3rd edition (New York: Sloan Publishing, 2007), p. 7.

24. Jessica Neuwirth, *Equal Means Equal: Why the Time for an Equal Rights Amendment Is Now* (New York: New Press, 2015), p. 88. For a rousing rebuttal to both arguments, see Christina Villegas, "The Modern Feminist Rejection of Constitutional Government," Heritage Foundation, August 8, 2016. http://www.heritage.org/political-process/report/the-modern-feminist-rejection-constitutional-government#_ftnref22

25. Stanley Fish, *There's No Such Thing as Free Speech: And It's a Good Thing, Too* (New York: Oxford University Press, 1994), p. 19.

26. Quoted in Daniel A. Farber and Suzanna Sherry, *Beyond All Reason: The Radical Assault on Truth in American Law* (New York: Oxford University Press, 1997), p. 25.

27. Raymond Aron, *The Opium of the Intellectuals* (New Brunswick, NJ: Transaction, 2011 [1957]), p. 26.

28. Isabel Knight, "Students Share Mixed Responses to George/West Collection," *Daily Gazette* (Swarthmore), February 13, 2014. http://daily.swarthmore.edu/2014/02/13/students-share-mixed-responses-to-georgewest-collection/

29. Sandra Y. L. Korn, "The Doctrine of Academic Freedom," *Harvard Crimson*, February 18, 2014. http://www.thecrimson.com/column/the-red-line/article/2014/2/18/academic-freedom-justice/?page=single#

30. Hank Berrien, "Yale Students Scream to Block Free Speech," *Daily Wire*, November 11, 2015. http://www.dailywire.com/news/1041/yale-students-scream-block-free-speech-hank-berrien

31. There is a rich tradition of this kind of writing, especially on the right, going back decades, starting with William F. Buckley's *God and Man at Yale*, running through *The Closing of the American Mind* by Allan Bloom and *Tenured Radicals* by Roger Kimball, and in full bloom today with such works as *Sex and God at Yale* by Nathaniel Harden, *End of Discussion* by Guy Benson and Mary Katherine Ham,

Silenced by Kirsten Powers, *The Victims' Revolution* by Bruce Bawer, *The Intimidation Game* by Kimberely Strassel, and many, many more.

32. See Charlotte Allen,"King of Fearmongers," *Weekly Standard,* April 15, 2013. http://www.weeklystandard.com/king-of-fearmongers/article/714573

33. See "ADL Report: Anti-Semitic Targeting of Journalists During the 2016 Presidential Campaign; A Report from ADL's Task Force on Harassment and Journalism," Anti-Defamation League, October 19, 2016, p. 6. https://www.adl.org/sites/default/files/documents/assets/pdf/press-center/CR_4862_Journalism-Task-Force_v2.pdf

34. Tariq Nasheed, Twitter, September 14, 2017. https://twitter.com/tariqnasheed/status/908463507246522368?lang=en. Tweets also available here, in case Mr. Nasheed ever removes them: https://twitchy.com/dougp-3137/2017/09/14/wait-what-tariq-nasheeds-take-on-how-ben-shapiro-masks-racist-rhetoric-sends-heads-to-desks/

35. Ayaan Hirsi Ali, "Why Is the Southern Poverty Law Center Targeting Liberals?," *New York Times*, August 24, 2017. https://www.nytimes.com/2017/08/24/opinion/southern-poverty-law-center-liberals-islam.html?mcubz=1

36. As one college student wrote: "In other words, punching someone in the face and making racist comments about them are similarly perceived by the brain, activating many of the same pain receptors. And it's clear from recent events that many UCLA students have been getting punched in the face." Keshav Tadimeti, "Hurtful, Discriminatory Comments Should Not Be Defended as Free Speech," *Daily Bruin*, May 16, 2016. http://dailybruin.com/2016/05/16/keshav-tadimeti-hurtful-discriminatory-comments-should-not-be-defended-as-free-speech/

37. Jencey Paz, "Hurt at Home," *Yale Herald*, November 6, 2015, removed since original publication but still available here: http://web.archive.org/web/20151107010454/http://yaleherald.com/op-eds/hurt-at-home/

38. Jonathan Holloway, "An Announcement from Campus," Yale College, April 28, 2016. http://yalecollege.yale.edu/deans-office/messages/announcement-campus

39. Some available organizations include: Learning and Interactive Vietnamese Experience; Asian American Students Alliance; Asian American Studies Task Force; Association of Native Americans at Yale, Undergraduate Organization; India at Yale; IvyQ (as in "Queer"); Japanese Undergraduate Students at Yale; Latina Women at Yale; Liberal Party; Reproductive Rights Action League at Yale; Sex and Sexuality Week Planning Board; Undergraduate First Generation Low Income Partnership; Women in Physics; Women's Leadership Initiative at Yale; Yale Queer+Asian; Yale Urban Collective; Black Solidarity Conference at Yale; Yale Women's Center; Yale Southeast Asian Movement; Q (again, as in "Queer") Magazine; Alliance for Southeast Asian Students; Arab Students Association; Association of Salvadoreñas at Yale Undergraduate; Black Student Alliance at Yale; Brazil Club; Canadian Students' Association at Yale [Talk about safe spaces!]; Chinese American Students' Association; Chinese Undergraduate Students at Yale; Club Colombia; Club of Argentine Students at Yale; Club of Romanian Students at Yale; Cuban-American Undergraduate Students' Association; Despierta Boricua, the Puerto Rican Student Organization at Yale; DisOrient; Eritrean and Ethiopian Student Association at Yale; In the Q[as in "Queer"]loset; Japanese American Students Union; Kasama: The Filipino Club at Yale; Korean American Students at Yale; La Revolucion; La Société Française; Lo Stivale; Malaysian and Singaporean Association; Organization for Racial and Ethnic Openness; Russian Cultural Club; Sisters of All Nations; South Asian Society; Southeastern European Society; Student Association of Thais at Yale; Students of Nigeria; Swiss Students and Affiliates at Yale; Taiwanese American Society; German Society of Undergraduates

at Yale University; Polish Students' Society of Yale College; Vietnamese Student Association; Yale African Students Association; Yale Black Women's Coalition; Yale British Undergraduates; Yale Caribbean Students' Organization; Yale College Black Men's Students Union; Yale College Student Czech and Slovak Society; Yale Dominican Student Association; Yale European Undergraduates; Yale Friends of Turkey; Yale Hawaii Institute; Yale Kala; Yale LGBTQ Cooperative; Yale Mexican Student Organization; Yale Scandinavian Society; Yale Undergraduate Portuguese Association; Lesbian, Gay, Bisexual, Transgender, and Queer+ Activism Collective; Margin: Student Perspectives from the Left; Middle Eastern Resolution through Education, Action & Dialogue; Party of the Left; Students for Justice in Palestine; and Yale NAACP.

40. See Rosalie Pedalino Porter, "The Case Against Bilingual Education," *Atlantic*, May 1998, https://www.theatlantic.com/magazine/archive/1998/05/the-case-against -bilingual-education/305426/; Peter J. Duignan, "Bilingual Education: A Critique," Hoover Institution. http://www.hoover.org/research/bilingual-education-critique

41. Lani Guinier, *Tyranny of the Majority: Fundamental Fairness in Representative Democracy* (New York: Free Press, 1994), pp. 5–6.

42. Lani Guinier, "The Triumph of Tokenism: The Voting Rights Act and the Theory of Black Electoral Success," *Michigan Law Review* 89, no. 5 (March 1991), p. 1108.

43. Ibid., p. 1103.

44. Ibid., p. 1107.

45. Paul Gigot, "Hillary's Choice on Civil Rights: Back to the Future," *Wall Street Journal*, May 10, 1993.

46. Yanan Wang, "A Course Originally Called 'The Problem of Whiteness' Returns to Arizona State," *Washington Post*, November 12, 2015. https://www.washingtonpost .com/news/morning-mix/wp/2015/11/12/a-course-originally-called-the-problem -of-whiteness-returns-to-asu-as-racial-tensions-boil-over-on-campuses/?utm _term=.6127c9c2182f

47. Preston Mitchum, Twitter, July 23, 2017. https://twitter.com/PrestonMitchum/ status/889165691529637888

48. Alia Wong, "Asian Americans and the Future of Affirmative Action," *Atlantic*, June 28, 2016. http://www.theatlantic.com/education/archive/2016/06/asian-americans -and-the-future-of-affirmative-action/489023/

49. "The Model Minority Is Losing Patience," *Economist*, October 3, 2015. http:// www.economist.com/news/briefing/21669595-asian-americans-are-united-states -most-successful-minority-they-are-complaining-ever

50. Lee Bollinger, "Pro: Diversity Is Essential," *Newsweek*, January 26, 2003. http:// www.newsweek.com/pro-diversity-essential-135143

51. Lyndon B. Johnson, "Commencement Address at Howard University: 'To Fulfill These Rights'—June 4, 1965," American Presidency Project, John Woolley and Gerhard Peters, eds. http://www.presidency.ucsb.edu/ws/index.php?pid=27021&st =Howard+University&st1=

52. Amy Wax and Larry Alexander, "Paying the Price for Breakdown of the Country's Bourgeois Culture," *Philadelphia Inquirer*, August 9, 2017. http://www.philly.com/ philly/opinion/commentary/paying-the-price-for-breakdown-of-the-countrys -bourgeois-culture-20170809.html

53. Penn Alumni & Students, "Guest Column by 54 Penn Students & Alumni: Statement on Amy Wax and Charlottesville," *Daily Pennsylvanian*, August 21, 2017. http://www.thedp.com/article/2017/08/guest-column-amy-wax-charlottesville

54. Jonathan V. Last, "Weekly Standard: Obamacare vs. the Catholics," NPR, February 7,

2012. http://www.npr.org/2012/02/07/146511839/weekly-standard-obamacare-vs-the-catholics

55. Chris Murphy, Twitter, July 28, 2017. https://twitter.com/ChrisMurphyCT/status/890924515999526912

56. "The Constitution of Japan," Prime Minister of Japan and His Cabinet. http://japan.kantei.go.jp/constitution_and_government_of_japan/constitution_e.html

57. Emma Green, "Bernie Sanders's Religious Tests for Christians in Public Office," *Atlantic*, June 8, 2017. https://www.theatlantic.com/politics/archive/2017/06/bernie-sanders-chris-van-hollen-russell-vought/529614/

58. Muslims believe that Jews and Christians who never heard the message of Muhammad—and who lead righteous lives—will go to heaven. Christians who have heard the Muslim message may still go to heaven so long as they believe that there is only one God. But if they reject the message of Muhammad, they are damned. See Camila Domonoske, "Is It Hateful to Believe in Hell? Bernie Sanders' Questions Prompt Backlash," NPR, June 9, 2017. http://www.npr.org/sections/thetwo-way/2017/06/09/532116365/is-it-hateful-to-believe-in-hell-bernie-sanders-questions-prompt-backlash

59. Sohrab Ahmari, "The Dogma of Dianne Feinstein," *New York Times*, September 11, 2017. https://www.nytimes.com/2017/09/11/opinion/the-dogma-of-dianne-feinstein.html?mcubz=1

60. "New PRRI/The Atlantic Survey Analysis Finds Cultural Displacement—Not Economic Hardship—More Predictive of White Working-Class Support for Trump," Public Religion Research Institute, May 9, 2017. https://www.prri.org/press-release/white-working-class-attitudes-economy-trade-immigration-election-donald-trump/

61. See, for example, Brenda Major et al., "The Threat of Increasing Diversity: Why Many White Americans Support Trump in the 2016 Election," *Group Processes & Intergroup Relations*, October 20, 2016. http://journals.sagepub.com/doi/pdf/10.1177/1368430216677304

62. Franklin D. Roosevelt, "Acceptance Speech for the Renomination for the Presidency, Philadelphia, Pa.—June 27, 1936," American Presidency Project, John Woolley and Gerhard Peters, eds. http://www.presidency.ucsb.edu/ws/?pid=15314

63. Max Roser, "Life Expectancy," Our World in Data. https://ourworldindata.org/life-expectancy

64. Max Roser, "Child Labor," Our World in Data. https://ourworldindata.org/child-labor/

65. Max Roser, "Life Expectancy."

66. Robert Nozick, *Anarchy, State, and Utopia* (New York: Basic Books, 2013 [1974]), p. 163.

11: POP CULTURE POLITICS

1. William Blake, "Chapter IX," *The [First] Book of Urizen*, 1794, Bartleby.com. http://www.bartleby.com/235/259.html

2. Max Weber, "Science as a Vocation," 1918. See p. 15 of http://anthropos-lab.net/wp/wp-content/uploads/2011/12/Weber-Science-as-a-Vocation.pdf. From H. H. Gerth and C. Wright Mills (trans. and eds.), *Max Weber: Essays in Sociology* (New York: Oxford University Press, 1946), pp. 129–56.

3. Tim Blanning, in his excellent book *The Romantic Revolution: A History*, Modern Library Chronicles (New York: Random House, 2011, Kindle edition), gives a brief history of just how elusive definitions of romanticism have been.

4.   Isaiah Berlin, *The Roots of Romanticism,* A. W. Mellon Lectures in the Fine Arts (Princeton, NJ: Princeton University Press, 1999 [1965]), p. 1.

5.   Blanning, *The Romantic Revolution,* Kindle location 281-90.

6.   David Brooks, *Bobos in Paradise: The New Upper Class and How They Got There* (New York: Simon & Schuster, 2010, Kindle edition), p. 67.

7.   "Whatever we may think about the merits or demerits of the movement usually dubbed Romanticism," he continues, "it certainly conveyed a deeper understanding of pre-capitalist society and of historical evolution in general and thus revealed some of the fundamental errors of utilitarianism and of the political theory for which utilitarianism served as base." Joseph A. Schumpeter, *Capitalism, Socialism and Democracy,* 3rd edition (New York: Harper Perennial Modern Thought, 2008 [1942]), p. 249.

8.   William Blake, "Auguries of Innocence," Poetry Foundation. https://www.poetry foundation.org/poems/43650/auguries-of-innocence

9.   See Richard Kieckhefer, "The Specific Rationality of Medieval Magic," *Historical Review* 99, no. 3 (June 1994), pp. 813-36; Gregory W. Dawes, "The Rationality of Renaissance Magic," *Parergon,* July 1, 2013; Valerie I. J. Flint, *The Rise of Magic in Early Medieval Europe* (Princeton, NJ: Princeton University Press, 1991).

10. On this point I heartily recommend Nobel Prize-winning psychologist Daniel Kahneman's *Thinking, Fast and Slow* (New York: Farrar, Straus and Giroux, 2011). He surveys a lifetime of research showing the innumerable ways our animal brain can mislead the human mind.

11. Maureen Cleave, "The John Lennon I Knew," *Telegraph,* October 5, 2005. http://www.telegraph.co.uk/culture/music/Rockandjazzmusic/3646983/The-John-Lennon-I-knew.html

12. Joe Bosso,"The Edge Interview: Memory Man," *Guitar World,* November 10, 2008. http://www.guitarworld.com/edge-u2-interview-memory-man

13. Victor Hugo, *William Shakespeare,* Part I, Book II, Chapter IV. https://archive.org/stream/williamshakespea00hugouoft/williamshakespea00hugouoft_djvu.txt

14. Nietzsche did say in *Thus Sprach Zarathustra*: "I would believe only in a God who could dance. One must still have chaos in oneself to be able to give birth to a dancing star," which does have a decidedly pantheist vibration to it. Friedrich Nietzsche, "VII. Reading and Writing," *Thus Sprach Zarathustra.* http://www.gutenberg.org/cache/epub/1998/pg1998.txt

15. Martha Bayless, *Hole in Our Soul: The Loss of Beauty and Meaning in American Popular Music* (Chicago: University of Chicago Press), p. 36.

16. Susan J. Wolfson, " 'This Is My Lightning' or, Sparks in the Air," *Studies in English Literature 1500-1900,* 55, no. 4 (Autumn 2015), p. 751.

17. B. F. Schonland, "Wilkins Lecture: Benjamin Franklin: Natural Philosopher," *Proceedings of the Royal Society of London* 235, no. 1203 (Series A, Mathematical, Physical, and Engineering Sciences, June 12, 1956), pp. 433-44: "Before he had heard about it Franklin was acclaimed in Europe as the modern Prometheus. The discovery was later described by Joseph Priestley, himself no mean judge of scientific experiment, as 'the greatest, perhaps, that has been made in the whole compass of philosophy since the time of Sir Isaac Newton.' The effect on the public mind was awe-inspiring and can be compared to that produced in our own time by the explosion of the atom bomb."

18. Chieko Tsuneoka, "A New Godzilla Faces a More Nationalistic Japan," *Wall Street Journal,* September 4, 2016. http://www.wsj.com/articles/a-new-godzilla-faces-a-more-nationalistic-japan-1472834845

19. William M. Tsutsui, "Review: *Shin Godzilla*," *ArkansasOnline*, October 7, 2016. http://www.arkansasonline.com/news/2016/oct/07/shin-godzilla-20161007/?f=entertainment

20. Tsuneoka, "A New Godzilla Faces a More Nationalistic Japan."

21. William Peter Blatty, "*The Exorcist* Script—Dialogue Transcript," 1973. http://www.script-o-rama.com/movie_scripts/e/exorcist-script-transcript-blatty-friedkin.html

22. William Peter Blatty, *The Exorcist* (New York: HarperCollins, 2011 [1971]), p. 345.

23. As Thomas Hibbs has noted, "Rather than straight horror, *The Exorcist* should be grouped with a number of classic Seventies dramas, films such as *Deliverance*, *Taxi Driver*, and *Chinatown* that disclose the chaos and evil lurking just beneath the surface of civilization. Both the book and the film are intimately connected to the cultural upheaval of the late 1960s; the film within the film that brings Chris MacNeil to Georgetown features a campus antiwar protest." Thomas Hibbs, "*The Exorcist* at 40," *National Review* online, October 31, 2013. http://www.nationalreview.com/article/362662/exorcist-40-thomas-hibbs

24. Helen Childress, "*Reality Bites* Script—Dialogue Transcript," 1994. http://www.script-o-rama.com/movie_scripts/r/reality-bites-script-transcript-stiller.html

25. Alan Ball, *American Beauty*, 1999. http://www.dailyscript.com/scripts/American Beauty_final.html

26. "*Point Break*: Quotes," IMDB. http://www.imdb.com/title/tt0102685/quotes

27. John Steinbeck, *The Grapes of Wrath* (New York: Penguin Books, 2006 [1939]), p. 33.

28. "*Mr. Robot* (2015–): Quotes," IMDB. http://www.imdb.com/title/tt4158110/quotes

29. Ibid.

30. "*Fight Club* (1999): Quotes," IMDB. http://www.imdb.com/title/tt0137523/quotes

31. Tom Schulman, "*Dead Poets Society*: Final Script," 1989. http://www.dailyscript.com/scripts/dead_poets_final.html

32. Kevin J. H. Dettmar, "*Dead Poets Society* Is a Terrible Defense of the Humanities," *Atlantic*, February 19, 2014. http://www.theatlantic.com/education/archive/2014/02/-em-dead-poets-society-em-is-a-terrible-defense-of-the-humanities/283853/

33. Berlin, *The Roots of Romanticism*, p. 12.

34. Ibid.

35. Carlyle fawned over Muhammad because, in Berlin's words, the prophet was "an elemental force, that he lives an intense life, that he has a great many followers with him; that something elemental occurred, a tremendous phenomenon, that there was a great and moving episode in the life of mankind, which Muhammad represents. The importance of Muhammad is his character and not his beliefs. The question of whether what Muhammad believed was true or false would have appeared to Carlyle perfectly irrelevant." Ibid., p. 13.

36. Allan Bloom notes in *The Closing of the American Mind* how so many of his left-leaning peers admire terrorists because of their commitment to radical self-assertion. Indeed, explain to a typical college student who wears a Che Guevara T-shirt that he is lionizing a cold-blooded murderer and he will roll his eyes. Guevara's appeal stems from his commitment to his cause. One finds echoes of this thinking in countless apologias to terrorists around the world: "At least they believe something!" Or, as Walter puts it in *The Big Lebowski*: "Say what you will about the tenets of national socialism. At least it's an ethos."

37. Compare the well-known Latin maxim *Fiat justitia ruat caelum*, or "Let justice be done though the heavens fall."

38. See Jonah Goldberg, "Life and Death on Basic Cable," *National Review* 65, no. 15, August 19, 2013. https://www.nationalreview.com/nrd/articles/354946/life-and -death-basic-cable

39. Paul MacInnes, "*Breaking Bad* Creator Vince Gilligan: The Man Who Turned Walter White from Mr. Chips into Scarface," *Guardian*, May 18, 2012. https://www .theguardian.com/tv-and-radio/2012/may/19/vince-gilligan-breaking-bad

40. See Jonah Goldberg, "Empty Integrity," *National Review* 66, no. 21, November 17, 2014. http://www.nationalreview.com/article/392395/empty-integrity-jonah-goldberg

41. Samuel Taylor Coleridge, "Chapter XIV," *Biographia Literaria*. http://www.english .upenn.edu/~mgamer/Etexts/biographia.html

42. See, for example, *They Live* or "A Most Unusual Camera" from *The Twilight Zone*.

12: THE FAMILY'S LOSING WAR AGAINST BARBARISM

1. Joseph A. Schumpeter, "The March into Socialism," *American Economic Review Papers and Proceedings of the Sixty-Second Annual Meeting of the American Economic Association* 40, no. 2 (May 1950), p. 450. (This was the last thing Schumpeter worked on during his lifetime. He died with it all but completed; it was finished by his wife.)

2. Nicholas Wade, *Before the Dawn: Recovering the Lost History of Our Ancestors* (New York: Penguin, 2007, Kindle edition), p. 169.

3. Ibid.

4. Joseph Henrich, Robert Boyd, and Peter J. Richerson, "The Puzzle of Monogamous Marriage," *Philosophical Transactions of the Royal Society B: Biological Sciences*, March 5, 2012, pp. 657–69. https://www.ncbi.nlm.nih.gov/pmc/articles/ PMC3260845/

5. Eric D. Gould et al., "The Mystery of Monogamy," *American Economic Review* 98, no. 1 (March 2008), pp. 333–34.

6. Robin Fox, *The Tribal Imagination: Civilization and the Savage Mind* (Cambridge, MA: Harvard University Press, 2011), p. 49.

7. Susan Dominus, "Is an Open Marriage a Happier Marriage?," *New York Times Magazine*, May 11, 2017. https://www.nytimes.com/2017/05/11/magazine/is-an -open-marriage-a-happier-marriage.html?mcubz=1&_r=0

8. Kathleen Doheny, "The Truth About Open Marriage," WebMD. http://www .webmd.com/sex-relationships/features/the-truth-about-open-marriage#1

9. W. Bradford Wilcox, "The Evolution of Divorce," *National Affairs*, Fall 2009. http:// www.nationalaffairs.com/publications/detail/the-evolution-of-divorce. I am deeply indebted to Wilcox's scholarship for much of my discussion of divorce.

10. Ibid., citing Barbara Dafoe Whitehead, *The Divorce Culture: Rethinking Our Commitments to Marriage and Family* (New York: Vintage Books, 1998).

11. Wilcox, "The Evolution of Divorce."

12. Wade F. Horn, "Wedding Bell Blues: Marriage and Welfare Reform," Brookings Institution, June 1, 2001. https://www.brookings.edu/articles/wedding-bell-blues -marriage-and-welfare-reform/

13. See "Table 15. Births and Birth Rates for Unmarried Women, by Age and Race and Hispanic Origin of Mother: United States, 2015," in *National Vital Statistics Reports* 66, no. 1 (January 5, 2017). https://www.cdc.gov/nchs/data/nvsr/nvsr66/ nvsr66_01.pdf. See also George A. Akerlof and Janet L. Yellen, "An Analysis of Out -of-Wedlock Births in the United States," Brookings Policy Brief Series, Brookings Institution, August 1, 1996. https://www.brookings.edu/research/an-analysis-of -out-of-wedlock-births-in-the-united-states/

14. Wilcox, "The Evolution of Divorce."

15. Due credit to Ben Shapiro for this pithy formulation.

16. W. Bradford Wilcox et al., "Mobility and Money in U.S. States: The Marriage Effect," Social Mobility Papers, Brookings Institution, December 7, 2015. https://www.brookings.edu/research/mobility-and-money-in-u-s-states-the-marriage-effect/ (quoting Sara McLanahan and Isabel Sawhill, "Marriage and Child Wellbeing Revisited: Introducing the Issue," *The Future of Children* 25, no. 2 [special issue: "Marriage and Child Wellbeing Revisited" [Fall 2015], p. 4).

17. Wilcox, "The Evolution of Divorce."

18. Andrew Cherlin, *The Marriage Go-Round: The State of Marriage* (New York: Vintage Books, 2009), pp. 5-6.

19. Steven Pinker, *The Blank Slate: The Modern Denial of Human Nature* (New York: Penguin, Kindle edition), p. 165.

20. Nicholas Zill, "The Paradox of Adoption," Institute for Family Studies, October 7, 2015. https://ifstudies.org/blog/the-paradox-of-adoption/

21. Pinker, *The Blank Slate*, p. 165.

22. Suzanne Woolley, "This Is How Much Your Kids Are Worth," Bloomberg Business, August 28, 2017. https://www.bloomberg.com/amp/news/articles/2017-08-28/this-is-the-best-long-term-care-insurance

23. Isabel V. Sawhill, "Beyond Marriage," *New York Times*, September 13, 2014. https://www.nytimes.com/2014/09/14/opinion/sunday/beyond-marriage.html?_r=0

24. W. Bradford Wilcox et al., "Strong Families, Prosperous States: Do Healthy Families Affect the Wealth of States?," American Enterprise Institute, October 19, 2015. http://www.aei.org/publication/strong-families-prosperous-states/

25. Jim Tankersley, "Why States with More Marriages Are Richer States," *Washington Post*, October 20, 2015. https://www.washingtonpost.com/news/wonk/wp/2015/10/20/why-states-with-more-marriages-are-richer-states/?utm_term=.9d08e445e746

26. Bryan Caplan, "What Is the Male Marriage Premium?," Library of Economics and Liberty, February 28, 2012. http://econlog.econlib.org/archives/2012/02/what_is_the_mar.html

27. See Pascal-Emmanuel Gobry, "Finally, Economists Acknowledge That They're Biased," *Forbes*, March 18, 2013. https://www.forbes.com/sites/pascalemmanuelgobry/2013/03/18/finally-economists-acknowledge-that-theyre-biased/#6543da0f1f57

    For males, the premium is 44 percent for marriage and only 34 percent for college. See Bryan Caplan, "The College Premium vs. the Marriage Premium: A Case of Double Standards," Library of Economics and Liberty, January 23, 2012. http://econlog.econlib.org/archives/2012/01/the_college_pre.html

28. See Gobry, "Finally, Economists Acknowledge That They're Biased."

29. Ron Haskins, "Three Simple Rules Poor Teens Should Follow to Join the Middle Class," Brookings Institution, March 13, 2013. https://www.brookings.edu/opinions/three-simple-rules-poor-teens-should-follow-to-join-the-middle-class/

30. Annie Kim, "Why Is Marriage Thriving Among (and Only Among) the Affluent?," *Washington Monthly*, March/April/May 2016. http://washingtonmonthly.com/magazine/maraprmay-2016/why-is-marriage-thriving-among-and-only-among-the-affluent/

31. Ibid.

32. Kim Parker and Renee Stepler, "As U.S. Marriage Rate Hovers at 50%, Education Gap in Marital Status Widens," Pew Research Center, September 14, 2017.

http://www.pewresearch.org/fact-tank/2017/09/14/as-u-s-marriage-rate-hovers-at
-50-education-gap-in-marital-status-widens/?utm_content=buffer2c241&utm
_medium=social&utm_source=facebook.com&utm_campaign=buffer

33. Jason DeParle, "Two Classes in America, Divided by I Do," *New York Times*, July
14, 2012. http://www.nytimes.com/2012/07/15/us/two-classes-in-america-divided
-by-i-do.html

34. See Milton Kurland, "Romantic Love and Economic Considerations: A Cultural
Comparison," *Journal of Educational Sociology* 27, no. 2 (October 1953), pp. 72-79;
Charles Lindholm, "Romantic Love and Anthropology," *Etnofoor* 19, no. 1 (2006),
pp. 5-21; Robert Levine et al., "Love and Marriage in Eleven Cultures," *Journal of
Cross-Cultural Psychology* 26, no. 5 (September 1995).

35. See Courtland Milloy, "Why Is Baseball Striking Out in the Black Community?,"
Washington Post, October 30, 2012. https://www.washingtonpost.com/local/
why-is-baseball-striking-out-in-the-black-community/2012/10/30/57fa1aca-22c
7-11e2-ac85-e669876c6a24_story.html?utm_term=.955c36217479. See also Mark
Armour and Daniel R. Levitt, "Baseball Demographics, 1947-2016," Society for
American Baseball Research. http://sabr.org/bioproj/topic/baseball-demograph
ics-1947-2012

36. See Barbara Dafoe Whitehead, "Dan Quayle Was Right," *Atlantic*, April 1993.
https://www.theatlantic.com/magazine/archive/1993/04/dan-quayle-was-right
/307015/

37. Joseph A. Schumpeter, *Capitalism, Socialism and Democracy*, 3rd edition (New
York: Harper Perennial Modern Thought, 2008 [1942]), p. 157.

13: THE TRUMPIAN ERA

1. Deirdre N. McCloskey, "Creative Destruction vs. the New Industrial State: Review
of McCraw and Galbraith," *Reason* (October 2007). Accessed via http://www.deir
dremccloskey.com/articles/galbraith.php

2. Franklin Delano Roosevelt, "4—State of the Union Message to Congress—January
11, 1944," American Presidency Project, John Woolley and Gerhard Peters, eds.
http://www.presidency.ucsb.edu/ws/?pid=16518

3. Lincoln Steffens, *The Autobiography of Lincoln Steffens, Volume II: Muckraking/
Revolution/Seeing America at Last* (New York: Harcourt, Brace & World, 1931),
p. 799. The line was later cleaned up and memorialized as "I've seen the future, and
it works."

4. In *Liberal Fascism*, I chronicle the infatuation the American progressive intellectuals had for governments that were willing to "experiment" with new and exciting
alternatives to liberal democratic capitalism. For instance, Rexford Guy Tugwell,
an influential member of FDR's Brain Trust, said of Italian Fascism, "It's the clean-
est, neatest, most efficiently operating piece of social machinery I've ever seen. It
makes me envious." "We are trying out the economics of Fascism without having
suffered all its social or political ravages," proclaimed the *New Republic*'s editor
George Soule, an enthusiastic supporter of the FDR administration. Stuart Chase,
the man who helped popularize the term "a New Deal," marveled how the Soviets
weren't guided by a "hungry group of stockholders" but were "informed by battal-
ions of statistics" and party bosses who had "no further incentive than the burning
zeal to create a new heaven and new earth which flames in the great of every good
Communist." As for the people being force-marched into this new order? What
of them? "The mass of peasants," Tugwell wrote of the Russian people, are not "to
be blamed for having dimly seen that the necessities for racial advance required

a drastic change, and for bringing it about—with ruthlessness if need be." Chase ended his book *A New Deal* asking, "Why should the Russians have all the fun of remaking a world?" Since my book remains anathema for some, for those interested in learning more, I recommend *Mussolini and Fascism: The View from America* by John Patrick Diggins, *Three New Deals: Reflections on Roosevelt's America, Mussolini's Italy, and Hitler's Germany, 1933–1939* by Wolfgang Schivelbusch, *The Forgotten Man* by Amity Shlaes, and the seminal 1962 essay "American Travelers to the Soviet Union 1917–32: The Formation of a Component of New Deal Ideology" by Lewis S. Feuer in the *American Quarterly*.

5. See, for example, William Easterly's *The Tyranny of Experts: Economists, Dictators, and the Forgotten Rights of the Poor* (New York: Basic Books, 2013) and his *The White Man's Burden: Why the West's Efforts to Aid the Rest Have Done So Much Ill and So Little Good* (New York: Oxford University Press, 2006). Also I highly recommend this discussion on Russell Robert's indispensable podcast "Econtalk": http://www.econtalk.org/archives/2011/05/easterly_on_ben.html

6. William Easterly, "Benevolent Autocrats," *National Bureau of Economic Research* (working paper), August 2011. https://williameasterly.files.wordpress.com/2011/05/benevolent-autocrats-easterly-2nd-draft.pdf

7. "Singapore Has Highest Death Penalty Rate," Associated Press, January 14, 2004. http://www.nbcnews.com/id/3958717/ns/world_news/t/singapore-has-highest-death-penalty-rate/#.WcFTprKGNhE

8. Thomas L. Friedman, "Our One-Party Democracy," *New York Times*, September 8, 2009. http://www.nytimes.com/2009/09/09/opinion/09friedman.html

9. Thomas L. Friedman, "The Power of Green," *New York Times Magazine*, April 15, 2007. http://www.nytimes.com/2007/04/15/magazine/15green.t.html

10. Donald J. Trump, "58—Inaugural Address—January 20, 2017," American Presidency Project, John Woolley and Gerhard Peters, eds. http://www.presidency.ucsb.edu/ws/index.php?pid=120000

11. Roberto Stefan Foa and Yascha Mounk, "The Democratic Disconnect," *Journal of Democracy* 27, no. 3 (July 2016), pp. 7–8.

12. Ibid., p. 9.

13. Ibid., p. 7.

14. Jacob Poushter, "40% of Millennials OK with Limiting Speech Offensive to Minorities," Pew Research Center, November 20, 2015. http://www.pewresearch.org/fact-tank/2015/11/20/40-of-millennials-ok-with-limiting-speech-offensive-to-minorities/

15. "The William F. Buckley Program at Yale: Almost Half (49%) of U.S. College Students 'Intimidated' by Professors When Sharing Differing Beliefs: Survey," McLaughlin & Associates. http://mclaughlinonline.com/2015/10/26/the-william-f-buckley-jr-program-at-yale-almost-half-49-of-u-s-college-students-intimidated-by-professors-when-sharing-differing-beliefs-survey/

16. See Michael Munger, "On the Origins and Goals of Public Choice," Independent Institute, June 29, 2017. http://www.independent.org/issues/article.asp?id=9115

17. For an attack on free speech as assault, see: http://dailybruin.com/2016/05/16/keshav-tadimeti-hurtful-discriminatory-comments-should-not-be-defended-as-free-speech/. For a defense of assault as a free speech, see: http://www.dailycal.org/2017/02/07/violence-helped-ensure-safety-students/

18. Samuel Earle, "Macron Shouldn't Misinterpret His Mandate," *Atlantic*, June 11, 2017. https://www.theatlantic.com/international/archive/2017/06/macron-france-election/529656/

19. Sohrab Ahmari, "Illiberalism: The Worldwide Crisis," *Commentary*, June 16, 2016. https://www.commentarymagazine.com/articles/illiberalism-worldwide-crisis/

20. Jonah Goldberg, "Days of Future Past," *National Review* 66, no. 18, October 6, 2014. http://www.nationalreview.com/article/388860/days-future-past-jonah-goldberg

21. Andras Kovacs, "Antisemitic Prejudice and Political Antisemitism in Present-Day Hungary," *Journal for the Study of Antisemitism: Eastern European Antisemitism* 4, no. 2 (2012), p. 445. http://web.ceu.hu/jewishstudies/jsa.pdf#page=93. See also Sam Sokol, "Ultra-Nationalist Jobbik Party's Gains Worry Hungarian Jews," *Jerusalem Post*, April 7, 2014. http://www.jpost.com/Jewish-World/Jewish-News/Ultra-nationalist-Jobbik-partys-gains-worry-Hungarian-Jews-347799

22. Ahmari, "Illiberalism."

23. Daphne Halikiopoulou, "Why the Golden Dawn Is a Neo-Nazi Party," Huffington Post, June 23, 2016. http://www.huffingtonpost.co.uk/daphne-halikiopoulou/golden-dawn_b_7643868.html

24. See, for example, Harriet Alexander, "Nicolas Maduro Threatens to Throw 'Bourgeois Parasite' Heinz Executives into Prison," *Telegraph*, December 2, 2015. http://www.telegraph.co.uk/news/worldnews/southamerica/venezuela/12029569/Nicolas-Maduro-threatens-to-throw-bourgeois-parasite-Heinz-executives-into-prison.html

25. Hubert Tworzecki and Radoslaw Markowski, "Why Is Poland's Law and Justice Party Trying to Rein in the Judiciary?," *Washington Post*, July 26, 2017. https://www.washingtonpost.com/news/monkey-cage/wp/2017/07/26/why-is-polands-law-and-justice-party-trying-to-rein-in-the-judiciary/?utm_term=.8eb83d5c10fb

26. Ahmari, "Illiberalism."

27. Maggie Haberman and David E. Sanger, "Transcript: Donald Trump Expounds on His Foreign Policy Views," *New York Times*, March 26, 2016. https://www.nytimes.com/2016/03/27/us/politics/donald-trump-transcript.html?_r=1&mtrref=www.theatlantic.com

28. Robert Costa, "Listening to Donald Trump Swear and Talk Politics on His Private Plane," *Washington Post*, July 12, 2015. https://www.washingtonpost.com/news/post-politics/wp/2015/07/12/listening-to-donald-trump-swear-and-talk-politics-on-his-private-plane/?utm_term=.467d43bf40f5

29. Bob Woodward and Robert Costa, "In a Revealing Interview, Trump Predicts a 'Massive Recession' but Intends to Eliminate the National Debt in 8 Years," *Washington Post*, April 2, 2016. https://www.washingtonpost.com/politics/in-turmoil-or-triumph-donald-trump-stands-alone/2016/04/02/8c0619b6-f8d6-11e5-a3ce-f06b5ba21f33_story.html?utm_term=.88433f6f2926

30. Jeremy Diamond, "Donald Trump: 'I Keep Whining and Whining Until I Win,'" CNN, August 11, 2015. http://www.cnn.com/2015/08/11/politics/donald-trump-refutes-third-party-run-report/

31. Donald J. Trump, "58—Inaugural Address—January 20, 2017."

32. Franklin D. Roosevelt, "130—Address at Oglethorpe University in Atlanta, Georgia—May 22, 1932," American Presidency Project, John Woolley and Gerhard Peters, eds. http://www.presidency.ucsb.edu/ws/?pid=88410

33. Jonathan Martin and Adam Nagourney, "Mocking Critics, Donald Trump Says He Can Win Without Republican Unity," *New York Times*, April 29, 2016. https://www.nytimes.com/2016/04/30/us/politics/trump-campaign.html

34. John Patrick Diggins, "Flirtation with Fascism: American Pragmatic Liberals and Mussolini's Italy," *American Historical Review* 71, no. 2 (January 1966), p. 495.

35. See Jonah Goldberg, *Liberal Fascism: The Secret History of the American Left from*

Mussolini to the Politics of Change (New York: Broadway Books, 2009 [2007]), pp. 166–67.

36. *Time* Staff, "Read President Trump's Interview with *Time* on Truth and Falsehoods," *Time*, March 23, 2017. http://time.com/4710456/donald-trump-time -interview-truth-falsehood/?xid=homepage

37. Donald J. Trump [and Tony Schwartz], *Trump: The Art of the Deal* (New York: Ballantine Books, 2015 [1987]), p. 58.

38. Timothy L. O'Brien, "How Much Is Trump Worth? Depends on How He Feels," *Newsweek*, October 19, 2015. http://www.newsweek.com/how-much-trump-worth -depends-how-he-feels-384720

39. Daniel White, "Donald Trump Tells Crowd to 'Knock the Crap Out of' Hecklers," *Time*, February 1, 2016. http://time.com/4203094/donald-trump-hecklers/

40. Mark Berman, "Trump Tells Police Not to Worry About Injuring Suspects During Arrests," *Washington Post*, July 28, 2017. https://www.washingtonpost.com/ news/post-nation/wp/2017/07/28/trump-tells-police-not-to-worry-about-injuring -suspects-during-arrests/?utm_term=.150e4947530e

41. Sophie Tatum, "Trump Defends Putin: 'You Think Our Country's So Innocent?,'" CNN, February 6, 2017. http://www.cnn.com/2017/02/04/politics/donald-trump -vladimir-putin/index.html

42. Steve Turnham, "Donald Trump to Father of Fallen Soldier: 'I've Made a Lot of Sacrifices,'" ABC News, July 30, 2016. http://abcnews.go.com/Politics/donald-trump -father-fallen-soldier-ive-made-lot/story?id=41015051

43. Trump carried the Electoral College—not, as he claims, in a historic landslide but by a relatively narrow margin. (It ranks as the forty-sixth best tally; see: https://www .nytimes.com/interactive/2016/12/18/us/elections/donald-trump-electoral-college -popular-vote.html). Moreover, were it not for five counties—four in Florida and one in Michigan—he would have lost to Hillary Clinton, who won the popular vote decisively. His margins in the historically "blue" states were also remarkably thin: 10,000 votes in Michigan, 22,000 in Wisconsin, and 46,000 in Pennsylvania. (See: http://www.thedailybeast.com/articles/2016/12/02/donald-trump-s-pollster-says -the-election-came-down-to-five-counties.html.)

44. Jan-Werner Muller, *What Is Populism?* (Philadelphia: University of Pennsylvania Press, 2016, Kindle edition), Kindle location 69–70.

45. Ibid., Kindle location 323–25.

46. Ibid., Kindle location 471–72.

47. See, for example, https://theoutline.com/post/1122/study-excluded-people-more -likely-to-believe-conspiracy-theories

48. William Jennings Bryan, "Bryan's 'Cross of Gold' Speech: Mesmerizing the Masses," History Matters, George Mason University. http://historymatters.gmu .edu/d/5354/

49. Goldberg, *Liberal Fascism*, p. 47.

50. "Populist Party Platform of 1892," July 4, 1892, Political Party Platforms, American Presidency Project, John Woolley and Gerhard Peters, eds. http://www.presidency .ucsb.edu/ws/index.php?pid=29616

51. Christopher Hitchens, "From Christopher Hitchens," Filmsnobs Reader Mail, Filmsnobs.com. http://www.filmsnobs.com/index.php?nowShowing=articles&by =Shimes&id=44

52. It would be grossly unfair and inaccurate to deny that sometimes populist feelings of resentment are warranted. The farmers of the Free Silver movement had

legitimate grievances. The masses that formed the initial ranks of Italian Fascism or Coughlin's National Union of Social Justice may have reached the wrong conclusions, but they were right to feel ill-served by their leaders. Even the hordes who swelled the rallies of Adolf Hitler had good reason to search for a better way, even if their searching led them in an evil and calamitous direction. The tide of populist nationalism that led to the victory of the Brexit movement had many sound arguments on its side. Similarly, here in America, many of the resentments that Donald Trump tapped into were wholly understandable.

53. Zeke J. Miller, "Donald Trump Has a Grand Unified Campaign Conspiracy Theory," *Time*, October 13, 2016. http://time.com/4530568/donald-trump-hillary-clinton-conspiracy/

54. Tim Hains, "Donald Trump's 'Argument for America' Ad Targets 'Failed and Corrupt Political Establishment,'" RealClearPolitics. https://www.realclearpolitics.com/video/2016/11/04/ad_donald_trumps_argument_for_america.html

14: THINGS FALL APART

1. Abigail Geiger, "For Many Voters, It's Not Which Presidential Candidate They're for but Which They're Against," Pew Research Center, September 2, 2016. http://www.pewresearch.org/fact-tank/2016/09/02/for-many-voters-its-not-which-presidential-candidate-theyre-for-but-which-theyre-against/

2. Nancy Knowlton, "Corals and Coral Reefs," Ocean Portal, Smithsonian National Museum of Natural History. http://ocean.si.edu/corals-and-coral-reefs

3. Jeremy T. Claisse et al., "Oil Platforms off California Are Among the Most Productive Marine Fish Habitats Globally," *Proceedings of the National Academy of Sciences of the United States of America* 111, no. 43 (September 22, 2014). http://www.pnas.org/content/111/43/15462.full

4. Jonathan Haidt, *The Righteous Mind: Why Good People Are Divided by Politics and Religion* (New York: Knopf Doubleday, 2012, Kindle Edition), p. 308.

5. Arthur C. Brooks, "America and the Value of 'Earned Success,'" *Wall Street Journal*, May 9, 2012, A13.

6. Arthur C. Brooks, "A Nation of Givers," American Enterprise Institute, March 11, 2008. https://www.aei.org/publication/a-nation-of-givers/

7. Barack Obama, "32—Inaugural Address—January 21, 2013," American Presidency Project, John Woolley and Gerhard Peters, eds. http://www.presidency.ucsb.edu/ws/?pid=102827

8. Yuval Levin, *The Fractured Republic: Renewing America's Social Contract in the Age of Individualism* (New York: Basic Books, 2016), p. 209.

9. Ibid., p. 4.

10. Joel Gehrke, "DNC: 'Government Is the Only Thing That We All Belong To,'" *Washington Examiner*, September 4, 2012. http://www.washingtonexaminer.com/dnc-government-is-the-only-thing-that-we-all-belong-to/article/2506923

11. The original website is no longer active, but curious readers can still access the statist slideshow here: https://web.archive.org/web/20120907070601/https://barackobama.com/life-of-julia

12. Nicholas Eberstadt, "Our Miserable 21st Century," *Commentary*, March 2017. https://www.commentarymagazine.com/articles/our-miserable-21st-century/

13. Ibid.

14. Ibid.

15. George F. Will, "America's 'Quiet Catastrophe': Millions of Idle Men," *Washington*

Post, October 5, 2016. https://www.washingtonpost.com/opinions/americas-quiet
-catastrophe-millions-of-idle-men/2016/10/05/cd01b750-8a57-11e6-bff0-d53f592
f176e_story.html?utm_term=.1c72ed7e3967

16. Stephen J. Rose, "The Growing Size and Incomes of the Upper Middle Class,"
Research Report, Urban Institute: Income and Benefits Policy Center, June 2016, p. 6.
http://www.urban.org/sites/default/files/publication/81581/2000819-The-Growing
-Size-and-Incomes-of-the-Upper-Middle-Class.pdf

17. Bernadette D. Proctor et al., "Income and Poverty in the United States," Current
Population Reports, U.S. Census Bureau, p. 23. https://www.census.gov/content/
dam/Census/library/publications/2016/demo/p60-256.pdf (I recommend printing
it out, or tilting your head.)

18. "The American Middle Class Is Losing Ground: Share of Adults Living in Middle-
Income Households Is Falling," Pew Research Center: Social & Demographic
Trends, December 8, 2015. http://www.pewsocialtrends.org/2015/12/09/the
-american-middle-class-is-losing-ground/st_2015-12-09_middle-class-03/

19. Ronald Bailey, "Natural Gas Ambush Killed Off Coal Mining Industry, Not Obama's
'War on Coal,'" *Reason*, October 11, 2016. http://reason.com/blog/2016/10/11/
natural-gas-ambush-killed-off-coal-minin

20. Scott Lincicome, "The Truth About Trade," *National Review* online, April 4, 2016.
http://www.nationalreview.com/article/433575/trade-american-economy-free
-trade-costing-american-jobs

21. See https://www.bea.gov/iTable/iTable.cfm?reqid=56&step=2&isuri=1#reqid=56&
step=51&isuri=1&5602=208

22. Ana Swanson, "A Single Chart Everybody Needs to Look at Before Trump's Big Fight
over Bringing Back American Jobs," *Washington Post*, November 28, 2016. https://
www.washingtonpost.com/news/wonk/wp/2016/11/28/theres-a-big-reason-trump
-might-not-be-able-to-keep-his-promise-on-jobs/?utm_term=.bde6c7d970f0

23. Rich Lowry and Ramesh Ponnuru, "For Love of Country," *National Review* 69, no.
3, February 20, 2017. https://www.nationalreview.com/magazine/2017-02-20-0000/
donald-trump-inauguration-speech-and-nationalism

24. ACS, "My Country Right or Wrong," American Chesterton Society. https://www
.chesterton.org/my-country-right-or-wrong/

25. Frederic Cople Jaher, *The Jews and the Nation: Revolution, Emancipation, State Formation, and the Liberal Paradigm in America and France* (Princeton, NJ: Princeton
University Press, 2002), p. 135.

26. Hans Kohn, "Napoleon and the Age of Nationalism," *Journal of Modern History* 22,
no. 1 (March 1950), pp. 21-37.

27. "Every people," Rousseau insisted in 1765, "has, or should have, a national character; and if a people did not, the first thing to do would be to provide it with one."
Jean-Jacques Rousseau, "Constitutional Project for Corsica," Constitution Society.
http://www.constitution.org/jjr/corsica.htm

28. Isaiah Berlin, "Herder and the Enlightenment," in *Three Critics of the Enlightenment: Vico, Hamann, Herder*, Henry Hardy, ed. (Princeton, NJ: Princeton University Press, 2013), p. 256.

29. Tim Blanning, *The Romantic Revolution: A History*, Modern Library Chronicles
(New York: Random House, 2011, Kindle edition), Kindle location 1856-58.

30. Donald J. Trump, "58—Inaugural Address," January 20, 2017, American Presidency Project, John Woolley and Gerhard Peters, eds. http://www.presidency.ucsb
.edu/ws/index.php?pid=120000

31. Ian Schwartz, "Trump: 'We Will Have So Much Winning If I Get Elected That You

May Get Bored with Winning," RealClearPolitics, September 9, 2015. https://www
.realclearpolitics.com/video/2015/09/09/trump_we_will_have_so_much_winning
_if_i_get_elected_that_you_may_get_bored_with_winning.html

32. Geoffrey Skelley, "Just How Many Obama 2012–Trump 2016 Voters Were There?,"
Sabato's Crystal Ball, University of Virginia Center for Politics, June 1, 2017.
http://www.centerforpolitics.org/crystalball/articles/just-how-many-obama-2012-
trump-2016-voters-were-there/

33. Publius Decius Mus [Mike Anton], "The Flight 93 Election," *Claremont Review of
Books*, September 5, 2016. http://www.claremont.org/crb/basicpage/the-flight-93
-election/

34. Quoted in George J. Borjas, *We Wanted Workers: Unraveling the Immigration Narrative* (New York: W. W. Norton, 2016), p. 15.

35. See ibid., pp. 13–31, for starters.

36. Ronald F. Inglehart and Pippa Norris, "Trump, Brexit, and the Rise of Populism:
Economic Have-Nots and Cultural Backlash," Faculty Research Working Paper
Series, Harvard Kennedy School, August 2016, pp. 4–5. https://research.hks.harvard
.edu/publications/getFile.aspx?Id=1401

37. David Card et al., "Immigration, Wages, and Compositional Amenities," Norface
Migration, Discussion Paper No. 2012-12. http://davidcard.berkeley.edu/papers/
immigration-wages-compositional-amenities.pdf

38. Hillary Clinton, Twitter, November 19, 2015. https://twitter.com/hillaryclinton/
status/667371059885301761?lang=en

39. Robert D. Putnam, "*E Pluribus Unum*: Diversity and Community in the Twenty-
First Century: The 2006 Johan Skytte Prize Lecture," *Scandinavian Political Studies*
30, no. 2 (June 2007), pp. 150–51.

40. Ibid., p. 149.

41. Fukuyama, *Trust: The Social Virtues and the Creation of Prosperity* (New York: Free
Press, 1996), p. 26.

42. "Chapter 5: U.S. Foreign-Born Population Trends," Pew Research Center, September 28, 2015. http://www.pewhispanic.org/2015/09/28/chapter-5-u-s-foreign-born
-population-trends/

43. Anna Brown and Renee Stepler, "Statistical Portrait of the Foreign-Born Population in the United States, 2014," Pew Research Center, April 19, 2016. http://www
.pewhispanic.org/2016/04/19/statistical-portrait-of-the-foreign-born-population
-in-the-united-states-2014-key-charts/#2013-fb-origin

44. "FFF: Back to School: 2015–2016," U.S. Census Bureau, September 2, 2014. https://
www.census.gov/newsroom/facts-for-features/2015/cb15-ff17.html

45. Robby Soave, "The University of California's Insane Speech Police," Daily Beast,
June 22, 2015. http://www.thedailybeast.com/the-university-of-californias-insane
-speech-police

46. Amanda Taub, "The Real Story About Fake News Is Partisanship," *New York Times*,
January 11, 2017. https://www.nytimes.com/2017/01/11/upshot/the-real-story-about
-fake-news-is-partisanship.html?_r=1

47. Ibid.

48. Carolyn Declerck and Christopher Boone, *Neuroeconomics of Prosocial Behavior:
The Compassionate Egoist* (San Diego, CA; Waltham, MA; Oxford, U.K.: Academic
Press, 2016), p. 158.

49. Taub, "The Real Story About Fake News Is Partisanship."

50. Tyler Cowen, "Move On—This Isn't True Here," Marginal Revolution, July 26, 2008.
http://marginalrevolution.com/marginalrevolution/2008/07/xxxxxxx.html

51. Amy Chozick, "Hillary Clinton Calls Many Trump Backers 'Deplorables,' and G.O.P. Pounces," *New York Times*, September 10, 2016. https://www.nytimes.com/2016/09/11/us/politics/hillary-clinton-basket-of-deplorables.html

52. Quoted in "Happiness," in Tyron Edwards, *A Dictionary of Thoughts: Being a Cyclopedia of Laconic Quotations from the Best Authors, Both Ancient and Modern* (Detroit: F. B. Dickerson Company, 1908), p. 215.

53. Allahpundit, "Confirmed: Republicans Like Democratic Ideas Better When They're Trump's," Hot Air, September 2, 2015. http://hotair.com/archives/2015/09/02/confirmed-republicans-like-democratic-ideas-better-when-they-think-theyre-trumps/?utm_source=Sailthru&utm_medium=email&utm_campaign=Gfile09042015&utm_term=GFile

54. Ariel Malka and Yphtach Lelkes, "In a New Poll, Half of Republicans Say They Would Support Postponing the 2020 Election If Trump Proposed It," *Washington Post*, August 10, 2017. https://www.washingtonpost.com/news/monkey-cage/wp/2017/08/10/in-a-new-poll-half-of-republicans-say-they-would-support-postponing-the-2020-election-if-trump-proposed-it/?utm_term=.b31482067e85

55. Gabby Morrongiello, "Conway Jokes CPAC Could Become 'TPAC' in Honor of Trump," *Washington Examiner*, February 23, 2017. http://www.washingtonexaminer.com/conway-jokes-cpac-could-become-tpac-in-honor-of-trump/article/2615550

56. "Celebs Pledge Allegiance to Obama," Fox News, September 20, 2012. http://video.foxnews.com/v/1852139055001/?#sp=show-clips. See also Francis Romero, "Celebs Pledge Allegiance," *Time*, January 20, 2009. http://content.time.com/time/arts/article/0,8599,1872644,00.html

57. Mark Morford, "Is Obama an Enlightened Being? Spiritual Wise Ones Say: This Sure Ain't No Ordinary Politician. You Buying It?," *San Francisco Gate*, June 6, 2008. http://www.sfgate.com/entertainment/morford/article/Is-Obama-an-enlightened-being-Spiritual-wise-2544395.php

58. Deepak Chopra, "Obama and the Call: 'I Am America,'" Huffington Post, May 25, 2011. http://www.huffingtonpost.com/deepak-chopra/obama-and-the-call-i-am-a_b_80016.html

59. Eve Konstantine, "The Obama Vibe," Huffington Post, February 5, 2008. http://www.huffingtonpost.com/eve-konstantine/the-obama-vibe_b_85143.html

60. Washington Free Beacon Staff, "Barbara Walters: We Thought Obama Was Going to Be 'The Next Messiah,'" Washington Free Beacon, December 18, 2013. http://freebeacon.com/culture/barbara-walters-we-thought-obama-was-going-to-be-the-next-messiah/

61. Hillary Rodham Clinton, "Remarks by First Lady Hillary Rodham Clinton, University of Texas, Austin, Texas, April 7, 1993," Liz Carpenter Lecture Series. https://clintonwhitehouse3.archives.gov/WH/EOP/First_Lady/html/generalspeeches/1993/19930407.html

CONCLUSION

1. Charles Krauthammer, "Decline Is a Choice," *Weekly Standard*, October 19, 2009. http://www.weeklystandard.com/decline-is-a-choice/article/270813

2. I am indebted to Larry Siedentop's *Inventing the Individual: The Origins of Western Liberalism* (Cambridge, MA: Belknap Press/Harvard University Press, 2014) for this discussion.

3. Linda C. Reader, "Augustine and the Case for Limited Government," *Humanitas* 16, no. 2, (2003), pp. 97–98.

4. Ibid., p. 98.

5. According to the American G. K. Chesterton Society, this is a good summation of his thinking, but he never said it so explicitly. See "When Man Ceases to Worship God," American Chesterton Society. https://www.chesterton.org/ceases-to-worship/

6. The year 2006 marked a watershed: According to the U.S. Census, that was the year when, for the first time in the history of the Republic, Americans preferred water to beer. As political scientist Susan McWilliams notes, beer is a socially oriented beverage and water is a privately oriented one. "There's a reason that beer commercials tend to include lots of people hanging out in a room together," she writes, "and bottled water commercials tend to include lone individuals climbing things and running around by themselves, usually on a beach at sunrise—even though they are not being chased." Susan McWilliams, "Beer and Civic Life," Front Porch Republic, March 20, 2009. http://www.frontporchrepublic.com/2009/03/beer-and-civic-life/

7. This line comes from the TV series *American Gods*. Based on the Neil Gaiman novel of the same name, the show posits that we've turned TV, technology, etc., into the new gods of our age. "You are what you worship," explains Vulcan, the ancient volcano god turned god of guns. "The screen is the altar. I'm the one they sacrifice to," Media, the new god of TV, explains. "Then till now. Golden Age to Golden Age. They sit side by side, ignore each other, and give it up to me. Now they hold a smaller screen on their lap or in the palm of their hand so they don't get bored watching the big one. Time and attention, better than lamb's blood. Huh?"

8. Kif Leswing, "The Average iPhone Is Unlocked 80 Times per Day," Business Insider, April 18, 2016. http://www.businessinsider.com/the-average-iphone-is-unlocked-80-times-per-day-2016-4

9. "Americans Are Poorly Informed About Basic Constitutional Provisions," Annenberg Public Policy Center of the University of Pennsylvania, September 12, 2017. https://www.annenbergpublicpolicycenter.org/americans-are-poorly-informed-about-basic-constitutional-provisions?utm_source=news-release&utm_medium=email&utm_campaign=2017_civics_survey&utm_term=survey&utm_source=Media&utm_campaign=e5f213892a-Civics_survey_2017_2017_09_12&utm_medium=email&utm_term=0_9e3d9bcd8a-e5f213892a-425997897

10. One member of this crowd is Facebook creator Mark Zuckerberg. Among various proposals for causes by which millennials can derive communal meaning, he asked: "How about modernizing democracy so everyone can vote online . . . ?" See: "Mark Zuckerberg's Commencement Address at Harvard," Harvard Gazette, May 25, 2017. https://news.harvard.edu/gazette/story/2017/05/mark-zuckerbergs-speech-as-written-for-harvards-class-of-2017/

11. John Courtney Murray, "The Return to Tribalism," Woodstock Theological Library at Georgetown University. http://www.library.georgetown.edu/woodstock/murray/1961d

12. "Idiocy" shares the same root word—*idios*—with "idiom" and "idiosyncratic." It means private, selfish, removed from the public good, alone. An *idiota* in modern Spanish means moron. But *idiota* in Latin means a layman or ordinary person. For the Greeks, the idiot was the opposite of the citizen who has both knowledge of, and appreciation for, the larger community. "An idiot," writes Walter C. Parker, "is one whose self-centeredness undermines his or her citizen identity, causing it to wither or never to take root in the first place. Private gain is the goal, and the community had better not get in the way. An idiot is suicidal in a certain way, definitely self-

defeating, for the idiot does not know that privacy and individual autonomy are entirely dependent on the community." I have problems with some of Parker's characterization and his politics, but I also agree with his core complaint. Education is all about turning barbarians and idiots into citizens. Walter C. Parker, "Teaching Against Idiocy," *Phi Delta Kappan* 86, no. 5 (January 2005), pp. 344–45.

13. Patrick J. Deneen, "How a Generation Lost Its Common Culture," Minding the Campus, February 2, 2016. http://www.mindingthecampus.org/2016/02/how-a-generation-lost-its-common-culture/

14. Neil Postman, Foreword to *Amusing Ourselves to Death: Public Discourse in the Age of Show Business* (New York: Penguin, 2005 [1985]), pp. xix–xx.

15. Irving Kristol, "On Conservatism and Capitalism," *Wall Street Journal*, September 11, 1975, p. 20.

16. Stan M. Haynes, *President-Making in the Gilded Age: The Nominating Conventions of 1876–1900* (Jefferson, NC: McFarland, 2016), p. 216.

17. Jonah Goldberg, *Liberal Fascism: The Secret History of the American Left, from Mussolini to the Politics of Change* (New York: Broadway, 2009 [2007]), pp. 143–44.

18. Eugene Peterson, *The Pastor: A Memoir* (San Francisco: HarperOne, 2012), p. 157.

19. Elias Canetti, *Crowds and Power*, Carol Stewart, trans. (New York: Farrar, Straus and Giroux, 1960), p. 18.

20. C. S. Lewis. *The Abolition of Man* (New York: HarperOne, 1974 [1944]), p. 26.

21. Ibid., p. 25.

22. Francis Fukuyama, "The End of History?," *National Interest*, no. 16 (Summer 1989), p. 18.

23. Julian Benda, *The Treason of the Intellectuals* (New York: Routledge, 2017 [1927]), p. 15.

24. Rebecca Savransky, "Eric Trump: 'Nepotism Is Kind of a Factor of Life,'" *The Hill*, April 4, 2017. http://thehill.com/homenews/news/327244-eric-trump-nepotism-is-kind-of-a-factor-of-life. He called it "a beautiful thing" separately. See: http://thehill.com/homenews/news/328201-eric-trump-nepotism-is-a-beautiful-thing

25. This is often attributed to the French labor activist and politician Alexandre Auguste Ledru-Rollin, though that attribution is apocryphal. Some sources attribute it to Gandhi, which seems even more unlikely.

26. "88. Shutting Down Media Outlets," Economist/YouGov Poll: July 23–25, 2017—1500 US Adults, YouGov, p. 98. https://d25d2506sfb94s.cloudfront.net/cumulus_uploads/document/u4wgpax6ng/econTabReport.pdf

27. See "More Americans Say Personal Immorality Not Disqualifying for Elected Officials," in "Clinton Maintains Double-Digit (51% vs. 36%) lead over Trump, PRRI/Brookings Survey," Public Religion Research Institute, October 19, 2016. https://www.prri.org/research/prri-brookings-oct-19-poll-politics-election-clinton-double-digit-lead-trump/

28. Calvin Coolidge, "Address at the Celebration of the 150th Anniversary of the Declaration of Independence in Philadelphia, Pennsylvania—July 5, 1926," American Presidency Project, John Woolley and Gerhard Peters, eds. http://www.presidency.ucsb.edu/ws/index.php?pid=408

29. "ingratitude," Merriam-Webster. https://www.merriam-webster.com/dictionary/ingratitude

APPENDIX

1. "Margaret Thatcher on Socialism: Did Margaret Thatcher Once Say That 'the Trouble with Socialism Is That Eventually You Run Out of Other People's Money'?," Snopes. http://www.snopes.com/politics/quotes/thatcher.asp

2. Yuval Noah Harari, *Sapiens: A Brief History of Humankind* (New York: Harper-Collins, 2015, Kindle edition), p. 4.

3. Ibid., p. 11.

4. Eric Beinhocker, *The Origin of Wealth: Evolution, Complexity, and the Radical Remaking of Economics* (Boston: Harvard Business School Press, 2006), p. 9.

5. Todd G. Buchholz, "Dark Clouds, Silver Linings," in *New Ideas from Dead Economists: An Introduction to Modern Economic Thought* (New York: Penguin, 2007 [1990]), p. 313.

6. Francisco Ferreira, "The International Poverty Line Has Just Been Raised to $1.90 a Day, but Global Poverty Is Basically Unchanged. How Is That Even Possible?," World Bank, October 4, 2015. http://blogs.worldbank.org/developmenttalk /international-poverty-line-has-just-been-raised-190-day-global-poverty-basically -unchanged-how-even

7. Beinhocker, *The Origin of Wealth*, p. 9.

8. David Landes, *Prometheus Unbound: Technological Change and Industrial Development in Western Europe from 1750 to the Present* (Cambridge, U.K.: Cambridge University Press, 1969), p. 5; quoted in Beinhocker, *The Origin of Wealth*, p. 11.

9. Douglass C. North et al., *Violence and Social Orders: A Conceptual Framework for Interpreting Recorded History* (New York: Cambridge University Press, 2009), p. 3.

10. I'm using 1700 as the year economic growth took off (and ending at the current year of 2018, so 318 years) and 365.25 days as the length of the year. By that measure, the vast majority of human progress has transpired in the last 13 hours and 56 minutes.

11. Confucius, "*The Analects—13: The Analects Attributed to Confucius [Kongfuzi], 551–479 BCE, by Lao-Tse [Lao Zi]* (trans. by James Legge (1815–1897)," USC U.S.-China Institute, Annenberg School for Communication and Journalism, University of Southern California. http://china.usc.edu/confucius-analects-13

12. Irving Kristol, "'When Virtue Loses All Her Loveliness'—Some Reflections on Capitalism and 'the Free Society,'" *Public Interest 33*, Fall 1970. https://www .nationalaffairs.com/public_interest/detail/when-virtue-loses-all-her-loveliness -some-reflections-on-capitalism-and-the-free-society

13. Robert J. Gordon, *The Rise and Fall of American Growth: The U.S. Standard of Living Since the Civil War* (Princeton, NJ: Princeton University Press, 2016), pp. 2–3.

14. Ronald Bailey, *The End of Doom* (New York: St. Martin's, 2015), pp. 67–69.

15. Deirdre N. McCloskey, *Bourgeois Dignity: Why Economics Can't Explain the Modern World* (Chicago: University of Chicago Press, 2010), p. 1.

16. See, for example, Chelsea German and Marian L. Tupy, "No, Capitalism Will Not 'Starve Humanity' by 2050," Human Progress, February 17, 2016. http://human progress.org/blog/no—capitalism-will-not-starve-humanity-by-2050

17. "Quantifying History: Two Thousand Years in One Chart," *Economist*, June 28, 2011. http://www.economist.com/blogs/dailychart/2011/06/quantifying-history

18. McCloskey, *Bourgeois Dignity*, p. 1.

19. Beinhocker, *The Origin of Wealth*, p. 9.

20. Ibid., p. 49.

21. "GDP, 1990 International Dollars," Human Progress. http://humanprogress.org/ f1/2128

22. Chelsea German, "Extreme Poverty's End in Sight," Human Progress, September 24, 2015. http://humanprogress.org/blog/extreme-povertys-end-sight
23. "Share of People Living in Extreme Poverty," Human Progress. http://humanprogress.org/static/3469
24. "Absolute Poverty Rates in East Asia and the World, Percent of Population," Human Progress. http://humanprogress.org/static/2636
25. "Towards the End of Poverty," *Economist*, June 1, 2013. http://www.economist.com/news/leaders/21578665-nearly-1-billion-people-have-been-taken-out-extreme-poverty-20-years-world-should-aim
26. Sebastien Malo, "World's 'Extremely Poor' to Fall Below 10 Percent of Global Population: World Bank," Reuters, October 4, 2015. http://www.reuters.com/article/2015/10/04/us-global-poverty-worldbank-idUSKCN0RY0WI20151004
27. Matt Ridley, *The Rational Optimist: How Prosperity Evolves* (New York: HarperCollins, 2010), p. 15.
28. Franklin Delano Roosevelt, "4—State of the Union Message to Congress—January 11, 1944," American Presidency Project, John Woolley and Gerhard Peters, eds. http://www.presidency.ucsb.edu/ws/?pid=16518
29. "Employment in Agriculture (% of Total Employment)," World Bank. https://data.worldbank.org/indicator/SL.AGR.EMPL.ZS
30. Gordon, *The Rise and Fall of American Growth*, pp. 52–53.
31. See, for example, "Agricultural Sector Employment, Percent of Total Employment," Human Progress. http://humanprogress.org/sharable/8249
32. "Hours Worked per Worker," Human Progress. http://humanprogress.org/story/2246
33. "Labor Productivity per Hour Worked," Human Progress. http://humanprogress.org/story/2254
34. Francis Fukuyama, *The Origins of Political Order: From Prehuman Times to the French Revolution* (New York: Farrar, Straus and Giroux, 2011), p. 463.
35. "Vegetables [sic] Yields," Human Progress. http://humanprogress.org/f1/2156
36. "Cereal Yields," Human Progress. http://humanprogress.org/f1/2413
37. Recorded in all four canonical gospels, but I am referencing the version that appears in the gospel of John. https://www.biblegateway.com/passage/?search=John+6&version=NIV
38. The median household income in the United States in 2015 was $55,775. See Kirby G. Posey, "Household Income: 2015," U.S. Census Bureau, September 2016, p. 2. https://www.census.gov/content/dam/Census/library/publications/2016/demo/acsbr15-02.pdf
39. Brian Wansink and C. S. Wansink, "The Largest Last Supper: Depictions of Food Portions and Plate Size Increased over the Millennium," *International Journal of Obesity* 34 (2010), pp. 943–44, doi:10.1038/ijo.2010.37. https://foodpsychology.cornell.edu/research/largest-last-supper-depictions-portion-size-increased-over-millennium
40. "Food, Net Production, Relative to 2004-2006," Human Progress. http://humanprogress.org/f1/2263
41. "Meat Consumption, Developing Countries, per Person," Human Progress. http://humanprogress.org/static/1897
42. "Food Supply, per Person, per Day," Human Progress. http://humanprogress.org/f1/2126
43. "Food Consumption Shortfall Among Food-Deprived Persons," Human Progress. http://humanprogress.org/f1/2107

44. "Undernourished Persons," Human Progress. http://humanprogress.org/f1/2339
45. "Access to Electricity," Human Progress. http://humanprogress.org/f1/3274
46. Ridley, *The Rational Optimist*, p. 236.
47. Mark J. Perry, "Each American Has the Energy-Equivalent of 600 Full-time 'Human Energy Servants,'" AEIdeas (American Enterprise Institute), December 2, 2015. https://www.aei.org/publication/each-american-has-the-energy-equivalent-of-nearly-600-full-time-human-energy-servants/
48. Bailey, *The End of Doom*, pp. 61–62.
49. Ridley, *The Rational Optimist*, p. 245.
50. Bailey, *The End of Doom*, p. 65.
51. Ibid., p. 62.
52. "Greenhouse Gases from Agriculture," Human Progress. http://www.humanprogress.org/f1/2176
53. Gordon, *The Rise and Fall of American Growth*, p. 129.
54. William Manchester, *A World Lit Only by Fire* (Boston: Little, Brown, 1993 [1992]), pp. 63–64.
55. Ibid., p. 142.
56. Robert Bryce, *Smaller Faster Lighter Denser Cheaper* (New York: PublicAffairs, 2014), p. 74.
57. Brink Lindsay, *Against the Dead Hand: The Uncertain Struggle for Global Capitalism* (New York: John Wiley, 2002), p. 63.
58. See, for example, "Passenger Kilometers Travelled," Human Progress, http://humanprogress.org/f1/2374. The figures are incomplete, but completing the figures would only increase the already impressive total and reinforce the already real trend.
59. According to science journalist Ronald Bailey, forest trend researchers stated in a 2006 article in the *Proceedings of the National Academy of Sciences* that "among 50 nations with extensive forests reported in the Food and Agriculture Organization's comprehensive Global Forest Resources Assessment 2005, no nation where annual per capita gross domestic product exceeded $4,600 had a negative rate of growing stock change." See Ronald Bailey, *The End of Doom*, p. 250.
60. Ridley, *The Rational Optimist*, p. 305.
61. Bailey, *The End of Doom*, p. 250.
62. "Forest Area, Square Kilometers," Human Progress. http://humanprogress.org/sharable/8143
63. Ronald Bailey, "Rage Against the Machines," *Reason,* July 2001. http://reason.com/archives/2001/07/01/rage-against-the-machines/1
64. "U.S. Energy-Related Carbon Dioxide Emissions," Human Progress. http://humanprogress.org/static/3391
65. Bailey, *The End of Doom*, p. xvii.
66. Ibid., p. 2.
67. Bryce, *Smaller Faster Lighter Denser Cheaper,* p. 59.
68. Manchester, *A World Lit Only by Fire*, p. 55.
69. "Life Expectancy at Birth," Human Progress. http://humanprogress.org/f1/2314
70. Bailey, *The End of Doom*, p. 2.
71. Gordon, *Rise and Fall of American Growth*, p. 322.
72. Max Roser, "Child Mortality," Our World in Data. http://ourworldindata.org/data/population-growth-vital-statistics/child-mortality/
73. "Infant Mortality Rate," Human Progress. http://humanprogress.org/f1/2386
74. "Death rate," Human Progress. http://humanprogress.org/f1/2104

75. See, for example, "Wealth & Health of Nations," Gapminder. http://www.gap
minder.org/world/#$majorMode=chart$is;shi=t;ly=2003;lb=f;il=t;fs=11;al=30;stl
=t;st=t;nsl=t;se=t$wst;tts=C$ts;sp=5.59290322580644;ti=2013$zpv;v=0$inc_x;m
mid=XCOORDS;iid=phAwcNAVuyj1jiMAkmq1iMg;by=ind$inc_y;mmid=YCOO
RDS;iid=phAwcNAVuyj2tPLxKvvnNPA;by=ind$inc_s;uniValue=8.21;iid=phAwc
NAVuyj0XOoBL_n5tAQ;by=ind$inc_c;uniValue=255;gid=CATID0;by=grp$map
_x;scale=log;dataMin=194;dataMax=96846$map_y;scale=lin;dataMin=23;data
Max=86$map_s;sma=49;smi=2.65$cd;bd=0$inds=;modified=60

76. Manchester, *A World Lit Only by Fire*, p. 62.

77. T. Anderson. "Dental Treatment in Medieval England," *British Dental Journal*
197, no. 7, October 9, 2004, p. 1. http://www.nature.com/bdj/journal/v197/n7/
pdf/4811723a.pdf

78. D. H. Robinson and A. H. Toledo, "Historical Development of Modern Anesthesia,"
Journal of Investigative Surgery 25, no. 3 (June 2012), pp. 141-49. http://www.ncbi
.nlm.nih.gov/pubmed/22583009

79. Bryce, *Smaller Faster Lighter Denser Cheaper*, p. 166.

80. Gordon, *The Rise and Fall of American Growth*, p. 226.

81. McCloskey, *Bourgeois Dignity*, p. 57.

82. Gordon, *The Rise and Fall of American Growth*, p. 228.

83. Max Roser, "Maternal Mortality," Our World in Data. https://ourworldindata.org/
maternal-mortality/

84. Bryce, *Smaller Faster Lighter Denser Cheaper*, p. xxiii.

85. Max Roser and Esteban Ortiz-Ospina, "Global Extreme Poverty," Our World in
Data (first published in 2013; substantive revision March 27, 2017). https://our
worldindata.org/extreme-poverty/

86. Jared Rhoads, "The Medical Context of Calvin Jr.'s Untimely Death," Calvin
Coolidge Presidential Foundation, July 7, 2014. https://coolidgefoundation.org/
blog/the-medical-context-of-calvin-jr-s-untimely-death/

87. Gordon, *The Rise and Fall of American Growth*, p. 214.

88. Chelsea German, "Modern Chemicals, Health, and Hunger," Human Progress
(January 13, 2016). http://humanprogress.org/blog/modern-chemicals—health—
and-hunger

89. Ridley, *The Rational Optimist*, p. 310.

90. Gordon, *The Rise and Fall of American Growth*, p. 214.

91. German, "Modern Chemicals, Health, and Hunger."

92. See "You Have Died of Dysentery," Know Your Meme. http://knowyourmeme.com/
memes/you-have-died-of-dysentery

93. "Heart Disease," NIH Research Portfolio Online Reporting Tools (RePORT).
https://report.nih.gov/NIHfactsheets/ViewFactSheet.aspx?csid=96

94. Bryce, *Smaller Faster Lighter Denser Cheaper*, p. 41.

95. Ridley, *The Rational Optimist*, p. 298.

96. Bailey, *The End of Doom*, pp. 97-98.

97. Ibid., pp. 116-17.

98. Ridley, *The Rational Optimist*, p. 18.

99. Max Roser and Esteban Ortiz-Ospina, "Literacy," Our World in Data. https://our
worldindata.org/literacy/

100. "Mean Years of Schooling," Human Progress. http://humanprogress.org/f1/3246

101. Gordon, *The Rise and Fall of American Growth*, p. 178.

102. Victor Davis Hanson, "Progressive Mass Hysteria," *National Review* online,

June 30, 2015. http://www.nationalreview.com/article/420496/progressive-mass-hysteria

103. "Battle of New Orleans," *Encyclopaedia Britannica*. https://www.britannica.com/event/Battle-of-New-Orleans-United-States-United-Kingdom-1815

104. Gordon, *The Rise and Fall of American Growth*, p. 178.

105. Ibid., p. 431.

106. "Mobile Cellular Subscriptions," Human Progress. http://humanprogress.org/fl/2537

107. Gordon, *The Rise and Fall of American Growth*, p. 431.

108. Ibid., p. 440.

109. See https://www.youtube.com/watch?v=ziVpqh9UXmI.

110. Bryce, *Smaller Faster Lighter Denser Cheaper*, p. 113.

111. James B. Meigs, "Inside the Future: How PopMech Predicted the Next 110 Years," *Popular Mechanics*, December 10, 2012. http://www.popularmechanics.com/technology/a8562/inside-the-future-how-popmech-predicted-the-next-110-years-14831802/

112. Gordon, *The Rise and Fall of American Growth*, p. 444.

113. Bryce, *Smaller Faster Lighter Denser Cheaper*, p. 111.

114. Gordon, *The Rise and Fall of American Growth*, p. 444.

115. Bryce, *Smaller Faster Lighter Denser Cheaper*, p. xxiii.

116. Ridley, *The Rational Optimist*, p. 24.

117. Bryce, *Smaller Faster Lighter Denser Cheaper*, p. 107.

118. Ibid., p. 117.

119. Ibid., p. 121.

120. "Internet Users," Human Progress. http://humanprogress.org/fl/2536

121. Tim Montgomerie, "Two: Capitalism Has Produced a $600 Billion Global Marketing Machine but It Has Completely Failed to Sell Its Enormous Achievements," Legatum Institute, Shorthand Social, November 9, 2015. https://social.shorthand.com/montie/3gPcCzNQ2uc/two

122. Quoted in Ridley, *The Rational Optimist*, p. 11.

Acknowledgments

Some people love writing books. Those people are strange, at least to me. Maybe if I didn't have to churn out columns and magazine articles on deadlines, I'd enjoy writing books more. After all, there's much to love about taking serious time to learn about a subject and think seriously about it. And if that was all I had to do professionally, maybe I would love writing books, too.

But that's not the life I have chosen. And for that reason, I am immensely grateful to a large number of people who helped make it possible for me to get this book done.

That list begins with my wife, Jessica Gavora, who is not only an accomplished writer and thinker in her own right, but the best confidante, friend, and partner I could ever hope for. She put up with a lot over the last few years—not to mention ever since she met me!—and my gratitude to her is boundless.

My research assistant, Jack Butler, has been a great boon to me as well. He has been indefatigable in helping me work through this process (a very generous term for the cacophonous ordeal that has been this whole experience). In particular, the section in the appendix on human material progress is more his baby than my own. He is as sharp-minded as he is decent and hardworking, and I look forward to taking undue credit for his inevitable successes in life. He also helped manage a talented string of interns who helped at various stages of this book: Chris Gavin, Matt Winesett, Robbie Rosamelia, and James Altschul.

My editor, Mary Reynics, has been heroically unflappable and inhumanly cheerful from day one. I know for a fact that some editors would go on a three-state killing spree if an author delivered two-and-half-times more words than contractually obliged. She has been a great asset and ally for me throughout, as has everyone at Crown.

My literary agent, Jay Mandel, has been the best sounding board, advocate, and friend one could hope for in the ever-changing landscape of publishing.

I consider myself one of the luckiest people in the world, for reasons too long and too saccharine to list here. But near the top of the list is the fact that I have a home at two institutions that I consider the best in the world at what they do. The first is *National Review,* where I am a senior editor at the magazine and a fellow at the National Review Institute. My friend Rich Lowry, the brilliant editor of *National Review,* hired me two decades ago, essentially on a hunch. Since then, *National Review* has become more than an employer, but my Burkean little platoon. Rich generously gave me the time and space to get this book done, with the full and generous support of the National Review Institute, and its profoundly talented president, Lindsay Craig.

The second institution I call home is the American Enterprise Institute, to my mind the best and most consequential think tank in the world. Arthur Brooks, the president of AEI, has been a patron, a mentor, a friend, and a role model. He, too, hired me on a hunch in 2010, and my life has been changed for the better ever since.

I also wish to express my sincere gratitude to Thomas and Diane Smith for their generous support for this project.

Institutions matter, a lot. But what matters more, and what truly is the measure of my good fortune, are my friendships. At AEI, NR, and beyond, I am blessed to have a group of people who are not just friends but intellectual lodestars and resources. They have helped me in large ways and small to get my thoughts (somewhat) organized for this book. Special thanks go to my friend John Podhoretz, who offered both brilliant insights and encouragement from the book proposal to the finished product, as did Charles Murray, another indispensable friend and resource. Toby Stock, vice president for development and academic programs at AEI, has been a tremendous advocate and source of encouragement and insight. Kevin Williamson, my infuriatingly talented *National Review* colleague, read the whole manuscript and offered extremely useful notes. Steven Teles of the Niskanen Center was also kind enough to offer some useful critical comments near the end as well.

Marian Tupy and his team at the Cato Institute's HumanProgress .org were simply a gold mine, particularly in the effort to compile data for the section on, well, human progress. I want to thank them for their generous help.

The last few years have been particularly trying, unsettling, and distracting in terms of the changing political landscape but also in more personal terms. Steven Hayes, A.B. Stoddard, Ramesh Ponnuru, Yuval Levin, Charles Cooke, Jack Fowler, Jay Nordlinger, Ronald Bailey, Bret Baier, Chris Stirewalt, James Rosen, Nick Schulz, Doug Anderson, Scott McLucas, Cliff Asness, Martin Eltrich, Harlan Crow, Chelsea Follett, Meg Cahill, Michael Pratt, Mark Antonio Wright, Reihan Salam, Scott Immergut, Rob Long, Patrick Fitzmaurice (the best syndicated column editor in the business), Drucilla Davida, Kirsten Reisz, and Ashley Koerber have helped me in ways large and small, either with book-related issues or with other demands on my brain, my work, or my time. I don't know if I could have gotten through the last few years without their collective friendship, counsel, and assistance. I should also thank the entire crew at Signature Cigars in Washington, D.C. It's been not just my office away from my offices but also a refuge in more ways than one.

I should also thank some intellectuals who have graciously taken the time to answer no doubt odd or silly questions from me. NYU's Jonathan Haidt and Yale's Paul Bloom were generous in their responses to email questions. I also want to thank Russ Roberts of the Hoover Institution. I have never met him, though we have emailed on occasion. But his podcast EconTalk not only saved me immense time in learning about and thinking about various complicated issues, but also taught me a great deal about how to think about some of the issues raised in this book.

Of course, all errors are my own (but don't tell Jack that).

Then, of course, there are the two Lucys in my life: my mom, Lucianne Goldberg, who taught me so much about how to fight for what matters, and my daughter, Lucy, who, more than anyone else, reminds me daily what really matters.

Index

social media, 202, 218, 251, 286, 323–24, 325, 335, 348
social science, 177–79, 182*n*, 183, 184
Social Security, 306
sociology, 179
Socrates, 5, 58
Sombart, Werner, 172
Sotomayor, Sonia, 213
Southern Poverty Law Center, 217–18
Soviet Union, 36, 82, 85, 86, 187, 197, 205, 231, 255, 279, 280
Sowell, Thomas, 34
Spacey, Kevin, 250
Spielberg, Steven, 224
sports, 274–75
Stalin, Joseph, 85
states, statism, 69–87, 152, 174–75, 304, 313–14
  administrative forms of, 175, 176–87, 188–208
  coercion and, 75–77
  division of labor in, 74, 75, 76, 86–87, 136–37, 140
  elites and, 53–56, 60, 165–75, 207–8, 280–81, 314
  exploitation and, 9
  familism in, 56–57
  family function of, 304, 306–7
  father figures of, 85–86, 280, 307
  government contrasted with, 173–75
  ideology and, 76
  institutions and, 83, 89–90, 229–33, 234, 262, 276, 277, 300–306, 309–10, 325, 333, 343, 344
  meaning and belonging in, 329–30, 340, 342–43
  nationalism in, 313–14
  nepotism in, 54–56
  population size and, 74
  progressivism and, 175, 176–87
  property rights and, 72, 74
  religion and, 83–84
  self-interest in, 81–82
  social constructions and, 82–83
  social contract and, 69–70
  stationary bandit model in, 70–73, 79, 81, 84, 90, 174
  torture and, 33
  violence and, 30, 76, 79
  warfare and, 73–74
  wealth creation in, 74–75
  writing and, 73, 77–80
stationary bandits, 70–73, 79, 81, 84, 90, 174
status, 38–41, 167, 172
Steffens, Lincoln, 280
Steinbeck, John, 251
Steuerle, C. Eugene, 268

Stone, Oliver, 38
subsidies, 198
Suicide of the West (Burnham), 115–16
Sumerians, 77
sumptuary laws, 157–58
Supreme Court, U.S., 9*n*, 146–47, 210, 213, 299
Sutherland, Kiefer, 260–61
Swayze, Patrick, 251
Syria, 279
Syriza, 285

Tacitus, 92
Tammany Hall, 64
tariffs, 173
Taub, Amanda, 323
taxes, taxation, 76, 77, 93, 95, 157, 170, 185, 189–90, 326
taxi industry, 202–3
Tea Party, 326
technology, 8, 77, 100, 106, 114, 183–84, 214, 235, 248, 249, 335, 342
teenagers, 244
teleology, 98–99, 100, 118
television, 250, 251–52, 256, 257, 260–61, 274, 276, 285
Ten Commandments, 4
terrorism, terrorists, 12, 231, 285, 316, 318–19, 329, 342–43
Theory of Moral Sentiments, The (Smith), 35*n*, 39
Thirteenth Amendment, 34
Thomas, Clarence, 192, 222
Thomas, Robert Paul, 74
Thoreau, Henry David, 254
Thunder, David, 258
Tiananmen Square Massacre (1989), 286, 340
Tibet, 264
Tilly, Charles, 73
Titans, 245, 246
Tocqueville, Alexis de, 90, 96, 156
tolerance, 221, 227–29, 333
torture, 260–61
totalitarianism, 5, 12, 46, 140, 141, 279, 334, 348
Toynbee, Arnold, 99*n*
trade, 8, 77, 173, 328
  deficits in, 295
  human interaction and, 11
  see also commerce
transgender rights, 315
Tribal Imagination, The (Fox), 266
tribalism, 10–11, 12–14, 21, 62, 66, 86–87, 307, 311, 319, 340, 343, 348*n*, 351
  politics and, 16, 43, 64, 209–36, 314, 322–26, 341, 346, 347–48

Tribe: On Homecoming and Belonging
(Junger), 13
Triumph of Vulgarity, The (Pattison),
242–43
Trump, Donald, 15–16, 44, 105, 121, 188,
232, 233, 234, 236, 287–98, 307, 325
conservatives' relationship with, 299,
315–16, 326, 344–49
Constitution and, 347
cult of personality of, 257, 328, 347–48
elites and, 291, 314
entertainment background of, 344
"fake news" as tool of, 288–89
family of, 291, 346–47
feelings and instincts of, 290–91, 298
health care issue and, 328
ideology and, 287, 288, 289–90, 291,
345–46
immigration and, 318–19, 347
inaugural address of, 314
Islam and, 318–19
loyalty and, 291
nationalism of, 286, 297, 314, 328
political rise of, 299, 309, 310, 322,
343–45
populism of, 292–98, 308, 326–27
slogans of, 287–88, 314, 315, 316, 345
trade issue and, 328
winning as chief aim of, 288–89, 327–28,
341
Trump, Eric, 346–47
truth, 5
Tsuneoka, Chieko, 247
Tsutsui, William, 248
Tunisia, 287
Turkey, 57, 58, 285, 286
24, 260–61
Twitter, 324, 335, 348
Two Treatises of Government (Locke), 124,
147
Tyranny of the Majority, The (Guinier), 222

Uber, 203
Uncomfortable Learning, 219
unemployment, 308, 318
unions, 196–97, 204–5, 276
United States:
administrative state and, 175, 176–87,
188–208
birth of state in, 175
charitable giving in, 302–3, 304
civil service reform and, 194–95
divorce in, 266, 267–70, 271, 273–74, 276
economic growth of, 160–62, 171, 176,
307, 308
employment in, 308
family analogy of, 301–2

foreign-born population of, 320–21
founding of, 142–62
identity politics in, *see* identity politics
manufacturing in, 309
marriage in, 272
nationalization in, 186–87
patriotism in, 310–11
population growth of, 171
populism and, *see* populism
progressivism in, 175, 176–87, 194, 195,
208, 294
universals, human, 26–28
USA Today, 196
Utopia, 86

value, labor theory of, 101, 111, 128, 295
Vanderbilt, Cornelius, 172
Venezuela, 86, 286
Venice, 169–70
Veterans Affairs Department (VA), U.S.,
195
violence, 11, 30–33, 49–50, 76
Violence and Social Orders (North), 59
Virginia Statute for Religious Freedom
(1786), 147–48
virtue, 50–51, 59
Voegelin, Eric, 182*n*
Voltaire, 133, 256
voting rights, 171, 224, 269, 336
Vought, Russell, 232

Wade, Nicholas, 31, 263–64
Wallace, George C., 293
Wall Street, 38
Wall Street Journal, 247
Walters, Barbara, 328
Warens, Françoise-Louise, Baroness de,
131–32
War Finance Corporation, 187
Warren, Elizabeth, 296
wars, warfare, 31–33, 42, 73–74, 311, 348*n*
see also names of specific wars
Washington, George, 9*n*, 85, 150, 154
Washington Post, 274, 288
Watchmen, 257
Watt, James, 200
Wax, Amy, 227–28
Wayne, John, 260
wealth, *8*, 14–15, 66, 74–75, 121, 129, 136,
157, 159, 171–72, 176
Weber, Max, 76, 100–101, 237, 243, 312
WebMD, 267
Wedgwood, C. V., 105
welfare, 268, 302
West, Benjamin, 150
West, Cornel, 216
Westphalia, Treaty of (1648), 62, 105

About the Author

JONAH GOLDBERG IS A Fellow at the American Enterprise Institute and a senior editor at *National Review.* A bestselling author whose nationally syndicated column appears regularly in over a hundred newspapers across the United States, he is also a weekly columnist for the *Los Angeles Times,* a member of the board of contributors to *USA Today,* a Fox News contributor, and a regular member of the "Fox News All-Stars" on *Special Report with Bret Baier.* He was the founding editor of *National Review Online. The Atlantic* magazine identified Goldberg as one of the top fifty political commentators in America. In 2011 he was named the Robert J. Novak Journalist of the Year at the Conservative Political Action Conference (CPAC). He has written on politics, media, and culture for a wide variety of leading publications and has appeared on numerous television and radio programs. He is the author of two *New York Times* bestsellers, *The Tyranny of Clichés* (Sentinel, 2012) and *Liberal Fascism* (Doubleday, 2008).

ALSO AVAILABLE FROM BESTSELLING AUTHOR JONAH GOLDBERG

Fierce, funny, and controversial, this #1 *New York Times* bestseller traces fascism back to its liberal roots, offering a surprising new perspective on the theories and practices that define fascist politics.

CROWN
FORUM

With humor and passion, this book explores how liberals cloak some of today's most radical arguments in homespun aphorisms, revealing how this dangerous game undermines reasoned political discourse.

SENTINEL

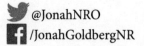